CHARACTER IN THE CRIMINAL TRIAL

Character in the
Criminal Trial

MIKE REDMAYNE

OXFORD
UNIVERSITY PRESS

OXFORD
UNIVERSITY PRESS

Great Clarendon Street, Oxford, OX2 6DP,
United Kingdom

Oxford University Press is a department of the University of Oxford.
It furthers the University's objective of excellence in research, scholarship,
and education by publishing worldwide. Oxford is a registered trade mark of
Oxford University Press in the UK and in certain other countries

© Mike Redmayne 2015

The moral rights of the author have been asserted

First Edition published in 2015
Impression: 1

Published in the United States of America by Oxford University Press
198 Madison Avenue, New York, NY 10016, United States of America

British Library Cataloguing in Publication Data
Data available

Library of Congress Control Number: 2014959904

ISBN 978–0–19–922889–8

Printed and bound by
CPI Group (UK) Ltd, Croydon, CR0 4YY

Cover image: The Accusers of Theft Adultery Murder by William Blake.
© The Trustees of the British Museum

For Helen Margaret Redmayne

General Editor's Introduction

There are few more contestable elements of the criminal trial than evidence of the defendant's character, bad or good. For many years the common law struggled with questions of the kinds of character evidence that should be admissible and the purpose for which it might be used. As a result of the Criminal Justice Act 2003 these controversies moved centre-stage in English law. Questions of propensity and prejudice remain contested, as does the ethical basis for admitting character evidence. In this erudite monograph Mike Redmayne not only conducts a searching examination of the relevant theoretical and empirical issues, but also broadens the debate by drawing parallels (and distinctions) with the relevance of an offender's character at the sentencing stage. This innovative approach to the subject takes a wide sweep, with the author going on to suggest ways in which character evidence has an influence in shaping the meaning and practical impact of elements of the criminal law itself. Thus, while the monograph makes an original contribution to the Law of Evidence, it also demonstrates criminal justice scholarship at its best.

Andrew Ashworth

Preface and Acknowledgments

I started writing about character without really realizing it. In 1999, I published a short note on the use of evidence to prove drug dealing ('Drugs, Money and Relevance' (1999) 3 *E & P* 128). Typical examples from the case law were the finding of a large amount of cash, or a small amount of drugs, in the house of a suspected drug dealer. I was interested in the relevance questions posed by such scenarios, and the way in which the courts analysed them. But it turned out that I was also writing about what the law classifies as character evidence, because if the drugs and money were relevant, they were relevant via an argument that they showed a propensity to deal in drugs. This got me thinking about patterns of reasoning in cases involving character, in particular claims about establishing probative value through unlikely coincidences, an area where it seemed to me that some of the received wisdom was wrong. I developed my thinking in a rather strange review article ('A Likely Story!' (1999) 19 *OJLS* 659). Having stumbled on an interest in character evidence, I then looked at the question of what empirical evidence on recidivism might have to say about the probative value of previous convictions. Around that time, there were moves to reform the admissibility of character evidence in England and Wales. These came to fruition in the Criminal Justice Act 2003, and I decided that developing some of the ideas I had already written about, and examining the legal changes brought about by the Act, would be a good topic for a book. I was also familiar with some of the literature on the use of previous convictions in sentencing, and there appeared to be some interesting similarities and differences between the debates about character in evidence law and sentencing, so the idea of combing the two topics emerged. The end result is this book about character in the criminal trial.

Especially on the evidence law side of things, there is much that this book does not cover. While I had grand ambitions when I started out, I found I needed to concentrate on particular issues in order to do them justice. Thus, I concentrate on defendants, rather than also looking at the use of bad character evidence against witnesses. Even where defendants are concerned, I leave much out. I do not discuss admissibility between co-defendants, nor do I look at explanatory evidence, evidence to rebut a false impression, or the issue of when evidence 'has to do with the alleged facts of the offence'. This book is not intended to be a guide to the Criminal Justice Act 2003, but an in-depth analysis of particular uses of character evidence in relation to defendants: good character and bad character evidence, used as evidence of propensity to commit crime and as evidence of credibility. When starting out, I had hoped to include comparative material, but later decided to keep the focus on the law in England and Wales. I hope that readers in other jurisdictions, who will know their own law better than I do, can draw out the implications of my arguments for the law elsewhere.

My work on character in the criminal trial has benefitted enormously from friends and colleagues. I am grateful to Neil Duxbury, David Hamer, Niki Lacey, Jill Peay, Federico Picinali, and Youngjae Lee for comments on draft chapters. Chapter 9 profited from discussion at a staff seminar in the Law Department at LSE, while a version of Chapter 4 was originally presented as a Current Legal Problems Lecture in the Faculty of Laws at UCL and published as 'The Ethics of Character Evidence' in the CLP annual volume for 2008. Parts of Chapter 8 were published as 'Recognising Propensity' [2011] Crim LR 177. Finally, thanks are due to Natasha Flemming, Elinor Shields, Sophie Rosinke, and the rest of the team at Oxford University Press for working on the manuscript so efficiently.

Mike Redmayne

August 2014

Contents

Table of Cases

Table of Statutes

Table of Statutory Instruments

Table of International Instruments

List of Abbreviations

ABH	actual bodily harm
ARAI	actuarial risk assessment instrument
ASBO	Anti Social Behaviour Order
AUC	area under the curve
CJA	Criminal Justice Act 2003
CPS	Crown Prosecution Service
CSDD	Cambridge Study in Delinquent Development
ECHR	European Convention on Human Rights
ECtHR	European Court of Human Rights
GBH	grievous bodily harm
IPP	imprisonment for public protection
JSB	Judicial Studies Board
LASPO	Legal Aid, Sentencing and Punishment of Offenders Act 2012
NCSC	National Centre for State Courts
NND	number needed to detain
OAPA	Offences Against the Person Act
OASys	Offender Assessment System
OVP	OASys Violence Predictor
PACE	Police and Criminal Evidence Act 1984
PPV	positive predictive value
RM2000	Risk Matrix 2000
VRAG	Violence Risk Appraisal Guide

1

Introduction

Somehow, in the history of jurisprudence, these issues—who people were, what they had done in the past—had come to be thought of as different in kind from the 'facts' of a case, different from blood on the wall and reams of phone company records. How had this idea gotten going, when it was so counterintuitive? I was being asked to decide if a crime had occurred—in other words, if someone did something to someone else. How could the nature of either 'someone' stand off-limits?

D. Graham Burnett, *A Trial By Jury* (2002)

We navigate through much of our day-to-day lives by assessing people on the basis of their past behaviour. I predict how my partner will react to my coming home late and drunk on the basis of how she has reacted before; when waiting to meet a friend, reminding myself that 'he's always late' provides some reassurance that he has not simply forgotten the arrangement; when deciding which restaurant to visit, I avoid the one where the staff were previously rude. This process of extrapolating from past to present and future behaviour informs how we deal with matters of greater moment too. When deciding whom to employ, we put considerable emphasis on CVs and references, and the past record of politicians plays an important role in elections. In all these things judgments of character play a central role. None of this is usually regarded as problematic.

This book examines the use of assessments of character in a particular institutional context: the criminal trial. Here, character sometimes becomes more controversial. The main issue I examine is the use of bad character evidence to prove guilt. This typically involves using evidence about a defendant's past behaviour—often in the form of previous convictions—to show how he acted at the time of the alleged offence. For example, if a defendant (D) is on trial for burglary, should the court hear evidence that he has a previous conviction for burglary on the grounds that it shows that he is more likely to have committed the current burglary? The common law has traditionally restricted this use of character evidence, and this explains Burnett's puzzlement in the quotation which introduces this chapter. The policy of restricting the use of character evidence to prove guilt is one which has generally been supported by academics writing about the law of evidence. The other topic addressed in this book is the use of character in sentencing: should judges take criminal record, or other evidence about the defendant's previous behaviour, into account when sentencing? If, for example, D is convicted of burglary, should his sentence be increased because he has a previous conviction for burglary? Here, the law has tended to be more permissive, and while the use of character in sentencing has been less controversial, commentators do disagree about whether, why, and to what extent character should affect sentence. In both evidence law and sentencing, there have been significant changes to legal policy in England and Wales in recent years. The Criminal Justice Act (CJA) 2003, in particular, puts more emphasis on the defendant's character in both domains. In this book I assess these reforms and the arguments for and against placing so much significance on the defendant's character in the criminal trial.

1.1 Character in the Criminal Process

In this section, I look beyond the criminal trial to sketch the ways in which a person's character may be relevant in various parts of the criminal process, thus both introducing the issues examined in this book and setting them in their larger context.[1] When a crime has been committed, we would expect the police to take criminal record into account when deciding whom to investigate.[2] Criminal record is also likely to play a role in some decisions to arrest, though here it would usually be supplemented by other evidence. Code A of the Police and Criminal Evidence Act 1984 explicitly states that a decision to stop and search cannot be based on criminal record alone.[3] But the assumption that previous offenders are suitable objects of suspicion is nowadays institutionalized in various ways, for example, by databases of DNA profiles and fingerprints which allow traces left at crime scenes to be searched against the prints and profiles of previous offenders. In fact, this example raises some of the controversies which recur, in various guises, throughout this book. It has become a matter of dispute just whose records the DNA and fingerprint databases should contain. At one point, prints and profiles were retained indefinitely, not just for those convicted of crime, but also for those who had only been arrested. This policy was held to infringe Article 8 of the European Convention on Human Rights (protecting the right to private life).[4] The details of this debate need not

---

[1] A useful account is J. Jackson and M. Wasik, 'Character Evidence and Criminal Procedure' in D. Hayton (ed), *Law's Futures* (Oxford: Hart Publishing, 2000).

[2] Much of the time a suspect will be identified by members of the public or be found near to the scene of crime. Steer's study found that in a small proportion of cases, 'local police knowledge', including knowledge of *modus operandi*, led to the identification of suspects: D. Steer, *Uncovering Crime: The Police Role* (London: HMSO, 1980). *Modus operandi* was also found to play a role in a small number of cases in C. Phillips and D. Brown, *Entry into the Criminal Justice System: A Survey of Police Arrests and Their Outcomes* (London: Home Office, 1998), 41–3, 198.

[3] Para 2.2.

[4] *S and Marper* v *United Kingdom* (2009) 48 EHRR 50. The law on the retention of DNA samples and fingerprints is found in the Police and Criminal Evidence Act 1984, ss 64–5, amended in

concern us—what matters is the broad question raised. The criminal process sometimes has a legitimate interest in people's past behaviour, but just how far should this scrutiny extend? Should it be confined to the discrete category of previous convictions, or extend to other instances of suspicious behaviour— here having been arrested, but in other contexts perhaps just living a particular lifestyle? And even with previous convictions, there are questions of staleness. Should people convicted of minor theft be included on the DNA database for the rest of their lives? In some contexts we recognize the importance of a person being able to put his past behind him. The Rehabilitation of Offenders Act 1974 allows those convicted of offences at the less serious end of the spectrum[5] to treat a conviction as 'spent' for employment purposes after a particular period,[6] a practice which helps to respect the right to private life.[7] To what extent should this idea of giving someone a fresh start inform other uses of character evidence?

Moving on through the criminal process, after investigation and arrest criminal record may be relevant to decisions about case disposal made by police and prosecutors. As an alternative to prosecution, Simple Cautions (for adults) are usually only available to offenders who have not committed similar offences in the last two years,[8] and similar principles apply to Youth Cautions for young offenders.[9] Once a suspect has been charged, assessments of character continue to play a role in deciding whether to 'discontinue' the prosecution. The Code for Crown Prosecutors lists as relevant public interest factors militating in favour of prosecution that 'the suspect's previous convictions or the previous out-of-court disposals which he or she has received are relevant to the present offence'[10] and 'there are grounds for believing that the offence is likely to be continued or repeated'.[11] The latter factor reminds us that, although the simple terms in which 'character' has been discussed so far equate character with past behaviour, character, as a

---

2012 in response to *Marper*. The current position is complex, but, in simple terms: anyone convicted of 'qualifying' offences (basically, serious violent, sexual, and terrorist offences) and adults convicted of any recordable offence will have their DNA profiles stored indefinitely. Those under the age of 18 convicted of a non-qualifying offence for the first time will have their profiles stored for five years (but on a second conviction the profile is stored indefinitely). Those charged with qualifying offences will have their profiles stored for three years; those arrested for such offences will have them stored for three years if permission is granted by the Biometrics Commissioner. The rules for fingerprints are similar.

[5] Offences resulting in custodial sentences of 30 months or less. For general discussion, see N. Padfield, 'Judicial Rehabilitation? A View from England' (2011) 3 *Eur J Probation* 36.

[6] There are exceptions for those working with children and vulnerable adults.

[7] *R (On the Application of T and another)* v *Secretary of State for the Home Department* [2014] UKSC 35.

[8] Ministry of Justice, *Simple Cautions for Adult Offenders* (2013), para 46.

[9] Ministry of Justice, *Youth Cautions: Guidance for Police and Youth Offending Teams* (2013), para 4.16.

[10] *The Code for Crown Prosecutors* (London: CPS, 2010), para 4.16 (p). 'Relevant to' is glossed as 'similar to' in the 'Easy Read' version of the Code. This factor presumably reflects the assumption that offending is more serious where it repeats past offending; this is usually an aggravating factor in sentencing.

[11] *Code for Crown Prosecutors*, para 4.16 (s).

disposition which persists over time, is also in play when we project current behaviour into the future. Character and risk are intertwined.

Once a suspect has been charged, in cases which cannot be dealt with at first court appearance there will be a decision about whether to remand the suspect in custody or release him on bail. Bail decisions are paradigmatically about risk: an assessment of the suspect's anticipated behaviour is key. Schedule 1 to the Bail Act 1976 provides for exceptions to the right to bail where there are grounds for believing that, if released, the defendant would fail to surrender to custody, commit an offence while on bail, or interfere with witnesses. The Schedule goes on to specify that in making decisions about bail, regard should be had to 'the defendant's record as respects the fulfilment of his obligations under previous grants of bail' and his 'character, antecedents, associations and community ties'. As a risk-based decision, it is uncontroversial that an assessment of the defendant's behavioural tendencies will feature in remand decision-making.[12] Where controversy does start to arise is over the way in which risk is read off the defendant's (suspected) behaviour. In 1994, the UK Government foreclosed the right to bail in cases where a defendant was charged with murder, manslaughter, or rape and had a previous conviction for such an offence.[13] The European Court of Human Rights found that this automatic removal of the right to bail infringed Article 5 of the Convention. Part of its reasoning was that the judge making the decision about bail:

> must examine all the facts arguing for and against the existence of a genuine requirement of public interest justifying, with due regard to the presumption of innocence, a departure from the rule of respect for the accused's liberty...For example, the danger of an accused's absconding cannot be gauged solely on the basis of the severity of the sentence risked. As far as the danger of re-offending is concerned, a reference to a person's antecedents cannot suffice to justify refusing release.[14]

What this seems to rule out is making strong presumptions on the basis of what the defendant has done: thus even if the defendant has pleaded guilty to armed robbery (as in *Muller* v *France*[15]), it should not be presumed that he presents a high risk of absconding or offending while on bail. The problem of balancing broad generalizations (such as 'armed robbers are likely to avoid appearing for trial') against more individualized information about a

---

[12] Although the particular risks which are deemed relevant are more controversial, the risk of offending while on bail being a case in point. See R. A. Duff, 'Pre-Trial Detention and the Presumption of Innocence' in A. Ashworth, L. Zedner, and P. Tomlin (eds), *Prevention and the Limits of the Criminal Law* (Oxford: Oxford University Press, 2013).

[13] Criminal Justice and Public Order Act 1994, s 25.

[14] *Caballero* v *UK* (2000) 30 EHRR 643, [40]. This is in fact the Commission's reasoning, but seems to have been endorsed by the Court which, the issue having been conceded by the UK, gave a very brief opinion. The last sentence in the quotation is probably best read as holding, not that previous convictions alone cannot establish a risk of reoffending sufficient to justify refusing bail, but that the judge should consider their seriousness. See *Muller* v *France* ECHR 17 March 1997, [43]–[44]; and *Clooth* v *Belgium* (1992) 14 EHRR 717, [4].

[15] ECHR 17 March 1997.

defendant is another recurring issue when character evidence is employed in the criminal process.

The trial is the focus of this book, and, as we have already seen, character may be relevant to both the fact-finding and sentencing phases of the trial. In this book, I discuss the use of the defendant's bad character to prove guilt in detail. I also look at the practice of telling the jury when the defendant is of good character. I shall not say more about those topics here, but it is worth noting that it is not only the defendant's character which can be relevant at trial. Witnesses can also have their previous bad—and occasionally good—character brought up, typically as a way of impugning their credibility.[16] And in trials for sexual offences, defendants sometimes seek to introduce evidence about the complainant's 'sexual history'—previous sexual behaviour—as evidence of consent.[17] At the sentencing stage of the trial, the defendant's presentation of mitigation will often allude to personal details, mentioning such things as jobs and relationships. An employer might provide a reference.[18] Previous convictions tend to be an aggravating factor in sentencing. Beyond such routine uses of a person's record, sentencing provisions in England and Wales have for some years included special provisions for 'dangerous' offenders: those considered to pose a particular risk of serious reoffending. And after sentence, some of those given a custodial sentence will have their criminal record and behaviour while in prison scrutinized by the parole board in deciding just when they should be released.[19]

Character may also be relevant to the criminal process by being part of the culpability structure of criminal law. Theories of criminal responsibility are controversial, but some commentators think that the fact that an action is 'out of character' might affect its culpability.[20]

Character, then, is relevant in various forms and in various ways to decision-making in the criminal process. Details of exactly what should be considered and for what purposes may be controversial, but the basic fact is that many instances of criminal justice decision-making concentrate not just on a suspect's, defendant's, or witness's current (alleged) behaviour, but also take into account past and likely future behaviour. Subjects of the criminal process are judged as actors in time, and not just as inhabitants of the present.

---

[16] Criminal Justice Act 2003, s 100. On witness good character, see C. Crinion, 'Adducing the Good Character of Prosecution Witnesses' [2010] *Crim LR* 570.

[17] See M. Redmayne, 'Myths, Relationships and Coincidences: The New Problems of Sexual History' (2003) 7 *E & P* 75; and L. Kelly, J. Temkin, and S. Griffiths, *Section 41: An Evaluation of New Legislation Limiting Sexual History Evidence in Rape Trials*, Home Office Online Report 20/06 (London: Home Office, 2006).

[18] See J. Shapland, *Between Conviction and Sentence: The Process of Mitigation* (London: Routledge, 1981), 7.

[19] See, generally, N. Padfield (ed), *Who to Release? Parole, Fairness and Criminal Justice* (Cullompton: Willan Publishing, 2007).

[20] See discussion in Chapter 11.

1.2 Defining Character

To this point, the idea of character has been used in a rather loose way, to refer to past behaviour and behavioural tendencies. But is it really apt to say that a tendency to, for example, abscond before trial is part of a person's character? In ordinary language, talk of character tends to be reserved for broad moral traits, such as selflessness, honesty, bravery, and the like. Less morally charged behavioural tendencies are often ascribed to personality: good sense of humour, reserved, impulsive.[21] A tendency to abscond, or to burgle, seems to fit neither of these categories. The law of evidence, however, employs a broad definition of character: character refers to any behavioural tendency or propensity.[22] The latter term has become current in English law after the introduction of the Criminal Justice Act 2003, which uses propensity (and to a lesser extent disposition) as key concepts. For the purposes of looking at character in the criminal trial, it is useful to include the propensity view in the conception of character. So, when I discuss character, I am often discussing the simple fact that a person has a propensity to commit a particular type of crime. In sentencing law, though, character often means something more than a propensity to commit a particular type of crime, something closer to the everyday meaning of character: when a defendant presents character evidence to mitigate sentence, he is often seeking to show that he is caring, or reliable, or some such.[23]

The propensity view of character has the virtue of being simple: if A is more likely than other people to do X, he has a propensity to do so. However, there might be concerns that this is too simple. One worry is that the propensity view may be blind to motivational aspects of behaviour. 'Character traits are not merely dispositions to behave in particular ways. They are also dispositions to be motivated in certain ways, by certain kinds of consideration.'[24] To be brave, for example, is not simply to react to danger in a particular way, it is also to perceive certain

---

[21] See, eg, J. Kupperman, *Character* (New York: Oxford University Press, 1991), ch 1. Kupperman defines character in the following manner: 'X's character is X's normal pattern of thought and action, especially with respect to concerns and commitments in matters affecting the happiness of others or of X, and most especially in relation to moral choices' (17). On character versus personality, see also P. Goldie, *On Personality* (London: Routledge, 2004), chs 1–2. Goldie notes that character exists at a deeper level than personality (in that bad character swamps pleasant personality), and concerns moral worth.

[22] B. J. Anderson, 'Recognizing Character: A New Perspective on Character Evidence' (2012) 121 *Yale LJ* 1912.

[23] While these examples still involve the idea of propensity or disposition, sentencing law may take an interest in character without assuming that it shows a propensity. Sometimes sentencers include as personal mitigation the fact that a person has done a good deed—such as saving someone's life—in the past. The basis for mitigation is unclear, but it may reflect a 'social accounting' view of sentencing whereby the offender is simply rewarded for the past good deed without any assumption that it reflects more broadly on his character. I discuss such cases in Chapter 11.

[24] R. A. Duff, 'Choice, Character, and Criminal Liability' (1993) 12 *Law & Philosophy* 345, 365. In a similar vein, the 'act frequency' approach to personality is sometimes criticized for ignoring motivation: J. Block, 'Critique of the Act Frequency Approach to Personality' (1989) 56 *J Personality & Soc Psychol* 234, 238.

situations as dangerous, and to be appropriately motivated when acting in the face of danger. The drunk who confronts an armed robber without grasping the gravity of the situation is not brave, nor is the bodyguard who intervenes only because he will receive a large bonus for doing so.[25] This is surely right, but it does not raise significant problems for the use of character in the criminal process, even when character means no more than propensity. Criminal law makes some concessions to the complexities of behaviour—a person will not be convicted of a violent offence if he was acting under duress, and evidence of intoxication can be used to negate intention. As a mechanism of social defence, however, the criminal law's concessions are limited. The standards for a successful claim of duress are set quite high, and the drunk can be convicted of crimes of recklessness. But at the end of the day it is the criminal law's categorizations which matter: a person with previous convictions for violence can rightly be treated differently—say, for sentencing purposes—from a person with no criminal record. To the extent that finer-grained motivations matter, these can be taken into account where appropriate. We might want to allow that the person with previous convictions for drunken violence is clumsy and thoughtless rather than truly vicious, and perhaps assume that he does not have a propensity for sober violence. The complexity of character is a useful reminder that we should be prepared to look past offence labels, but is not a significant objection to a propensity view.

A different criticism of the propensity view is that it treats propensities as real even when they have not been manifested. Consider the prediction of offending. Because 'offending is one element of a larger syndrome of anti-social behaviour that arises in childhood and tends to persist into adulthood with numerous different behavioural manifestations,'[26] we might be able to predict that someone who exhibits anti-social behaviour in childhood will later commit crime. Such a person could therefore be said to have a propensity to commit crime. Indeed, we might say that a person has a propensity to offend even in the absence of evidence about their own anti-social behaviour: if all we knew, for example, was that they fitted certain risk factors, such as having separated parents and attending an unruly school.[27] One view of character, which is endorsed by Duff, may block this way of thinking: possession of a character trait necessarily involves the trait's manifestation in action.[28] We cannot describe someone as brave if they have never acted bravely. This view is sometimes tied to an anti-realist view of dispositions in general: we cannot describe a glass as fragile until it breaks, or a rubber band as elastic until it is stretched.[29] Whatever the answer to such metaphysical questions,

[25] Because of this, character traits are best seen as complex sets of dispositions, which include motivational and perceptual aspects: D. Butler, 'Character Traits in Explanation' (1988) 49 *Philosophy and Phenomenological Research* 215.

[26] D. Farrington, 'Human Development and Criminal Careers' in M. Maguire, R. Morgan, and R. Reiner (eds), *Oxford Handbook of Criminology* (Oxford: Oxford University Press, 1997), 380.

[27] Identified as risk factors in J. Hales, C. Nevill, S. Pudney, and S. Tipping, *Longitudinal Analysis of the Offending, Crime and Justice Survey 2003–06* (London: Home Office, 2009), 2.

[28] Duff, 'Choice, Character, and Criminal Liability', 372. See also J. Gardner, 'The Gist of Excuses' (1998) 1 *Buffalo Criminal L Rev* 575.

[29] See S. Mumford, *Dispositions* (Oxford: Oxford University Press, 2003). As Mumford notes, the anti-realist view is not especially intuitive: 'The concept of a disposition is a concept of

no one can deny our ability to predict the behaviour of objects and of people. If that is all that a propensity view of character picks out, it is still significant: the criminal law is often interested in prediction, or in the question of whether certain factors make a person likely to have behaved in a certain way.

It may be obvious that there is ultimately more at stake here than questions of definition. There is something disturbing about saying that a person who fits certain risk factors, such as attending an unruly school or having separated parents, has a propensity to commit crime, and something even more disturbing in using these factors as evidence that a person has committed a crime. There are certainly difficult and controversial issues lurking here, and I discuss them in Chapters 4 and 12. But it seems better to confront the ethical and inferential issues underlying such examples directly, rather than ruling them out of a propensity view of character by definitional fiat.

1.3 The Structure of the Book

Chapters 2 to 10 of this book concentrate on the use of character evidence in guilt adjudication, Chapters 10 to 12 cover sentencing, and Chapter 13 concludes. The focus of much of the book, then, is on the law of evidence. This is partly because the conceptual, doctrinal, and theoretical issues underlying character evidence are complex and deserve to be discussed at length. It is also because, given the common law's long resistance to relying on character to prove guilt, the burden of argument is greater (as noted above, the use of character in sentencing is less controversial—which is not to say uncontroversial). But chapters 2 to 10 also prepare the ground for the discussion of sentencing, in particular Chapters 2 and 4.

In more detail, Chapter 2 looks at the empirical debates underlying character evidence, examining psychological research on the stability of character and the criminological evidence on recidivism. Chapter 3 examines one of the key objections to admitting character evidence: that it is prejudicial. This chapter also explains the concept of comparative propensity, which I rely on when explaining the relevance and probative value of character evidence. Chapter 4 then moves on to consider another objection to using character evidence: that it is somehow incompatible with the moral framework of the criminal trial, in particular because the trial should treat defendants as autonomous.

Chapter 5 shifts the focus to more doctrinal issues. At this point, some more terminological clarification is necessary. Character evidence can be used to prove guilt in different ways. It can be used as evidence of propensity to commit crime or as evidence of lack of credibility. For example, if D is on trial for burglary and

something that lies behind what occurs and what is verifiable. We accept the possibility of particulars possessing dispositions which they never manifest and we accept the possibility of kinds possessing dispositions though no kind-member has ever manifested them. The ordinary notion of a disposition permits these as significant propositions, though anti-realism questions the appeal to evidence-transcendent truth-conditions' (63).

has a previous conviction for burglary, the conviction might be admitted to show that he has a propensity to burgle, or it might be used to show that he is dishonest and therefore prone to lie, and that his defence in court should therefore be given less credit. I refer to the former situation as involving propensity evidence, and the latter as involving credibility evidence. Obviously, credibility evidence involves propensity too: the assumption is that D has a propensity to lie. But it is important to distinguish between the two uses of character evidence, and the propensity/credibility terminology is useful for this purpose. Chapter 5, then, looks at the doctrinal history of propensity evidence, covering the development of the common law up until its replacement by the provisions in the Criminal Justice Act 2003. This chapter not only allows a more informed assessment of the CJA—was it better or worse than what it replaced—but also sets the stage for the detailed analysis, in Chapter 6, of reasoning about propensity and the problems of the common law admissibility tests.

With Chapter 7, the focus moves on to the CJA. I explain and assess the Act's admissibility scheme for propensity evidence. While the assessment in this chapter is largely favourable, Chapter 8 gives a more critical analysis of some of the ways in which the courts have analysed propensity evidence. Here, the shadow of the common law can be seen. This chapter also examines the use of acquitted misconduct evidence to prove guilt. The assessment of the CJA continues in Chapter 9, but this time the focus is on credibility evidence. Then, in Chapter 10, I examine the use of good character evidence.

Good character evidence is an important topic in its own right, but Chapter 10 also helps to set the stage for the initial analysis of sentencing law in Chapter 11. Just as good character—which may mean no more than a lack of previous convictions—is said to reflect favourably on defendants in the guilt-adjudication stage of the trial, so it is an important mitigating factor in sentencing. Chapter 11 explores this practice, as well as the justification for the 'recidivist premium'—the practice of sentencing defendants with criminal records more harshly than those without. The analysis also touches on character theories of criminal liability. Chapter 12 completes the discussion of sentencing by looking at the CJA's treatment of 'dangerous' offenders. Here, questions of evidence rise to the surface again, as I look at the evidence for the reliability of risk assessment. Chapter 13 concludes by summarizing the arguments and reflecting briefly on the significance of the law's increasing emphasis on character in the criminal trial.

2

The Relevance of Character

Chapter One began with the observation that we commonly form judgments of character in everyday life when predicting how people will act, and that this is generally regarded as unproblematic. It is no doubt true that such character ascriptions are uncontroversial in daily life, but in philosophy and psychology they are contested. Gilbert Harman, for example, has observed that it 'seems that ordinary attributions of character traits are often deeply misguided and it may even be the case that there is no such thing as character, no ordinary character traits of the sort people think there are, none of the usual moral virtues and vices.'[1] Harman's assessment is informed by work in social and personality psychology, and this literature has sometimes been drawn upon to argue against the use of character evidence in the criminal trial.[2] In this chapter, I review the psychological literature on which Harman draws, and then turn to the criminological evidence on recidivism, to examine issues about the relevance and probative value of character evidence.

2.1 People and Situations

There is a considerable body of research in social psychology which suggests that people do not behave very consistently from one situation to another, and that situations are powerful determinants of behaviour. The latter view is often referred to as 'situationism', contrasted with 'personism' (the view that personality is more important), and the debate between the two views is known as the person-situation debate. In the 1920s, Hartshorne and May conducted a large study on honesty in schoolchildren. They found that the children's honesty varied between different situations, such as cheating on a test, lying, and stealing.

---

[1] G. Harman, 'Moral Philosophy Meets Social Psychology: Virtue Ethics and the Fundamental Attribution Error' (1999) 99 *Proc Aristotelian Soc* 315, 316.

[2] See, eg, R. G. Spector, 'Rule 609—A Last Plea for Its Withdrawal' (1979) 32 *Oklahoma L Rev* 334, 351. For more measured assessments, see S. M. Davies, 'Evidence of Character to Prove Conduct: A Reassessment of Relevancy' (1991) 27 *Criminal Law Bulletin* 504; M. A. Mendez, 'The Law of Evidence and the Search for a Stable Personality' (1996) 45 *Emory LJ* 221; and R. Munday, 'Reflections on the Criminal Evidence Act 1898' (1985) 44 *CLJ* 62. The Law Commission carried out a (rather dated) review of the literature in *Evidence in Criminal Proceedings: Previous Misconduct of a Defendant*, LCCP No 141 (London: HMSO, 1996), 97–106.

While there was considerable consistency between similar situations—a child would persistently cheat on a particular type of test—there was little consistency across different situations: the same child would not lie or steal (and would even be less likely to cheat on a different type of test), and very few children were always honest or dishonest. Hartshorne and May concluded that honesty was not a unified character trait, but a function of situations.[3] Around the same time, a study of extraversion/introversion among children came to similar conclusions.[4]

Three classic social psychology experiments feature regularly in the writings of those who doubt the existence of character.[5] Milgram's disturbing experiments on obedience to authority found that a majority of subjects could be made to inflict what they believed to be a 450-volt electric shock on a person who had screamed in agony when they had administered lower levels of shock.[6] The experimenter's insistence that they 'must' do this as part of a (sham) experiment on negative reinforcement of learning seemed to overwhelm basic norms against inflicting pain. Less dramatically, Isen and Levin found that whether or not a person had just found a coin in a phone box influenced whether they would help someone pick up dropped possessions,[7] and Darley and Batson found that whether seminary students would come to the aid of a person apparently in need of medical attention was best predicted by whether or not they were late for an appointment.[8] Where experiments such as these have included some test of personality variables, those variables are found to be only weakly correlated with the target behaviour.

The results of these and other experiments are certainly striking, but one needs to be careful in drawing conclusions from them. Various details of the experimental set-ups may be significant. For example, in the Milgram experiment, the existence of a slippery slope, whereby subjects gave at first mild but then progressively higher levels of shock, may have made it harder for subjects to refuse to cooperate. Darley and Batson's person in need of medical attention was carefully presented so as to look ambiguous: a potential threat. While it is surprising that such a small thing as finding a coin can affect our behaviour, helping someone

[3] H. Hartshorne and M. May, *Studies in The Nature of Character, Vol 1: Studies in Deceit* (New York: MacMillan, 1928), 381.

[4] T. M. Newcomb, *The Consistency of Certain Extrovert-Introvert Behavior Patterns in 51 Problem Boys* (New York: Columbia University, 1929).

[5] See Harman, 'Moral Philosophy Meets Social Psychology'; J. Doris, *Lack of Character: Personality and Moral Behavior* (Cambridge: Cambridge University Press, 2002); and P. B. M. Vranas, 'The Indeterminacy Paradox: Character Evaluations and Human Psychology' (2005) 39 *Noûs* 1. Some philosophers draw less sceptical conclusions from the literature, eg R. Kamtekar, 'Situationism and Virtue Ethics on the Content of Our Character' (2004) 114 *Ethics* 458; and R. M. Adams, *A Theory of Virtue: Excellence in Being for the Good* (Oxford: Oxford University Press, 2006). It should be noted that the philosophical debate revolves around virtue ethics, which may require a relatively robust conception of character.

[6] S. Milgram, *Obedience to Authority* (New Yorker: Harper & Row, 1969).

[7] A. Isen and P. Levin, 'Effect of Feeling Good on Helping' (1972) 21 *J Personality & Soc Psychol* 384.

[8] J. Darely and D. Batson, '"From Jerusalem to Jericho": A Study of Situational and Dispositional Variables in Helping Behavior' (1973) 27 *J Personality & Soc Psychol* 100.

pick up dropped possessions is hardly the greatest test of our moral fibre, and it is possible that the coin works by affecting mood and hence attentiveness. The Milgram and Darley experiments can also be said to unveil the same—no doubt under-appreciated—factor: our fear of social embarrassment in disobeying the orders of an authority figure or being late for an appointment. That this factor can disorient our moral compass does not mean that countless situational factors can have the same effect and that moral character is therefore an illusion.[9]

While the experiments just discussed play a prominent role in philosophical discussions of moral character, the more general psychological literature is equally important in an assessment of the potential relevance of character to the criminal process. The person-situation debate of the 1970s and 1980s was partly instigated by an influential review of personality studies by Walter Mischel, which found that personality variables were only weakly correlated with behaviour.[10] A correlation of 0.3 is sometimes said to be the 'personality ceiling'[11] because few studies have found an effect size for personality greater than this, and most considerably lower. However, low correlations are not necessarily unimpressive; in some contexts they may have significant implications.[12] What is more, analyses of the effect sizes of situational variables find similarly low correlations: there is little basis for arguing that situations are more determinative than personality.[13]

Today, the person-situation debate is more or less over.[14] The rather predictable consensus is that both persons and situations are important factors in explaining behaviour ('interactionism'). When one looks at behaviour over significant time periods, aggregating across situations, even the psychologists who tend to be associated with situationism agree that there are inter-individual differences in behaviour: 'people differ significantly on virtually any dimension, showing stable overall individual differences: on the whole, some people are more sociable than others, some are more open minded, some are more punctual, and so on.'[15] The importance of such differences can be seen in the fact that personality measures are predictive of life outcomes,[16] and can be of some use in predicting job performance.[17] However, viewing behaviour across

---

[9] For the points in this paragraph, see J. Sabini and M. Silver, 'Lack of Character? Situationism Critiqued' (2005) 115 *Ethics* 535.

[10] W. Mischel, *Personality and Assessment* (New York: Wiley, 1968).

[11] See L. Ross and R. E. Nisbett, *The Person and the Situation: Perspectives of Social Psychology* (London: Pinter and Martin, 2011), ch 4. Cf D. C. Funder, *The Personality Puzzle* (5th edn, New York: Norton, 2010), 121, who takes the figure to be 0.4.

[12] See Funder, *Personality Puzzle*, 125–6; Sabini and Silver, 'Lack of Character?', 541–2.

[13] D. C. Funder and D. J. Ozer, 'Behavior as a Function of the Situation' (1983) 44 *J Personality & Soc Psychol* 107; and F. D. Richard, C. F. Bond, and J. J. Stokes-Zoota, 'One Hundred Years of Social Psychology Quantitatively Described' (2003) 7 *Review of Gen Psychol* 331.

[14] See G. V. Caprara and D. Cervone, *Personality: Determinants, Dynamics, and Potentials* (Cambridge: Cambridge University Press, 2000), 64, 110.

[15] W. Mischel, 'Toward an Integrative Science of the Person' (2004) 55 *Ann Rev Psychol* 1, 3.

[16] D. J. Ozer and V. Benet-Martínez, 'Personality and the Prediction of Consequential Outcomes' (2006) 57 *Ann Rev Psychol* 401; and B. W. Roberts et al, 'The Power of Personality: The Comparative Validity of Personality Traits, Socioeconomic Status, and Cognitive Ability for Predicting Important Life Outcomes' (2007) 2 *Perspectives on Psychol Sci* 313.

[17] See Funder, *Personality Puzzle*, 222–5.

long time periods can be said to 'remov[e] the situation by aggregation':[18] two people who display the same average level of a particular behaviour, such as aggressiveness, can have very different patterns of behaviour when situational variation is taken into account. One person may be aggressive towards intimates but polite to strangers, whereas the other may behave in the opposite way. This sort of variation was in fact found in Mischel and Shoda's study of aggressiveness in children.[19] However, there is stability within this variation: while aggressive behaviour in one situation may not predict it in another, 'individuals are characterized by distinctive and stable patterns of behaviour variability across situations',[20] what Mischel and Shoda refer to as '*if . . . then . . .*' patterns. So while we cannot say that S is aggressive *tout court*, we can say that S tends to be aggressive if he finds himself in situation X.

While situations are an important influence on behaviour, their significance should not be overemphasized, in part because situations are not distinct from personalities.[21] Situations are not entirely objective: a social gathering which for one person is intimidating may be pure fun for another, yet these different characterizations of situations are themselves a product of personality. Further, people have some control over the situations they find themselves in: the shy can avoid social gatherings and the extroverted can seek them out. Nor are situations static, they are themselves shaped by people: the extrovert may help to turn a muted social gathering into raucous one.[22] Thus, as a recent study confirms, people's behaviour may be more consistent in everyday life than in the manipulated world of the psychology experiment.[23]

If psychologists have, by and large, come to a consensus on interactionism, this does not mean they all believe in character in the classical sense. Mischel remains sceptical of 'descriptions of people in terms of broad traits . . . using situation-free adjectives'.[24] No doubt he would reject descriptions of people as 'extroverted', 'aggressive', or 'honest'. Doris's conclusion is that 'personality should be conceived as *fragmented*: an evaluatively disintegrated association of situation-specific local traits'.[25] For Adams, 'virtue in human beings is fragmentary and frail in various ways'.[26] Miller rejects traditional character traits

[18] Mischel, 'Toward an Integrative Science', 3.

[19] W. Mischel and Y. Shoda, 'Reconciling Processing Dynamics and Personality Dispositions' (1998) 49 *Ann Rev Psychol* 229.

[20] Mischel, 'Toward an Integrative Science', 7.

[21] See D. C. Funder, 'Towards a Resolution of the Personality Triad: Persons, Situations and Behaviors' (2006) 40 *J Research in Personality* 21; and Ross and Nisbett, *The Person and the Situation*, ch 6.

[22] For emphasis of these points in relation to offending, see P.-O. H. Wikström, 'Individuals, Settings and Acts of Crime: Situational Mechanisms and the Explanation of Crime' in P.-O. H. Wikström and R. J. Sampson (eds), *The Explanation of Crime: Context, Mechanisms and Development* (New York: Cambridge University Press, 2006).

[23] R. A. Sherman, D. S. Nave, and D. C. Funder, 'Situational Similarity and Personality Predict Behavior' (2010) 99 *J Personality & Soc Psychol* 330.

[24] 'Toward an Integrative Science', 18.

[25] *Lack of Character*, 64.

[26] *Theory of Virtue*, 115 (but note the clarification in R. M. Adams, 'A Theory of Virtue: Response to Critics' (2010) 148 *Philos Stud* 159, 162). See also Vranas, 'The Indeterminacy Paradox'.

such as honesty and compassion, but concludes that people have 'mixed traits' which are: 'highly sensitive to different features of situations and can adjust their causal activity from one activity to the next. Seemingly small changes in a situation can have a surprisingly large impact on behavior, whereas seemingly major changes might not.'[27]

What are the implications of all this for character evidence? This depends on exactly what character evidence is being used to prove. 'Situational variables are relevant to how people will act under specific circumstances; personality traits are better for describing how people act in general.'[28] That it is hard to predict how S will act on a particular occasion is not too surprising. But often this is not what character evidence is being used to prove. In sentencing, a common use of information about a person's past behaviour is to assess their risk of reoffending, and this relates not to one specific occasion, but to any point in the future, and here the observation that people often pick the situations they find themselves in is also relevant.[29] This does not mean that prediction of reoffending is always easy, but the problems of predicting reoffending are not necessarily due to the fragility of personality. Predicting rare behaviour is always difficult: that a person convicted of rape will rape again is much less certain than that a person convicted of theft will steal again.

The use of previous convictions to prove guilt during the fact-finding stage of the trial, though, looks to be far more problematic. For here we are using information about past behaviour to determine what happened on a particular occasion: just what social psychology warns against. However, there are various reasons why the fact-finding exercise at trial is different from the situation in a typical social-psychology experiment. One is that, as we will see in the next section, we have a different set of data to draw on. Crime statistics, and criminology generally, provide us with a huge amount of information on the repetition of criminal behaviour (information which has been overlooked in philosophical discussions of moral psychology). While talk of 'the criminal personality' may be outmoded, recidivism is well recognized as a brute fact of criminology. And here the fragmentation of character seems to be less marked: propensity to commit crime is general, in that those who rape also have a propensity to steal. Of course, the rapist and the thief spend most of their time not raping and stealing, which returns us to the problem of using past behaviour to determine what S did on a specific occasion. But a further difference between the social psychology experiment and the trial is that (in contrast also to the purely predictive sentencing scenario) we are not trying to use a single source of information to

---

[27] C. B. Miller, *Character and Moral Psychology* (Oxford: Oxford University Press, 2014), 100. Miller would probably not accept the language of character being fragmentary: his is critical of Doris's idea of local character traits (198–202). For him, mixed traits may show consistent behaviour when judged from the actor's point of view, but to observers they may be interpreted as producing inconsistent behaviour because subtle changes in mood and motivation affect behaviour. For present purposes, these differences are not significant.

[28] Funder, *Personality Puzzle*, 135.

[29] As Ross and Nisbett put it: 'clerics and criminals rarely face an identical or equivalent set of situational challenges' (*The Person and the Situation*, 19).

determine what D did. There will inevitably be other evidence: character will be just one part of a bigger picture.[30]

Even if we are talking of small effect sizes of the sort associated with personality psychology, character evidence may be sufficient to turn a moderately strong case into a very strong one. This is partly because evidence combines by multiplication. But it is also because the way to think about character evidence in the context of a trial appears to be comparatively. When we learn that D has a previous conviction for rape, we learn something we did not know before. If we started off thinking that D did not have any previous convictions, then the relevant question now is how much more likely D is to commit rape than someone without a criminal record. We will look at ways of answering this question quantitatively later in this chapter. Sticking to the present context—small effect sizes in personality research—here is the thinking of Ross and Nisbett, writers strongly associated with situationism:

Consider Tom, Dick and Harry—three participants in a hypothetical study of... extraversion. Suppose we know that on a single randomly sampled occasion Tom scored two standard deviations below the mean, that is, at roughly the 2nd population centile... And suppose we know that Harry scored two standard deviations above the mean, at the 98th centile... Given just these two 'items' of information, we can make some rather striking inferences about their subsequent behaviour. In particular, we can already estimate that Harry is roughly five times as likely as Tom (probabilities of 4.5 and .9 per cent, respectively) to be doing something truly extroverted (that is, in the top 2 per cent) when they are next encountered. Harry also is more than twice as likely to show a truly extroverted response than a randomly selected individual or than Dick, whose level of extraversion on the one previous time it was observed proved to be perfectly average.[31]

This suggests that information about past behaviour can be powerful evidence in a comparative exercise.

Other uses of character evidence might be rather more dubious on the basis of the research reviewed here. In sentencing, personal mitigation can sometimes range widely over a person's life, with a sentence discounted where a defendant has done some significant good deed. While the theoretical basis for such aspects of mitigation remains opaque,[32] the fragmented, or mixed, nature of character

---

[30] Sometimes probative value will be increased by similarity in *modus operandi*, as with Mullen, the blow-torch burglar, and Straffen, the child killer (*Mullen* [1992] Crim LR 735; and *Straffen* [1952] 2 QB 911). Here, probative value seems to flow through something more than a simple personality factor which could be described in broad terms ('aggressive', 'selfish'): motivational and aptitudinal factors play a part. Ross and Nisbett, *The Person and the Situation*, 20, note that the former play a role in enhancing predictability in everyday life.

[31] *The Person and the Situation*, 116. The authors go on to note: 'these differences in relative likelihood become greater when we are able to make our assessments on the basis of aggregated data' (117).

[32] See A. Ashworth, 'Re-evaluating the Justifications for Aggravation and Mitigation at Sentencing' in J. V. Roberts (ed), *Mitigation and Aggravation at Sentencing* (Cambridge: Cambridge University Press, 2011), and discussion in Chapter 11 of this book.

traits would appear to mean that a person's exemplary action in, say, saving a drowning child should not be seen as reflecting on his likelihood of reoffending. More equivocal are those character-based theories of criminal responsibility which attach significance to the notion of actions which are out of character, or the idea of a 'settled disposition'.[33] If character is fragmented, we should be wary of the notion of out-of-character actions, unless we have information about D's behaviour in similar situations to the present one.[34] That D is kind to his colleagues may not tell us much about whether his aggressiveness to a stranger is out of character. On the other hand, where we know that D has committed a crime, we might be on safer ground in saying that committing crime is not out of character for him, in part because, as Ross and Nisbett note, extreme behaviour gives a better basis for prediction.[35] The problem of drawing an inference from non-criminal behaviour to criminal behaviour can also occur in evidence law. Consider Dolan, who reacted with destructive rage when his possessions—his car, the shower—malfunctioned.[36] This evidence was used at his trial for murder of his child, the prosecution theory being that he had lost his temper in a similarly violent way. Situational specificity might mean that we should be cautious of drawing such an inference.

2.2 Recidivism and the Relevance of Previous Convictions

Character evidence can take various forms, but in the criminal trial it most often involves the use of evidence of previous offending (typically previous convictions) to prove that the defendant has committed the offence for which he is on trial or that he may reoffend in the future. It is the former which is the focus here—although the discussion is of obvious relevance to sentencing questions too. The questions to be examined, then, concern the relevance of previous convictions to the defendant's guilt. To think about this, we need to model the way in which evidence of previous convictions might be used to prove guilt. Above, it was noted that as evidence of guilt previous convictions operate comparatively. It may be easier to understand this by way of an example involving a different type of evidence. Suppose D is on trial for murder, and that there is some evidence linking him to the crime: for example, he was seen close to the scene of crime and fibres similar to those in one of his sweaters are found on the victim. This evidence establishes a certain probability of guilt. If it is then revealed that D had a motive to kill V (for example, V was having an affair with D's wife), then the probability of D's guilt increases. This is despite the fact that the vast majority of people with a motive to kill do not go on to commit murder. The motive evidence contributes to the case against D because people with a motive

---

[33] See discussion in Chapter 11.
[34] See J. M. Doris, 'Out of Character: On the Psychology of Excuses in Criminal Law' in H. LaFollette (ed), *Ethics in Practice* (3rd edn, Oxford: Blackwell, 2006).
[35] *The Person and the Situation*, 138–9.
[36] *Dolan* (2003) 1 Cr App R 18, [2003] EWCA Crim 1859.

Table 2.1 Reoffending rates by number of previous convictions

Number of previous offences	Proportion of offenders who reoffend within one year
0	11.4
1–2	21.2
3–9	28.4
10–24	33.6
>25	47.9
All offenders	26.5

to kill are more likely to kill than those without: it is this comparative element which creates probative value.[37]

As evidence of guilt, previous convictions work in a similar way to motive evidence. Previous convictions are probative because people with previous convictions are more likely to commit crime than those without previous convictions. If, in the example above, what is revealed is not that D had a motive but that he had a previous conviction for serious violence, the probability of D's guilt still increases. But what basis is there for believing that people with a criminal record are more likely to offend? It is not uncommon for people—especially males—to have previous convictions. 33 per cent of the male population born in 1953 had been convicted by age 53. Most of these—52 per cent—had only been convicted once.[38] This suggests that many people have previous convictions and that recidivism is the exception rather than the rule. As with motive, however, that does not mean that previous convictions are not probative of guilt: the pertinent question is whether people with previous convictions are more likely to offend than those without. Looking at all those who were convicted in 2009 to 2010, 26.5 per cent were reconvicted within a year.[39] What is more, the likelihood of reoffending in this period was linked to the number of previous convictions, as Table 2.1 shows.[40]

These figures are suggestive, but they provide little detail. When previous convictions are used in court to prove guilt, they are being used as evidence that D committed a specific offence—say burglary—while the figures in Table 2.1 cover any offence at all. More detail is provided in Table 2.2, which

[37] See R. D. Friedman and R. C. Park, 'Sometimes What Everybody Thinks They Know Is True' (2003) 27 *Law & Human Behavior* 629.
[38] *Conviction Histories of Offenders Between the Ages of 10 and 52 England and Wales* (London: Ministry of Justice, 2010), 7. For females, the figures are 7 and 75 per cent.
[39] *Proven Re-Offending Statistics Quarterly Bulletin October 2009 to September 2010, England and Wales* (London: Ministry of Justice, 2012). The cohort in this study is broad: all offenders who were released from custody, received a non-custodial conviction, or a caution, reprimand/warning, or who tested positive for opiates/cocaine between October 2009 and September 2010.
[40] Data from *Quarterly Bulletin October 2009 to September 2010*, table 6C (the tables are contained in a separate Excel document).

Table 2.2 Number of convicted offences committed during the one-year follow-up period, by index offence group and reoffence group, 2009 cohort

Index offence group	Number of offenders	Violence (serious)	Violence (non-serious)	Robbery	Public order or not	Sexual	Sexual (child)	Soliciting or prostitution	Domestic burglary	Other burglary	Theft
Violence (serious)	1,343	8	121	11	71	1	–	–	7	6	82
Violence (non-serious)	14,444	130	3,354	126	2,319	65	10	9	192	154	1,917
Robbery	1,147	7	168	43	118	1	–	1	55	55	244
Public order or riot	3,306	30	669	20	812	14	–	2	51	49	467
Sexual	568	3	42	1	51	115	26	–	6	5	82
Sexual (child)	712	–	17	–	8	44	136	–	–	2	8
Soliciting or prostitution	32	–	3	–	1	–	–	19	–	–	8
Domestic burglary	2,043	13	312	64	194	9	–	4	397	214	783
Other burglary	1,736	15	363	35	221	2	3	2	206	543	1,093
Theft	9,611	50	1,678	116	1,563	54	9	32	387	633	16,320
Handling	914	1	138	10	89	1	–	1	75	72	436
Fraud and forgery	2,333	6	120	5	67	4	1	4	25	22	308
Absconding or bail offences	1,023	4	242	36	236	6	3	20	33	38	370
Taking and driving away and related offences	1,227	21	214	22	142	4	2	3	61	57	268
Theft from vehicles	565	4	102	10	66	3	–	2	41	93	347
Other motoring offences	3,685	13	401	26	182	7	7	5	74	100	401
Drink driving	3,470	8	179	6	123	9	1	–	9	11	114
Criminal or malicious damage	2,387	29	638	27	544	17	12	1	40	58	533
Drugs import/export/production/supply	1,244	3	57	7	59	3	–	–	15	11	141
Drugs possession/small-scale supply	3,100	21	314	17	210	8	1	1	61	53	515
Other	1,726	12	303	32	402	14	2	16	25	36	402
Total	56,616	378	9,435	614	7,478	381	213	122	1,760	2,212	24,839

Italics means less than or equal to 50 offenders—treat the data with caution.

– Data based on less than or equal to 10 offences are removed as they make the data unreliable for interpretation.

Handling	Fraud and forgery	Absconding or bail offences	Taking and driving away and related offences	Theft from vehicles	Other motoring offences	Drink driving	Criminal or malicious damage	Drugs import/export/production/supply	Drugs possession/small-scale supply	Other	Total number of offences
5	9	39	10	6	87	16	46	12	46	37	620
107	197	905	165	78	1,095	330	1,175	154	816	546	13,884
22	32	67	26	27	152	26	79	33	79	39	1,274
31	53	233	33	24	256	72	315	27	175	204	3,537
3	11	28	1	–	18	1	27	1	15	14	450
1	1	3	2	3	10	3	4	–	4	5	251
1	–	6	–	–	–	–	4	–	4	10	56
98	72	194	89	78	296	41	143	44	233	125	3,403
84	67	244	75	102	346	29	214	19	235	142	4,040
260	436	2,246	137	232	875	112	655	190	1,257	963	28,205
65	65	126	34	74	198	26	83	12	143	41	1,690
11	261	92	9	5	148	22	51	12	75	50	1,298
22	29	246	31	20	179	30	122	13	96	114	1,890
49	36	147	147	44	514	40	107	18	120	84	2,100
53	12	111	22	179	157	16	57	9	104	76	1,464
87	54	198	110	61	1,437	110	171	38	278	71	3,831
5	11	63	36	10	532	114	72	10	66	21	1,400
22	31	215	50	30	207	70	483	7	140	172	3,326
8	22	40	7	9	39	14	32	22	146	16	651
37	36	200	28	27	310	55	122	102	826	75	3,019
24	28	152	39	38	162	25	146	12	102	1,226	3,198
995	1,463	5,555	1,051	1,047	7,018	1,152	4,108	735	4,960	4,031	79,547

Table 2.3 Offender: offence ratios for one-year follow-up, 2009 cohort

	Serious violence	Robbery	Sexual	Domestic burglary	Theft	All offences
Serious violence	**168:1**	122:1	1,343:1	192:1	16:1	2:1
Robbery	164:1	**27:1**	1,147:1	21:1	5:1	0.9:1
Sexual	189:1	568:1	**5:1**	95:1	7:1	1.3:1
Domestic burglary	157:1	32:1	227:1	**4:1**	3:1	0.6:1
Theft	192:1	83:1	178:1	25:1	**0.6:1**	0.3:1

shows the number of offences of various types committed by offenders with previous convictions for a range of specific offences.[41] The first thing to say about these data is that they track a differently defined cohort than the figures above. The cohort is adults released from custody or commencing a court order under probation supervision in the first quarter of 2009—so offenders who had, for example, been fined or cautioned are not included. This study, then, tracked a reasonably serious group of offenders, many of whom no doubt already had previous convictions.[42] Overall, the 56,616 offenders committed nearly 80,000 offences—so some committed more than one offence, though in fact the majority (60 per cent) committed no offences during the one-year follow-up period.[43] These figures tell us something about how reoffending varies between those recently convicted of different offences.[44] Of particular interest for the purposes of evidence law is the rate of reoffending for the same offence—because similarity between previous offence and current charge is a significant trigger for the admissibility of previous convictions. The ratio of offenders for crime X to new offences of crime X varies, from 168:1 for serious violence to 0.6:1 for theft. Table 2.3 shows the offender: offence ratios for several crimes.

Much of the pattern here can be explained by how common the different offences are. As serious violence is much rarer than theft, it is not surprising that theft reoffending is frequent among all groups, but serious violence much less frequent. The ratios suggest a degree of specialization; ignoring theft reoffending, there is a tendency for same-offence recidivism to be more frequent than recidivism for any other specific offence. At the same time, there is quite a degree

[41] From *Adult Re-convictions: Results from the 2009 Cohort England and Wales* (London: Ministry of Justice, 2011), 40.

[42] Reflected in the fact that nearly 40 per cent were reconvicted during the year (*Adult Re-convictions 2009*, 3).

[43] See *Adult Re-convictions 2009*, 3.

[44] It is important to note, however, that the index offences tell us nothing about the offenders' previous histories: those whose index offence is violence may have criminal records for a variety of other offences. The index offence simply picks out an offence committed at a particular point in time.

Table 2.4 Number of previous convictions/cautions for same offence (%)

	0	1	2	3+
Actual bodily harm/grievous bodily harm	70	18	6	5
Common assault	53	25	11	11
Shoplifting	16	13	9	62
Rape, sexual assault, unlawful sexual intercourse	87	6	3	4
Burglary	40	15	9	37
Robbery	77	12	5	6

of promiscuity, and while those convicted of theft are the most prolific overall, the ratios for all offences show much less variation than the same-offence ratios. Reoffending is common among all groups.[45] Table 2.4 shows elements of the same pattern from a different angle: the number of previous convictions/cautions for the same offence possessed by those convicted of particular offences in 2009.[46] Again, there seems to be more recidivism for the more common/less serious offences, such as common assault and shoplifting.

The figures presented here combine males and females. Because males commit much more crime than females, trends in male offending dominate the figures. In general, females are less likely to reoffend than males: in 2010, the one-year reoffending rates were 28 per cent for males and 19 per cent for females.[47] But this distinction may be less significant than it appears. For the more serious group of offenders in the 2009 cohort, the difference is less marked: 42 versus 36 per cent, and female offenders were slightly more prolific, committing more offences per reoffender.[48] One analysis of this issue concluded that, once age and criminal history are taken into account, a similar proportion of males and females reoffend.[49] It is therefore a reasonable assumption that the trends identified in this chapter apply to women as much as to men.

In light of the fact that recidivism is generally less common for more serious offences, some writers have argued that previous convictions for these offences have little probative value if used to prove commission of the same offence.[50] This implies, counter-intuitively, that if a person on trial for murder has a previous

[45] For similar results, see C. Lloyd, G. Mair, and M. Hough, *Explaining Reconviction Rates: A Critical Analysis*, Home Office Research Study No 136 (London: Home Office, 1994), 47–9. The authors note that there was a tendency for a defendant to be convicted of a less serious offence than he was initially convicted for, explaining this as the result of regression to the mean.
[46] *Sentencing Statistics: England and Wales 2009 Statistics Bulletin* (London: Ministry of Justice, 2010), table 6.4.
[47] *Proven Re-Offending Statistics Quarterly Bulletin October 2009 to September 2010, England and Wales* (London: Ministry of Justice, 2012), table 3.
[48] *Adult Reconvictions 2009*, 14 and table A1.
[49] See Lloyd et al, *Explaining Reconviction Rates*, 29–30.
[50] See C. H. Rose, 'Should the Tail Wag the Dog? The Potential Effect of Recidivism Data on Character Evidence Rules' (2006) 36 *New Mexico L Rev* 341; E. J. Imwinkelried, 'Undertaking the Task of Reforming the American Character Evidence Provision: The Importance of Getting

conviction for murder, that conviction would say little about whether he had committed the current offence. The argument fails to grasp that what really matters is, as noted above, a comparative judgment: whether the person with the murder conviction is more likely than other people to commit murder. In Park's terms, the question is whether the person has a comparative propensity to commit crime.[51] While the data reviewed so far are suggestive, they do not really answer this question. What we need to do is compare offending rates between those with convictions and those without. That is not easy, because it is difficult to find comparable datasets. Any evaluation will have to be somewhat rough and ready.

For purposes of comparison, a reasonable proxy for crime rates among those without previous convictions is the general criminal statistics, which show the number of convictions among the population of England and Wales in any given year. The population of England and Wales above the age of 10 (the minimum age for criminal liability) is about 48 million. This allows the calculation of ratios similar to those in Table 2.3. The ratios for the population are given in Table 2.5.[52]

The figures mean that, for example, during the one-year period there was one offence of violence for every 433 people in the population (figures for common assault are included, so the majority of these are not very serious offences). The data from Table 2.2 can be combined into comparable categories (see Table 2.6), to contrast offending rates among the population at large with offending rates for those with particular previous convictions. This shows that, for example, for every 4.4 people in the cohort who had committed an offence of violence, there was one offence of violence committed during the one-year follow-up.

The differences between the 2009 cohort—which, as was emphasized above, is a group of fairly serious offenders—and the general population are marked. They are summarized in Table 2.7, which shows the factor by which offence rates among the different offence groups in the 2009 cohort exceeded those among the general population. What this means is that violent offenders in the 2009 cohort were 98 times more likely to commit an offence of violence than a member of the general population.

In earlier work I conducted a similar comparison, using data from a two-year reconviction study.[53] The data were split between those whose initial offence had led to custodial and non-custodial sentences (Table 2.8). The figures show how

---

the Experiment Off on the Right Foot' (1995) 22 *Fordham Urban LJ* 285, 297–8; and T. R. Lave and A. Orenstein, 'Empirical Fallacies of Evidence Law: A Critical Look at the Admission of Prior Sex Crimes' (2013) 81 *U Cincinnati L Rev* 795. For a less serious version of the same error, see L. Laudan and R. J. Allen, 'The Devastating Impact of Prior Crimes Evidence and Other Myths of the Criminal Justice Process' (2011) 11 *J Crim L & Criminol* 493, 521.

[51] R. C. Park, 'Character at the Crossroads' (1998) 49 *Hastings LJ* 717.

[52] Data from *Criminal Statistics: England and Wales 2009 Statistics Bulletin* (London: Ministry of Justice, 2010), 62. Figures for violent offences include the summary offences of common assault and assault on a police constable (data from supplementary table S5.1).

[53] M. Redmayne, 'The Relevance of Bad Character' (2002) 61 *CLJ* 684, drawing on C. Kershaw, J. Goodman, and S. White, *Reconvictions of Offenders Sentenced or Discharged from Prison in 1995, England and Wales* (London: Home Office, 1999).

Table 2.5 Population:offence ratios, England and Wales 2009

Violence	433:1
Sexual offences	9,412:1
Burglary	2,087:1
Robbery	5,581:1
Theft and handling stolen goods	429:1
All offences	34:1

Table 2.6 Offender:offence same-crime reoffending ratios for one-year follow-up, 2009 cohort

Violence	4.4:1
Sexual offences	4:1
Burglary	2.7:1
Robbery	27:1
Theft and handling stolen goods	0.6:1
All offences	0.7:1

much more likely the study group was to commit the offence they had originally been sentenced for than the general population.

For the most part, these figures are considerably lower, and are closer to Park's calculations, based on US data.[54] There are various possible explanations for the differences, and some significant ones are worth mentioning.[55] As has been emphasized, the 2009 cohort data measure number of offences, not the number of offenders who reoffended. Because some offenders commit more than one offence in the relevant period, this increases the difference between the offending sample and the general population.[56] The 2009 study also involved a sample of a slightly more serious group of offenders, given the sentences which led to inclusion in the cohort, so a higher rate of reoffending is to be expected. Finally, the 2009 figures involved a one-year follow-up. The probability of reconviction is greatest straight after sentencing/release from custody, and declines quite quickly. The one-year focus in the 2009 study thus shows comparative propensity at its highest.[57]

[54] 'Character at the Crossroads'. Park's comparative propensity figures are: homicide, 224; rape, 163; burglary, 56; larceny, 19; and drug offence, 24. These are based on arrest (not conviction) rates.
[55] One factor points in the other direction: reconviction rates have fallen by 24 per cent from 2000 to 2009 (though there has been a rise in the proportion of serious reconvictions): *Adult Re-convictions 2009*, 8.
[56] This may explain, in particular, why the comparative figures for theft and handling based on the 2009 study are much higher than in the earlier one.
[57] The difference in the figures for sexual offences is notable. In my earlier work, I remarked that the figure for sexual offending was low for the custody sample, but even ignoring that the comparison between the 2009 cohort and the general population is striking. This does not appear to be a

Table 2.7 2009 cohort compared with the general population

Violence	98
Sexual offences	2,353
Burglary	773
Robbery	206
Theft and handling stolen goods	715
All offences	49

Table 2.8 Two-year same crime comparative propensity

	Custody sample	Non-custody sample
Violence	29	55
Sexual offence	80	250
Burglary	125	131
Robbery	185	400
Theft and handling	38	35

It is plainly pointless to look for a 'true' measure of comparative propensity, especially with the available data. The figures here are certainly not intended to be presented in court, but they are nevertheless informative. They suggest that a person with a recent previous conviction for a particular offence is considerably more likely than a person without a previous conviction to commit such an offence: previous convictions therefore have considerable probative value as proof of guilt.

Of course, criminal statistics, such as the ones relied on here, are notoriously problematic. Only a tiny proportion of known crimes result in conviction[58]—yet conviction rates are what is measured in the data presented in this section. The main problem with relying on a comparison of conviction rates between those with previous convictions and the general population as a proxy for actual differences in offending is that to the extent that there is a tendency to 'round up the usual suspects',[59] the statistics will exaggerate reoffending compared with first-time offending. While this is no doubt a factor in the comparative figures given in Tables 2.7 and 2.8, it seems unlikely that the difference in offending rates

freak figure—the rate of sexual reoffending was similar in other years. The figure reflects the fact that sexual offending was common among those in the 2009 cohort who had been convicted of a sexual offence, but rare in the general population.

[58] About 2 per cent of crime recorded by the British Crime Survey: see R. Garside, *Crime, Persistent Offenders and the Justice Gap* (London: Crime and Society Foundation, 2004).

[59] See R. Reiner, *Law and Order: An Honest Citizen's Guide to Crime and Control* (Cambridge: Polity, 2007), 11–13. For empirical evidence of this process in Scotland, see L. McAra and S. McVie, 'Youth Justice? The Impact of System Contact on Patterns of Desistance from Crime' (2007) 4 *Youth Justice* 315.

is a complete artefact of policing practices. Suspects are often identified by members of the public or are caught in the act.[60] Sometimes, suspects are identified by other processes over which the police have little control, as when there is a match from a crime scene sample to a profile on the DNA database—something which occurs in around 60 per cent of cases where a sample is submitted,[61] suggesting that those on the database (who are there because of police decision-making) are responsible for a reasonable proportion of crime. Further, other sources of information about offending, such as self-report studies, suggest that the criminal justice system targets the more serious recidivists.[62]

It should again be emphasized that no great claims are being made about the comparative figures presented here. They give us some idea about the differences between those with previous convictions and those without, but cannot be taken to be anything like exact. However, even if the figures are all reduced by a factor of ten, they still represent significant differences. If a person with previous convictions is only twice as likely to offend as someone without, that is still significant in terms of probative value.

2.3 Criminal Careers

The statistics presented in the previous section say something about the significance of previous convictions as a risk factor for offending. But it is important to put them in perspective by placing them in the context of what else is known about offending trajectories. As was noted, many people, especially men, gain a criminal conviction, but the majority do not go on to be reconvicted.

Perhaps the most important context in which to place recidivism statistics is the relationship between age and crime. Offending is most common in the late teenage years, and the age-crime curve has a very sharp peak—a typical example is presented in Figure 2.1.[63] Offending increases rapidly in the mid-teens, peaking

---

[60] M. McConville and J. Baldwin, 'The Role of Interrogation in Crime Discovery and Conviction' (1982) 22 *Brit J Criminol* 165, 168. The 2000 British Crime Survey found that in two-thirds of violent incidents the offender was known to the victim: *The 2000 British Crime Survey England and Wales* (London: Home Office, 2000), 38.

[61] See <http://www.npia.police.uk/en/13340.htm>. Not all matches result in conviction, as sometimes an innocent explanation for the presence of DNA is accepted. One cannot expect the match rate to be too high because of 'churn': the age-crime curve, discussed below, means that offenders on the database will continually be dropping out of crime, to be replaced by new offenders. See D. Leary and K. Pease, 'DNA and the Active Criminal Population' (2003) 5 *Crime Prevention & Community Safety* 7.

[62] In their study of young people's offending in Peterborough, Wikström et al found that those with a police record tended to report higher levels of offending than those without a record: P.-O. H. Wikström, D. Oberwittler, K. Treiber, and B. Hardie, *Breaking Rules: The Social and Situational Dynamics of Young People's Urban Crime* (Oxford: Oxford University Press, 2012), 119. See also M. Maguire, 'Crime Statistics, Patterns and Trends: Changing Perceptions and Their Implications' in M. Maguire, R. Morgan, and R. Reiner (eds), *The Oxford Handbook of Criminology* (2nd edn; Oxford: Oxford University Press, 1997), 175; and C. Coleman and J. Moynihan, *Understanding Crime Data: Haunted by the Dark Figure* (Milton Keynes: Open University Press, 1996), ch 2.

[63] For detailed discussion of such curves, and the difficulties in interpreting them, see D. P. Farrington, 'Age and Crime' (1986) 7 *Crime and Justice* 189; and S. B. van Mastrigt and D. P. Farrington, 'Co-offending, Age, Gender and Crime Type: Implications for Criminal Justice Policy' (2009) 49 *Brit J Criminol* 552.

at age 17 to 18 and then dropping off rather less sharply than it rose. Age is significant for our purposes because the statistics which were used earlier to generate figures for comparative propensity were based on one- and two-year follow-ups. This
is a crucial point. Recent convictions may have considerable probative value, but
that value fades the longer the gap between current charge and previous offence.
And the probability of recidivism declines most quickly after the late teens.

How long does it take for a previous conviction to lose all value as a predictor
of future offending? Soothill and Francis conducted a study which helps to answer
this question.[64] Using official data, they studied 'hazard rates' for groups of
offenders born in 1953 and compared them to the non-offending population. The
groups were studied from age 20 on, and comprised those with no convictions,
those who had only been convicted between the ages of 10 and 16, those who had
only been convicted between the ages of 17 and 20, and those who had been convicted in both of these periods. The hazard rate represents the probability of conviction at a particular age given that there had been no conviction from age 20 up
until that age. The results are represented in Figure 2.2. The comparison group,
those who have never offended, do not have zero probability of conviction: a few
will be convicted relatively late in life. As the authors put it, they have 'a small and
declining risk of being convicted within the next year—from around 1 in 100 at
the age of 21 years, around 1 in 200 at the age of 25 years, around 1 in 300 at the
age of 30 years and around 1 in 700 at the age of 35 years.'[65] Unsurprisingly, the
probability of conviction for the offending groups declines with time, the decline
roughly echoing the age-crime curve. Although the probabilities of offending for
all groups become close, they never quite converge. Nevertheless, there is little
to choose between most of the groups by age 30. Soothill and Francis conclude
that, for the purposes of employment and the like, 'it is time to wipe the slate
clean for most offenders with convictions for minor offences after, say, ten years if
ex-offenders have managed such a significant crime-free period.'[66]

Note the caveat: 'offenders with convictions for minor offences'. Reconviction
hazard rates vary with different types of offences. A recent study of hazard rates
for a variety of offences concludes that:

Hazards for all types of reoffending were highest in the first few months following sen-
tence/discharge, but some types of reoffending were more persistent than others. The
hazards for violent and sexual reoffending were more persistent than the hazards for non-
violent reoffending (although violent reoffending remained less frequent than nonviolent
reoffending, and sexual reoffending remained far less frequent). Among violent offences,
homicide and wounding, other assault, weapon possession and criminal damage hazards
were more persistent, while the robbery hazard was less persistent. Among nonviolent

---

[64] K. Soothill and B. Francis, 'When Do Ex-Offenders Become Like Non-Offenders?' (2009)
48 *Howard J* 373. See also M. C. Kurlychek, R. Brame, and S. D. Bushway, 'Scarlet Letters and
Recidivism: Does an Old Criminal Record Predict Future Offending?' (2006) 5 *Criminol & Public
Policy* 483.
    [65] 'When Do Ex-Offenders Become Like Non-Offenders?', 383.
    [66] 'When Do Ex-Offenders Become Like Non-Offenders?', 385.

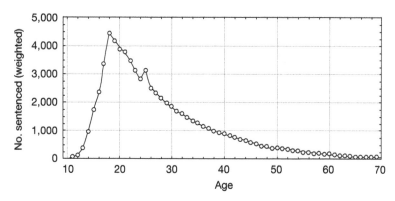

Figure 2.1 Age-crime curve 1997 sentencing sample (from J. F. Macleod, P. G. Grove, and D. Farrington, *Explaining Criminal Careers: Implications for Justice Policy* (Oxford: Oxford University Press, 2012), 109). The secondary peak at age 25 is almost certainly an artefact of the way in which ages were recorded—individuals of unknown age were recorded by the courts as being age 25. The points on the graph show court appearances resulting in one or more convictions

offences, drugs offences, drink driving and fraud hazards were persistent, while theft, absconding, other motoring and burglary hazards were less persistent.[67]

As this passage notes, base rates are part of the picture. Because sexual offending is rare, sexual reoffending is much less frequent than theft reoffending. Nevertheless, because the hazard rate for sexual reoffending declines slowly compared to theft, an offender will remain at greater risk of sexual offending compared to members of the general population long after his chances of committing theft have more or less converged with those of the general population.

We have seen that age, time-lapse, and type of offence are all part of the bigger picture of recidivism. And in the previous section the significance of the number of previous convictions was noted. The figures in Table 2.1 show that chances of reconviction increase with number of reconvictions. Data from the Cambridge Study in Delinquent Development (CSDD) paint a similar picture (Table 2.9).[68] Piquero et al explain: 'recidivism probabilities begin at .399 (the prevalence of offending in the CSDD) and jump quickly (because of the large proportion of one-time offenders who do not recidivate) to .682'.[69] The curve then flattens out, but jumps to 0.82 at offence four before flattening again. From offence four to

---

[67] P. Howard, *Hazards of Different Types of Reoffending* (London: Ministry of Justice, 2011), iv. The study did not divide the offenders into different groups on the basis of the type of offences they tended to commit, thus these findings tell us about the chances that any offender will commit, for example, a violent offence after x months without offending.

[68] From A. Piquero, D. Farrington, and A. Blumstein, *Key Issues in Criminal Career Research: New Analyses of the Cambridge Study in Delinquent Development* (Cambridge: Cambridge University Press, 2007), 133.

[69] Piquero et al, *Key Issues in Criminal Career Research*, 133.

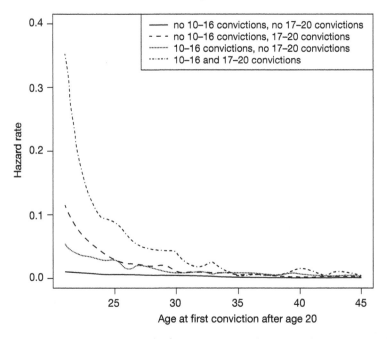

Figure 2.2 Conviction hazard rates for four groups using the 1953 Offenders Index cohort data (from Soothill and Francis, 'When Do Ex-Offenders Become Like Non-Offenders?' (2009) 48 *Howard J* 373)

ten, an average of 84.5 per cent reoffend. Again, though, the age–crime relationship should not be forgotten: although these recidivism probabilities are high, the general trend for all offenders appears to be gradual desistance.[70]

One reason why Piquero et al, and other criminologists, are interested in these changing recidivism probabilities is that the flattening of the curve after offence four, with a high probability of recidivism, may mark out a particular group of 'chronic' offenders. For our purposes, the wider point is that, beneath the general probabilities of recidivism we have been considering so far, there may be different types of offenders. Table 2.9 suggests that a distinction might be drawn between those who desist relatively early in their criminal career, and those who are convicted a fourth time, who then have a low probability of desisting. One well-known typology was developed by Moffitt, who suggests a broad distinction between 'adolescent-limited' and 'life course persistent' offenders.[71] Analysing the

---

[70] See J. H. Laub and R. J. Sampson, *Shared Beginnings, Divergent Lives: Delinquent Boys to Age 70* (Cambridge, MA: Harvard University Press, 2003).

[71] T. E. Moffitt, '"Life-Course-Persistent" and "Adolescent Limited" Antisocial Behavior: A Developmental Taxonomy' (1993) 100 *Psychol Rev* 674. The consensus appears to be that this taxonomy fails: all offenders gradually desist, so there is none who persists at a constant rate, and in any case two groups is two few for the purposes of grouping offenders. See, eg, T. Skardhamar, 'Reconsidering the Theory on Adolescent Limited and Life-Course Persistent Anti-Social Behaviour' (2009) 49 *Brit J Criminol* 863.

Table 2.9 Recidivism probabilities from CSDD: first ten convictions

Offence number	Recidivism probability
1	0.399
2	0.682
3	0.696
4	0.820
5	0.828
6	0.830
7	0.840
8	0.891
9	0.909
10	0.800

CSDD data, Piquero et al suggest that their subjects might be divided into five groups: non-offenders, low adolescence peaked, very low rate chronics, high adolescence peaked, and high rate chronics, all exhibiting distinct age-crime curves and risk factors.[72] Laub and Sampson identify six offender typologies, but are sceptical of linking these to childhood risk factors.[73] Many other examples could be given: this is a contested and methodologically complex area of criminology, but it is certainly common currency that a small group of offenders is responsible for a disproportionate amount of crime.[74]

Typologies are potentially significant for our purposes. It may be wrong to make assumptions about a particular defendant's risk of offending based on general data about reoffending when that defendant may belong to a distinct group with a lower or higher risk than the norm. There are many issues here, some of which are discussed in later chapters. For now, a simple response seems appropriate. As was stressed earlier, attempts to quantify comparative propensity are inevitably inexact, and no argument is being made that any figures be presented in court. For now, the argument is simply that those with recent previous convictions are significantly more likely to offend than those without. To the extent that the largest group of offenders comprises those who only offend once, we should be cautious about reading much into a single previous conviction, at least unless it is for a serious offence. When a defendant has serious, or multiple, convictions, it is important to bear in mind the age-crime curve and the significance of the increasing number of previous convictions. These factors go some way towards

---

[72] Piquero et al, *Key Issues in Criminal Career Research*, ch 10.
[73] *Shared Beginnings, Divergent Lives*, ch 5.
[74] Piquero et al, *Key Issues in Criminal Career Research*, 3. This finding occurs in both self-report studies and in studies using reconviction (or re-arrest) rates. For an example from a self-report study, see J. Hales, C. Nevill, S. Pudney, and S. Tipping, *Longitudinal Analysis of the Offending, Crime and Justice Survey 2003–06* (London: Home Office, 2009), 1.

placing the defendant into one of the common typologies, such as adolescent limited and chronic.

The argument above might be put slightly differently: even if there was widespread agreement that there were, say, five distinct types of offender, this would be more complexity than the law could manage given the purposes for which previous convictions are used at the fact-finding stage of the trial and the information available to the court. Nevertheless, there is one typology the law appears to insist on, though admittedly it is one which is easily handled. This is the typology of specialization in offending. As we will see in later chapters, the law's assumption is generally that people stick to particular types of offending: violence, property offending, sexual offending, and the like. Thus, if a defendant with previous convictions for sexual and property offences is on trial for GBH, those convictions are unlikely to be admissible as evidence of propensity to be violent.

Is there any evidence that offenders specialize?[75] In discussing Table 2.2, it was noted that there is a fair degree of promiscuity in offending, but also some specialization.[76] When this data was used to generate comparative propensities for the 2009 cohort (Table 2.7), it turned out that any offender in the cohort was 49 times more likely to commit any offence in the one-year period than was a member of the general population. Francis and Soothill examined the link between sex offending and homicide, and estimated that in a 21-year period, sex offenders were seven times more likely to commit homicide than members of the general population.[77] Other criminological literature by and large agrees: offenders show considerable versatility, and a person who has committed one offence is at risk of committing further different offences,[78] though some offenders may specialize in less serious offences.[79] What specialization there is increases with age, but a particular finding of the CSDD study is that there is little evidence of specialization in violence; violence is simply something which is likely to occur in any prolonged offending career. 'The number of offenses is the strongest predictor of whether an individual is a violent offender.'[80] This is reflected in the figures in the first column of Table 2.3: there is little difference in the frequency of serious violence among different offender groups. Overall, the best conclusion may be that offenders are 'specialized generalists', tending to commit a range of offences, but (perhaps with the exception of violence) being more likely to commit their specialization offence than any other particular offence.

[75] See generally K. Soothill, C. Fitzpatrick, and B. Francis, *Understanding Criminal Careers* (Cullompton: Willan, 2009), ch 6.

[76] See also Lloyd et al, *Explaining Reconviction Rates*, 46–9.

[77] B. Francis and K. Soothill, 'Does Sex Offending Lead to Homicide?' (2000) 11 *J Forensic Psychiatry* 49. See also K. Soothill, B. Francis, and J. Liu, 'Does Serious Offending Lead to Homicide? Exploring the Interrelationships and Sequencing of Serious Crime' (2008) 48 *Brit J Criminol* 522.

[78] Piquero et al, *Key Issues in Criminal Career Research*, ch 6; Wikström et al, *Breaking Rules*, 122; and J. F. Macleod, P. G. Grove, and D. Farrington, *Explaining Criminal Careers: Implications for Justice Policy* (Oxford: Oxford University Press, 2012), 91–105.

[79] R. B. Felson and D. W. Osgood, 'Violent Crime' in E. Goode (ed), *Out of Control: Assessing the General Theory of Crime* (Stanford: Stanford University Press, 2008).

[80] Piquero et al, *Key Issues in Criminal Career Research*, 81.

2.4 Conclusion

This chapter has reviewed a range of evidence about how past behaviour relates to future behaviour. Research in social psychology suggests that character is fragmentary, and that may create problems for some uses of character evidence in the criminal process. But when it comes to the use of character evidence—typically in the form of previous convictions—to prove guilt, social psychology's concerns seem to have little purchase. The best evidence about whether past criminal behaviour is indicative of future criminal behaviour comes from criminal statistics and criminology more generally. Here there is little doubt: prior offending is among the most significant predictors of future offending.[81] Of course, no one offends all the time, and situational factors must be important in explaining why particular criminal acts occur. A sceptic might leap from this to the claim that crime statistics are an artefact of situations—that people reoffend simply because they are more likely than others to find themselves in criminogenic situations. Although this critique concedes the predictive power of criminal record, it is worth responding to. Criminology has its own person-situation debate: is offending caused by personal factors or environmental factors?[82] It is no surprise that, just as with psychology generally, criminal actions turn out to depend on an interaction between people and situations. In a large-scale study of young people in Peterborough, Wikström et al measured a criminal propensity variable, which was based on responses to questions about morality and self-control. Criminal propensity explained about 50 per cent of the variation in self-reported crime involvement; a measure of exposure to criminogenic settings was also predictive of self-reported offending, but less so (explaining about 20 per cent of variance).[83] Criminogenic situations, however, were not criminogenic for everyone, but only for those with medium or high propensity: 'criminogenic exposure', the authors conclude, 'is only relevant to crime prone people.'[84] Young people with high propensity also spent more time in criminogenic settings than those with low propensity,[85] reflecting the point made above in relation to the personality literature: people may choose the situations they find themselves in, and these choices are likely to be related to underlying

---

[81] See, eg, P. Gendreau, T. Little, and C. Goggin, 'A Meta-Analysis of the Predictors of Adult Offender Recidivism: What Works!' (1996) 34 *Criminology* 575; Lloyd et al, *Explaining Reconviction Rates*; and Macleod et al, *Explaining Criminal Careers*, 72. One needs to be cautious in claiming that criminal history is the best predictor of future offending because of the significance of the age-crime curve: a 90-year-old with hundreds of convictions but none in the last 20 years is unlikely to reoffend.

[82] Person-environment interactions are undoubtedly complex. Criminal propensity may be shaped by environmental factors such as upbringing, but the focus in this discussion is on finer-grained situational factors that may cause offending (eg confrontational situations; situations where there is a temptation to commit crime). Somewhere between the two levels are factors such as place of residence. There is evidence that change of residence can curb offending (see, eg, D. S. Kirk, 'Residential Change as a Turning Point in the Life Course of Crime: Desistance or Temporary Cessation?' (2012) 50 *Criminology* 329), but for most offenders place of residence does not change.

[83] Wikström et al, *Breaking Rules*, 140, 151.

[84] *Breaking Rules*, 319.

[85] *Breaking Rules*, 311.

dispositions. A further reason to doubt that situations are all-powerful in creating crime is the evidence on versatility, noted above. It is not obvious how situational factors explain why X is not only more likely to steal than other people, but also more likely to commit sexual and violent offences.

One important point to emerge from the person-situation debate in psychology is that when we aggregate over individuals, differences in behaviour between individuals may disappear, to re-emerge when we return to a finer level of focus. The statistics reviewed here no doubt wash out many significant differences between offenders: to say that offenders tend to be versatile is not to say that there are no offenders who are complete specialists. I touched on this above, in relation to the existence of distinct groups of offenders, but the issue deserves re-emphasis. On the basis of a long-term study of US males, Sampson and Laub comment that there 'is enormous variability in peak ages of offending...and age at desistance varied markedly'; 'variability in individual age-crime curves...renders the aggregate curve descriptive of few people'—though they also emphasize that a decline in offending with age was common to all offenders in their study.[86] They note the difficulty of predicting patterns of offending for individuals: 'human agency and random processes are ever-present realities, making prediction...problematic.'[87] I return to this issue in later chapters, but the basic point is that one must always be careful in interpreting a criminal record: offending behaviour can, and does, change rapidly. Even so, given that the use of criminal records in fact-finding does not involve fine-grained prediction, the data reviewed here do offer some useful general lessons. While previous offending is one of the best predictors of future offending, most offenders are convicted only once. A single previous conviction for an offence of modest seriousness says little about future risk. After the late teens, offending declines with age, the decline being most rapid immediately after the late teen peak. One should be wary of thinking that a few convictions gained by the age of 19 says much about a person at age 24 if they have not offended since. Here, Soothill and Francis's research offers a useful rule of thumb: after ten years without conviction, minor offenders should be treated like non-offenders as far as the risk of offending is concerned.

[86] R. J. Sampson and J. H. Laub, 'A Life-Course View of the Development of Crime' (2005) 602 *Annals American Academy Pol & Soc Sci* 12, 17.

[87] Sampson and Laub, 'A Life-Course View', 40. At the same time, Sampson and Laub acknowledge the reality of individual differences. For similar findings, see M. E. Ezell and L. E. Cohen, *Desisting from Crime: Continuity and Change in Long-Term Crime Patterns of Serious Chronic Offenders* (New York: Oxford University Press, 2005). On the difficulty of prediction, see also L. Kazemian, D. P. Farrington, and M. Le Blanc, 'Can We Make Accurate Long-Term Predictions about Patterns of De-escalation in Offending Behavior?' (2009) 38 J *Youth & Adolescence* 384.

3
Character and Prejudice

The standard objection to admitting bad character evidence is that it is prejudicial to the defendant—that it will undermine his right to a fair trial by making it more likely that he will be convicted even if innocent. Two different mechanisms of prejudice are often identified: reasoning prejudice and moral prejudice. Reasoning prejudice involves the fact-finder giving too much weight to bad character evidence. With moral prejudice, the fact-finder may give the correct weight to the evidence, but take a dislike to the defendant on the basis of his past criminal record and therefore convict him when not convinced beyond reasonable doubt that he is guilty. This chapter examines whether character evidence is likely to be prejudicial in these ways. It also considers whether it might undermine other criminal justice policies, such as deterrence.

The claim that certain evidence is prone to being given too much weight, or that it will prejudice the fact-finder (especially a jury) in some other way, is a common one in evidence law. It has underpinned many exclusionary rules such as the rule against hearsay, the practice of not telling the jury that the defendant's failure to answer police questions is suspicious, and rules excluding confessions which are thought to be unreliable. There is an obvious difficulty in grounding the law of evidence on this sort of argument: we trust jurors enough to have—and we often vigorously defend—a jury system, allowing them to make momentous decisions about guilt and innocence. So it is odd that we are reluctant to trust the jury properly to evaluate certain types of evidence, especially when judicial directions can be used to warn jurors to evaluate such evidence carefully. The difficulty of arguing that juries both are and are not competent to evaluate evidence is no doubt one reason why, in England and Wales at least, exclusionary rules are much less prominent than they were. Today, we admit considerable amounts of hearsay evidence and inform the jury that it can, in some circumstances, attach weight to a failure to answer police questions or to testify in court. However, bad character evidence may differ from the examples of hearsay and silence in a way which makes it more coherent to argue that, while we trust the jury, we should not inform it about the defendant's criminal record.[1] With hearsay and silence, the difficulty is in deciding what weight to give the evidence, and the fear is that the jury will fail to attend to the 'hearsay dangers'—the factors which should make

---

[1] See R. D. Friedman, 'Minimizing the Jury Over-Valuation Concern' (2003) *Michigan State L Rev* 967.

us suspicious of hearsay—or the possible innocent reason for silence. While there may be similar problems with character evidence, there is also the concern that knowing that the defendant is a bad person will affect the jury at a less conscious level, leading it to lower the standard of proof (moral prejudice) or to give more weight to other prosecution evidence than it otherwise would—a subtle form of reasoning prejudice.

Whether the concern is the classic one of the jury over-weighting bad character evidence, or that character evidence causes harm in more subtle ways, the claim that character evidence is prejudicial is in principle capable of empirical assessment. This chapter examines the evidence for prejudice, focussing on the use of character evidence as evidence of propensity to commit crime.

There is one preliminary point which is worth dealing with before proceeding. It can be argued that 'moral prejudice' is not really prejudice at all.[2] If jurors lower the standard of proof when the defendant has a criminal record, this might be said to be perfectly rational. The previous chapter shows that the probability of recidivism increases with the number of convictions. If the standard of proof is understood in utilitarian terms, then, the argument goes, it is worse to acquit a serial offender than a first-time offender.[3] The serial offender is more likely to reoffend, so the extra cost of acquitting the guilty recidivist should be offset by lowering the standard of proof. There are many complex issues here, but in this work I take the view that lowering the standard of proof in such a case is an example of prejudice. As we will see in Chapters 11 and 12, in England and Wales, as in most jurisdictions, previous convictions are likely to lead to a longer sentence, especially if the offender is classified as 'dangerous'. Taking the utilitarian view, then, there is a risk of double-counting the risk of recidivism, treating the defendant more harshly both when deciding to convict and when sentencing. It is therefore not obvious that the utilitarian approach should lead to a lower standard of proof for defendants with several previous convictions.[4] In any case, the utilitarian approach to the standard of proof is controversial, both as a matter of political morality,[5] and particularly as an interpretation of the current 'beyond reasonable doubt' standard of proof.[6] For those reasons, I take the standard view

---

[2] See L. Laudan and R. J. Allen, 'The Devastating Impact of Prior Crimes Evidence and Other Myths of the Criminal Justice Process' (2011) 101 *J Crim L & Criminol* 493, 513; and C. W. Sanchirico, 'Character Evidence and the Object of Trial' (2001) 101 *Columbia L Rev* 1227, 1248.

[3] The utilitarian approach is elaborated in L. Laudan, 'The Rules of Trial, Political Morality, and the Costs of Error: Or, is Proof Beyond a Reasonable Doubt Doing More Harm than Good?' in L. Green and B. Leiter (eds), *Oxford Studies in the Philosophy of Law: Volume 1* (Oxford: Oxford University Press, 2011).

[4] The utilitarian juror would also need to take into account the likely enhanced sentence when deciding on the appropriate standard of proof: convicting an innocent defendant is worse if a longer than normal sentence is the probable result. This in itself would tend to offset the decision to lower the standard of proof because of the risk of recidivism. Further, the claim that it is worse to acquit a recidivist presumably depends on conviction having a crime-reducing effect: on the basis of the evidence discussed in Chapter 11, this is at least questionable.

[5] A more subtle analysis, but one that still allows some scope for utilitarian considerations, is A. Wertheimer, 'Punishing the Innocent – Unintentionally' (1985) 48 *Philosophical Studies* 589.

[6] See F. Picinali, 'Two Meanings of "Reasonableness": Dispelling the "Floating" Reasonable Doubt' (2013) 76 *MLR* 845.

that lowering the standard of proof for a defendant with previous convictions would be prejudicial.

3.1 Integrating Comparative Propensity

It will be helpful to begin by revisiting the model of the relevance of previous convictions sketched in Chapter 2. The basic idea is that if D has a recent previous conviction, then he can be said to have a comparative propensity to commit similar crimes: he is more likely to offend than someone without a previous conviction. This, of course, does not prove that he is guilty of the specific crime he is charged with. The analogy of motive was used in the previous chapter: if D is on trial for murdering V and we learn that he had a motive to murder V, that should make us think it more likely that D killed V than we thought it was before we heard the evidence of motive. Learning that D has a previous conviction works in the same way. This can be modelled more formally, in Bayesian terms. The standard Bayesian model for integrating a piece of evidence into an assessment of guilt is:

$$\frac{P(G)}{P(I)} \quad \times \quad \frac{P(E\,|\,G)}{P(E\,|\,I)} \quad = \quad \frac{P(G\,|\,E)}{P(I\,|\,E)}$$

Prior odds   Liklihood ratio for   Posterior odds
on guilt   the evidence   on guilt

Here, we start with the prior odds on guilt: our assessment of how likely D is to be guilty before we hear the relevant evidence. The odds are represented as the probability of guilt divided by the probability of innocence: ($P(G)/P(I)$). When we introduce the evidence—here represented by a likelihood ratio—we can combine this with the prior odds to get the posterior odds: how likely D is to be guilty after considering the evidence. The likelihood ratio—a comparison of the probability of the evidence occurring if D is guilty and the probability of it occurring if he is innocent—is a useful measure of the probative value of evidence.

To give a simple example, suppose D is on trial for burglary and part of the evidence against him is that a shoe print matching the pattern of a pair of trainers owned by D was found at the crime scene. The expert testifies that about 5 per cent of people in the relevant population wear trainers with the same sole pattern. If, before it considers the shoe-print evidence, the jury thinks that the probability of D's guilt is 0.4, then after considering the shoe print it should update that probability to 0.93. Assuming that D's shoe was bound to match if he had indeed committed the crime, then the likelihood ratio for the shoe evidence is 1/0.05; the evidence makes guilt 20 times more likely than it was before.[7]

---

[7] In the example, the prior odds on guilt are 0.4:0.6; the likelihood ratio is 1/0.05; thus the posterior odds on guilt are 0.4:0.03, which equates to a probability of guilt of 0.93.

When it comes to previous convictions, however, things are slightly different. The measure of the probative value of previous convictions used in Chapter 2 was comparative propensity: the probability that a person will offend given that he has a previous conviction compared to the probability that he will offend given that he does not. We might think of this as $P(O|E)/P(O|\bar{E})$.[8] That is not a likelihood ratio; indeed, it more or less reverses the standard likelihood ratio: $P(E|G)/P(E|I)$. Is this significant? It would be possible to provide a likelihood ratio for evidence of prior offending, with the question being 'what is the probability that a guilty/innocent defendant will have a previous conviction of the relevant type?' But the data available make it easier to explore probative value by thinking in terms of $P(O|E)/P(O|\bar{E})$, and, more significantly, this seems to be a more natural way to think about evidence of prior convictions. The same goes for motive evidence: 'how likely is it that he would kill her if he had/did not have this motive?' is easier to grasp than 'how likely is it that he would have had this motive if he did/did not kill her?' This may be the general rule for 'prospective' evidence, evidence which is connected to the crime by a direction of causation from evidence to crime. In contrast, with trace evidence—evidence which exists because the crime was committed, such as a shoe print found at the crime scene or a witness's report that the culprit was wearing a brown shirt—the likelihood ratio, $P(E|G)/P(E|I)$, is the appropriate way to analyse the evidence. But the likelihood ratio is not the only—or always the most useful—means of analysing probative value within a probabilistic framework.[9] A ratio along the lines of $P(O|E)/P(O|\bar{E})$ is a perfectly proper way of analysing probative value in certain situations, and of combining prospective evidence with other evidence in a case.[10] Because of the emphasis on updating probabilities, most of which will be partially subjective, it is not too misleading to describe this as a Bayesian model even though Bayes's theorem is not involved.

To see how the Bayesian model for previous convictions works, let us return to the burglary example used above, where the jury initially thinks that the probability that D is guilty is 0.4. If instead of shoe-print evidence the prosecution introduces evidence that, within the last year, D was released from custody after serving a sentence for burglary, then, if we accept the figures in Table 2.7 of the previous chapter, the jury should now think it is 773 times more likely that D committed the burglary he is now charged with. Probability of guilt would change from 0.4 to 0.99. This suggests that evidence of a recent criminal conviction might be powerful evidence.

---

[8] $\bar{E}$ denotes the negative of E, ie D does not have a previous conviction.

[9] R. D. Friedman, 'Assessing Evidence' (1996) 94 *Michigan L Rev* 1810, 1829.

[10] Suppose, for example, that we are interested in whether a person will die from heart disease, and we have evidence that he is a smoker. Suppose we know that in a population of 1,000 people, 200 are smokers and the rest non-smokers. Suppose also that epidemiological studies suggest that 40 of the smokers will die of heart disease, compared to 60 non-smokers. X is a member of a similar population; if this is all we know we should rate the probability that he will die from heart disease as 0.1. If we learn that he is a smoker, then we should revise the probability that he will die of heart disease: we should think that it is 2.5 times more likely than we initially did. Thus, we should revise the probability to 0.2.

There are various reasons for setting out a normative model for combining bad character evidence with other evidence in some detail. One is that, as just noted, it suggests that bad character evidence can be powerful, which in turn implies that we need convincing reasons to exclude it. But the model is also useful because it exposes the assumptions which are being made in the argument for the relevance and probative value of previous convictions. The remainder of this section explores various criticisms which might be made of the Bayesian model illustrated in the previous paragraph. The first point to note is that the model depends on the assumption that the evidence about the previous conviction tells the jury something completely new. The probative value of the burglary conviction is based on a judgment of comparative propensity: a comparison of offending rates between people with recent previous convictions for burglary and the general population, in which committing burglary is much rarer. However, if the jury starts the trial with the assumption that D probably has a recent previous conviction for some crime or other, then informing it that he has a previous conviction for burglary would have substantially less impact than in the example above. That is because, on the evidence reviewed in Chapter 2, all offenders have a comparative propensity to burgle (ie are more likely to do so than members of the general population). Because offenders do specialize to some extent, the conviction would still have some weight, but not as much as when the initial assumption is that D is simply the average person. This shows that what might be termed the jury's 'default assumption'—its beliefs about the defendant's character before it hears any evidence on the issue—is important in assessing how much probative value previous convictions have in actual trials. We will see in section 3.5.2 that there is evidence that the default assumption is that D has previous convictions. This is not to say that bad character evidence is irrelevant, just that its power may be rather less than in the numerical example given above.

Another criticism which might be made of the Bayesian model of the impact of previous convictions is that it ignores selection effects. If the defendant was arrested because he had a criminal record, or if the police trawled through their records until they found someone with a similar *modus operandi*, some might think that this reduces the probative value of any previous convictions: whether innocent or guilty, the defendant is likely to have a criminal record. Indeed, in the DNA context it has been argued that, where D is located through a database search, DNA evidence is less powerful because the probability of finding a person with matching DNA increases in proportion to the size of the database (just as getting a run of heads when tossing a coin becomes more probable the longer one spends tossing the coin).[11] This, however, is not a convincing argument.[12] The

---

[11] See National Research Council, Committee on DNA Forensic Science, *The Evaluation of Forensic DNA Evidence* (Washington, DC: National Academy Press, 1996), 133–5; and N. E. Morton, 'The Forensic DNA Endgame' (1997) 37 *Jurimetrics J* 477, 487–93.

[12] See D. H. Kaye, 'Rounding up the Usual Suspects: A Legal and Logical Analysis of DNA Database Trawls' (2009) 87 *North Carolina L Rev* 425; and P. Donnelly and R. D. Friedman, 'DNA Database Searches and the Legal Consumption of Scientific Evidence' (1999) 97 *Michigan L Rev* 931.

probability of finding a DNA match might increase with the size of the database, but the DNA match still has the same probative value—it still singles D out from other members of the population to the extent that it does in non-database cases. The same is true of previous convictions.

There is, however, a slightly different way of making the argument that selection effects matter. Evidence of past crimes, Lempert argues:

is likely to be redundant because it probably has influenced the decisions to arrest and prosecute and so has figured in the jurors' initial estimation of the odds on the defendant's guilt. Even if jurors could be made aware of the way in which this type of evidence enters into their initial estimation of the odds on guilt, the task of separating the redundant portion of such evidence from the nonredundant poses an insoluble estimation problem.[13]

The idea is that the jury will start the trial by thinking that there is a reasonable chance that D is guilty—because he must have been brought to trial for good reason, such as because he has previous convictions. This takes us back to the problem of default assumptions: Lempert's argument is basically that the default assumption is that D has previous convictions. As noted above, this may well be the case, but if so, it does not necessarily have the implications Lempert suggests. One problem is that the argument is too general: it would justify excluding much more than previous convictions. If the case involved a street robbery, for example, the jury may well start the case thinking that part of the evidence which led to D being tried is an identification by the victim. Should evidence that the victim did identify D be excluded as redundant? Further, why should we think that the jury is incapable of dealing with redundancy, an argument which, after all, might justify excluding much evidence, such as multiple eyewitness identifications? Speculation about default assumptions and jury reasoning is not a very satisfactory basis for an exclusionary rule.[14]

---

[13] R. O. Lempert, 'Modeling Relevance' (1977) 75 *Michigan L Rev* 1021, 1052.

[14] A slightly different version of the 'usual suspects' argument is made in R. O. Lempert, S. R. Gross, and J. S. Liebman, *A Modern Approach to Evidence: Text, Problems, Transcripts and Cases* (3rd edn, St Paul, Minn: West Group, 2000), 327–8. The authors think of the problem in terms of P(E|G)/P(E|I). They suggest that jurors may think about the denominator of the ratio in terms of the proportion of adult citizens with robbery convictions. 'Because the proportion is very low, and the proportion of guilty robbery defendants with prior records is quite high, the jurors will conclude that a prior record is very probative of guilt.' The authors go on to note that this would be a mistake, because the police tend to focus on the usual suspects: '[a] particularly important aspect of this process is that the photographs shown to crime victims and other eyewitnesses for the purposes of identifying the criminal usually come from files on people with records for similar crimes. When mistakes are made and innocent defendants are prosecuted, they will, by definition, be innocent defendants *with* prior similar records'. The problem with this argument is that, however the defendant was selected, the previous conviction is still probative to the same extent. Consider an analogy: the issue in a trial is identity and evidence establishes that the crime was committed by a person with red hair. One in 20 people in the relevant population have red hair, thus the LR for evidence of red hair is 20. It makes no difference if the police only looked for suspects in a particular village where everyone has red hair; on the hair-colour evidence alone, everyone in the village would still be 20 times more likely to have committed the crime than anyone else in the population. Of course, it would be different if the village was an isolated one and the crime had been committed there, making it implausible that anyone outside the village had committed the crime. Then having red hair would be irrelevant, because it would not distinguish D from anyone else in the population of possible perpetrators. The wider lesson is that when thinking about P(E|I) one has to frame the

The Bayesian model depends on an assessment of comparative propensity. It is because defendants with recent previous convictions are much more likely to offend than those without that bad character is taken to be probative. But there may be a concern about this way of conceptualizing comparative propensity. As we saw in Chapter 2, just over half of those who are convicted do not reoffend. Even in scenarios where reoffending is common, as with the cohort of relatively serious theft offenders represented in Table 2.3 of that chapter (within a year of conviction or release from custody there were nearly two offences of theft for every theft offender in the cohort), it will doubtless be the case that some offenders in the cohort did not reoffend: the high reoffending rate will be due to the actions of some especially prolific recidivists. The objection, then, is that comparative propensity is too undiscriminating. The defendant we are dealing with may be one of those who is unlikely to reoffend, yet we are judging him on the basis of an assessment which is skewed by the actions of the recidivists. Because of this, it might be thought that comparative propensity is potentially unreliable evidence.

This critique of comparative propensity raises complex issues. Some of these are more moral than inferential—do we mistreat the defendant by judging him on the basis of other people's actions?—and are therefore dealt with in the next chapter. Here, the focus is on the inferential issue raised by the reference to unreliability (although the moral and the inferential are not always easy to separate in these contexts). To start, we need to be clear just what the inferential criticism is. Figures for comparative propensity do not focus exclusively on the actions of those who reoffend. The figures are average reoffending rates: we are assessing the probability that D is guilty on the basis of what all those in the cohort did. The fact that some do not reoffend actually makes the comparative propensity figures smaller than they otherwise might be. The criticism, then, is that even using figures for average behaviour in the cohort is problematic, because if the cohort contains distinct groups of low- and high-risk offenders, then we are drawing an untenable inference if we assume that D is the average offender rather than a low risk one. In slightly more formal terms, we are judging D on the basis of an inappropriate reference class.[15]

There is a stock response to this line of argument. The reference class problem can be raised as an objection to all sorts of evidence. When an eyewitness testifies and we place some weight on her evidence, we are presumably treating her as the

question carefully, conditioning the probability of finding the evidence on the hypothesis that D is an innocent member of the population of possible perpetrators, not on the hypothesis that he is an innocent member of the pool of people suspected by the police. None of this is to deny that a process whereby witnesses are shown mugshots of possible perpetrators is unproblematic; among other things, the witness is likely to know that people in the photographs have criminal records and this may make her more likely to make a false identification. On mugshot trawls, see further D. M. Risinger and L. C. Risinger, 'Innocence Is Different: Taking Innocence into Account in Reforming Criminal Procedure' (2011–12) 56 *NY Law School L Rev* 869, 900–6.

[15] For discussion of the reference class problem in legal contexts, see Special Issue on the Reference Class Problem (2007) 11 *E & P* 243–317; R. J. Allen and M. S. Pardo, 'The Problematic Value of Mathematical Models of Evidence' (2007) 36 *J Legal Studies* 107; and M. Redmayne, 'Exploring the Proof Paradoxes' (2008) 14 *Legal Theory* 281, 285–9.

average eyewitness: neither especially good nor especially bad, though no doubt there are factors which, were we aware of them and their significance, would allow a more fine-grained analysis of her abilities, and hence of the significance of her evidence, to be made. And, to return to the example of motive, though no doubt some people are more or less likely to act on a motive to kill, we still take motive into account as evidence against the defendant. With the eyewitness, though, we do have the chance to probe the evidence to see if the witness is more or less likely to have made a misidentification: this is the point of examination and cross-examination during the trial, and of any contextual information on witnessing conditions and the like, information which allows us to refine the reference class and make a more discriminating inference. However, it is not so easy to evade the motive analogy on this point—asking the defendant whether he is more or less likely to have acted on his motive to kill makes about as much sense as asking the defendant if he is the sort of person likely to reoffend.[16] In fact, bad character evidence may be more amenable to probing than motive. As we saw in Chapter 2, information about the number of previous convictions, how recent they are, and the age at which they were gained will help to refine the strength of inference we draw from bad character evidence. Admittedly, there will still be variation which is not captured by these factors. We noted evidence that offenders might be divided into distinct groups such as 'adolescent limited' and 'life course persistent'. If a young defendant has just one or two previous convictions, we will have little idea which group he belongs to. It is not obvious, however, that we could ever assign a person to a particular subgroup until after the fact—until a distinct offending pattern has been established over the course of time. Perhaps delving into things such as childhood risk-factors could help, but just as with the eyewitness there comes a point at which we cannot reasonably probe any further—and it should be emphasized that even after questioning the eyewitness we are fooling ourselves if we think we 'really' know what weight to put on her evidence. While this does raise a question about how far it is reasonable to probe into the likelihood that D will reoffend (should we look at childhood risk factors, or question his probation officer?), an issue discussed briefly in the next chapter, as far as inferential concerns go there does not seem to be anything wrong in relying on the notion of comparative propensity to offend.

There may be a more radical objection to the Bayesian model outlined above. The Bayesian model of evidence evaluation has its critics, who would argue that it is simply the wrong starting point for thinking about evidence. This is not the place for a thorough review of the debate about Bayesianism.[17] For present purposes,

---

[16] It might just be argued, though, that everyone who has a motive to kill their rich uncle has the same strength of reason to kill. What may vary with motive are countervailing factors, such as how strong D thinks the countervailing reasons are. In contrast, the argument would go, those who offend will have different propensities to reoffend.

[17] My view is that most of the criticism of Bayesian models of evidence and proof misses the target. For discussion, with references to the literature, see M. Redmayne, 'The Structure of Evidence Law' (2006) 26 *OJLS* 805. For recent critical accounts, see M. S. Pardo, 'The Nature and Purpose of Evidence Theory' (2013) 66 *Vanderbilt L Rev* 547; and S. Haack, 'The Embedded Epistemologist: Dispatches from the Legal Front' (2012) 25 *Ratio Juris* 206.

the most significant criticism is that the Bayesian model does not describe how jurors actually reason, because juries assess evidence by means of stories or explanations.[18] Pardo and Allen's explanatory model of evidence might seem to suggest that bad character evidence is normally irrelevant, because for them 'an item of evidence is... relevant if it is explained by the particular explanation offered by the party offering the evidence';[19] 'in every case, the probative value of evidence will be determined by what best explains it'.[20] The fact that the defendant murdered the victim, however, does not explain his having a previous conviction for GBH. With prospective evidence such as character evidence, the direction of explanation is reversed: D's having a conviction for GBH forms part of the explanation of why he killed V (it shows that he has a propensity to do so). Pardo and Allen's thoughts on such examples remain unclear, although there are hints that they would include prospective evidence in their model.[21] Certainly, there is plenty of evidence (reviewed in section 3.5, below) that juries put weight on previous convictions, and Pennington and Hastie seem to accept that bad character has a place in the story model,[22] so we should not doubt the descriptive accuracy of the claim that previous convictions are integrated in the evaluation of evidence in real trials. If jurors use character evidence in evaluating cases, we need a normative model to decide when it is appropriate to allow them to do so (although the model needs to be sensitive to the ways in which evidence may actually be used: hence the concern about issues such as default assumptions, and prejudice more generally). Any normative model must surely reflect the fact that some previous convictions are more probative than others, and once that is conceded it is hard to see why the Bayesian framework outlined above is inappropriate.

The foregoing has explored, and responded to, possible criticisms of the model of bad character evidence and its integration in the criminal trial that is relied on in this book. Before turning to the standard criticisms of bad character evidence—that juries will give it too much weight or that it will distort their reasoning in other ways—a slightly different type of argument will be considered.

3.2 Undermining Deterrence

The standard arguments against using bad character evidence conceive its negative impact in terms of adjudicative accuracy: fact-finders may be led astray. But there is another way in which character evidence might undermine the criminal trial. The threat of conviction is one aspect of the criminal law's power of deterrence.

---

[18] See N. Pennington and R. Hastie, 'The Story Model for Juror Decision Making' in R. Hastie (ed), *Inside the Juror: The Psychology of Juror Decision Making* (Cambridge: Cambridge University Press, 1993); and M. S. Pardo and R. J. Allen, 'Juridical Proof and the Best Explanation' (2008) 27 *Law & Philosophy* 223.

[19] Pardo and Allen, 'Juridical Proof', 241.

[20] Pardo and Allen, 'Juridical Proof', 263.

[21] See their discussion of accident rates: Pardo and Allen, 'Juridical Proof', 259.

[22] Pennington and Hastie, 'Story Model', 205.

But because, as noted above, bad character evidence is 'prospective', it exists whether or not the defendant committed the crime for which he is on trial. This contrasts with trace evidence—such as fingerprints or eyewitness reports—which are generated by the crime itself. A person with previous convictions who is contemplating whether or not to commit a crime might be deterred by the thought that committing the crime will generate trace evidence, but previous convictions, it has been argued, can play no role in deterrence, because they exist whether or not the person commits the contemplated crime. In fact, if previous convictions are admissible evidence they may even undermine deterrence, because the defendant may think along the lines of 'I'm damned if I do and damned if I don't'. In more technical terms:

> In the extreme case, there may be a self-reinforcing equilibrium where juries are very willing to convict habitual criminals, whatever the evidence matching the criminal to the crime, and the police are very willing to arrest them. Since the criminal saves nothing by avoiding crime, there is no deterrence. In equilibrium the punitive police and jury reinforce criminal behaviour, and criminal behaviour reinforces their inclination to be punitive.[23]

The extreme case described here is sufficiently extreme to tell us little about real trials. The argument that admissibility of previous convictions reduces deterrence has, however, been put with more subtlety by Sanchirico.[24] Sanchirico suggests that where character evidence is inadmissible, more trace evidence will be needed to secure conviction. He also supposes that whereas it might not be that difficult to find a single piece of trace evidence against an innocent suspect, finding two incriminating traces will be much more difficult, but that for a guilty suspect a second piece of trace evidence will not be so much more difficult to find. The result is that if two pieces of evidence are needed to secure a conviction, then in a system which excludes character evidence there is a considerable disincentive to commit crime: the innocent are very unlikely to have two pieces of evidence incriminating them, whereas for the guilty this is rather more likely. But, keeping the assumption that two pieces of evidence are needed to convict, a person with a previous conviction has rather less disincentive, because, there already being one piece of evidence against him (his record), only one piece of trace evidence is needed to secure a conviction, and that is reasonably likely to exist whether he is innocent or guilty.[25] The key assumption in this model is that committing a crime increases the chance of there being at least two pieces

[23] J. Schrag and S. Scotchmer, 'Crime and Prejudice: The Use of Character Evidence in Criminal Trials' (1994) 10 *J Law, Economics & Organization* 319, 323.
[24] Sanchirico, 'Character Evidence'.
[25] Sanchirico ('Character Evidence', 1275) provides the following table, which may help to clarify the argument:

Eyewitnesses	D offends	D does not offend
At least 1	20%	10%
At least 2	19%	1%

of trace evidence more than it increases the chance of there being at least one piece of trace evidence.[26]

There are numerous problems with this argument. Because most jurisdictions do not have a corroboration rule, a defendant can be convicted on a single piece of trace evidence such as a confession or an eyewitness identification, so if a single piece of trace evidence is easy to come by, even a person without a criminal record might think that actually committing a crime will not make that much difference to the chances of conviction.[27] More fundamentally, Sanchirico assumes that the criminal trial is solely concerned with shaping the incentives of potential offenders; the fact that admitting previous convictions can increase fact-finding accuracy plays no role in his model. One can appreciate how bizarre this perspective is by noting that for Sanchirico evidence of motive should be excluded, because as prospective evidence its admission will undermine deterrence for those who have a motive to offend.[28] Even if we take Sanchirico's model on its own terms, it makes little sense empirically. For the admission of previous convictions to undermine deterrence, potential offenders will need to know about the relevant rule of evidence and take the fact that it increases their chance of conviction into account when deciding whether to commit crime. Given that criminal record will, in the vast majority of cases, only play a supporting role in gaining a conviction, surely even the rational calculator will focus more or less exclusively on the chances of generating trace evidence when deciding whether or not to offend. However, even this ignores the fact that offenders do not appear to be rational calculators. Offenders tend not to think about the criminal justice consequences of their actions, putting them out of their minds as far as they are able to and instead concentrating on the potential rewards of crime.[29] In the real world,

---

[26] It is hard to assess how plausible this is. Sanchirico's assumption is that a graph plotting the amount of evidence against the probability of finding it would show a curve declining more sharply for the innocent than the guilty. This may be plausible: perhaps it is rare for a crime to generate just one trace, and two or three traces is more likely, after which the curve declines. For the innocent the curve may well decline straight away. However, in some innocence cases there will be dependencies: eg, being misidentified by one eyewitness may increase the probability of being misidentified by a second, because the first misidentification suggests that D looks like the culprit. Sanchirico in fact argues that the difference between the evidence distributions for the innocent and the guilty need not always occur (at 1276); his overall argument is that increasing sentences for repeat offenders is a more reliable way of deterring recidivists, because sentencing is conditioned on conviction and thus (in his scheme) on trace evidence, and that in some cases character evidence will undermine deterrence.

[27] In England and Wales, *Turnbull* [1977] QB 224 does mean that a case should be withdrawn from the jury if it depends on 'weak' eyewitness identification evidence alone. However, it is rare for eyewitness evidence to be classified as 'weak'.

[28] Sanchirico, 'Character Evidence', 1291: motive 'is prone to foul incentive setting if used to establish conduct, and so should be employed, if at all, only in sentencing'.

[29] See A. N. Doob and C. M. Webster, 'Offenders' Thought Processes' in A. von Hirsch, A. Ashworth, and J. Roberts (eds), *Principled Sentencing: Readings on Theory and Policy* (3rd edn, Oxford: Hart Publishing, 2009); N. Shover, *Great Pretenders: Pursuits and Careers of Persistent Thieves* (Boulder, CO: Westview Press, 1996), 152–61, 175–80; and R. T. Wright and S. Decker, *Burglars on the Job: Streetlife and Residential Break-Ins* (Boston, MA: Northeastern University Press, 1994), 127–33.

admitting criminal record simply will not have any effect on crime rates, whatever a rational-choice model may suggest.

A final objection to Sanchirico's model is that if a person with a criminal record does not offend, there is no crime he can be falsely convicted of.[30] While this sort of argument would certainly hold for most cases involving motive—if X does not murder his rich uncle in order to inherit under the will, it is unlikely that anyone else will murder him, so the motive will not be used as evidence against X—the case of previous convictions is more complex. For volume crime, like burglary, X, who has a criminal record for burglary, may reason that the police will try to associate him with any burglary committed in the neighbourhood, so he may as well commit a burglary: damned if he does, damned if he doesn't. X cannot prevent the fact that other people will commit crimes which fit his profile. However, to the extent that there are other burglars who will commit crimes fitting X's profile, it is less probable that the police will knock on X's door: they have many other 'usual suspects' to choose from. So X's chance of being associated with burglary simply because of his criminal record is small in volume crime cases, and therefore even if we accept Sanchirico's rational actor model, X has reason to concentrate on the likelihood that he will generate trace evidence if he does offend. Things are different, of course, for signature crimes. Straffen knows that he will be a prime suspect whenever a young girl is strangled to death, not sexually molested and no attempt is made to hide the body.[31] But this should not encourage Straffen to offend on the thinking that he will be convicted whatever he does. Because very few people commit crimes which fit Straffen's profile (perhaps only Straffen), by desisting, Straffen can drastically reduce the probability that there is a crime fitting his profile which he can be convicted of. In short, both Straffen and the potential burglar are only prone to be damned if they do.

Sanchirico's argument is made with considerable ingenuity and a fair degree of subtlety. However, for numerous reasons it provides no justification for excluding bad character evidence. His argument bears some similarity with those made by Harcourt against various forms of profiling.[32] One of Harcourt's claims is that basing criminal justice decision-making on factors associated with offending may increase crime. Thus, if people with previous convictions are targeted by the police more than those without criminal convictions, those without convictions might offend more.[33] I doubt this argument has much leverage on policy as regards admitting previous convictions in court, which, as already noted, is unlikely to feature in the decision-making of potential offenders. A different concern voiced by Harcourt is the 'ratchet effect': targeted groups, such as those with

---

[30] For this point in a slightly different context, see D. Enoch, L. Spectre, and T. Fisher, 'Statistical Evidence, Sensitivity, and the Legal Value of Knowledge' (2012) 40 *Phil & Pub Aff* 197, 218–19.

[31] *Straffen* [1952] 2 QB 911.

[32] B. E. Harcourt, *Against Prediction: Profiling, Policing, and Punishing in an Actuarial Age* (Chicago, IL: University of Chicago Press, 2007).

[33] Harcourt makes this argument in relation to sentencing in *Against Prediction*, 139–44. He does not necessarily endorse the rational choice model on which the argument is based, but is meeting the arguments of those who suggest that targeting recidivists will deter reoffending.

previous convictions, will become over-represented in the prison population, with various negative social consequences as they become stigmatized and find re-entry to society more difficult, making them even more likely to recidivate.[34] This argument is worth taking seriously, especially in contexts such as sentencing. But when it comes to evidence, the argument could apply to any factor which bears on the chances of conviction: there could be a ratchet effect for having a motive to commit crime, for being prone to confessing, or for acting suspiciously.[35] Granted, these factors are less likely to become stigmatizing than is having a criminal record, but the unruly nature of the ratchet argument should at least give us pause in applying it to evidence law. Further, given that criminal record will usually play only a minor role in conviction decisions, the ratchet argument has limited force in this context. To the extent that there are concerns about stigmatization, we should pursue policies, such as those underlying the Rehabilitation of Offenders Act, which help offenders reintegrate in society, rather than excluding evidence which can help convict the guilty.

3.3 Confusing Coincidence

In the Australian case *Perry*,[36] Perry was tried for attempting to kill her husband by poisoning. The prosecution introduced evidence that three other people whom Perry had been associated with had died of poisoning. In allowing Perry's Appeal against conviction, Murphy J commented that:

Common assumptions about improbability of sequences are often wrong. A suggested sequence, series or pattern of events is often incorrectly regarded as so extremely improbable as to be incredible. However, highly improbable, as well as merely improbable, sequences and combinations are constantly occurring. In random tossing the occurrence of a run of ten consecutive heads or tails is generally regarded as highly improbable. But this will occur on the average once in every 512 tosses, and the lesser sequences more frequently (2 runs of 9; 4 runs of 8; 8 runs of 7). If one randomly tosses a coin 257 times, more likely than not there will be a sequence of ten heads or tails. Although it is extremely improbable that any particular ticket will win a large lottery, it is certain that one will.[37]

This seems to identify a source of prejudice, and is therefore worth exploring.

While the typical use of bad character evidence examined in this book is the introduction of previous convictions to prove guilt, cases like *Perry* are also regarded as involving character evidence. The other incidents suggest that Perry may have a bad character, and thus that she may have murdered her husband, or, in more legal terms, they are 'uncharged misconduct evidence'. This type of case

---

[34] The argument is made—again in relation to sentencing—in Harcourt, *Against Prediction*, 168–9, 192.

[35] As Harcourt notes: '[p]rofiling even on innocuous traits has the effect of marginalizing anyone who deviates from the norm' (*Against Prediction*, 191).

[36] [1982] HCA 75.

[37] *Perry*, [11]. See also A. Cossins, 'The Legacy of the *Makin* Case 120 Years on: Legal Fictions, Circular Reasoning and Some Solutions' (2013) 35 *Sydney L Rev* 731.

is often distinguished from the one involving previous convictions, as involving 'coincidence' rather than propensity reasoning. The classic example of a coincidence case is *Smith*, where Smith was tried for murder after the discovery that three of his wives had drowned in the bath; the idea is that this pattern of events is so improbable that it cannot be a coincidence.[38] As we will see in Chapter 5, it is not always easy to distinguish between coincidence and propensity cases. For example, in *Straffen*, the fact that Straffen had strangled two young girls could be used to show that he had a propensity to murder young girls, or we could say that it just cannot be a coincidence that Straffen was found in proximity to three strangled young girls.[39] Both processes of reasoning come to the same conclusion: that Straffen murdered the third girl.

The difficulty of distinguishing coincidence cases from other cases suggests one response to the concern expressed by Murphy J. Imagine a case where D is identified by an eyewitness as the person who murdered V, fibres matching D's sweater are found at the crime scene, and D had a motive to kill V. In such a case, we might say that it 'cannot be a coincidence' that all these three links between D and the crime should occur, and therefore that D is guilty. If we are prone to misjudge the probability that a pattern of events would occur by chance, then we appear to have a reason to doubt the accuracy of jury reasoning in almost any case.[40] The objection to character evidence becomes an objection to all evidence.

Murphy J's concern is, however, worth taking seriously. Cases like *Smith* do seem to invoke a particular pattern of reasoning where we rely heavily on rejecting chance as the explanation for a series of events. Moreover, in *Smith* and *Perry* we are rejecting chance in order to conclude that a crime was committed, rather than knowing that there has been a crime and trying to attribute responsibility for it: the 'cannot be a coincidence' reasoning is doing much more work here than in the eyewitness, fibre and motive case described above. There are also some well-known cases which fit the coincidence pattern and in which reasoning about the improbability of patterns has proved problematic. In the case of Sally Clark, two of Clark's young children died, the deaths initially being attributed to 'cot death'—ie there was no obvious explanation for them.[41] Clark was convicted of murder, but the conviction was eventually quashed amid much criticism of the statistical evidence which had been presented on the improbability of a family suffering two cot deaths.[42] The Dutch nurse, Lucia de Berk, was convicted of murder

---

[38] *Smith* [1914–15] All ER 262. For a detailed account of the case, see J. Robins, *The Magnificent Spilsbury and the Case of the Brides in the Bath* (London: John Murray, 2010).

[39] *Straffen* [1952] 2 QB 911.

[40] This sort of response is made in K. Amarasekara and M. Bagaric, 'The Prejudice against Similar Fact Evidence' (2001) 5 *E & P* 71, 95–6.

[41] See *Clark (Sally) (Appeal against Conviction (No 1)* CA 2 October 2000; *Clark (Sally) (Appeal against Conviction) (No 2)* [2003] 2 FCR 447, [2003] EWCA Crim 1020. A decent narrative account is L. Schneps and C. Colmez, *Math on Trial: How Numbers Get Used and Abused in the Courtroom* (New York: Basic Books, 2013), ch 1; for more legal detail, see R. Nobles and D. Schiff, 'A Story of Miscarriage: Law in the Media' (2004) 31 *JLS* 221.

[42] Whether the statistical evidence did play a significant role in the conviction is a difficult question. The first appeal judgment concluded that the statistical evidence had played little role in the

when it was noticed that her shifts coincided with what appeared to be an unusually large number of patient deaths.[43] Her conviction was also quashed, and in this case too there has been criticism of the courts' reliance on the improbability of de Berk's having been present at so many deaths.

Psychological research lends some support to the claim that we are not very good at recognizing when patterns are due to chance. 'We are predisposed', according to Gilovich, 'to see order, pattern and meaning in the world...As a consequence, we tend to "see" order where there is none, and we spot meaningful patterns where only the vagaries of human chance are operating.'[44] The evidence for this includes the fact that people expect a series of tosses of a fair coin to contain fewer runs of heads and tails than the typical series actually does;[45] that we believe in a 'hot hand' in basketball and other sports, whereby players have runs of good form during a game when they are 'hot' or 'in the zone' (in fact, such runs of good form occur no more than is expected by chance);[46] and that geographical clusters of particular forms of cancer have often triggered cancer scares when, once again, such clusters occur randomly.[47] Accounts of the de Berk case suggest that mistakes about the patterns which can be found in chance sequences played a role in building a case against de Berk: fellow nurses, then hospital administrators, prosecutors, and experts, became convinced that de Berk simply had too many unexplained deaths on her watch.[48]

All this suggests that coincidence cases are potentially problematic, and that they may lead to false convictions. But this probably does not have significant implications for the rules of evidence. Relatively few cases are pure coincidence

trial, and that the jury had been warned against relying on it. The second appeal (after a referral by the Criminal Cases Review Commission) quashed the conviction largely because medical evidence, suggesting a possible natural cause of death for one of the children, had not been disclosed to the defence. But in a brief discussion of the statistical evidence, the Court commented that 'we rather suspect that with the graphic reference by Professor Meadow to the chances of backing long odds winners of the Grand National year after year [the statistical evidence] may have had a major effect on [the jury's] thinking notwithstanding the efforts of the trial judge to down play it' (*Clark (No 2)* [2003] 2 FCR 447, [178]).

[43] An overview of the case appears in Schneps and Colmez, *Math on Trial*, ch 7. See also T. Dersken and M. Meijsing, 'The Fabrication of Facts: The Lure of the Incredible Coincidence' in H. Kaptein, H. Prakken, and B. Verheij (eds), *Legal Evidence and Proof: Statistics, Stories, Logic* (Dartmouth: Ashgate, 2009). For discussion of other 'statistical coincidence' cases, several involving nurses, see S. E. Fienberg and D. H. Kaye, 'Legal and Statistical Aspects of Some Mysterious Clusters' (1991) 154 *J R Statist Soc A* 61.

[44] T. Gilovich, *How We Know What Isn't So: The Fallibility of Human Reason in Everyday Life* (New York: Free Press, 1991), 9.

[45] See A. T. Oskarsson, L. Van Boven, and G. H. McClelland, 'What's Next? Judging Sequences of Binary Events' (2009) 135 *Psychol Bull* 262.

[46] The classic study is T. Gilovich, A. Tversky, and R. Vallone, 'The Hot Hand in Basketball: On the Misperception of Random Sequences' (1985) 3 *Cognitive Psychol* 295. This article led to a number of studies on similar phenomena in sports; not all researchers agree that the hot hand is a myth. For evidence of the hot hand in volleyball (a sport where defensive strategies are less prone to break the shooter's 'flow' than in basketball), see M. Raab, B. Gula, and G. Gigerenzer, 'The Hot Hand Exists in Volleyball and Is Used for Allocation Decisions' (2012) 18 *J Experimental Psychol: Applied* 81.

[47] A. Gawande, 'The Cancer-Cluster Myth' *The New Yorker*, 8 February 1999, 34.

[48] See Dersken and Meijsing, 'Fabrication of Facts'.

cases—where a suspicious pattern is used to prove that there has been a crime as opposed to an innocent coincidence. Still, even if problem cases are rare, we might try to formulate a high admissibility threshold for the evidence. Tests which have featured in the case law (although they have not been confined to coincidence cases) include: does the evidence 'make coincidence an affront to common sense?'[49] and 'the improbability of [the evidence] having some innocent explanation is such that there is no reasonable view of it other than as supporting an inference that the accused is guilty'.[50] But these formulations do not really solve the problem, because if there is a bias which makes us see design where there is mere chance it will have done its work by the time we apply such tests. After all, the courts in *Clark* and *de Berk* would presumably have said that the pattern of deaths they saw could not have been a coincidence. In any case, the difficulty of distinguishing between coincidence cases and other ones would probably mean that this test would have to be applied in all cases involving bad character evidence, a position which—we will see as the argument develops—would be hard to defend.

This does not mean that we should be complacent. No doubt there are lessons to be learned from *Clark* and *de Berk*, and it is important that those involved in the criminal process—not least expert witnesses, who seem to have been the main culprits in these cases—are aware of them. What is not so obvious is that some sort of cognitive bias whereby we read randomness as design was the main problem in these cases. In both *Clark* and *de Berk* there were deeper problems: in *Clark*, evidence that one of the children had died of natural causes was initially missed, and Meadows, the expert who gained some notoriety because of the case, assumed that cot deaths were independent events when he testified that the probability of two cot deaths in the same family was around 1 in 73 million. In *de Berk*, there were numerous errors in gathering the data relating to de Berk—for example, because one of the hospitals where she had worked had changed its name, data which undermined the prosecution case were not taken into account. And as in *Clark*, evidence emerged that some of the supposedly suspicious deaths were due to natural causes. One problem does link the two cases, and this is more closely related to mistakes about probability. Even if we take the figures used in court to describe the probability of chance occurrence at face value—1 in 73 million for Clark, 1 in 342 million for de Berk—it is not obvious what to make of them. Something very improbable has happened, but improbable things happen every day. We do not arrest lottery winners on suspicion of fraud. One way to put the figures in perspective is to bear in mind that evidence evaluation is a comparative exercise. It does not matter that the defence story is improbable, what matters is whether it is much less probable than the prosecution story. But how likely is it that a mother would kill both of her babies or that a nurse would be a serial killer? One answer to the former question is 1 in 8.4 billion,[51] a figure which puts the prosecution's double cot-death statistic into perspective.

---

[49] *Boardman* [1975] AC 421, 453, 444, 439.   [50] *Pfennig* (1995) 127 ALR 99, 113.
[51] A. P. Dawid, 'Bayes's Theorem and Weighing Evidence by Juries' in R. Swinburne (ed), *Bayes's Theorem* (Oxford: Oxford University Press, 2002), 76.

Does this have implications for *Smith*, the brides in the bath case? The intuitive reaction to *Smith* is that it is obvious that Smith was a murderer, but might this be a result of our tendency to see design where there is only chance, or to fail to appreciate that it is unlikely that a man should kill three wives? In *Smith*, however, there was other incriminating evidence. Smith went to great lengths to encourage his wives to take baths, and he had made sure he would profit financially from each of the deaths. He also changed his name between drownings. Further, accidental adult bath drownings are presumably much rarer than cot death.[52] The recent English nurse case of *Norris* also relied heavily on establishing an unlikely pattern: several patients apparently dying of spontaneous hypoglycaemia.[53] The prosecution expert testified that spontaneous hypoglycaemia was extremely rare, and that to see five cases of it in a short period was 'extraordinary'.[54] This case too was stronger than *de Berk*. The pattern of deaths, along with in one of the cases a missing dose of insulin on the same ward, made it very likely that someone had killed the patients by injecting insulin. Norris was then the only person whose shifts easily gave him the opportunity to have done so. In *de Berk*, the shift pattern was doing far more work; without de Berk's presence at the deaths there was no reason to suspect that anything was amiss.

The lesson seems to be that where we have to rely on an unlikely coincidence to do the vast majority of the work to prove that a crime has been committed and that it was committed by D, we should be circumspect about convicting. But it is probably not all that useful to think of these cases in terms of prejudice and reasoning errors, nor in terms of rules of evidence that might guard against false conviction. Cases like *de Berk* are not easy to analyse—statisticians do not have an agreed model for assessing the probabilities in them[55]—and need to be carefully handled by all involved. Exclusionary rules are not an appropriate way of achieving this.

3.4 Attributing Error

In Chapter 2, we reviewed some of the psychological debates about character and personality. We saw that experiments in social psychology suggest that behaviour can be heavily influenced by situational factors. Some social psychologists also argue that this fact is under-appreciated: observers will conclude that X failed to help the person in distress because he is mean rather than because he was in a rush. The tendency to attribute behaviour to personality rather than to situation is sometimes termed the 'fundamental attribution error' or 'correspondence

---

[52] Despite autopsies, there was no obvious cause of drowning such as slipping and hitting the head (which would have left bruising).

[53] *Norris* [2009] EWCA Crim 2697.   [54] *Norris*, [39].

[55] See R. Meester, M. Collins, and R. Gill, 'On the (Ab)Use of Statistics in the Legal Case against the Nurse Lucia de B' (2006) 5 *Law, Probability & Risk* 233; D. Lucy, 'Commentary on Meester et al.' (2006) 5 *Law, Probability & Risk* 251; and Fienberg and Kaye, 'Legal and Statistical Aspects'.

bias'—the latter because people presume that behaviour corresponds to character.[56] So, for example, when subjects read either pro- or anti-Castro essays, knowing that the essay writers had not chosen but had been assigned to write an essay putting forward a particular view, they still presumed that the essay told them something about the speaker's politics.[57] In Darley and Batson's good Samaritan experiment, discussed briefly in Chapter 2, the seminary students had been asked whether their interest in a religious vocation was based on a desire to help others or a desire for personal salvation. There was no correlation between their answers and the likelihood that they would stop to help the person in distress, yet people expect there to be such a correlation, with altruistic seminarians more likely to help.[58] 'Laypeople', Ross and Nisbett conclude, 'fail to appreciate the power and subtlety of the situational control of behaviour and are guilty of a sort of naïve dispositionism, seeing traits where there are none.'[59] Unsurprisingly, this supposed psychological bias is sometimes used to bolster the claim that jurors will give too much weight to character evidence.[60]

The implications for the use of character evidence are fairly obvious. If the jury is told that D has a previous conviction for burglary, it will attribute a disposition to burgle and then expect D to act on that disposition in relevant circumstances. The concern is that both the attribution of the disposition and the inference from it to behaviour would be mistaken, because they fail to take situational factors into account. One source of evidence suggests lay people do attribute dispositions in this manner, and that in doing so they fall into error by seeing criminal dispositions as more powerful than they are. Roberts and White questioned members of the public in Canada about the likelihood that a first-time offender would reoffend. Estimates were far higher than official statistics: the public thought that property offenders had a 49 per cent chance of reoffending when the official rate was 27 per cent; for offences against the person the figures were 60 per cent versus 17 per cent and for sex offenders 58 per cent versus 14 per cent.[61] Roberts and White suggest that this is an instance of attribution error.[62]

There are many reasons to doubt that studies like Roberts and White's, or the more general literature on attribution error, show that previous convictions are

---

[56] D. T. Gilbert and P. S. Malone, 'The Correspondence Bias' (1995) 117 *Psychol Bull* 21.

[57] E. E. Jones and V. A. Harris, 'The Attribution of Attitudes' (1967) 3 *J Experimental Psychol* 1.

[58] P. Pietromonaco and R. Nisbett, 'Swimming Upstream against the Fundamental Attribution Error: Subject's Weak Generalizations from the Darley and Batson Study' (1982) 10 *Social Behavior & Personality* 1.

[59] L. Ross and R. E. Nisbett, *The Person and the Situation: Perspectives of Social Psychology* (New York: McGraw-Hill, 1991), 119.

[60] See, eg, Law Commission, *Evidence in Criminal Proceedings: Previous Misconduct of a Defendant*, LCCP No 141 (London: HMSO, 1996), 101; and Lempert et al, *A Modern Approach to Evidence*, 325.

[61] J. Roberts and N. White, 'Public Estimates of Recidivism Rates: Consequences of a Criminal Stereotype' (1986) 28 *Canadian J Criminology* 229, 233. The public's estimates and official statistics did converge, however, for second- and third-time offenders.

[62] Roberts and White, 'Public Estimates of Recidivism Rates', 239. See further J. V. Roberts, *Punishing Persistent Offenders: Exploring Community and Offender Perspectives* (Oxford: Oxford University Press, 2008), 185–90.

prejudicial when used as evidence of propensity to commit crime.[63] The subjects in Roberts and White's research are being asked to predict the likelihood of future offending, whereas comparative propensity focusses on how much more likely D is to offend than someone without the relevant previous conviction(s). While the research subjects make the mistake of thinking that more serious offenders are more likely to reoffend (perhaps ignoring the low base-rate for serious offending), comparative propensity does tend to increase in line with offence seriousness. The D with a previous conviction for rape is much more likely to commit rape, compared to other people, than the D with a previous conviction for theft is to commit theft, compared to other people. What is more, we saw in the previous chapter that there is plenty of evidence for the robustness of comparative propensity: if we attribute criminal dispositions we do not seem to be falling into error. Ross and Nisbett would probably not disagree; they note that trait-based predictions can be accurate in some situations, including when 'the prediction deals with the relative likelihood of extreme outcomes or events, and the actors have in the past shown themselves to be extreme relative to others' and when 'the predictions are mindful of population base-rates'.[64] Judgments of comparative propensity fit these criteria well. In short, if we want evidence that previous convictions are prejudicial, we need to look elsewhere than the general research on attribution errors.

3.5 Empirical Studies of Bad Character

There are several empirical studies examining the impact of previous convictions on fact-finders' assessments of guilt and innocence. Some of these are mock jury studies, some are studies of real trials. First, though, it is worth looking at some recent research on the impact of character on blame attribution. This research does not involve previous convictions, and in that respect is rather different from the other studies surveyed here. Nevertheless, the research may be useful for the way in which it explores the mechanisms through which character might impact on the criminal trial.

---

[63] The concept of a fundamental attribution error has been devastatingly critiqued in J. Sabini, M. Siepmann, and J. Stein, 'The Really Fundamental Attribution Error in Social Psychological Research' (2001) 12 *Psychol Inquiry* 1. The major problem is that the research provides no good way of distinguishing situations from dispositions, because each can be re-described in terms of the other. For example, in the Castro experiment the situational force of obeying instructions can be re-described as a disposition to do what one is told. Sabini et al conclude that the error the research may have uncovered is a tendency to underestimate the power of certain dispositions, such as wanting to avoid embarrassment. For other criticisms of the research, see D. C. Funder, 'Errors and Mistakes: Evaluating the Accuracy of Social Judgment' (1987) 101 *Psychol Bull* 75; and C. B. Miller, *Character and Moral Psychology* (Oxford: Oxford University Press, 2014), 158–70. For evidence that in realistic conditions people do use situational hedges when describing other people's behavioural tendencies, see J. C. Wright and W. Mischel, 'Conditional Hedges and the Intuitive Psychology of Traits' (1988) 55 *J Personality & Soc Psychol* 454.

[64] Ross and Nisbett, *The Person and the Situation*, 138–9.

Nadler, working alone and with McDonnell, conducted a series of experiments on lay people's judgements of blame in relation to scenarios where D does or does not have bad character or a bad motive.[65] A typical example discussed by the authors is a case where D crashes into another car while speeding, and was speeding to get back home before his parents in order to: (a) hide drugs; or (b) hide a present he had bought for his parents. Subjects found D more responsible for the accident in the drugs condition than in the gift condition.[66] This might be interpreted as evidence that bad character is prejudicial, because D's motive for speeding does not seem to be relevant to his responsibility. In perhaps the most interesting of the experiments, a character called Nathan causes a serious accident while skiing.[67] In one condition, 'good Nathan' is a model citizen: a responsible and reliable employee who volunteers at an animal shelter when not working. 'Bad Nathan', in contrast, is feckless and lazy. Bad Nathan tended to be judged as more responsible for the accident and more deserving of punishment than good Nathan; the accident was also thought to be more foreseeable in the bad Nathan condition. But these differences disappeared when each subject was asked to judge both good Nathan and bad Nathan at the same time: then the two were treated equally. Nadler and McDonnell conclude that:

Human beings inside and outside of the jury box often make intuitive judgments of blame and responsibility very quickly and automatically as they first process the story about a transgression. Our initial inclinations about whether to categorize the person we are judging as 'good' or 'bad' can motivate us to blame or exculpate him or her. This initial motivation, in turn, can influence our interpretation of the person's actions in a way that allows us to excuse their responsibility or to find them blameworthy for the harm they caused.[68]

It is not easy to assess the significance of Nadler's experiments. The experimental materials are very thin—a brief description of an event and some information about character—in contrast to the richer evidence base in a criminal trial. And, as the authors admit, not all of the findings can easily be depicted as prejudice. Recklessness involves unjustifiable risk-taking, and arguably the driver's speeding is less justified when he wants to hide cocaine than when he wants to hide a present. Recklessness can also be interpreted as 'indifference', and bad Nathan's character is evidence that he, unlike good Nathan, is indifferent to other people's interests. Further, what the experiments may show is that ordinary processes of blame attribution are character-based, rather than purely cognitive, a state of affairs some theorists think is perfectly proper. But even under a purely cognitive model, subjects may reason that the bad person is more likely to have taken a foreseen risk than the good person, and thus that the risk was less likely to have been

---

[65] J. Nadler, 'Blaming as a Social Process: The Influence of Character and Moral Emotion on Blame' (2012) 75 *Law & Contemporary Problems* 1; and J. Nadler and M.-H. McDonnell, 'Moral Character, Motive, and the Psychology of Blame' (2012) 97 *Cornell L Rev* 255.

[66] Nadler, 'Blaming as a Social Process', 5–6. While similar to Nadler and McDonell's experiments, this one was actually conducted by Alicke: M. Alicke, 'Culpable Causation' (1992) 63 *J Personality & Soc Psychol* 368.

[67] Nadler, 'Blaming as a Social Process', 15–27.

[68] Nadler and McDonnell, 'Moral Character', 303–4.

foreseen in the good character scenario (although this is more plausible in the driver case than in Nathan's, because Nathan's level of awareness was specified). All the same, Nadler's findings are suggestive, showing that 'even mild virtue deficits lead to more severe blame judgments',[69] and some of the results—such as that bad Nathan's accident was more foreseeable than good Nathan's—are hard to rationalize even under a character-based conception of responsibility. Nevertheless, it may be significant that good Nathan and bad Nathan are judged equal when seen alongside each other. This suggests that even if prejudice operates against those with bad character, such prejudice can be overcome by conscious effort.

Nadler and McDonnell's experimental scenarios are not a very close fit for the use of bad character evidence to prove guilt. Their subjects were asked questions about blame and *mens rea*: how much was D to blame? How intentional was his conduct? The typical use of bad character evidence in a criminal trial is to show that D did what he is accused of having done. It might be used to show that behaviour was deliberate rather than accidental, but this is a starker, more bivalent decision than 'how responsible was D?'[70] What is more, character is clearly probative of guilt in many scenarios where it is introduced: the jury often would not be wrong to think it more likely that D committed the crime if he had bad character than if he did not. The experiments do suggest, however, that character evidence with a legitimate use might 'spill over', affecting other issues, such as *mens rea*, to which it is arguably less probative.

3.5.1 Mock-jury studies

There have been several experimental studies on the impact of bad character—almost always previous convictions—on judgments of the likelihood that D committed an offence.[71] These studies use a mock-jury format of varying degrees of sophistication. A trial scenario with evidence incriminating D is given to subjects, with the key variable being whether or not D has previous convictions. Subjects are asked to rate the likelihood of guilt (or, sometimes, whether they would convict), and differences between the 'previous convictions' and 'no previous convictions' conditions are

[69] Nadler, 'Blaming as a Social Process', 3.
[70] Nadler and McDonnell, 'Moral Character', 303, also note that the use of previous convictions to prove guilt may involve a more analogical process of reasoning, with jurors asking: how similar is the current crime to the past one?
[71] A. N. Doob and H. M. Kirshenbaum, 'Some Empirical Evidence on the Effect of s 12 of the Canada Evidence Act upon an Accused' (1972–73) 15 *Crim LQ* 88; A. P. Sealy and W. R. Cornish, 'Juries and the Rules of Evidence' [1973] *Crim LR* 208; V. P. Hans and A. N. Doob, 'Section 12 of the Canada Evidence Act and the Deliberations of Simulated Juries' (1975–76) 18 *Crim LQ* 235; E. G. Clary and D. R. Shaffer, 'Effects of Evidence Withholding and a Defendant's Prior Record on Juridic Decisions' (1980) 112 *J Soc Psychol* 237; E. G. Clary and D. R. Shaffer, 'Another Look at the Impact of Juror Sentiments toward Defendants on Juridic Decisions' (1985) 125 *J Soc Psychol* 637; R. L. Wissler and M. J. Saks, 'On the Inefficacy of Limiting Instructions: When Jurors Use Prior Conviction Evidence to Decide on Guilt' (1985) 5 *Law & Human Behavior* 1; E. Greene and M. Dodge, 'The Influence of Prior Record Evidence on Juror Decision Making' (1995) 19 *Law & Human Behavior* 67; and J. S. Hunt and T. L. Budesheim, 'How Jurors Use and Misuse Character Evidence' (2004) 89 *J Applied Psychol* 347.

noted. The studies are often set up so that in the 'no previous conviction' condition subjects rate guilt as about 50 per cent likely (or about half of subjects would vote to convict). This maximizes the sensitivity of the study, avoiding 'floor' and 'ceiling' effects: if, for example, the evidence was very weak, previous convictions might be considered probative by subjects, but still have no effect on conviction rates and little discernible effect on likelihood of guilt.[72] It is worth bearing this in mind, because this aspect of the studies means that it will not be too surprising to find that previous convictions have an effect, especially on verdicts.

Most of the studies find that where D has a previous conviction which is similar to the current charge, this increases perceived likelihood of guilt and the chance of a guilty verdict.[73] There is considerable evidence that this effect is impervious to judicial instructions to ignore bad character evidence.[74] Some studies find that where the previous conviction is dissimilar, it has minimal effect or is actually helpful to D, in that it decreases likelihood of guilt compared to the control condition;[75] a prior acquittal for a similar crime has also been found to have no effect.[76] While these findings are often interpreted as showing that similar previous convictions are prejudicial, one has to be cautious about drawing that conclusion. As has been emphasized, previous convictions for similar crimes can be powerful evidence of guilt; jurors are perfectly right to let them affect their judgments. The studies might, of course, reveal that jurors put too much weight on previous convictions: that they are more prejudicial than probative. It is plainly no simple matter to decide what 'too much weight' means, but in most of the studies the effects are relatively modest, at least when compared to the comparative propensity figures given in the previous chapter. In Doob and Kirshenbaum's study, a previous conviction for burglary in a burglary case led to a roughly one-point shift in ratings on a seven-point scale of likelihood of guilt;[77] in Hunt and Budesheim's, the shift was about 1.5 points on a ten-point scale.[78] Sealy and Cornish found that guilty verdicts increased from 25 to 51 per cent when similar convictions were introduced in a theft case;[79] Wissler and Saks found that such convictions increased the percentage of guilty verdicts from 35 to 80 in an auto-theft case and from 50 to 70 in a murder case.[80] Perhaps the most dramatic increase was 0 per cent guilty verdicts increasing to 40 per cent when a previous conviction for burglary was introduced in a burglary case in Hans and Doob's experiment.[81] But if, as noted above, these studies involve cases which are

[72] When combined with other evidence probative of guilt, probabilities of guilt will increase most when they are around 0.5. Suppose evidence with a likelihood ratio of 2 in favour of the prosecution. If the jury initially thinks that $P(G) = 0.1$, the posterior probability will be 0.18; for $P(G) = 0.5$ the increase is to 0.66; and for $P(G) = 0.9$ it is to 0.94.

[73] The exception is Doob and Kirshenbaum, 'Some Empirical Evidence'. A similar previous conviction had no effect in the condition where there was no deliberation.

[74] The exception is Sealy and Cornish, 'Juries and the Rules of Evidence'.

[75] Sealy and Cornish, 'Juries and the Rules of Evidence'; Wissler and Saks, 'On the Inefficacy of Limiting Instructions'.

[76] Greene and Dodge, 'Influence of Prior Record Evidence'.

[77] 'Some Empirical Evidence'.   [78] 'How Jurors Use and Misuse Character Evidence'.

[79] 'Juries and the Rules of Evidence'.   [80] 'On the Inefficacy of Limiting Instructions'.

[81] 'Section 12 of the Canada Evidence Act'.

reasonably strong to begin with, a significant increase in the percentage of guilty verdicts is not surprising. While it tells us that bad character evidence can make the difference between conviction and acquittal, other sorts of evidence, such as motive, would presumably produce similar results.

It should, however, be noted that in many of these studies juries were told to ignore previous convictions, but generally did not do so. Further, in Hans and Doob's study, mock juror deliberations were examined, and it was found that previous convictions operated indirectly, by changing the way in which other evidence was interpreted: 'It seems that the actual facts of the case—their salience, their strength, their plausibility—were subtly altered by the presence of record.'[82] This sort of 'spill-over' is similar to the effects identified by Nadler and McDonnell, and may suggest that previous convictions operate in unconscious ways which are hard to control. But it is unlikely that character evidence is unique in this respect: other studies have found that introducing one type of evidence can increase the weight accorded to another. Thus, circumstantial evidence against D is viewed as more convincing when eyewitness evidence is introduced,[83] and the defendant's testimony can make jurors give more weight to other evidence.[84] Further, that juries use evidence indirectly when told not to use it does not necessarily tell us what they will do with it if told that they can in fact use it for its obvious purpose: as evidence of the defendant's propensity to commit crime.

One of the mock-jury studies is worth more detailed analysis. Lloyd-Bostock's experiments, conducted for the Law Commission, involved jury-eligible subjects in England and Wales, and used a realistic video of a criminal trial as the experimental material.[85] The study also included an impressive number of variables; different crimes were studied and previous convictions were varied: some were for a similar crime, some for a dissimilar one, some were recent (18 months old) and some old (five years old). Lloyd-Bostock's findings are summarized in Table 3.1 (in the base condition, the trial included no explicit information about previous convictions).

There are several significant findings here. Compared to the base condition, jurors gave no weight to old convictions, and as in some of the other studies a dissimilar conviction, even a recent one, actually seems to have favoured the defendant. Focussing on likelihood of guilt, a recent similar conviction does count against the defendant, but the impact is modest. Where verdicts are concerned, the impact cannot even be detected (though as Lloyd-Bostock notes, if the other evidence against D had been stronger, an effect might have been found[86]).

---

[82] 'Section 12 of the Canada Evidence Act', 245.

[83] D. M. Saunders, N. Vidmar, and E. C. Hewitt, 'Eyewitness Testimony and the Discrediting Effect' in S. M. A. Lloyd-Bostock and B. R. Clifford (eds), *Evaluating Witness Evidence* (Chichester: Wiley, 1983).

[84] B. C. Smith, S. D. Penrod, A. L. Otto, and R. C. Park, 'Jurors' Use of Probabilistic Evidence' (1996) 20 *Law & Human Behavior* 49, 72.

[85] S. Lloyd-Bostock, 'The Effects on Juries of Hearing about the Defendant's Previous Criminal Record: A Simulation Study' [2000] *Crim LR* 734.

[86] Lloyd-Bostock, 'Effects on Juries', 744. The study was designed to produce a likelihood of guilt of around 50 per cent in base condition, but unsurprisingly this did not make it a closely balanced case in terms of conviction.

Table 3.1 Effect of previous convictions on jurors

Likelihood of guilt, individual jurors, after deliberation	
Recent dissimilar	42.41
Old dissimilar	46.58
Good character	48.22
Old similar	50.80
Base	**51.47**
Recent similar	66.00
Percentage guilty verdicts, individual jurors, after deliberation	
Old dissimilar	2.8
Recent dissimilar	2.9
Old similar	5.6
Good character	16.7
Base	**22.2**
Recent similar	22.9

If we are concerned about moral prejudice, then Lloyd-Bostock's results are reassuring. If jurors were prepared to convict those with a criminal record on less than full proof, we would expect to see dissimilar, and perhaps old, previous convictions having an impact, but they do not.[87] One finding, however, does provide evidence of moral prejudice. In a variation where the previous conviction was for indecent assault on a child, the rate of guilty verdicts rose to 25 per cent. Still, this remains a relatively low conviction rate.

Lloyd-Bostock also repeated her research using magistrates rather than jury-eligible subjects.[88] The findings are shown in Table 3.2. As with juries, previous convictions had most effect when recent and similar. But magistrates put more weight on old similar convictions than did juries.[89] What is initially surprising is the effect of old dissimilar convictions, a finding that Lloyd-Bostock traces to the impact of a conviction for serious violence (OAPA, section 18). Given the significance of such a serious conviction, magistrates cannot be criticized for this tendency. What is more surprising is that a recent dissimilar conviction does not have the same effect. Where previous convictions do have an impact, Lloyd-Bostock notes that 'as in the jury study,

[87] Greene and Dodge, 'Influence of Prior Record Evidence', explicitly tested the standard of proof in their study. They found that the probability required for conviction did not decrease when D had previous convictions, although it did increase when D had a prior acquittal.

[88] S. Lloyd-Bostock, 'The Effects on Lay Magistrates of Hearing that the Defendant is of "Good Character", Being Left to Speculate, or Hearing that He Has a Previous Conviction' [2006] *Crim LR* 189.

[89] Recall that 'old' is five years old: the convictions are not especially stale. The discussion in Chapter 2 suggests that a ten-year crime-free period is good evidence of desistance.

Table 3.2 Effect of previous convictions on magistrates

Likelihood of guilt, individual magistrates, after deliberation	
Recent dissimilar	34.9
Base	**37.8**
Good character	41.5
Old dissimilar	58.5
Recent similar	59.1
Old similar	65.3
Percentage guilty verdicts, benches of magistrates, after deliberation	
Good character	0
Base	**0**
Recent dissimilar	0
Old similar	12.5
Old dissimilar	20
Recent similar	25

the effects...are not large'.[90] There is little in these studies to show that previous convictions are prejudicial.

3.5.2 Studies of real trials

There are several studies which examine conviction rates in actual trials, with previous convictions as a variable. All of these involve data from the United States and have recently been reviewed in an insightful paper by Laudan and Allen.[91] In Kalven and Zeisel's study from the 1960s, *The American Jury*, defendants with a criminal record were substantially more likely to be convicted than those without: 58 versus 75 per cent.[92] In the 1970s, Myers also found that previous convictions were a good predictor of likelihood of conviction.[93] More recently, in the early 2000s, the National Centre for State Courts organized a detailed study of trials in an attempt to explore the phenomenon of hung juries. This generated a rich dataset, including questionnaires filled out by jurors, judges, and lawyers,

[90] 'Effects on Lay Magistrates', 211.
[91] Laudan and Allen, 'The Devastating Impact of Prior Crimes Evidence'.
[92] H. Kalven and H. Zeisel, *The American Jury* (Chicago, IL: University of Chicago Press, 1966), 160. These figures are not quite based on the distinction between having and not having a criminal record. Kalven and Zeisel included in the criminal record category those defendants who did not take the stand, but the jury was not told that they had no record, the rationale being that in such cases there would be the suspicion of a criminal record, even if defendants in this group in fact had no record (159–60).
[93] M. Myers, 'Rule Departures and Making Law: Juries and Their Verdicts' (1979) 13 *Law & Soc Rev* 781, 792–3.

which has been analysed in several studies, some of which focus on criminal record.

Laudan and Allen's analysis of the NCSC data confirms the finding of the earlier studies. The conviction rate for defendants with no criminal record is 56 per cent, compared to 76 per cent for those who do have a record.[94] But as the authors note, it would be premature to conclude that revealing previous convictions to the jury has a substantial impact on the defendant's chances of acquittal. Delving deeper into the data, it turns out that the conviction rate for defendants with previous convictions does not vary depending on whether or not the convictions are revealed to the jury.[95] Telling the jury about the defendant's criminal past, then, appears to make no difference. Just having a criminal record is what counts. This is a striking finding.

Before turning to possible explanations of the puzzle uncovered by Laudan and Allen, one caveat is worth noting. In another analysis of the NCSC data, Eisenberg and Hans also examined the impact of criminal record.[96] Focussing on defendants with a criminal record, their basic finding was the same: 'there was no meaningful difference in the overall conviction rate between cases in which juries learned of the criminal record and cases in which they did not.'[97] But these authors also controlled for the strength of the case against the defendant, a factor which could be tracked through post-verdict questionnaires filled out by jurors. The strength of evidence probe involved a seven-point scale, with four being the mid-point on the scale. Eisenberg and Hans comment that:

> The most striking conviction rate is for cases with evidence strength equal to three in which the jury learned about a criminal record. Despite the relatively weak evidence, the conviction rate exceeded 60%, far greater than the rate for cases with evidentiary strength equal to three in which the jury did not learn about a criminal record, and far greater than the conviction rate for evidentiary strength equal to two.[98] ... [T]he presence of a criminal record increases the probability of conviction from less than 20% to about 50% or greater... [I]n the strongest of weak cases, the existence of a prior criminal record can cause a jury to convict.[99]

Eisenberg and Hans's finding might not seem too surprising. As has been noted, if a case is close to the tipping point at which juries are prepared to convict, then any additional evidence is apt to produce a significantly greater conviction rate. However, juries were asked to grade evidence strength after delivering a verdict, so any assessment of the weight of previous convictions should already have been incorporated in that grading. Hence Eisenberg and Hans's conclusion that criminal record was most likely to have been operating as moral prejudice, by lowering

---

[94] 'The Devastating Impact of Prior Crimes Evidence', 504.

[95] Laudan and Allen, 'The Devastating Impact of Prior Crimes Evidence', 506.

[96] T. Eisenberg and V. P. Hans, 'Taking a Stand on Taking the Stand: The Effect of a Prior Criminal Record on the Decision to Testify and on Trial Outcomes' (2009) 94 *Cornell L Rev* 1353.

[97] 'Taking a Stand on Taking the Stand', 1380.

[98] 'Taking a Stand on Taking the Stand', 1382.

[99] 'Taking a Stand on Taking the Stand', 1385.

the threshold required for conviction.[100] This, then, is some evidence that previous convictions can be prejudicial, although the finding does need to be seen in the context of: first, Allen and Laudan's conclusion that all defendants with a criminal record are more likely to be convicted, whether or not the jury is told about the record; and, second, that in most of the cases where criminal record was revealed, the jury would have been told to use it as evidence of the defendant's lack of credibility,[101] so it is difficult to tell what would happen if the jury was told that criminal record could be used as evidence of propensity to offend.

That first piece of context brings us back to the puzzle: why, in the NCSC data, should the dominant effect of previous convictions be to increase the chance of conviction of all defendants with previous convictions, even when the jury is not explicitly told about them? There are several possible explanations, but a promising one is that the jury either presumes that the defendant has previous convictions, or works it out from the defendant's tactical choices at trial. In the United States, defendants without previous convictions can announce this fact to the jury, can call good character evidence, and can testify without worrying that their previous convictions will be revealed to the jury (defendants with previous convictions risk having those convictions revealed when they testify).[102] In England and Wales, the current position is that if a defendant has no previous convictions, the judge should give a 'good character' direction to the jury.[103] In either jurisdiction, there is a decent chance that one or more jury members will know that the absence of information about criminal record signals that the defendant does have previous convictions. Even if this does not occur, jurors may simply presume that the defendant is likely to have previous convictions. The experimental research lends some support to this latter possibility. Lloyd-Bostock asked her subjects, in the condition where no information about previous convictions was given, whether they thought that the defendant had previous convictions: 66 per cent said they thought he had at least one.[104] A default assumption that the defendant has previous convictions would help to make sense of other research findings. As we have seen, several studies, including Loyd-Bostock's, find that dissimilar previous convictions are favourable to the defendant. This may be because the default assumption is that the defendant has a criminal record for offences similar to the current charge, and the dissimilar conviction indicates that D is better than he was thought to be.[105] It may also be significant that, where verdicts were concerned, Lloyd-Bostock found that a recent similar conviction had no effect, as if it simply confirmed what juries already supposed.

---

[100] 'Taking a Stand on Taking the Stand', 1386–7.

[101] Eisenberg and Hans found no evidence that criminal record worked in this way, a result they describe as 'deeply troubling': 'Taking a Stand on Taking the Stand', 1388.

[102] See Laudan and Allen, 'The Devastating Impact of Prior Crimes Evidence', 508.

[103] *Aziz* [1996] AC 41.

[104] Lloyd-Bostock, 'Effects on Juries', 753. There was a similar finding in the magistrates study: Lloyd-Bostock, 'Effects on Lay Magistrates', 195.

[105] Note that this speaks to Lempert's concern that juries will not be able to recognize that evidence undermines assumptions they have already made (Lempert, 'Modeling Relevance'); in Lloyd-Bostock's study, it appears that juries do recognize this.

3.6 Conclusion

Is bad character evidence prejudicial? No one can answer that question with complete confidence. The experimental studies produce somewhat disparate findings, and there will always be doubts about their external validity. The data on real trials also provides a slightly mixed picture, with the additional problem that the studies are from the United States, leaving a question mark about their applicability to England and Wales, especially now that, under the Criminal Justice Act 2003, bad character evidence is widely admissible as evidence of propensity. In fact, an empirical study was carried out to examine the workings of the 2003 Act, but on this issue the methodology was sufficiently unsophisticated that the results are of very limited value. For what it is worth, however, practitioners thought that bad character had limited impact on trials, while Crown Court judges:

> reported that the juries that have heard bad character evidence appear to have been extremely careful not to allow this to prejudice their view of the defendant. The judges considered, therefore, that the juries are listening to the directions issued by the trial judge and were regarding bad character evidence appropriately and giving it modest weight. There was some anecdotal evidence that the defendant's bad character has led the jury to consider that the defendant has been treated unfairly and to be unwilling to convict him or her. There was also some anecdotal evidence of juries acquitting a defendant even when damaging bad character evidence had been presented.[106]

Nevertheless, some conclusions can be drawn. The experimental studies provide little evidence that bad character evidence is prejudicial. While previous convictions for a similar crime do affect ratings of guilt and verdicts, the impact is generally moderate and not out of line with the—often considerable—probative value of criminal record. The data on real trials suggest that jurors will work out whether a defendant has previous convictions and therefore that evidential rules excluding such evidence have little impact. On the more negative side, Lloyd-Bostock's study suggests that some previous convictions—her example being indecent assault on a child—can be prejudicial when introduced in cases not involving that type of offending.[107] Eisenberg and Hans found that, where criminal record was introduced, jurors seemed to lower the standard of proof in 'the strongest of weak cases'.[108]

In my view, these findings do not support anything like a strict exclusionary rule for bad character evidence. One reason for this is that, even if we focus on the more negative findings, it is not easy to exclude character evidence. Juries

---

[106] Morgan Harris Burrows LLP, *Research into the Impact of Bad Character Provisions on the Courts*, Ministry of Justice Research Series 5/09 (London: Ministry of Justice, 2009), 34.

[107] While I presume that that is evidence of prejudice, that is not necessarily the case. As we saw in Chapter 2, criminals tend to be generalists. People who indecently assault children may well be more likely than the average person to commit other crimes too. However, juries probably do not appreciate this fact, so it is likely that the effect operates through simple dislike of the defendant, the sort of mechanism explored in Nadler and McDonnell's research.

[108] 'Taking a Stand on Taking the Stand', 1385.

appear to presume that defendants have previous convictions, or to work out that they do from the absence of information about good character. Character may enter the trial in other ways too. Nadler and McDonnell observe that 'juries are likely to extrapolate information about character from evidence about a person's priorities, choices and motivations.'[109] And as Gross puts it: 'what we regulate as "character evidence" is only a small part of the evidence and arguments that lawyers use to develop competing versions of the characters of the actors in the events that are subject to litigation.'[110] Character may even enter fact-finders' judgments without lawyers' efforts. Research suggests that judgments of character are rapid, automatic processes which we are prone to make on the basis of appearance alone: hence the finding in some studies that less attractive people are more likely to be found guilty and are sentenced more harshly.[111] Judgments of traits, including honesty, can be made on extremely brief exposure to a face.[112] And people are reasonably good at telling criminals from non-criminals by appearance alone (although they are not able to tell which crimes the targets have committed).[113] We think in terms of character with very little prompting.

It is likely that criminal trials are awash with character inferences whether we like it or not. The best policy is surely not to ignore this by not mentioning character—and therefore letting whatever inferences fact-finders draw do their work uncorrected—but to let fact-finders know about a defendant's previous convictions, at least when they are relevant to guilt. Where a defendant's criminal record is not as bad, or as recent, as jurors suspect, this may well work to the defendant's advantage. Where previous convictions are recent and similar, juries will probably put weight on them in their deliberations, but there is very little evidence that they will put too much weight on them. Telling the jury about previous convictions also allows the judge to explain what they are relevant to and to warn against over-weighting. While some of the research suggests that previous convictions work unconsciously, spilling over into the assessment of other evidence or leading jurors to lower the standard of proof, there are also signs that jurors can control and moderate their reasoning when such dangers are made explicit—as when good and bad Nathan are judged alongside each other.[114]

[109] 'Moral Character', 297–8.

[110] S. R. Gross, 'Make-Believe: The Rules Excluding Evidence of Character and Liability Insurance' (1998) 49 *Hastings LJ* 843, 845–6.

[111] J. J. Gunnell and S. J. Ceci, 'When Emotionality Trumps Reason: A Study of Individual Processing Style and Juror Bias' (2010) 28 *Behavioral Sciences & Law* 850.

[112] See J. Willis and A. Todorov, 'First Impressions: Making Up Your Mind after a 100-ms Exposure to a Face' (2006) 17 *Soc Psychol* 592. See also R. J. W. Vernon, C. A. M. Sutherland, A. W. Young, and T. Hartley, 'Modeling First Impressions from Highly Variable Facial Images' (2014) 111 (32) *Proc Nat'l Acad Sci US* E3353.

[113] J. M. Valla, S. J. Ceci, and W. M. Williams, 'The Accuracy of Inferences about Criminality Based on Facial Appearance' (2011) 5 *J Social, Evolutionary & Cultural Psychol* 66. See also S. Mishra and R. Sritharan, 'Personality and Behavioral Outcomes Associated with Risk-Taking Are Accurately Inferred from Faces' (2012) 46 *J Research in Personality* 760.

[114] Some of the evidence on racism points in a similar direction: when the issue of race is brought to people's attention, they are able to monitor and control the tendency to be biased against people of a different race. Thus, in research in the United States, blacks and whites are treated equally in

In England and Wales, the current position is, roughly, that juries will be told about any previous convictions which show a propensity to commit the crime currently charged; in practice, this means that only convictions for similar offences are admitted (see Chapter 7). Previous convictions for any—even a non-similar—offence may be admitted under the 'tit for tat' rule if the defendant attacks a prosecution witness or co-defendant (see Chapter 9). This is some way away from being a scheme of automatic admissibility, and it might therefore be open to criticism in the light of the evidence reviewed here. If D is on trial for burglary, but has a previous conviction for assault, and D does not trigger the tit for tat rule, the jury will probably not be told anything about D's criminal record. Because of the assault conviction, however, the judge will not instruct the jury to regard D as a person of good character. The concern, therefore, is that jurors will presume or infer that D has previous convictions, and will therefore be more likely to convict D than they otherwise would be. Under a scheme of automatic admissibility, however, the jury would be aware that D had a previous conviction for assault and, if the mock-jury research is right, this would be advantageous to D.

On the evidence reviewed here, a scheme of automatic admissibility is not unthinkable.[115] However, the current English position is not as unattractive as it might first look. If jurors do make inferences on the basis of what they know about admissibility rules, then in time English juries will understand that when there is neither a good character direction nor mention of a previous conviction, the defendant has a previous conviction for a non-cognate offence. Further, it is not obvious that disadvantaging the burglary defendant with an assault conviction is an example of prejudice: as we saw in the previous chapter, criminals tend to be generalists, so an assault conviction *is* evidence that the defendant has committed burglary; in any case, D is free to reveal his non-cognate record to the jury.[116] Finally, there is some evidence that jurors regard it as unfair to introduce evidence of previous convictions which they regard as irrelevant,[117] and that is something to be avoided.

In reviewing the evidence for the prejudicial nature of previous convictions, this chapter has concentrated on their use as evidence of the defendant's propensity to commit crime. While the evidence is incomplete, it gives us little reason to adopt a predominantly exclusionary policy. Little has been said about the second way in which previous convictions are used against defendants: as evidence of

---

trials where race is made a salient issue: S. R. Sommers and P. C. Ellsworth, 'How Much Do we Really Know about Race and Juries? A Review of Social Science Theory and Research' (2003) 78 *Chicago-Kent L Rev* 998, 1010–16.

[115] Or automatic admissibility with occasional exceptions, such as where the previous conviction is for child abuse.

[116] See, eg, *Speed* [2013] EWCA Crim 1650 (D, on trial for a sexual offence, let the jury know about his record for offences of dishonesty).

[117] See the quotation from the Morgan Harris Burrows study, *Research into the Impact of Bad Character Provisions on the Courts*. This conclusion was also drawn by Greene and Dodge, 'Influence of Prior Record Evidence', owing to the finding that a prior acquittal reduced likelihood of guilt.

their lack of credibility. Suffice it to say that here the research is much less equivocal. Juries do not use previous convictions as a way of assessing credibility,[118] and limiting instructions telling juries to use criminal record as a gauge of credibility but not of propensity do not work. The empirical evidence provides a strong case for dropping credibility uses of bad character evidence. That argument is taken up in Chapter 9.

---

[118] See, eg, Lloyd-Bostock, 'Effects on Juries', 747–8, 754; and Eisenberg and Hans, 'Taking a Stand on Taking the Stand', 1387–8.

4

The Ethics of Character Evidence

> So many people are employed in positions of trust; so many people, out of so many, will be dishonest. I have heard you talk, a hundred times, of its being a law. How can I help laws?
>
> Charles Dickens, *Hard Times* (1854)

In Chapter 3, we explored the question of whether admitting bad character evidence is prejudicial in the sense that admitting it is likely to distort the fact-finding process. The conclusion was that there is little evidence that admitting bad character does cause prejudice. There may, however, be other ways in which character evidence can have a negative impact on the criminal trial. Criminal trials are not just about accurate fact-finding: they are widely understood to have a moral dimension as well. Practices such as excluding improperly obtained evidence, respecting the privilege against self-incrimination, and—on some accounts—allowing defendants to confront the witnesses against them tend to be explained in terms of their contribution to fairness rather than to adjudicative accuracy. The topic of this chapter is whether using a defendant's past actions as evidence against him might also undermine the fairness of the trial; whether, in other words, such a practice is morally problematic.

At the very start of this book it was noted that judging people on the basis of their past behaviour—even past bad behaviour—is not usually considered to be something to be avoided in everyday life. Criminal trials, however, may be different. The criminal trial is a morally freighted event, where judgments about blameworthiness are central. It is reasonably uncontroversial to claim that, in the event of a guilty verdict, the criminal trial communicates censure to a defendant, and that criminal trials should treat defendants as responsible agents.[1] Some writers, especially Duff, take the 'communicative' view of criminal trials further, and argue that the trial calls defendants to account for their wrongdoing.[2] In

---

[1] On the latter, see L. Fuller, *The Morality of Law* (New Haven, CT: Yale University Press, 1969), 162: 'To embark on the enterprise of subjecting human conduct to the governance of rules involves of necessity a commitment to the view that man is, or can become, a responsible agent, capable of understanding and following rules, and answerable for his defaults.'

[2] R. A. Duff, *Punishment, Communication and Community* (Oxford: Oxford University Press, 2001). The view is applied to the trial in Duff's *Trials and Punishments* (Cambridge: Cambridge University Press, 1986), ch 4, and at greater length in R. A. Duff, L. Farmer, S. Marshall, and V. Tadros, *The Trial on Trial: Volume 3: Towards a Normative Theory of the Criminal Trial*

what follows, I shall not make much of the differences between the various moral accounts of the trial, but take it as given that there is a communicative aspect to trials.[3] Whether trials express censure, or call defendants to account, it can hopefully be appreciated that, as a communicative enterprise, the trial may face constraints on the information it uses to produce a verdict. For example, by relying on evidence obtained via serious state wrongdoing, the court might undermine its own attempts to convey a moral judgment to the defendant. This then hints at the sort of argument which might be made against using previous convictions to prove guilt: that doing so would undermine the message of censure by implying that the defendant is not a responsible agent or that he will not be able to understand and respond to the message of blame being conveyed to him.

This chapter explores moralized accounts of the exclusion of bad character evidence. While the focus remains on the law of evidence and the use of character evidence to prove guilt, some of the arguments touch on the use of character evidence in sentencing, and therefore help to set the stage for the discussion in Chapters 11 and 12.

4.1 Exclusion and Exceptions

Before looking at moral arguments against bad character evidence in more detail, something should be said about one of the challenges they face: the need to explain their own defeasibility or limited applicability. If there is an ethical objection to bad character evidence, it probably has to allow for exceptions. *Straffen*[4] provides a useful example. Straffen had previous convictions for murdering young girls by strangulation.[5] The attacks were non-sexual and Straffen made no attempt to hide the bodies. When the strangled, unhidden, unmolested body of a young girl was found close to where Straffen had just escaped from prison, his previous convictions were admitted as the primary evidence against him at his trial for the girl's murder, and led to his conviction. A rule which excluded Straffen's criminal record on moral grounds would pay a very high price in terms of failing to convict the guilty, so high that an exceptionless rule is unattractive. Unsurprisingly, the common law recognized exceptions to the *prima facie* rule that bad character evidence was inadmissible as proof of guilt, and an exception was held to apply (not very convincingly, it must be said) in *Straffen* itself.[6]

(Oxford: Hart Publishing, 2007). Duff also expands on the theme, with particular reference to the criminal law, in *Answering for Crime* (Oxford: Hart Publishing, 2008).

[3] For more detailed discussion, see M. Redmayne, 'Theorizing the Criminal Trial' (2009) 12 *New Crim L Rev* 287.

[4] [1952] 2 QB 911.

[5] In fact, Straffen had been found unfit to plead, but this detail is not important for the purposes of the present discussion. Given the repeated use of *Straffen* as an example, and as one where guilt is obvious, it should be noted that not everyone is convinced of Straffen's guilt: see B. Woffinden, 'Insane, Guilty, or Neither?' *The Guardian*, 26 May 2001.

[6] See further the discussion in Chapter 5.

The most obvious way in which an exception to a moralized character evidence prohibition could be justified is in terms of balancing the probative force of the evidence and the seriousness of the offence charged against the moral cost of using the evidence. In England and Wales, the common law seemed to settle on something like this balancing test when the House of Lords decided *DPP* v *P*.[7] The test for admissibility of bad character evidence, it was held, was whether 'its probative force in support of the allegation that an accused person committed a crime is sufficiently great to make it just to admit the evidence, notwithstanding that it is prejudicial to the accused in tending to show that he was guilty of another crime'.[8] While a balancing test makes some sense when the probative value of character evidence is being balanced against its prejudicial effect on the fact-finder—one can conceptualize both in terms of their effect on truth-finding—things are rather trickier when probative value is being balanced against moral harm. These two values do not seem to be easy to compare. Even if one accepts that some sort of comparison is theoretically possible, it is very hard to know what a moralized exclusionary rule would look like under balancing: perhaps the need to convict the guilty would always outweigh the moral cost involved in admitting character evidence; perhaps it never would. It may be that we simply have to accept this sort of vagueness and do the best we can, but proponents of a moralized exclusionary rule for bad character evidence would at least need to accept that under balancing identifying a moral cost to admitting character evidence would not lead to any obvious pattern of exclusion. In particular, this approach would not easily justify the sort of exclusionary rule found at common law.

The common law approach to bad character evidence does, however, hint at a different way of justifying exceptions. As we will see in Chapter 5, a prominent strand in the thinking about bad character evidence, especially before *DPP* v *P*,[9] was that cases where bad character evidence was admissible were different in kind, rather than just in degree. Sometimes what was said to be excluded was a particular argument linking bad character evidence to probable guilt, with bad character evidence being admissible where this argument could be avoided. The idea of 'forbidden reasoning' (often identified as 'propensity reasoning') fits rather well with the idea that the exclusionary rule has a moral basis. If some bad character cases do not involve forbidden reasoning, there is simply no moral cost in these cases and no need to engage in balancing. A forbidden reasoning approach does face other problems, though. Chapters 5 and 6 suggest that, at least in the common law scheme, it is not possible to identify any distinction in the evidential reasoning in cases where bad character evidence was held to be admissible and those where it was not.

None of the foregoing poses insurmountable objections to developing a moralized justification for the exclusion of bad character evidence. But the discussion does identify points to bear in mind as we proceed.

---

[7] [1991] 2 AC 447.   [8] *DPP* v *P*, 460.   [9] [1991] 2 AC 447.

4.2 Putting the Defendant's Life on Trial

The moral accounts we will examine all seem to revolve around similar themes, though the themes get developed in various different ways. The central theme is the significance of desistance from crime. Chapters 2 and 3 noted that those who have been convicted of crime have a comparative propensity to offend, and that it is comparative propensity which provides the argument in favour of admitting previous convictions to prove guilt. But desistance was also seen to be an important aspect of offending patterns: most offenders are only convicted once, and even prolific offenders tend to desist from crime at some stage. In Chapter 3, the question was raised whether this might pose a problem for drawing inferences from previous convictions; I argued that it did not, at least if the problem was conceived in purely inferential terms. We are now ready to consider the moral side of the problem.

One way of being more confident that a particular defendant does have a high comparative propensity to offend would be to consider risk factors. Is D employed and/or in a stable relationship?[10] Are there any childhood risk factors such as having separated parents or attending an unruly school?[11] What is his probation officer's view? But while the identification of risk factors might help us to be more confident about a judgment of propensity, this strategy opens up another line of criticism. The worry is that the trial will become a general moral enquiry into D's life, something we would find distasteful.[12] Our fears about this sort of trial are captured in Camus's *L'Etranger*, where the central character has his lack of emotion at his mother's funeral used against him in court.[13] They also seem to be reflected in Holt LCJ's response to the prosecution's attempt to introduce evidence of the defendant's previous offending in *Harrison's Trial*: '[h]old, what are you doing now? Are you going to arraign his whole life? Away, away! That ought not to be; that is nothing to the matter.'[14]

While this is an interesting line of objection to character evidence, there are reasons to be sceptical of its ability to provide a foundation for a policy of exclusion. While our initial reaction might be that the criminal trial should not be a general enquiry into a person's life, it turns out that something like this occurs in France. Field's research on the French criminal trial shows that in more serious cases the trial starts by presenting the accused's life story. Previous convictions are freely admitted.[15] Still, that occurs in a particular political, cultural, and

---

[10] The importance of employment and marriage in sustaining desistance is emphasized in J. H. Laub and R. J. Sampson, *Shared Beginnings, Divergent Lives: Delinquent Boys to Age 70* (Cambridge, MA: Harvard University Press, 2006).

[11] Identified as risk factors in J. Hales, C. Nevill, S. Pudney, and S. Tipping, *Longitudinal Analysis of the Offending, Crime and Justice Survey 2003–06* (London: Home Office, 2009), 2.

[12] This is the concern ultimately raised by Peter Tillers in 'What is Wrong with Character Evidence?' (1998) 49 *Hastings LJ* 781.

[13] A. Camus, *L'Étranger* (Paris: Gallimard, 1942).   [14] (1692) 12 How St Tr 833, 864.

[15] S. Field, 'State, Citizen and Character in French Criminal Process' (2006) 33 *JLS* 522. See also J. H. Wigmore, *A Treatise on the Anglo-American System of Trials at Common Law* (3rd edn, Boston: Little, Brown & Co, 1940), § 193.

procedural context, and we might think that French practice tells us little about the proprieties of the common law trial. It would certainly be a significant change in our practices if the trial (at least at the guilt-adjudication stage)[16] were to start ranging so widely over a person's life, and pointing out that this happened elsewhere would be unlikely to quell objections. In fact, the use of previous convictions in the modern common law trial might be thought to work precisely because it does not involve a broad moral enquiry. Unlike at the time of *Harrison's Trial*, official criminal records make it easy to check whether D has offended before. Some information to contextualize the previous conviction will be easy to present, such as how long ago it occurred and D's age at the time. While, as we have seen, there may be an argument that the inference will be sounder if we go further, this could raise issues which are difficult to prove, potentially opening up a series of further questions. Given that the question of D's propensity is rarely central to the trial, introducing his criminal record along with—as under the Criminal Justice Act 2003—a warning against placing undue reliance on previous convictions and a reminder to take into account anything the defendant has said about them may be a perfectly reasonable position to take.[17] Where a question about the defendant's propensity, proved through previous convictions, really is central to the case, then perhaps there is an argument of fairness in favour of allowing the defendant to introduce other sorts of evidence to cast doubt on his continuing propensity, in which case the prosecution might be permitted to respond in kind. If the defendant wants to turn the trial into a general moral enquiry, that might be a decision we should respect.

What has been said here does not exhaust arguments about the significance of desistance which, as noted, run through attempts to develop an ethical objection to bad character evidence. All that is claimed so far is that there is no reason to think that the introduction of previous convictions must be accompanied by a wide-ranging moral audit of the defendant.

4.3 Autonomy

We do not have to look far to find a further objection to using bad character evidence to prove guilt. A series of arguments focus on the defendant's autonomy. According to Wasserman, courts are reluctant to base verdicts 'on the frequency of misconduct by others or by the defendant himself', because this is 'inconsistent with law's commitment to treat the defendant as an autonomous individual, free to determine and alter his conduct at each moment'.[18] Similar ideas about

---

[16] As we will see in Chapter 11, the sentencing stage can engage more deeply with the defendant's character, although typically this involves good character evidence, not bad character evidence.

[17] See *Hanson, Gilmore, and P* [2005] 2 Cr App R 21, [2005] EWCA Crim 824, [18].

[18] D. T. Wasserman, 'The Morality of Statistical Proof and the Risk of Mistaken Liability' (1991) 13 *Cardozo L Rev* 935, 943–53.

character evidence can be found in work by Tillers,[19] Ho,[20] Acorn,[21] and by Duff and his colleagues.[22]

Autonomy-based objections to bad character evidence face a number of initial problems. First, the fact that behaviour is predictable does not necessarily imply a lack of autonomy: I am regularly to be found in a particular pub on a Tuesday night, but the fact that my presence there can be predicted with a fair degree of reliability does not say much about my autonomy. Second, there is something rather paradoxical in the claim that offending behaviour, in particular, is non-autonomous. 'Autonomous' means, literally, making one's own law, and there is an obvious sense in which criminals are better at doing that than the law-abiding. Indeed, the criminological literature identifies a certain rebellious, anti-authoritarian streak in many persistent offenders.[23] There is, third, a marked asymmetry in the worries about autonomy here. As it often is, motive is a useful counter-example. When we say that the fact that the defendant had a motive for murdering his rich uncle increases the probability that he did so, the autonomy concern does not seem to be engaged, even though, in Wasserman's terms, we are basing a verdict on the frequency of misconduct by others, for motive is only evidence of guilt because we know that there is a general tendency to act on motive. Similarly, when the defendant offers good character evidence in his favour, we do not worry about the possibility that he has suddenly demonstrated his autonomy by becoming a bad person.

We should resist jumping from these objections to the conclusion that there is nothing to the autonomy objection. There is plenty to niggle with in the points above; further, autonomy is a vague concept,[24] so perhaps the clearest lesson to draw from the foregoing is that the autonomy objection needs to be refined and expressed more carefully. First, though, a slight side-track is in order.

[19] Tillers, 'What is Wrong with Character Evidence?'. Although raising the autonomy issue, Tillers ends up attaching little significance to it.

[20] H. L. Ho, *A Philosophy of Evidence Law: Justice in the Pursuit of Truth* (Oxford: Oxford University Press, 2008), ch 6, which builds on H. L. Ho, 'Justice in the Pursuit of Truth: A Moral Defence of the Similar Facts Rule' (2006) 35 *Common Law World Rev* 51.

[21] A. E. Acorn, 'Similar Fact Evidence and the Principle of Inductive Reasoning: Makin Sense' (1991) 11 *OJLS* 63–91, 68.

[22] Duff et al, *The Trial on Trial*. A very brief sketch of the arguments developed in this book appears in Duff, *Trials and Punishments*, 131.

[23] See N. Shover, *Great Pretenders: Pursuits and Careers of Persistent Thieves* (Boulder, CO: Westview Press, 1996), ch 4; and S. Maruna, *Making Good: How Ex-Offenders Reform and Rebuild Their Lives* (Washington, DC: American Psychological Association, 2001).

[24] See, eg, N. Arpaly, 'Which Autonomy?' in J. K. Campbell, M. O'Rourke, and D. Shier (eds), *Freedom and Determinism* (Cambridge, MA: MIT Press, 2004), 173–88; and O. O'Neill, 'Autonomy: The Emperor's New Clothes' (2003) 77 *Proceedings of the Aristotelian Society (Supplement)* 1. Duff et al note the problem of the vagueness of the term (*The Trial on Trial*, 130 fn 5), and suggest that it is better to talk in terms of responsibility. Nevertheless, 'autonomy' is used in their discussion of character evidence, perhaps because in that context replacing it with 'responsibility' would make the arguments sound less intuitively persuasive.

4.4 Motives and Reasons

Above, and in Chapter 3, I have deployed the example of motive to blunt certain objections that might be made to the use of character evidence. The strategy is to note that since a particular objection to character evidence also applies to motive evidence, and because excluding motive evidence is counter-intuitive, that particular objection to character evidence fails. This strategy, however, might be undermined if there was a significant difference between evidence based on the existence of a motive and evidence based on previous convictions. In fact, in the present context, both Ho and Duff et al suggest that there is a difference between the two types of evidence, a difference which has moral resonance.[25] Their argument proceeds along the following lines: when we say that D has a motive for committing crime—he killed his wife because she was having an affair, or his rich uncle in order to inherit under the will—we are offering an explanation for his behaviour with reference to the reasons why he committed it. While motive evidence may have a similar inferential structure to bad character evidence—we look at the behaviour of others to infer the likely behaviour of D—the explanatory structure in motive cases, in particular the fact that it taps into D's reasons for action, might be thought to be significant. This sort of inferential structure does seem to respect D as a responsible agent, in the sense of someone who can respond to reasons. It does not treat D as simply having some opaque and ungovernable urge to commit crime.

This is an intriguing argument, but it relies on distinctions which do not really hold up. An initial question is: why should the fact that D responds to reasons be significant in the context of the moral structure of the trial? The answer might seem obvious: only those who respond to reasons are appropriate subjects of criminal responsibility. But this response will collapse the distinction between character and motive. If we use D's previous conviction for burglary as evidence that he has committed burglary, there is no obvious sense in which we are treating him as unresponsive to reason (that is, unless we interpret reason in the Kantian sense of right reason, but surely the D who murders his unfaithful wife also does not respond to reason in this sense either). Indeed, while it might seem obvious that saying 'D has a propensity to burgle' does not provide a reason for D's burgling V's house, surely 'propensity' is a place-holder for something more complex. Underlying D's propensity to burgle may be something like the following: D enjoys the thrill of burglary as well as its material rewards, and gives little thought to the impact of burglary on the victim.[26] Propensity, in other words, should not

---

[25] Duff et al, *The Trial on Trial*, 254–6; and Ho, *Philosophy*, 298–306. Ho's account is especially significant because, he argues, it can be used more generally to explain why some previous convictions are different in kind from others; in other words, it could explain why a moral account of the character evidence prohibition does not apply to all uses of character evidence.

[26] See J. Katz, *Seductions of Crime: Moral and Sensual Attractions of Doing Evil* (New York: Basic Books, 1988), ch 2; R. T. Wright and S. Decker, *Burglars on the Job: Streetlife and Residential Break-Ins* (Boston, MA: Northeastern University Press, 1994), ch 2; and N. Shover, *Great Pretenders: Pursuits and Careers of Persistent Thieves* (Boulder, CO: Westview Press, 1996), 77–111, 164–7.

be understood as an opaque and ungovernable urge, but as a complex set of sensibilities and reasons for action.

There is little reason to think that morality gives us grounds to distinguish between character and motive for the purposes of an exclusionary rule. But a different way of framing the objection to bad character might be developed from the preceding discussion. If D's responsiveness to reasons is important to the criminal trial, this might be because the reasons-responsive are able to respond appropriately to the censuring message in the criminal verdict. If we use D's previous conviction as evidence that he has a propensity to burgle, might we be implying that D has not responded to censure, and hence reason, in the appropriate way?

4.5 Moral Improvement

In the initial assessment of the autonomy argument against previous convictions, I noted that autonomy concerns do not seem to surface when it comes to good character evidence, and that there is a sense in which criminals are more autonomous than the law-abiding. I suggested that, rather than taking these to be knock-down objections to the autonomy argument, we might instead respond to them by trying to refine the concept of autonomy. Perhaps, then, what is really important is not autonomy per se, but the freedom to change our ways, or, slightly different, to become better people than we already are. Some writers provide resources for thinking that this particular sort of freedom may be morally significant. There is a bizarre, but intriguing, philosophical debate on whether pre-punishment is permissible: that is, whether it could be appropriate to punish someone for a crime before he commits it.[27] To make sense of this question we have to suppose that we have strong evidence that a person will commit a crime, and that after the event it will not be practicable to punish him, perhaps because he will leave the jurisdiction. We also need to be clear that we are talking about retributive punishment, not preventive detention. Smilansky suggests that there are moral reasons for not allowing pre-punishment in this situation.[28] For him, the unacceptability of pre-punishment flows from deep Kantian intuitions about respecting autonomous moral personality and choice. Pre-punishment would treat people as objects, as if they had no choice, as if they could not change their minds. In a similar vein, though on a different topic—decency—Margalit argues that

---

[27] See C. New, 'Time and Punishment' (1992) 52 *Analysis*; S. Smilansky, 'The Time to Punish' (1994) 54 *Analysis*; C. New, 'Time and Punishment' (1995) 55 *Analysis*; D. Statman, 'The Time to Punish and the Problem of Moral Luck' (1997) 14 *J Applied Philosophy*; R. Sorensen, 'Future Law: Prepunishment and the Causal Theory of Verdicts' (2006) 40 *Noûs*; and G. Yaffe, 'Prevention and Imminence, Pre-Punishment and Actuality' (2011) 48 *San Diego L Rev* 1205. The problem of pre-punishment is taken in a slightly different direction in S. Smilansky, 'Determinism and Prepunishment: The Radical Nature of Compatibilism' (2007) 67 *Analysis*; and I. Haji, 'Libertarian Openness, Blameworthiness, and Time' in Campbell et al, *Freedom and Determinism*.
[28] Smilansky, 'The Time to Punish'.

there is a deep link between respect and the possibility of change: respecting people preserves the idea that the future is open; even hardened criminals, Margalit suggests, deserve respect because of the possibility that they might change.[29]

When Duff et al and Ho talk of autonomy in relation to character evidence, it seems that this is what they really have in mind. Duff et al argue that '[t]o take the fact of prior wrongdoing as evidence of... guilt of a new offence is inconsistent with... respect for the defendant as a responsible agent: as a responsible agent she could have put her past crime behind her, and come to guide her actions by the appropriate reasons that the law provides or expresses; but we treat her as if her past conduct determines her present conduct'.[30] For Ho, '[r]espect for the accused requires that the court must not be dismissive of his capacity to revise, or act against, his bad character.'[31] There are arguments with a similar structure in the wider criminal law literature: it is wrong to criminalize conduct, or incapacitate people, on the basis of predictions of future wrongdoing, for to do so would dismiss people's capacity to choose rightly. For example:

When harmless conduct is proscribed merely because the actor, if she perpetrates it, may then be tempted to commit further acts that are harmful, she is being treated as one might a child: as someone who lacks the insight or self-control to resist the later temptation. Assuming she is a competent actor, such treatment would fail to respect her as a moral agent, capable of deliberation and self-control.[32]

These arguments are mistaken. In what follows, I concentrate on character evidence and the capacity to change, but the arguments apply equally to claims like the one above about pre-emptive criminalization.[33]

There is much to be said for the idea that we should respect people's capacity for moral improvement, and that such respect should be embedded in our criminal justice institutions. But it really is not clear that using bad character evidence against defendants is inconsistent with respect for their ability to change. How exactly does the inference from previous conviction to present propensity involve treating the defendant 'as if past conduct determines present conduct'? We are not treating the defendant's actions as predetermined, we are just saying that there

---

[29] A. Margalit, *The Decent Society* (trans N. Goldblum, Cambridge, MA: Harvard University Press, 1996), 70–5.

[30] Duff et al, *The Trial on Trial*, 113–14. See also V. Tadros, 'Distinguishing General Theory, Doctrine and Evidence in Criminal Responsibility: A Response to Lacey' (2007) 1 *Crim Law & Philosophy* 259, 264 ('[a] process that is respectful of D's agency requires that D's conduct is not prejudged from his previous conduct if it has been communicated to D, as it will be if he was convicted, that the conduct was worthy of condemnation. For D should be treated as capable of responding to public moral condemnation in the appropriate way'). Tadros has now distanced himself from these arguments: see his 'Controlling Risk' in A. Ashworth, L. Zedner, and P. Tomlin (eds), *Prevention and the Limits of the Criminal Law* (Oxford: Oxford University Press, 2013). In his essay in the same volume ('Pre-Trial Detention and the Presumption of Innocence'), Duff argues against prediction in slightly different terms from those used in *The Trial on Trial*, and discusses the use of prior actions more cautiously (at 127–30).

[31] Ho, *Philosophy*, 300.

[32] A. Simester and A. von Hirsch, *Crimes, Harms and Wrongs: On the Principles of Criminalisation* (Oxford: Hart Publishing, 2011), 62.

[33] For sustained critique of the latter, see Tadros, 'Controlling Risk'.

is a certain probability that he has done something.[34] An analogy may be useful. Suppose, as sometimes happens, that during building work an unexploded Second World War bomb is found in London.[35] It may be that, so long after the bomb was dropped, there is very little chance of it now exploding. But when bomb disposal experts clear the area, they are not dismissing the possibility of the bomb being safe; they might even take it into account in deciding what degree of precautions to take. What they are doing, though, is allowing the possibility that the bomb remains dangerous. In the same way, when using the previous conviction against the burglar we should take into account both the possibility that he no longer has a propensity to burgle as well as the possibility that he remains dangerous. But that is exactly how the concept of comparative propensity works, because it averages over recidivists and desisters. So when we presume that the defendant remains somewhat more likely to burgle than other people, we are taking into account his capacity to change, not dismissing it. We can also, and should, take the possibility of change into account by noting such things as the length of time between the previous conviction and the present charge. It is true that the bomb analogy is in some ways inapt; people obviously are not inanimate objects. But introducing agency makes no difference to the argument, which is simply a conceptual one about probability.[36]

Might it be argued, though, that we demean the defendant by treating his conduct as partially determined? Determination is usually taken to be a bivalent, all or nothing concept: something is either determined or it is not. But we could talk instead of the defendant's choice being influenced by his character; influence is something which can come in degrees and may be what the arguments under consideration have in mind. But it seems that those arguments need the strong, bivalent concept of determinism if they are to work: the argument of Duff et al, which objects to treating the defendant as if his past determines his future, loses its pull if expressed in terms of influence.[37] As the unexploded bomb analogy shows, the inference that there is a possibility that the defendant has burgled again does not involve assuming that he is unable to change. Moreover, there does not seem anything wrong, or disrespectful, in treating the defendant as less than fully free. Radical autonomy, where we choose more or less arbitrarily, is not an attractive vision of the world, nor does it seem respectful to think of a defendant

[34] For a similar point in a different context, see R. Reiner, *Law and Order: An Honest Citizen's Guide to Crime and Control* (Cambridge: Polity, 2007), 18–20.

[35] This example intentionally reflects a debate in punishment theory about incapacitative punishment. Various views are usefully collected in A. von Hirsch and A. Ashworth (eds), *Principled Sentencing Readings on Theory and Policy* (Oxford: Hart Publishing, 1998), 88–140. The bomb example is used by Norval Morris at 108.

[36] See Tadros's helpful hostel example, 'Controlling Risk', 146–8. Corrado has also confronted the argument that 'where crime is predictable, it is to that extent unfree' in 'Punishment and the Wild Beast of Prey: The Problem of Preventive Detention' (1996) 86 *J Criminal Law & Criminol* 778 (the passage quoted is at 795).

[37] If we treat D's present conduct as being influenced by her past, we are not denying that 'she could have put her past crime behind her, and come to guide her actions by the appropriate reasons'. Nor does there seem to be any conflict with treating D as a responsible agent.

as autonomous in this way. Incomplete autonomy has got to be the realistic start-ing point for any theory which values autonomy.[38]

It is, however, possible to reframe the argument about the significance of change in a way that avoids the problems just described. When we take precau-tions in dealing with the unexploded bomb, even though we are not dismissing the possibility that the bomb is harmless, we are presuming that the bomb has not completely changed. Similarly, when we use previous convictions against the burglar, we are presuming that he has not completely reformed. So what has just been said might seem to be splitting hairs. Duff et al and Ho could argue that it is the presumption that the defendant has not completely reformed which is incompatible with the censuring function of the criminal verdict, and that this presumption fails to treat the defendant as a responsible agent. Put differently, the argument might be that we should treat the defendant as being morally autono-mous in the sense of someone who would make the correct moral choice.[39] To assess that claim, we need to look in more detail at the concept of censure, to see if criminal verdicts do express a message that is incompatible with the use of character evidence to prove guilt.

4.6 Censure and Reform

Should the criminal trial operate on a presumption that a defendant has responded to the censure of a previous conviction by reforming completely?[40] In everyday morality, we do not appear to be under any obligation to presume that people who have behaved badly on some occasion in the past have completely changed. If you invite an acquaintance to dinner and he spends the evening telling racist jokes, you do not seem to do anything wrong by not inviting him again. In acting in that way, you do not disrespect him in the way that concerns Smilansky and Margalit: they talk in terms of possibilities, not presumptions. You can allow that the dinner guest may have changed, but still decide not to take the risk that he will behave offensively if invited again. Of course, the criminal trial is very dif-ferent from a dinner invitation, and once again it may be in a theory of the trial, and in particular in the censuring functions of the verdict, that we find support for the presumption we are interested in. The obvious way to find some support

---

[38] See J. Raz, *The Morality of Freedom* (Oxford: Oxford University Press, 1986), 155–6.
[39] The interpretation sometimes put on Kant's use of the term autonomy: see O. O'Neill, *Bounds of Justice* (Cambridge: Cambridge University Press, 2000), ch 2.
[40] The arguments analysed in this section put considerable emphasis on the process of censure embodied in a guilty verdict; they thus apply very much to previous convictions rather than to other types of bad character evidence. It might seem odd to have a theory that justifies the exclusion of just one type of bad character evidence; but then again, if the arguments are thought convinc-ing, the feeling of oddness will doubtless wear off. At times, it seems as though the courts took this approach—being more prone to exclude previous convictions than other types of bad charac-ter evidence—before the CJA 2003 came into force: see C. Tapper, *Cross and Tapper on Evidence* (9th edn, London: Butterworths, 1999), 349. Tapper draws an analogy with the double jeopardy principle.

for the presumption is to look to sentencing theory to deepen our understanding of the way in which verdicts communicate the censuring message to defendants. In fact, Duff et al take this route, in a proposal which supplements the analysis explored above.[41] If the criminal verdict is seen as part of a process of moral communication with the defendant, then we might suppose that, when the defendant was previously convicted of burglary, he should have taken the message of moral censure seriously. He should have responded to the moral message by taking on board the wrongness of burglary and desisting from future offending. This might provide the foundation for various objections to the use of previous convictions. By using the previous conviction we might, as Duff et al suggest, be failing to treat the defendant as a responsible agent, as someone who responds properly to censure. The criminal process might also be thought to be acting cynically, or hypocritically, if it punished people in the expectation that they would reform, but then presumed that they had not done so by using their previous convictions against them once they were suspected of a later crime.[42]

The difficulty facing this analysis is that it does not easily mesh with sentencing theory. If we look at two influential theories of sentencing, which both emphasize the communicative nature of punishment, we do not find anything as strong as a normative expectation that the defendant will respond to censure by changing. Duff himself argues that while punishment aims to modify conduct by persuading offenders to recognize and repent their wrongdoing, a commitment to the autonomy of defendants means that punishment must leave them 'free to reject its message'.[43] Perhaps it could be argued that ideal defendants would take the moral message on board and relinquish any propensity to commit crime. But to treat someone as a responsible agent—which is what is motivating us here—does not seem to mean that we should treat them as an ideal agent. Indeed, there would be something rather odd about a theory of the trial and punishment that treated defendants as ideal moral agents—why would such angelic people commit crime in the first place? And why would they need hard treatment, rather than simple censure?

Like any change in behaviour, desistance from crime is something which is not easy to achieve.[44] We need to take this on board if our theory of the trial is to be psychologically realistic, and doing so underlines the point just made. Von Hirsch's account of punishment actually embraces this psychological realism as one of its central features. For von Hirsch, punishment treats us as 'moral but fallible' agents.[45] Punishment operates as censure because the defendant, as a moral

[41] Duff et al, *The Trial on Trial*, 114–15.

[42] While the focus here is on retributive theories of punishment, a similar argument might be made under a deterrence framework: if punishment is justified on grounds of individual deterrence, then the use of previous convictions might be thought to conflict with that justification. The response would be that, given that deterrence does not usually claim to prevent crime—only to deter it to an appropriate degree—there is again no incompatibility.

[43] Duff, *Trials and Punishments*, 122.   [44] See Maruna, *Making Good*.

[45] A. von Hirsch and A. Ashworth, *Proportionate Sentencing: Exploring the Principles* (Oxford: Oxford University Press, 2005), 23. See also A. von Hirsch, *Censure and Sanctions* (Oxford: Clarendon Press, 1993), 13.

agent, can respond to moral criticism, but because the defendant is not an ideal agent the censure is supplemented by hard treatment. This conception of the subject of criminal law is prominent in von Hirsch's account of why first-time offenders should receive lighter sentences than recidivists.[46] As we will see in Chapter 11, desert theory, which tends to focus on crime seriousness as the key variable in determining sentence severity, generally rejects the claim that repeat offenders deserve longer sentences; repetition does not increase seriousness. But von Hirsch argues that first-time offenders should have their sentences reduced below the level indicated by the seriousness of the offence. Initial sentences should be mitigated because, as a fallible moral agent, the defendant can be presumed to take censure seriously. His first crime is regarded as a lapse rather than as a serious commitment to wrongdoing. To quote von Hirsch—in a passage which resonates with the themes we are exploring—'[t]he first-offender discount reflects...an ethical judgement: it is a way of showing respect for any person's capacity, as a moral agent, for attending to the censure in punishment... [P]eople's capacity to take condemnation of their acts seriously is something that has a moral dimension and should be acknowledged in the criminal law.'[47] But, von Hirsch suggests, as the defendant returns to court we have reason to increase the emphasis on hard treatment because he has, to some extent, proved deaf to the moral message.

We should certainly take from this that moral opportunity—people's ability to change, and to improve themselves morally—is something which deserves particular respect in criminal justice. But that merely emphasizes the points drawn from Margalit and Smilansky, and it takes the argument for a moral objection to bad character evidence no further. To spell it out: in using previous convictions against a defendant, the court seems to be acknowledging that he might not have taken the censuring message to heart when previously sentenced. That does not really conflict with the new message of censure when he is tried and convicted, a message which calls on him to recognize the moral wrong he has done and to mend his ways—but does not demand that he does or presume that he will. It is true that, when the defendant is convicted of burglary with a previous conviction being part of the evidence against him, the court appears to be acknowledging that he did not mend his ways. But it would look like this even if the previous conviction had not been admitted, and, in any case, the acknowledgment that he did not change is not to suggest that he could not have done so, or cannot in the future. The only way to generate a conflict between the censuring message and the use of previous convictions is to read a much more authoritarian message

---

[46] A. von Hirsch, 'Desert and Previous Convictions' in von Hirsch and Ashworth, *Proportionate Sentencing*. For helpful discussion, see J. V. Roberts, *Punishing Persistent Offenders: Exploring Community and Offender Perspectives* (Oxford: Oxford University Press, 2008), chs 3–4; and J. V. Roberts and A. von Hirsch (eds), *Previous Convictions at Sentencing: Theoretical and Applied Perspectives* (Oxford: Hart Publishing, 2010).

[47] Von Hirsch, 'Desert and Previous Convictions', 195–6. It should be noted that von Hirsch tentatively goes further: perhaps punishment 'asserts that the offender has a duty to attend to the censure and make extra efforts at self-restraint' (196). But even recognizing such a duty does not seem incompatible with using previous convictions to prove guilt.

into censure: a demand that the defendant reforms, along with a firm expectation that he will do so.[48] But that view of censure is, as we have seen, unattractive to both von Hirsch and Duff. And it is interesting that the reason why censure is not viewed in this forceful way is a concern for autonomy. So a respect for the autonomy of defendants, which was the starting point for the ideas pursued up to this point, turns out to be one of the things which makes the use of character evidence permissible, rather than, as the arguments surveyed suppose, problematic.

There is, however, a different argument against the use of previous convictions which might be drawn from von Hirsch's discussion of progressive loss of mitigation. As we have seen, von Hirsch suggests that an initial offence—and perhaps some subsequent ones—should be seen as lapses rather than as displaying a serious commitment to offending. If that is how we should view a defendant, then after an initial crime we should not consider him more likely to offend than other people. He remains like the rest of us, a basically good though flawed moral agent who lapsed on one occasion. The initial censure does not ask him to change his moral personality so much as to be more careful, to exert better self-control. As von Hirsch notes, however, the theory of progressive loss of mitigation may not apply to more serious crimes, and this seems right.[49] It would be odd to view Straffen's first child killing as a lapse from an otherwise moral life. It will be difficult, however, to say how serious a crime needs to be before we should see it as something more than just a lapse.

Von Hirsch's theory of progressive loss of mitigation is controversial.[50] However, because it raises wider issues about the role of character in sentencing, it will be discussed in more depth in Chapter 11.

4.7 Non-Criminal Bad Character

To this point, I have concentrated on the morality of using previous convictions to prove guilt. Bad character evidence extends further than this: evidence of previous non-criminal actions might also be used to prove guilt if they can be said to show a propensity to commit crime ('non-criminal bad character'). The case law provides various examples. In *Dolan*,[51] the prosecution tried to use evidence of Dolan's destructive temper when faced with malfunctioning objects as evidence that he had lost his temper and killed his young child. In *Saleem*,[52] possession of photographs of violently inflicted injuries was part of the evidence used to show

---

[48] Cf Lee's account of the recidivist premium (Y. Lee, 'Repeat Offenders and the Question of Desert' in Roberts and von Hirsch, *Previous Convictions at Sentencing*), discussed in Chapter 11. Lee suggests that conviction creates a 'normative expectation' that offenders will make an effort to desist, but even this does not assume that they will change—simply that they are at fault if they do not try to.

[49] Von Hirsch, 'Desert and Previous Convictions', 196.

[50] See Roberts, *Punishing Persistent Offenders*; and Roberts and von Hirsch, *Previous Convictions at Sentencing*.

[51] [2003] EWCA Crim 1859.   [52] [2007] EWCA Crim 1923.

that Saleem had participated in a violent attack. Evidence that the 39-year-old D had recently had a consensual relationship with a 16-year-old girl was used, in *Manister*,[53] as evidence that he had indecently assaulted a 13-year-old girl. In *Lewis*,[54] the fact that Lewis was a member of the Paedophilic Society was admitted as evidence that he had indecently assaulted children. When Vincent Tabak was prosecuted for the murder of Joanna Yeates—a crime which was hard to explain unless it had a sexual motivation—the prosecution was in possession of, but did not introduce at trial, evidence of Tabak's interest in violent pornography.[55] And in *Norris*,[56] the evidence that Norris was guilty of the murder of Stephen Lawrence included a video of Norris expressing extreme racist views. Moving beyond the case law, various other examples are worth considering. Research has shown that young men who have served in the armed forces are three times more likely to commit crimes of violence than members of the general population: thus, they have a comparative propensity for violence.[57] If a solider is on trial for a violent offence, should this study be brought to the attention of jurors? And, to move to a hypothetical example, what if studies showed that members of a certain racial or ethnic group were more likely to offend than the general population?

In the discussion so far, we have found little reason to think that using previous convictions to prove guilt has a moral cost. But might non-criminal bad character evidence be different? It should be obvious why it might be tempting to draw a distinction between cases involving convictions and cases that do not: if we do not do so, we look to be on a slippery slope, for if we think in terms of comparative propensity we seem to have no objection to admitting the evidence in the race example, something which is intuitively troubling. The wider criminal justice literature also provides some resources for the argument that we should not infer criminal conduct from non-criminal conduct. 'A disposition to engage in non-criminal conduct', Duff argues, 'is not yet a disposition to break the law'.[58] Moreover, Duff and others suggest that a presumption of harmlessness should govern decision-making in aspects of criminal justice; the presumption rules out preventive detention absent proof of criminal wrongdoing, but it might also have implications for non-criminal bad character evidence.

It would be easy to respond to the thought emerging here—that we should not infer criminal conduct from non-criminal conduct—by ridiculing it. If D, a collector of antique coins, is on trial for stealing an antique coin, surely the

---

[53] *Weir and Others (Manister)* [2006] 1 Cr App R 19, [2005] EWCA Crim 2866.

[54] (1983) 76 Cr App R 33.

[55] 'Vincent Tabak and the porn searches the jury did not hear about', *Guardian*, 28 October 2011. In what follows, I presume that this pornography was not illegal, although there was some suggestion that Tabak might be open to prosecution for it. Possession of 'extreme' pornography is an offence under the Criminal Justice and Immigration Act 2008, ss 63–7. Some unpleasant forms of pornography, such as depictions of rape, remained legal under this legislation.

[56] [2013] EWCA Crim 712.

[57] 'Soldiers more likely to be convicted of violent offences, report reveals', *Guardian*, 15 March 2013.

[58] R. A. Duff, 'Choice, Character, and Criminal Liability' (1993) 12 *Law & Philosophy* 345, 373. I discuss this aspect of Duff's views in more detail in Chapter 11.

prosecution should be able to rely on his interest in collecting coins to help prove guilt. The coin collector case, however, is different from those introduced above. What is doing the inferential work in this example is the interest in coins, not an interest in theft. So while it is true that the coin collector has a comparative propensity to steal antique coins (he is more likely than other people to do so), we are not treating him as someone who, *qua* coin collector, has less ability to resist offending than others. This is rather like the defendant in *Butler* who was charged with forcing a woman to fellate him while driving.[59] Evidence that he had engaged in the same conduct consensually with his girlfriend was admitted. Here, the taste for a particular form of sexual behaviour seems similar to the taste for antique coins.[60] The cases introduced above, however, seem to involve inferences which—unlike the one in the coin case—are potentially morally problematic. If the evidence in *Saleem* is relevant, then it is relevant because those who collect images of violent injuries have an interest in violence, which makes them more likely than other people to participate in violent attacks.[61] If it is relevant, the evidence shows an interest in crime in a way that an interest in coins does not. If Tabak's interest in violent pornography is relevant, it is relevant because it shows a propensity to sexual violence—likewise, Lewis's interest in paedophilia.[62] Unlike the coin collector's, these propensities are necessarily criminal.

One might of course argue that people who enjoy violent pornography, express paedophile views, or collect photographs of violent injuries are no more likely than others to commit crimes of sexual violence, abuse children, or participate in violence, because there is a sharp distinction between thinking and doing, especially when doing involves harming others and breaking the law. Fantasy is one thing, reality another.[63] If we take this as a factual argument, then to draw such a distinction is to argue that the evidence is irrelevant. It is true that the empirical argument in some of these cases is tricky: does Dolan's violence towards inanimate objects make him more likely to harm babies?[64] For present purposes, though, the

[59] (1987) 84 Cr App R 12.

[60] Sometimes it may be difficult to say whether a case fits the coin collector model. Imagine a case where D, who has racist views, is charged with assaulting a black person. Here, the distinguishing feature is not morally neutral, but we might treat the case like the coin collector case, along the lines that D's racism does not make him more likely to commit crime, but that if he were to commit crime he is likely to pick a black victim. However, it is doubtful that the analogy really works, because the racist mindset presumably involves views such as that people of certain races are worth less than those of other races, and this suggests a propensity to care less about victimizing them. If the racist convinced us that his views did not go beyond separatism—different races are of equal worth but should not mix—then it is doubtful that we would see the racism as relevant to the question of whether he had committed the assault.

[61] Assuming, of course, no alternative hypothesis such as that Saleem is a medical student.

[62] The facts of *Lewis* are slightly complex. Lewis self-defined himself as a paedophile, 'expressing the view that all love and affection is sexually motivated, whilst drawing a sharp distinction between being a paedophile and being a molester of children' ((1983) 76 Cr App R 33, 35). But the Paedophilic Society literature went rather further than that, arguing that sex between adults and children was a good thing (see at 37).

[63] The Court of Appeal appears to adopt this view in *R v D, P, and U* [2012] 1 Cr App R 8, [2011] EWCA Crim 1474, arguing that possession of child pornography is not evidence of child abuse. See the discussion in Chapter 7.

[64] I questioned this in Chapter 2.

cases become interesting when we accept that the evidence is relevant and ask whether there may be a moral objection to admitting the evidence, an objection different from the ones considered above in relation to previous convictions.

Having distinguished coin collector type cases, then, what moral arguments are there for refusing to draw an inference in a case like *Dolan, Tabak, Lewis,* or *Saleem*? Writing about preventive detention—the practice of confining the dangerous in order to stop them from committing crime—Duff has argued that:

> Respect for autonomy, and the 'presumption of harmlessness' which follows from it, forbid us to ascribe criminal dangerousness to anyone, unless and until by his own criminal conduct he constitutes himself as having such a character. Until then, even if we have good empirical grounds for predicting that he will come to manifest such a criminal character, we owe it to him to presume that he will not: to presume that he will, when it comes to the point, refrain from crime even if tempted to commit it.[65]

Walen has developed a similar argument. For him, preventive detention may be justified, but only once someone has committed an offence. If people:

> show sufficient disrespect for the law, then they no longer deserve to receive one of the benefits that normally flow from being an autonomous and accountable person. In particular, they no longer deserve to have the status of a person who must be presumed to be law-abiding. A state must normally accord its autonomous and accountable citizens this presumption as a matter of basic respect for their autonomous moral agency.[66]

These views appear to have implications for non-criminal bad character evidence. Both arguments take it that the state should respect citizens by presuming that they will obey the law until it has been proved that they have committed a crime. Unlike the presumption of innocence, which simply demands a certain degree of proof, the presumption of harmlessness (or law-abidingness) makes an assumption about how people will behave. It must apply to probabilistic conclusions—that a person is likely to offend—otherwise it could not block preventive detention, which demands a level of risk rather than certainty of offending. It seems then that the presumption must rule out an inference to guilt which depends on an assessment of comparative propensity based on non-criminal bad character evidence, because this involves assuming that a person who has not offended is likely to offend. Presuming that someone is law-abiding does not, however, rule out using eye-witness evidence (and other sorts of trace evidence) to prove guilt, because

---

[65] R.A. Duff, 'Dangerousness and Citizenship' in A. Ashworth and M. Wasik (eds), *Fundamentals of Sentencing Theory: Essays in Honour of Andrew von Hirsch* (Oxford: Oxford University Press, 1998), 155.

[66] A. Walen, 'A Punitive Precondition for Preventive Detention: Lost Status as a Foundation for a Lost Immunity' (2011) 48 *San Diego L Rev* 1229, 1230–1. Walen is careful to restrict his argument to 'long-term preventive detention': he allows that suspects and accused people may be deprived of their liberty for shorter periods without having lost the presumption of law abidingness through having been convicted. But it is at least plausible that, if the state really should presume its citizens to be law-abiding, this should impose restrictions on the evidence that can be used to convict, especially in serious cases where long custodial sentences are likely. This does not involve the sort of 'small sacrifice' which Walen thinks justifiable 'for the sake of the general welfare' (1238).

the inference would not involve an assessment of D's criminal propensity.[67] Nor would it rule out an inference in a coin collector type case.

How plausible, then, is the idea of a presumption of harmlessness or law-abidingness? One reason why it is attractive is that it provides a convenient explanation for why we should not use the fact that D is a soldier or a member of a certain racial group as evidence of guilt, or allow such things to trigger preventive detention.[68] But beyond this, it is not easy to make the case for the principle.[69] Walen admits that the presumption is not absolute: the state, for example, 'has an obligation to police its residents, arresting and prosecuting them if it finds sufficient evidence of criminal activity'.[70] What the presumption does do is prevent the state from depriving citizens of their liberty for a long period of time unless they have been convicted of a serious crime. But if the presumption of law-abidingness is a matter of the state's 'basic respect for [citizens'] autonomous moral agency',[71] it is puzzling why the presumption is due in some contexts and not others. There is plainly a greater impact on the citizen's freedom when she is subject to long-term detention than when she is arrested. This gives the state a greater burden of justification, but does the greater infringement of liberty really switch on a presumption that the citizen is law-abiding? This is not to say that there is no merit in a presumption of law-abidingness. Perhaps we should presume that the people we meet will make the correct moral choices, and perhaps the state should accord us a similar presumption. But why should such a presumption be a strong one which can only be overcome by proof that a person has committed a crime? The presumption might instead be a default assumption which is eroded to the extent that evidence suggests that it is unfounded. This would allow the presumption to apply in the case of arrest, but arrest would be justified so long as there was sufficient evidence to suggest that the person arrested had committed a crime. Similarly, in a criminal trial, the presumption would be eroded by evidence that D has a tendency to offend—such as his possessing violent pornography.

If a presumption of harmlessness cannot justify excluding the evidence in cases like *Manister*, *Saleem*, and *Tabak*, it presumably cannot play a role in the soldiers and race cases. Yet, as I have emphasized, these cases are disturbing, for intuitively

---

[67] Although the way it is put in the text hopefully suffices to make the point without too much complexity, it is not quite right. If D is presumed to have no propensity to commit crime, then there would be a zero prior probability that he offended and guilt could never be proved. What the presumption of law-abidingness must involve, then, is a presumption that D does not have a greater propensity to offend than any other non-offender. The presumption can allow that we all have some propensity to offend—perhaps even that we have the average propensity to offend.

[68] Walen may be attracted to the presumption of law abidingness for similar reasons: it helps 'to make sense of the principled reluctance to subject an autonomous person . . . to preventive detention'. A. Walen, 'A Unified Theory of Detention, with Application to Preventive Detention for Suspected Terrorists' (2011) 70 *Maryland L Rev* 871, 873. For further discussion, see his response to Tadros, 'Controlling Risk', in his book review, 'Prevention and the Limits of the Criminal Law' at: <http://clcjbooks.rutgers.edu/books/prevention-and-the-limits-of-the-criminal-law.html>.

[69] The idea of a presumption of harmlessness has its roots in Floud and Young's work on dangerousness, but there it is simply posited rather than argued for. See J. E. Floud and W. Young, *Dangerousness and Criminal Justice* (London: Heinemann, 1981), 44.

[70] Walen, 'A Punitive Precondition', 1231.   [71] Walen, 'A Punitive Precondition', 1230–1.

it seems very problematic to allow, in court, the argument that being a soldier or a member of a certain racial group makes one more likely to offend. These examples are especially significant because they may offer a *reductio* of the whole comparative propensity enterprise. We saw in Chapters 2 and 3 that the basic argument for the relevance of previous convictions relies on the fact that offenders have a higher crime rate than those who have not been convicted. The soldiers and race examples seem to employ just the same logic.

This is a complex area. There are well-known puzzle cases in evidence theory which may have some affinity with the examples we are considering.[72] In the blue bus case, Mrs X has been run over by a bus. The only information we have as to liability is that the blue bus company owns 60 per cent of buses which use the relevant road. Is this enough to establish liability in a civil case? In the prisoners hypothetical, a prison guard has been attacked by a group of prisoners. All we know is that one prisoner in this 100-strong group did not participate in the attack. Could we pick any of the prisoners and secure a conviction on the basis that it is 99 per cent likely that he is guilty? *Shonubi*,[73] a real case, caused controversy when the average amount of heroin smuggled by balloon-swallowing heroin smugglers was used to calculate the amount of heroin smuggled by Shonubi, a balloon-swallowing heroin smuggler, on smuggling trips where he had not been caught (this was done for sentencing purposes). These cases—especially the first two—trigger strong intuitions that liability (or the amount smuggled) has not been satisfactorily proved. But there is no agreed solution to these 'proof paradoxes'. In the previous chapter, I briefly discussed the inferential side of such paradoxes—via a discussion of the 'reference class problem'.[74] Here, it is the moral aspects which are germane.

The connection between the proof paradoxes and the examples we are considering has been made by Duff. Duff supposes a case where a defendant is a young, male, unemployed drug user, and there is actuarial evidence to show that such people are much more likely to commit crimes than others. Duff argues that this kind of evidence cannot be used in a criminal trial:

> To respect the defendant as a responsible citizen, we must treat him and judge him as an autonomous agent, who determines his own actions in the light of his own values or commitments. His membership of this actuarial group is part of the context of that self-determination; and as observers, we might think it very likely that he will have determined himself as a criminal. As judges of his guilt, however, we must rely only on evidence related to him as an individual agent, not on evidence related to him only as a member of an actuarial group.[75]

---

[72] See M. Redmayne, 'Exploring the Proof Paradoxes' (2008) 14 *Legal Theory* 281.

[73] *US* v *Shonubi* 998 F2d 84 (1993).

[74] Part of the inferential problem is that D may find it hard to defend himself by showing that he is not a typical member of the reference class. While it was suggested that this was not a very powerful objection to the use of previous convictions, partly because generic factors such as the staleness of the conviction can be considered easily, it may be more of a problem in cases like the race and soldier ones.

[75] 'Dangerousness and Citizenship', 156.

The example is a good one, but the arguments do not convince. As we have seen, autonomy is of no help here. The appeal to evidence related to D as an individual is intuitively attractive—the Court of Appeals in *Shonubi* demanded 'specific' evidence of the amount smuggled—but it is hard to make this idea work. Any inference we draw from evidence depends on generalizations. If D is seen running away from the scene of the crime, we think this is suspicious because we believe that, in general, this behaviour is more common among the guilty than the innocent. If D has a motive, we take this to add weight to the case against him because people with motives are more likely to commit crime than those without. If an eyewitness identifies D, this evidence can only be assessed by drawing on generalizations about eyewitnesses.

I suspect that there is no simple solution to the proof paradoxes: there is a variety of factors (perhaps different ones in different cases) which make us uneasy about ascribing liability in the examples.[76] In this spirit, then, I shall point to a series of grounds on which we might distinguish the troubling examples—the soldiers, the race example, and Duff's actuarial evidence example—from cases like *Saleem* and *Lewis*, and indeed from cases involving previous convictions. While I am not sure this leaves us with any definitive way of drawing the line between 'good' and 'bad' inferences, I hope that what follows will dissolve some of the tensions in this area.

One difference between the 'problem' cases and the others is that they will require some sort of expert evidence. The jury may well be perfectly aware of D's race, or that he is a soldier, or that he is a young, male, unemployed drug user, but the radical suggestion is that we present evidence about the criminal tendencies associated with these attributes. In the ordinary case, we just let the jury know that D has a criminal record, or that he likes violent pornography, and let it work out the significance for itself (albeit perhaps with a warning not to read too much into the evidence). That seems very different from saying 'D is a soldier and soldiers are three times more likely to commit violent crime than civilians'. But suppose it was general knowledge that soldiers have a propensity to commit violent crime. I am not sure we would think it morally problematic for jurors to take this into account as having some weight in a case involving a soldier accused of assault.[77] Admittedly, this still leaves tricky questions. If the jury did not know that D was a soldier, should the prosecution be able to reveal this? And why does the mode of presentation of the evidence make such a difference, especially as we seem to be happy with quantification in some contexts, as with DNA evidence? Perhaps when we present the evidence in some sort of statistical form, our concerns about autonomy (misplaced though they are) worry us more.

If we focus on the race example, or on other examples such as that attending an unruly school and having separated parents are associated with criminality,[78]

---

[76] See Redmayne, 'Exploring the Proof Paradoxes'.

[77] I suspect we would be concerned if we switched the attribute to race. For reasons why this might be the case, see below.

[78] See Hales et al, *Longitudinal Analysis of the Offending*.

it will be very tempting to say that choice is significant; using these attributes to prove guilt is problematic because they are unchosen. It seems a sensible principle of criminalization that we should not criminalize on the basis of factors over which people have no control. This, as Husak explains, 'would rule out including a great many characteristics in penal offences, even when they accurately predict harm. Race, gender, or age, for example, could not be among the elements of…crimes, notwithstanding their predictive power'.[79] The reason may well be that 'those who are punished should have had the opportunity to avoid punishment by choosing appropriately'.[80] But we cannot transfer a control or choice principle wholesale into the evidential domain. Hubert did not choose to look like Robert the burglar, and Harry did not choose to share a DNA profile with Larry the serial killer, yet we happily use eyewitness and DNA evidence to convict people, and this could result in Hubert and Harry being falsely convicted because of factors they could not control.[81] There may, however, be a way to take something like a choice principle and adapt it to the evidential problem which concerns us. In fact, a presumption of harmlessness might be invoked: the idea would be that in a criminal trial, and perhaps in everyday morality, we should presume that people are no more likely than the average person to have offended simply by virtue of their membership in a particular group, unless group membership itself displays a dubious moral choice. This, then, would rule out an argument that race shows a propensity to offend. The same goes for being a soldier (I am assuming that joining the army is not a dubious moral choice), but being a member of a gang associated with crime would be different, as would possessing violent pornography or expressing support for paedophilia.[82]

---

[79] D. Husak, 'Preventive Detention as Punishment? Some Possible Obstacles' in Ashworth et al, *Prevention and the Limits of the Criminal Law*, 190.

[80] T. M. Scanlon, *What We Owe to Each Other* (Cambridge, MA: Harvard University Press, 1998), 267. Cf Husak, who justifies this principle on the unconvincing basis that breaching it would 'treat people as though they lack free will or exhibit disrespect for their status as autonomous, rational agents' ('Preventive Detention as Punishment?', 190).

[81] This raises the question of why evidence should differ from criminalization, in that defining offences based on characteristics beyond our control is problematic, whereas convicting people on the basis of characteristics they cannot control is not, or at least not always. The obvious answer is that the criminal law creates rules intended to guide behaviour, whereas evidence law does not. But I doubt that this is the whole of the answer, because the law/procedure distinction is not always clear-cut: a presumption that anyone in possession of drugs is knowingly in possession might be justifiable on the grounds that it creates an incentive for people to be very careful about coming into possession of drugs. Even if rules of evidence are not intended to offer guidance, the control issue might worry us because of the way it makes it difficult to avoid conviction: a presumption that people who attended unruly schools and had separated parents were guilty of crimes of violence would be far more objectionable than the drug possession presumption on this score. Hubert and Harry, though, are caught out by case-specific factors which could not plausibly be taken to offer guidance on avoiding conviction. 'Do not look like Robert', or even 'do not look like a burglar' do not offer useful guidance, nor does 'do not share the DNA profile of a serial killer'. 'Do not act like a burglar', however, might offer useful guidance. What is more, most of us do not know whether we look like burglars or share DNA profiles with serial killers, so being liable to conviction on this basis is less worrying: it will not be hanging over us as we go about our lives.

[82] In the text, I have been using the concepts of choice and control more or less interchangeably, but control is probably the more useful concept: see Husak, 'Preventive Detention as Punishment?', 189–90. While Lewis (the defendant in the case involving possession of paedophile literature) may

While I find a principle of this sort attractive, there are complexities. Age is an unchosen characteristic, yet it does not seem ethically problematic to assume that a young person is more likely to commit crime than an old one. Age, however, is a universal attribute in that everyone will be considered more likely to offend in their late teens. If the moral principle here is connected with equality—we should all be deemed to have equal moral capital unless we do something to erode this assumption—then age is not a problematic factor. But gender is more troubling. In *Watters*,[83] the prosecution, in a rather desperate attempt to make a weak DNA case look strong enough to support a burglary conviction, argued that the fact that D was male was evidence against him, because most safe-crackers are male. If that argument strikes us as odd, it may be because D's sex would have been obvious to the jury, who might already have taken it into account, albeit at some unconscious level (they might well have been more reluctant to convict had Watters been a woman). But do we really want to say that the prosecutor's argument is morally impermissible? Perhaps—and things now risk becoming rather ad hoc—we can make an exception for gender because, rather like age, it is such a universal and basic characteristic.

A further difficulty for an account based on choice is motive. If D's wife is having an affair, D seems to have found himself, through no dubious moral choice of his own, with a motive to kill his wife's lover, and he is therefore in a group of people who are more likely to commit crime. Surely we cannot start excluding motive evidence on moral grounds? But there is a possibility that motive can be distinguished from race, being a soldier, and the like. As we noted above, a person with a motive has a reason to commit crime. While in the earlier discussion we saw that it was difficult to draw a sharp distinction between motive and previous convictions, a factor such as race does look to be very different. There may be something to this line of thought, but it brings yet further complexities. The motive model would appear to allow evidence of poverty to prove theft. Here, though, one more possible distinction can be brought in, one which potentially has considerable leverage on our puzzles. Some accounts of discrimination are based on the idea that discrimination is only wrongful when a distinction is made on the basis of traits which are connected to a 'history of mistreatment or current social disadvantage'.[84] Appointing job applicants on the basis of their star signs does not discriminate wrongfully, but appointing on the basis of race or gender does. That could explain why we would have qualms about using poverty evidence, but would be less worried about evidence that a particular person had suddenly come into financial difficulties being used to show a motive to commit a crime for financial gain. In particular, mistreatment/disadvantage suggests why

---

not have chosen his sexual preferences, they may be under his control in that he could modify or resist them.

[83] *Watters* CA 19 October 2000.

[84] See D. Hellman, *When is Discrimination Wrong?* (Cambridge, MA: Harvard University Press, 2008), 21. See also A. Wertheimer, 'Reflections on Discrimination' (2006) 43 *San Diego L Rev* 945.

we react so strongly to the idea of using race as evidence of propensity to commit crime.[85]

I do not pretend to be able to give a watertight explanation of why it might be wrong to use certain factors as evidence of a propensity to commit crime. I suspect there are no bright lines to be drawn here, and that the explanation for our intuitions lies somewhere in the mix of factors discussed above. I hope, though, to have shown that arguing for the admissibility of previous convictions (or non-criminal propensity evidence) does not commit one to accepting any and all propensity evidence, such as that based on race or being a soldier. In any case, anyone who accepts that the use of bad character evidence is sometimes permissible (say, in cases like *Straffen*) faces a similar problem: can they find good reasons to isolate admissibility to such exceptional cases, or will they be forced to admit that admissibility might be justified in a wide range of cases? Such people may be much further up the slippery slope than I am, but they are still on it.

In summary, there generally do not seem to be strong reasons to treat non-criminal propensity evidence differently from propensity evidence which relies on criminal behaviour. There are, however, exceptions to this rule, with the hypothetical example of race being the most obvious. This is not to deny that the inferences in some of the cases raise difficult issues: is there really a link between violent pornography and sexual violence? Or between smashing up furniture and battering babies? We may also have reason to be cautious about non-criminal propensity evidence for some of the reasons discussed above: that it risks turning the trial—and the criminal investigation—into an investigation of the defendant's life and attitudes. In *Dolan*, the Court of Appeal remarked that: 'Those of us who are hamfisted or over ambitious DIY enthusiasts would be horrified to learn that frustration in this difficult field of endeavour could be used against us.'[86] While this observation was framed as being about relevance, it also highlights the concern that the state might dredge up any unpleasant behaviour in our lives and use it to convict us.

4.8 Labelling

The discussion so far has suggested that it is not easy to develop a coherent moral objection to the use of previous convictions to prove guilt. Accounts which suggest that such a practice is somehow incompatible with the moral framework of

---

[85] There are other reasons. Race is an unhelpful reference class, because if there is a connection between race and crime, it is presumably explained by factors such as social disadvantage rather than by race itself. More generally, there are obvious connections between the discussion in the text and the literature on racial profiling. In particular, some writers presume that it is race rather than profiling itself that is problematic: F. Schauer, *Profiles, Probabilities, and Stereotypes* (Cambridge, MA: Harvard University Press, 2003), ch 7; and R. Kennedy, 'Suspect Policy', *New Republic*, Sept 13/20 1999, 30. Cf B. E. Harcourt, *Against Prediction: Profiling, Policing, and Punishment in an Actuarial Age* (Chicago, IL: University of Chicago Press, 2007).

[86] [2003] EWCA Crim 1859, [23].

the trial have failed to pay close attention to the reasoning underlying the use of previous convictions to prove a propensity to commit crime. The reasoning is not dismissive of the defendant's autonomy or capacity for moral improvement, it merely assumes that he has not completely changed. Nevertheless, the very fact that it is easy to misread the reasoning involved may be significant. We could modify the arguments slightly, so that what is emphasized is not the precise inferential structure of reasoning from bad character, but the way in which the use of previous convictions is likely to be interpreted by defendants.

Accounts of the criminal trial which emphasize the communicative role of the criminal verdict have tended to be rather armchair-based affairs, with scholars speculating about how various practices—such as the admission of improperly obtained evidence—might be interpreted by defendants, or by the public. Of course, proponents of the communicative view can easily move to the normative plane, and argue that what matters is how certain trial practices *should* be interpreted, not how they *are* interpreted. There are difficult questions here about the relationship between the normative and the empirical, but surely any account which stresses communication must have one eye on how trial practices are actually experienced. That, however, is something we know little about.

There is, however, some empirical evidence on how, in some situations, the use of previous convictions is understood by defendants. In research on the experiences of ethnic minority defendants in the courts, Shute, Hood, and Seemungal noted that when it came to sentencing, 'some felt that their past records when they had been "young and wild" were being given too much weight in sentencing policy. Not enough attention had been paid to them "as they were now", due to a failure properly to take into account the social and cultural circumstances in which they had grown up.'[87] As one defendant put it: 'The judge didn't look at my past to my present, he looked at the offence. He said it was my way of life, but I've changed from a drug user, I've found a job.'[88] And another: 'They think that if you have been in trouble before you are still the same person. I've been out of trouble for six years... I am a family man. I've changed. They don't care... They think I'm the same person.'[89] Similar comments about the importance of interpreting previous convictions in the light of the potential to change can be found in Roberts's research on offenders' reactions to sentencing.[90] In the context of our discussion, these responses are striking. Some defendants do seem to feel that insufficient recognition has been given to their efforts to change, and one can imagine similar reactions being made to the use of previous convictions to prove guilt.[91] A cynical response would be that, given that these defendants have been convicted, they

---

[87] S. Shute, R. Hood, and F. Seemungal, *A Fair Hearing? Ethnic Minorities in the Criminal Courts* (Cullompton: Willan, 2005), 45–6.

[88] Shute et al, *A Fair Hearing?*, 46.   [89] Shute et al, *A Fair Hearing?*, 49.

[90] Roberts, *Punishing Persistent Offenders*, ch 7. All the offenders interviewed did seem to accept that weight should be put on previous convictions at sentencing; the objection was to doing this too automatically.

[91] Defendants do seem to be sensitive to the fairness of the criminal process. See, generally, T. R. Tyler and Y. J. Huo, *Trust in the Law: Encouraging Public Cooperation with the Police and the Courts* (New York: Russell Sage Foundation, 2002); and Roberts, *Punishing Persistent Offenders*, ch 6.

have not in fact changed; people tend to be over-optimistic about their ability to change, so these reactions could be self-serving delusions.[92] Even taking this view, however, we might still feel that there is something significant here. If what matters is how defendants interpret trial practices, then these negative reactions may be noteworthy in themselves. If the courts are too readily dismissive of the possibility of moral change, might there be a danger that defendants come to adopt this bleak attitude too?

Vohs and Schooler found evidence that undermining subjects' belief in free will increased propensity to cheat on a simple test.[93] The relevance of this is that if, through their use of previous convictions, courts give defendants the impression that they are prisoners of their past lives, then defendants may come to think this way about themselves, and this will make them more likely to commit crime. Criminologists in fact have a similar concern: labelling or interactionist theory suggests that the process of being labelled a criminal may reinforce deviance.[94] The High Court of Australia may have been thinking along these lines when it worried that 'rehabilitation schemes might be undermined if the accused's criminal record could be used in evidence against him or her',[95] and the Law Commission, in its Consultation Paper on character evidence, echoed this line of thought: 'We should be wary of exaggerating the likelihood that those convicted will reoffend, or of assuming that individuals cannot change. High conviction rates for those with previous convictions do not make reconviction inevitable ... Such change is clearly something the law should encourage, rather than presuming it does not occur.'[96]

A wider body of psychological research underlines the importance of labelling, and Alfano has drawn on this to argue for what he terms 'factitious moral virtue'.[97] Taking the pessimistic lessons from situationist personality psychology seriously (see the discussion in Chapter 2), Alfano concludes that character does not exist in a form which would satisfy the needs of virtue ethics. Nevertheless, he suggests that our use of virtuous moral labels is useful, because it encourages

---

[92] M. Dhami, D. Mandel, G. Loewenstein, and P. Ayton, 'Prisoners' Positive Illusions of Their Post-Release Success' (2006) 30 *Law & Human Behavior* 631–47; and R. Moore, 'Adult Offenders' Perceptions of Their Underlying Problems: Findings from the OASys Self-Assessment Questionnaire', Home Office Research Findings 284 (London: Home Office, 2007).

[93] K. D. Vohs and J. W. Schooler, 'The Value of Believing in Free Will: Encouraging a Belief in Determinism Increases Cheating' (2006) 19 *Psychological Science* 49–54.

[94] See, eg, D. Downes and P. Rock, *Understanding Deviance* (5th edn, Oxford: Oxford University Press, 2007), ch 7. For evidence of this, see T. Chiricos, K. Barrick, W. Bales, and S. Bontrager, 'The Labelling of Convicted Felons and Its Consequences for Recidivism' (2007) 45 *Criminology* 547; L. McAra and S. McVie, 'Youth Justice? The Impact of System Contact on Patterns of Desistance' in S. Farrall, M. Hough, S. Maruna, and R. Sparks (eds), *Escape Routes: Contemporary Perspectives on Life After Punishment* (London: Routledge: 2011); and M. E. Ezell and L. E. Cohen, *Desisting from Crime: Continuity and Change in Long-Term Crime Patterns of Serious Chronic Offenders* (Oxford: Oxford University Press, 2005), 255. See also M. S. Adams et al, 'Labeling and Delinquency' (2003) 38 *Adolescence* 172.

[95] *Pfennig* (1995) 182 CLR 461, 513.

[96] *Evidence in Criminal Proceedings: Previous Misconduct of a Defendant*, LCCP No 141 (London: HMSO, 1996), 124 fn 10.

[97] M. Alfano, *Character as Moral Fiction* (Cambridge: Cambridge University Press, 2013).

people to act in the way they are labelled. Thus, when a group of schoolchildren was falsely told that it was keeping its classroom tidy, they began to keep it tidy, tidier even than another group who were simply exhorted to keep their classroom tidy.[98] When researchers visited households asking for a donation to charity, they labelled some of those who failed to donate 'uncharitable'. These negatively labelled people were less likely to make a donation on a repeat visit than non-givers who had not been labelled.[99]

Does any of this give us reason to reject bad character evidence? The remarks from defendants quoted above should certainly give us pause, but the defendants might have been expressing a legitimate concern that their previous convictions were too stale to warrant any inferences about whether the latest offence was part of a pattern of offending as opposed to—to return to von Hirsch's terms—a lapse from an otherwise successful attempt to go straight.[100] As we saw in Chapter 2, time-lapse is very significant, especially when previous offences were committed at the peak offending age of the late teens. The Law Commission is certainly right that we should not exaggerate the likelihood of reoffending. Alfano's work and the criminological literature on labelling take us slightly further than this, for they suggest that we should avoid negative labels even when they are true. Alfano notes that factitious virtue is best induced by '*plausible, public* announcements to an audience that has a *correct* conception of what is entailed by the virtue in question', and that labelling has most effect when it 'comes directly on the heels of trait-consonant behaviour'.[101] Telling a serial killer that he is virtuous will probably not do much good, but telling a persistent thief that he has put his past behind him just after he has failed to give in to temptation might be helpful, especially if this person's associates come to share the perception that he has changed. But if we are worried about negative labels, then the trial's primary labelling mechanism is the verdict of guilty or not guilty. Labelling may also be important in the sentencing process, which can place considerable emphasis on the defendant's chances of reoffending (a point to which I return in Chapter 11). In comparison, the use of previous convictions to prove guilt will probably not be a very significant factor in labelling, especially if a warning is given—as is standard practice in England and Wales—about placing too much significance on the evidence.[102] These worries about labelling effects might, however, help to explain why it would not be a good idea to present the jury with explanatory evidence along the lines of 'people with a recent previous conviction for burglary are x times more likely to commit burglary than those without a conviction'. If, as suggested above, this sort

---

[98] R. Miller, P. Brickman, and D. Bolen, 'Attribution Versus Persuasion as Tools for Modifying Behavior' (1975) 31 *J Personality & Soc Psychol* 430.

[99] R. Kraut, 'Effects of Social Labelling on Giving to Charity' (1973) 9 *J Experimental Soc Psychol* 551.

[100] It is worth underlining the significance of this for sentencing. If one is attracted by von Hirsch's account of the first-offence discount, then it seems that it is not only the first offence that should receive a discount, but also ones committed after a significant break in offending. A lapse can occur during, as well as at the beginning of, an offending career.

[101] Alfano, *Character as Moral Fiction*, 91.

[102] See *Hanson*, [2005] 2 Cr App R 21, [2005] EWCA Crim 824.

of comment prompts concerns about lack of autonomy, it would be wise to avoid it for fear of its effects on defendants.

4.9 Conclusion

In this chapter I have explored whether there are moral reasons to avoid using bad character evidence in a criminal trial. The conclusion is that arguments which have been put forward for a 'moralized' exclusionary rule are unconvincing. This does not mean that the ethical issues analysed in this chapter give no cause for concern. Von Hirsch's argument that we treat an initial conviction as no more than a lapse provides grounds to avoid using a single previous conviction as evidence of propensity to offend. But we also have empirical reasons for such a practice: as we saw in Chapter 2, about half of offenders are convicted only once. Concerns about labelling and offenders' perceptions of the fairness of the criminal process also give us grounds not to exaggerate the power of previous convictions, although of course rationality demands this anyway. Finally, there is a legitimate concern that, if we allow bad character evidence, the trial will become a general moral audit of the defendant's life. This is a concern to be aware of as the focus turns, in the chapters which follow, to the current law on the admissibility of bad character evidence.

5

Propensity's History
English Law before the Criminal Justice Act 2003

[T]he common sense to which the judge had recourse here was of a special kind. It posits that if two daughters say that their father behaved indecently towards them, this makes it more likely that he was guilty than if one had said so. Many citizens would agree. Yet this is precisely the reasoning which for more than 100 years the courts in England have said is too dangerous to adopt.

R v Inder (1991)

This chapter traces the history of the propensity evidence rule from its early development up until the introduction of the Criminal Justice Act 2003. There are several reasons for spending some time on a case law which has now been largely superseded by statute. If we understand what was going on before 2003, we will be in a better position to evaluate the impact of the CJA and to assess whether various criticisms of it—which inevitably assume that there is a better way of going about things—are valid. For this reason, the analysis in this chapter will pay most attention to the situation just prior to the introduction of the CJA. The case law is also significant for other reasons: it gives us a rich set of illustrations of situations in which questions about the admissibility of propensity evidence arise, and of how courts have responded. In this way, the case law provides a foundation for the next chapter in which the various factors which mould the probative value of propensity evidence—and which should therefore be central to admissibility even after the CJA—are assessed. The response of the courts to the cases is also significant for what it tells us about common ways of reasoning about similar fact evidence and their rights and wrongs. Finally, this chapter and the next one justify some of the claims made in Chapter 4, where I argued that attempts to distinguish a morally problematic 'forbidden' type of reasoning about character from a morally acceptable type are unconvincing.

Before moving on to the case law, some explanation is needed. When analysing probative value, earlier chapters have tended to concentrate on the example of previous convictions. But many of the cases analysed in the current chapter involve a slightly different question: cross-admissibility. D may be tried for more than one crime at the same time. In technical terms, more than one count (alleged offence) can be joined in a single indictment. The current test for joinder is whether the allegations: when taken together amount to a course of conduct; are founded on the same facts; or form a series of offences of the same or similar character.[1] Where different counts are joined together in an indictment, the question may arise as to whether the evidence supporting different counts is 'cross-admissible', that is, whether evidence introduced to prove count A is admissible to prove count B. For example, D may be charged with two different burglaries. If an eyewitness identifies him as the person who committed the burglary in count A, the question is whether this evidence can support the claim that D committed the burglary on count B. The more similar the two crimes, the more it makes sense to treat the evidence as cross-admissible on the grounds that evidence suggesting that D committed burglary A shows that he has a propensity to burgle, making it more likely that he committed burglary B.

Another important piece of terminology is 'similar fact' evidence: this was the term which tended to be used to describe bad character evidence (and 'similar fact rule' the principles of admissibility) prior to the introduction of the CJA. The language of propensity which has taken hold since the CJA came into force barely figures in earlier doctrine. Insofar as it does, it was often used negatively: what was to be excluded was evidence showing a propensity to commit crime. But, as I suggest in this chapter, and argue in the next, whatever the language used, courts which talked about similar fact evidence were dealing with propensity evidence.

As doctrine developed over the course of the twentieth century, courts had a number of different admissibility rules to choose from when deciding questions about the admissibility of propensity evidence. In what follows, this leads to a rather confusing narrative, but it should be apparent that, especially towards the end of the period in which admissibility questions were governed by the common law, courts were making, if imperfectly, a judgment about the probative value of bad character evidence, and using this as a guide to admissibility.

5.1 Early Cases

Although judicial objections to propensity evidence can be found as far back as the seventeenth century,[2] use of the evidence in the courts seems to have been common at least until the early nineteenth century.[3] Indeed, Lacey suggests that: 'Throughout the eighteenth century, trials were dominated by evidence

---

[1] Criminal Procedure Rules 2014, para 14.2.

[2] eg *Hampden's Trial* (1684) 9 How St Tr 1053; and *Harrison's Trial* (1692) 12 How St Tr 833.

[3] This summary of the early history of the rule against propensity evidence draws heavily on D. P. Leonard, *The New Wigmore: Evidence of Other Misconduct and Similar Events* (Frederick, MD: Aspen, 2009), chs 2–3. For other useful historical material, see J. Stone, 'The Rule of Exclusion of Similar Fact Evidence: England' (1933) 46 *Harvard L Rev* 954; T. P. Gallanis, 'The Rise of Modern Evidence Law' (1999) 84 *Iowa L Rev* 499; and J. H. Langbein, *The Origins of Adversary Criminal Trial* (Oxford: Oxford University Press, 2003), 190–6.

about the accused's (and witnesses') standing and reputation.'[4] At this time, one justification for using a local jury was that it would be expected to know something about the character of the parties, and more could be discovered by questioning the accused's witnesses: 'did he work regularly; did he support his family; was he sober and honest in his dealing with others; did he, in other words, have an established place in a community, and was he known to his respectable neighbours as a man who could be trusted.'[5] 'A man who could produce no witnesses was likely to have a difficult time in court.'[6]

The emergence of something like the modern rule of exclusion is usually traced to the 1810 decision in *Cole*.[7] But any exclusionary rule that had developed by this date was not sufficiently obvious to always be noticed—there was no mention of the rule in Hawkins's 1824 treatise.[8] The rule which did materialize was subject to exceptions from the moment of its birth. As Leonard puts it, albeit with his own gloss:

At the very least, a rule admitting evidence of other wrongdoing for non-character purposes, especially to demonstrate guilty knowledge, arose at about the same time as the firm establishment of the general character rule, and might even have predated it. From this time, cases carving out specific purposes for which such evidence might be admitted began to proliferate.[9]

During the nineteenth century, then, the 'categories' approach which came to influence the law for much of the twentieth century began to develop, the idea being that propensity evidence was admissible for certain specific purposes (categories of admissibility). It is not easy to say why a categories view of admissibility emerged. In this period, treatise writers tended to write about the law of evidence as a whole in narrow terms, organizing their analysis on the basis of type of crime or type of issue to be proved, rather than by reflecting on broad principles, and this approach may have moulded the treatment of propensity evidence.[10] The categories may also have appealed to a judicial mindset of cautious incrementalism.

When it came to rationalizing the exclusion of character evidence, there is little sign in the early case law that jury prejudice was considered a problem. Judges most often explained exclusion on the grounds that evidence of uncharged

---

[4] N. Lacey, 'The Resurgence of Character: Responsibility in the Context of Criminalisation' in R. A. Duff and S. Green (eds), *Philosophical Foundations of Criminal Law* (Oxford: Oxford University Press, 2011), 159.

[5] J. M. Beattie, *Crime and the Courts in England, 1660–1800* (Oxford: Oxford University Press, 1986), 440.

[6] Beattie, *Crime and the Courts in England*, 440.

[7] Unreported. See Leonard, *The New Wigmore*, 4.

[8] Hawkins wrote that 'after a crime hath been proved in the county in which it is laid, evidence may be given of other instances of the same crime in another county, in order to satisfy the jury' (cited in Leonard, *The New Wigmore*, 22).

[9] *The New Wigmore*, 35. The interpretation of the exceptions as allowing evidence for non-character (ie roughly, 'specific' propensity) purposes is Leonard's own.

[10] *The New Wigmore*, 28.

misconduct would take the defendant by surprise.[11] In an era before criminal
record keeping, previous misconduct was hard to prove and the defendant would
have had difficulty in defending himself against allegations of prior wrongdoing,
especially as he could not give evidence in his own defence until late in the nineteenth century. But this was probably not the whole story. In *Cole*, even though
D had admitted the previous behaviour (presumably homosexuality) and his tendency towards it, the prosecution was unable to use this admission against him.[12]
It may well be that the problem was conceptualized in terms of relevance, it being
thought that previous conduct was irrelevant. That was certainly Stone's interpretation of the history.[13] By the early twentieth century, however, jury prejudice
began to feature in rationalizations of the rule.[14] In *Bond*, for example, Kennedy J
complained that:

Nothing can so certainly be counted upon to make a prejudice against an accused upon
his trial as the disclosure to the jury of other misconduct of a kind similar to that which
is the subject of the indictment, and, indeed, when the crime alleged is one of a revolting
character, such as the charge against Bond in the present case, and the hearer is a person
who has not been trained to think judicially, the prejudice must sometimes be almost
insurmountable.[15]

But this strong statement sat alongside reference to the problem of surprise,[16] and
most of the argument in *Bond* revolved around relevance.

If propensity evidence was regarded as problematic, how was admissibility
rationalized in cases which fell into the right category? To the extent that propensity evidence was regarded as irrelevant, it may be that the categories were simply
seen as examples of relevant evidence being admitted, and thus as needing no
particular justification. But many statements suggest that something more pragmatic was going on. Propensity evidence was often admitted in cases involving
forgery and poisoning, where a defence of lack of knowledge or accident might
have been plausible.[17] Necessity, then, provided a justification for admission.[18] As
one judge put it:

Where the proof of an offence involves proof of such matters as intent to defraud, or guilty
knowledge, or the like, the evidence of other transactions is often the only evidence by
which that essential part of the offence can be proved. If the transaction is an isolated one
a jury would seldom be satisfied of the prisoner's guilt.[19]

---

[11] *The New Wigmore*, 8; and J. H. Wigmore, *A Treatise on the Anglo-American System of Trials at Common Law* (3rd edn, Boston, MA: Little, Brown & Co, 1940), § 194.
[12] Quoted in Leonard, *The New Wigmore*, 28.   [13] 'Rule of Exclusion'.
[14] See also Wigmore, *A Treatise on the Anglo-American System*, §194, arguing that prejudice is a reason for exclusion.
[15] [1906] 2 KB 389, 398.   [16] [1906] 2 KB 389, 397.
[17] Poisons were widely available and widely used in the nineteenth century; indeed, arsenic was voluntarily taken on health grounds. It also seems that poisons were a popular instrument of mur-der. See J. C. Wharton, *The Arsenic Century: How Victorian Britain was Poisoned at Home, Work, and Play* (Oxford: Oxford University Press, 2010).
[18] Leonard, *The New Wigmore*, 39.   [19] *Ollis* (1900) 2 QBD 758, 781 (Channell J).

5.2 *Makin*

Before the Introduction of the Criminal Justice Act 2003, the House of Lords considered the admissibility of propensity evidence in criminal cases on eight occasions.[20] Despite this, the 1894 decision of the Privy Council in *Makin* v *Attorney General for New South Wales*[21] influenced the case law right up until the CJA came into force. The Makins were convicted of the murder of a child whose body had been found buried, along with the bodies of other children, in the backyard of the house they were living in.[22] Evidence of the finding of the other bodies, as well as of the discovery of yet more children's corpses at other addresses where the Makins had resided, was admitted against the couple. Given the lack of consistency in the case law on the admissibility of evidence of other bad acts, the case came to the Privy Council, which found the evidence rightly admitted and upheld the convictions. As to the principles which should govern the admissibility of such evidence, Lord Herschell's judgment was brief and cryptic:

It is undoubtedly not competent for the prosecution to adduce evidence tending to shew that the accused has been guilty of criminal acts other than those covered by the indictment, for the purpose of leading to the conclusion that the accused is a person likely from his criminal conduct or character to have committed the offence for which he is being tried. On the other hand, the mere fact that the evidence adduced tends to shew the commission of other crimes does not render it inadmissible if it be relevant to an issue before the jury, and it may be so relevant if it bears upon the question whether the acts alleged to constitute the crime charged in the indictment were designed or accidental, or to rebut a defence which would otherwise be open to the accused.[23]

While this endorsed an approach to admissibility based on categories which had considerable authority in the previous case law, Lord Herschell's attempt to present an overview of principles of admissibility was problematic. As has been pointed out on numerous occasions,[24] it is not easy to understand how the two sentences in the quoted passage relate to each other. Is the evidence specified as relevant in the second sentence taken to be admitted for some purpose other than showing that the accused is likely to have committed the offence because of his character? Or is the idea that where character evidence is relevant, it is admissible despite the fact that it is being used as the basis for a propensity inference?

---

[20] *Ball* [1911] AC 47; *Thompson* [1918] AC 221; *Harris* [1952] AC 694; *Boardman* [1975] AC 421; *DPP* v *P* [1991] 2 AC 447; *R* v *H* [1995] 2 AC 596; *R* v *Z* [2000] 2 AC 483; and *Randall* [2004] 1 WLR 56, [2003] UKHL 69.

[21] [1894] AC 57.

[22] For a narrative account of the case and its historical background, see A. Cossins, *The Baby Farmers: A Chilling Tale of Missing Babies, Shameful Secrets and Murder in 19th Century Australia* (Sydney: Allen & Unwin, 2013).

[23] [1894] AC 57, 65.

[24] The passage has been said to 'contain an internal logical contradiction which would appear to render it unworkable': C. R. Williams, 'The Problem of Similar Fact Evidence' (1979) 5 *Dalhousie LJ* 281, 283.

Whatever Lord Herschell intended, in practice *Makin* was taken to establish an approach under which what matters is whether the evidence can be fitted into a particular category. *Makin* itself is vague as to what the categories were: rebutting accident, and then a broad category of 'rebutting a defence'. But, while it was established that the categories were not closed,[25] judges were reasonably cautious about expanding them, and a 'defence' had to be more specific than a simple plea of not guilty.[26] In 1906, Bray J in *Bond* referred to categories of proving system, rebutting accident, and proving knowledge,[27] and this was probably a reasonable interpretation of the nineteenth-century case law. As various commentators have noted,[28] the solidification of the categories is not a surprising turn of events; lawyers, after all, are fond of rules, and categorization is a way of crafting a rule which will appear to be relatively determinate, and which will enable judges to avoid asking the perhaps more difficult question of whether the evidence is more prejudicial than probative.

The categories approach is best illustrated by way of example. In *Harrison Owen*,[29] D was tried for burglary. Using keys found in a car left outside, he had let himself in to the victim's house. At trial, his defence seemed to be that he was in a state of automatism, perhaps through intoxication. The trial judge had admitted his many previous convictions for larceny and housebreaking, but the Court of Appeal held that this was an error, and quashed the conviction. D's defence did not fall into the recognized category of accident, but was instead that he was acting involuntarily. If bad character evidence were to be admissible in a case such as this, thought the Court, 'the results would be very startling'.[30] Contrast *Mortimer*,[31] where D was charged with deliberately driving his car into a female cyclist. Evidence that he had knocked other female cyclists from their bicycles was admitted to show that the incident was no accident. The defendant in *Flack*[32] was tried on counts of having committed incest with each of his three sisters. Given that his defence was a complete denial, and therefore '[n]o question of identity, intent, system, guilty knowledge, or of rebutting a defence of innocent

---

[25] *Harris*, [1952] AC 694, 705.

[26] See *Thompson*, [1918] AC 221, 232: 'The mere theory that a plea of not guilty puts everything material in issue is not enough for this purpose.' Lord Sumer continued: 'No doubt it is paradoxical that a man, whose act is so nakedly wicked as to admit of no doubt about its character, may be better off in regard to admissibility of evidence than a man whose acts are at any rate capable of having a decent face put upon them, and that the accused can exclude evidence that would be admissible and fatal if he ran two defences by prudently confining himself to one. Still, so it is' (232–3). Cf *Noor Mohammed* [1949] AC 182, 191–2: 'An accused person need set up no defence other than a general denial of the crime alleged. The plea of not guilty may be equivalent to saying "Let the prosecution proves its case, if it can," and having said so much the accused may take refuge in silence. In such a case it may appear (for instance) that the facts and circumstances of the particular offence charged are consistent with innocent intention, whereas further evidence, which incidentally shows that the accused has committed one or more other offences, may tend to prove that they are consistent only with a guilty intent. The prosecution could not be said, in their Lordships' opinion, to be "crediting the accused with a fancy defence" if they sought to adduce such evidence.'

[27] [1906] 2 KB 389, 414.

[28] eg P. Mirfield, 'Similar Facts—*Makin* Out?' [1987] *CLJ* 83, 88.

[29] (1951) 35 Cr App R 108.   [30] *Harrison Owen*, 113.

[31] (1936) 25 Cr App R 150.   [32] [1969] 1 WLR 937.

association ever arose',[33] the evidence on one count was not admissible on another. But in *Hall*,[34] where several young men alleged that Hall had committed acts of gross indecency on them, the evidence was admissible, because Hall put forward a defence of innocent association when he alleged that he had been giving the boys medical treatment. Hall, it seems, was damned whatever defence he put forward. On one count, he denied even having met the complainant, but this merely tipped that count into the 'identity' category.[35] *Lewis* provides a striking example of the difference the exact defence put forward by D can make.[36] Lewis was accused of indecently assaulting his partner's daughters. In response to one allegation, he admitted having dried one girl after a bath, but denied having done so indecently. However, when it came to an allegation that he had masturbated in front of both girls, Lewis, unsurprisingly, made a complete denial. The Court of Appeal held that evidence of Lewis's interest in paedophilia could be admitted to prove the towelling incident, but not the masturbation incident.

These cases give a decent idea of how the categories worked. As to exactly what categories were recognized by the middle of the twentieth century, given that the categories were not closed,[37] no list is likely to be complete. The brief list given by the Court of Appeal in *Flack*, quoted above, is indicative. Cross, writing soon after the categories were undermined by the House of Lords in *Boardman*, suggested the following: rebutting a defence of accident or involuntary conduct, rebutting the accused's plea of ignorance or mistake of fact; rebutting an innocent explanation of a particular act or of the possession of incriminating material; proving identity; and rebutting a defence of innocent association.[38] Whatever the categories were, enough has been said to show some of the difficulties in this way of determining admissibility: why should it matter whether Harrison-Owen alleged mistake or involuntariness? Had the complainants in *Flack* not been the defendant's sisters, and he had therefore had to explain his having met them, then perhaps the evidence would have been admitted under the 'innocent association' category, as in *Hall*.[39] But why should this detail in the case make a difference?

5.3 *Boardman*

After *Makin*, questions about the admissibility of propensity evidence reached the House of Lords in *Ball*,[40] *Thompson*,[41] and *Harris*,[42] but, beyond endorsing

[33] *Flack*, 943. [34] [1952] 1 KB 302. [35] *Hall*, 308.
[36] (1983) 76 Cr App R 33. [37] See *Harris*, [1952] AC 694, 705.
[38] R. Cross, *Evidence* (5th edn, London: Butterworths, 1979), 378–93.
[39] The description of the facts in *Hall* is sparse but we are told that D 'was attached to an institution which young men used to attend' (*Hall*, 302), which makes the distinction between the cases even thinner: it is not as if there was necessarily anything suspicious about Hall's association with the complainants which might have given the prosecution case some initial plausibility. And as Lord Cross noted in *Boardman* ([1975] AC 421, 458), it is not really fair to categorize a case as 'innocent association' when D's profession gives him a reason for having known the complainants.
[40] [1911] AC 47. [41] [1918] AC 221. [42] [1952] AC 694.

Makin, these decisions did little to develop the law. In 1975, however, the House of Lords delivered its judgment in *Boardman*,[43] which undertook a more detailed rethinking of the principles. Boardman was the headmaster at a male boarding school; he was tried on three counts involving sexual behaviour with the pupils. The evidence on two of the counts was held to be cross-admissible, and on conviction Boardman challenged this ruling.[44] His defence was that there had been no impropriety. The case might have been forced into the category of 'innocent association', but the House of Lords was reluctant to take this course (as Lord Cross noted, in a sense Boardman had no choice but to associate with the boys because of his job).[45] There was also some authority that cases involving homosexuality were subject to different principles; however, the House of Lords was unanimous in rejecting this view of the law. All of the judgments warned against an inflexible approach to the categories. Beyond this, it is not easy to say what the House of Lords agreed on, but as a whole the decision lends support to a new approach to similar facts: it was certainly heralded as such by commentators.[46] Drawing on the Court of Appeal's attempt to rethink the law in *Sims*,[47] emphasis was placed on the concept of 'striking similarity', the idea being that one (alleged) instance of misconduct could be used to prove another if they were linked by sufficient resemblance. Most of the judgments suggest that this was meant to be a demanding test. This can be seen by references made to the test in *Kilbourne*:[48] is there such underlying unity between the allegations of the witnesses 'as to make coincidence an affront to common sense'?[49] If the evidence excludes coincidence, of course, then unless the witnesses have colluded, the defendant is almost certainly guilty. The idea seems to be that 'striking similarity' is just a way of expressing this high standard. Thus, Lords Hailsham and Salmon gave the example of a burglar who leaves an unusual written mark in the properties he burgles, and Lord Hailsham suggested a case where sexual acts are performed while wearing 'the ceremonial head-dress of a Red Indian chief'.[50] After such examples, the similarity on the facts of *Boardman* itself was bound to disappoint. Lords Wilberforce and Cross emphasised that the case was borderline. The trial judge had put some emphasis on the fact that on both counts Boardman had been said to have shown an interest in being the passive partner in an act of buggery, but the House of Lords was less impressed by this. Other similarities, such as the fact that Boardman had woken the boys up at night and spoken to them in a quiet voice, were emphasised. The evidence was held to have been properly admitted.

[43] [1975] AC 421.
[44] The conviction on the third count had been quashed in the Court of Appeal, on account of an insufficiently careful direction on the corroborating role of distress.
[45] [1975] AC 421, 458.
[46] L. H. Hoffmann, 'Similar Facts after *Boardman*' (1975) 91 LQR 193, describing the decision as an 'intellectual breakthrough' (at 193). It must be said that it is a rather sad indictment of the state of evidence law when the reconceptualization of an issue in terms of relevance is hailed in this way. See also M. E. Turcott, 'Similar Facts: The Boardman Legacy' (1978–79) 21 *Crim LQ* 43.
[47] [1946] KB 531.   [48] [1972] 1 WLR 1365.
[49] See *Boardman*, [1975] AC 421, 453, 444, 439.   [50] [1975] AC 421, 454.

We also find another approach in *Boardman*. According to Lord Hailsham's judgment—the most thorough in dealing with the previous law—the first sentence in *Makin* sets out an absolute prohibition:

evidence of bad character is not admissible for the purpose of leading to the conclusion that a person, from his criminal conduct or character, is likely to have committed the offence for which he is being held...[W]hat is *not* to be admitted is a chain of reasoning...If the inadmissible chain of reasoning is the only purpose for which the evidence is adduced...the evidence itself is not admissible. If there is some other relevant, probative purpose [and this is what the second half of the *Makin* rule sets out]...the evidence is admitted, but should be made subject to a warning from the judge that the jury must eschew the forbidden reasoning.[51]

Similarly, for Lord Salmon: '[T]he test must be: is the evidence capable of tending to persuade a jury on some ground other than his bad character and disposition to commit the sort of crime with which he is charged.'[52]

5.4 From *Boardman* to *P*

It is difficult to find a single coherent message in *Boardman*. Some of the judgments emphasise striking similarity, others forbidden reasoning. While all stress that the admissibility standard is set high—a policy perhaps most clearly symbolized by the test of excluding coincidence—this was immediately undercut by the fact that the House of Lords held the evidence rightly admitted. Perhaps this is one reason why the House of Lords was later to describe the admissibility test in *Boardman* as 'somewhat unprincipled'.[53] It is not surprising, then, to find conflicting impulses in the cases which followed *Boardman*.

Soon after *Boardman*, in *Scarrott*,[54] the Court of Appeal appeared to read down the test of striking similarity by suggesting that it was synonymous with a criterion of 'positive probative value'. But, while cited in a few cases involving, like *Scarrott*, multiple allegations of sexual offences, this new test was not terribly influential.[55] This may have been because the admissibility criteria found in *Boardman* are sufficiently vague, and subject to manipulation, that they often did not thwart judicial intuitions about what bad character evidence should be admitted. For its part, the forbidden reasoning test frankly invited abuse. The idea here is that the jury must not reason to guilt via the proposition that the defendant has a propensity to commit crime. Because most bad character evidence does involve propensity

---

[51] [1975] AC 421, 451–3.   [52] [1975] AC 421, 462.
[53] *O'Brien* v *Chief Constable of South Wales Police* [2005] 2 AC 534, [2005] UKHL 26, [6].
[54] [1977] 3 WLR 629. This approach was prefigured in *Rance and Herron* (1976) 62 Cr App R 118.
[55] It played some role in *Inder* (1987) 67 Cr App R 143 (although here it did not seem to result in any relaxation of the admissibility standard); *Lunt* (1987) 85 Cr App R 241; *Barrington* [1981] 1 WLR 419; and *Wilmot* (1989) 89 Cr App R 12. Taking the statement out of context—ie as being other than a synonym for striking similarity—was cautioned against in *Brooks* (1991) 92 Cr App R 341.

reasoning (an argument made in more detail in Chapter 6), judges who relied on the *Boardman* forbidden reasoning doctrine had to find a way of obscuring the role of the propensity inference. Sometimes, propensity was banished by mere assertion; in *Rance*, for example, the fact that Rance had passed other bribes than the one he was on trial for 'went beyond merely showing a tendency on the part of Rance to commit the offence'[56] (there was no explanation why). Less bluntly, judges often used the old idea of the categories to provide them with language which enabled them to describe what the evidence was being used to do, such as to rebut a defence, rather than how it did so, which was almost always via propensity. This linguistic sleight of hand enabled courts to give the impression that the bad character evidence did not engage forbidden reasoning. One of the most brazen examples of this strategy pre-dates *Boardman*. Straffen was charged with the murder by strangulation of a young girl, and evidence that he had strangled other young girls was used to prove his guilt.[57] This was powerful evidence, and was more or less the only evidence against him. Yet according to the Court of Appeal, while it was an 'irrefragable rule' that such evidence was not admissible to prove that the accused has a 'propensity for committing the particular type of crime with which he is being charged',[58] this evidence did not infringe that rule, because it 'tended to rebut a defence which was otherwise open to the accused, that is, that he was not the person who committed the murder'.[59] A more mundane example is *Saunders*,[60] where evidence that D had acted aggressively towards the victim was said to be more than evidence of propensity, because it was 'admissible to rebut some of the defences put forward'.[61] And in *Baird*, the Court of Appeal rejected the argument that diaries, which detailed the defendant's fantasies, 'were evidence of inclination and no more...The expressions of sexual attraction and motive...went far to rebut the defence of innocent association.'[62] As these decisions show, *Boardman* did not kill off the categories approach. It remained popular with courts which read *Boardman* as a ban on propensity reasoning.

Boardman's striking similarity test was also open to manipulation. Here, for example, is the list of similarities noted by the trial judge in *Shore*, a case involving allegations of indecent assault by a headmaster:

(1) That all the incidents complained of arose during the course of the appellant's duty as a headmaster.

(2) That all the incidents concerned girls and not boys, though on occasions boys were present as well.

(3) That the incidents took place in circumstances which cropped up again and again, that is, either in the hall (which was used for PE) or in a bus or at the swimming pool.

(4) That all the incidents took place, with one or two exceptions, when other children and sometimes adults were in the vicinity.

---

[56] (1976) 62 Cr App R 118, 121.   [57] *Straffen* [1952] 2 QB 911.
[58] *Straffen*, 914.   [59] *Straffen*, 914–15.   [60] [1986] 1 WLR 1163.
[61] *Saunders*, 1165.   [62] (1993) 97 Cr App R 308, 317.

(5)   That on each occasion the appellant's hand would stray into the child's clothing and would move towards, though (with one exception) it never reached, the child's private parts.[63]

The Court of Appeal was unimpressed by (4), but thought that the other details showed a 'strikingly similar pattern'.[64] The number of allegations against Shore may have meant that the case was a strong one, but it is hard to see how the common features here can be described as 'striking'. In particular, Shore's employment as headmaster is not something which can have much more significance than his date of birth; it is rather like the significance attributed to the fact that the defendant drove 'a similar car' in each of the incidents in *Wilmot*,[65] a case in which identity was not disputed. In *Grant*,[66] the defendant's hurried departure from the scene was said to be one of the significant similarities between a series of burglaries where D gained entry on a pretext. In *Boardman* itself, the fact that two complainants were woken in their dormitory at night by the defendant speaking in a quiet voice was emphasised; although, if the complainants were fabricating, they were hardly likely to say that Boardman had shouted. Although not tightly linked to the striking similarity test, a wonderful example of finding distinctiveness where there is none is *Johanssen*, where the defendant's 'particular homosexual propensities' were described as being 'to handle the boys' penises and getting them to do the same with his, fellatio and buggery'.[67] Significantly, this was a case where the evidence gained much of its power through multiple allegations (eight complainants) rather than through especially distinctive behaviour. But because the available admissibility tests did not obviously accommodate this feature, it was tempting to exaggerate the distinctiveness of the behaviour.

While the striking similarity test was susceptible to manipulation, it would be wrong to suggest that it never presented a barrier to admissibility. In *Novac*,[68] the allegations that the defendant had met the complainants in an amusement arcade, offered them a bed for the night, and then attempted to bugger them were said to be 'commonplace',[69] while in *Inder* the common features in the allegations were described as no more than the 'stock in trade of the seducer of small boys', appearing in the 'vast majority of cases that come before the courts'.[70] Another element in *Boardman* which nudged towards a strict standard was the 'exclusion of coincidence' test.[71] In *Novac*, the common element of being picked up in an amusement arcade was not 'inexplicable on the basis of coincidence' and thus could not secure admissibility.[72] It was this strand in the case law, taking the admissibility test to be a demanding one, which created pressure to revisit it.

---

[63] (1989) 89 Cr App R 32, 38. For another example, see Pattenden's discussion of *Mustafa* (1977) 65 Cr App R 26: Rosemary Pattenden, 'Similar Fact Evidence and Proof of Identity' (1996) 112 *LQR* 446, 466–7.

[64] *Shore*, 42.   [65] (1989) 89 Cr App R 341, 348.

[66] [1996] 2 Cr App R 272, 274.   [67] (1977) 65 Cr App R 101, 103.

[68] (1977) 65 Cr App R 107.   [69] *Novac*, 112.   [70] (1978) 67 Cr App R 143, 149.

[71] The coincidence test was sometimes interpreted as a less demanding standard, eg in terms of 'unlikelihood of coincidence' in *Osmanioglu* [2002] EWCA Crim 930, [20].

[72] (1977) 65 Cr App R 107, 112.

The Court of Appeal's 1990 decision in *Brooks*[73] seems to have created some unease about the striking similarity test—or at least about applying the test seriously. The case involved allegations of sexual abuse made by the defendant's three daughters.[74] The trial judge, referring to the 'positive probative value' dictum in *Rance*, had ruled the allegations cross-admissible, commenting that 'it would be flying in the face of common sense to suggest that those matters ought to be tried in isolation'.[75] The Court of Appeal, however, disagreed with this decision, and quashed the convictions. Warning against reading too much into the positive probative value formulation of the rule, it stressed the need to locate striking similarities in the allegations. But in this case, it could not find any; as in *Inder*, the commonalities were little more than the stock in trade for this type of crime: 'there is nothing...except that the offences were alleged to have happened at home and that the daughters submitted and kept silent through fear. Sadly, these are the common coin of evidence in cases of father daughter incest. There is nothing striking about them.'[76] As for the trial judge's reference to common sense:

the common sense to which the judge had recourse here was of a special kind. It posits that if two daughters say that their father behaved indecently towards them, this makes it more likely that he was guilty than if one had said so. Many citizens would agree. Yet this is precisely the reasoning which for more than 100 years the courts in England have said is too dangerous to adopt.[77]

At the time, sexual child abuse was becoming an increasingly prominent public concern. Because the reasoning in *Brooks* suggested that it would be difficult to prosecute cases of familial child abuse, it was not surprising that it was soon to be challenged.

This is not to suggest that there were no resources for justifying admissibility in a case such as *Brooks*. The case law was complex enough that few decisions were inevitable. Six months after *Brooks*, the Court of Appeal decided *Bedford*, a case where admissibility of bad character evidence was approved, although described as 'borderline'.[78] The defendant had pleaded guilty to sexual offences against two boys, and these admissions were used as evidence against him in respect of a third allegation. There was little that was striking in the connections between the allegations, and unsurprisingly the defence argued 'stock in trade'. But with three allegations the lack of similarity was not felt to be an obstacle, because the 'cannot be coincidence' test could be used to overcome it (there was also a hint that the 'rebut innocent association' category could have been used). This time, the Court of Appeal was less disdainful of common sense: the combination of facts made 'the explanation of coincidence in relation to a similar allegation by the third boy an affront to common sense'.[79] *Bedford* was certainly a stronger case than *Brooks*, but it does illustrate the flexibility of the accumulated case law.

[73] (1991) 92 Cr App R 36.
[74] One of the three withdrew her allegation during the trial.   [75] *Brooks*, 39.
[76] *Brooks*, 42–3.   [77] *Brooks*, 43.   [78] (1991) 93 Cr App R 113, 117.
[79] *Bedford*, 117.

Soon after *Brooks*, a very similar case reached the House of Lords. In *DPP* v *P*,[80] P's two daughters alleged sexual abuse. In the light of *Brooks*, the Court of Appeal reluctantly held that the evidence was not cross-admissible, but encouraged an appeal. Lord Mackay delivered the single judgment of the House, holding that the evidence of each daughter could properly support the other. Although overruling the stock in trade cases, Mackay was otherwise respectful of previous authority. The famous *Makin* passage was quoted with no disapproval,[81] and long quotations from all of the *Boardman* speeches were given. However, the gist of the judgment was that striking similarity was not always a necessary criterion for admissibility. The clever move here, which helped to justify this without disapproving of *Boardman*, was to quote not just from the statements of principle in that case, but also from the passages where the judges had reviewed the facts and held the evidence admissible: for, as we saw, the application to the facts very much undercut the lofty statements found elsewhere in the *Boardman* judgments. Lord Mackay's summary of the law was as follows:

the essential feature of evidence which is to be admitted is that its probative force in support of the allegation that an accused person committed a crime is sufficiently great to make it just to admit the evidence, notwithstanding that it is prejudicial to the accused in tending to show that he was guilty of another crime. Such probative force may be derived from striking similarities in the evidence about the manner in which the crime was committed... But restricting the circumstances in which there is sufficient probative force to overcome prejudice of evidence relating to another crime to cases in which there is some striking similarity between them is to restrict the operation of the principle in a way which gives too much effect to a particular manner of stating it, and is not justified in principle... I consider that the judge must first decide whether there is material upon which the jury would be entitled to conclude that the evidence of one victim, about what occurred to that victim, is so related to the evidence given by another victim, about what happened to that other victim, that the evidence of the first victim provides strong enough support for the evidence of the second victim to make it just to admit it notwithstanding the prejudicial effect of admitting the evidence. This relationship, from which support is derived, may take many forms and while these forms may include 'striking similarity' in the manner in which the crime is committed, consisting of unusual characteristics in its execution the necessary relationship is by no means confined to such circumstances. Relationships in time and circumstances other than these may well be important relationships in this connection. Where the identity of the perpetrator is in issue, and evidence of this kind is important in that connection, obviously something in the nature of what has been called in the course of the argument a signature or other special feature will be necessary. To transpose this requirement to other situations where the question is whether a crime has been committed, rather than who did commit it, is to impose an unnecessary and improper restriction upon the application of the principle.[82]

In closing, Lord Mackay noted the criticism, made in argument, that admissibility decisions had become a lottery. In the light of his guidance, he thought: 'Judgments

---

[80] [1991] 2 AC 447.   [81] *DPP* v *P*, 454.   [82] *DPP* v *P*, 460–2.

properly made in the light of the appropriate principles should not...yield results which could properly be described as a lottery.'[83]

If all one were to take from *P* was that the admissibility test for bad character evidence depends on whether the evidence is more prejudicial than probative, it would be hard to criticize the decision. But *P* made no clean sweep of the law. The various views in *Boardman* were all quoted, seemingly with approval. And while striking similarity was sidelined, at least in cases not involving identity, Lord Mackay's judgment still seemed to emphasise something like similarity in its references to the importance of a relationship between the items of evidence.[84] It is no surprise, then, to find that *P* did little to solve the problems of the law, nor to end the admissibility lottery.

5.5 After *P*

It is not easy to generalize about the law in the wake of *P*. In the case law we find all of the tests which we have come across so far still being used. The post-*P* position, therefore, can only be appreciated by examining a number of cases.

One point is fairly straightforward. In *P*, Lord Mackay had suggested that the test of striking similarity would still play a role in cases where identity was in issue. No doubt he had in mind 'hallmark' cases like *Straffen*, where the prosecution case largely depended on character evidence and thus on showing that D had a peculiar *modus operandi*, one shared by very few people. But where there is evidence other than the character evidence to link D to the current crime, there is no need for striking similarity.[85] In *John W*,[86] D was charged with two attacks in which he had grabbed young women with what appeared to be a sexual motivation. He denied any involvement. There was identification evidence on one count, and a decent amount of circumstantial evidence on the other count. The attacks were similar, but there was nothing linking them which could be described as striking. The Court of Appeal held that the evidence on each count was cross-admissible, and rightly so. Unlike the situation in *Straffen*, the character evidence did not have to do nearly all of the work by itself, so there was no need for a strong connection in terms of the similarity of the attacks.

The simplest reading of *P* (and one endorsed in subsequent House of Lords decisions[87]) is that the admissibility test involves balancing probative force against

---

[83] *DPP* v *P*, 463.   [84] See Mackay's later interpretation of *P*, noted at n 87.

[85] See Pattenden's astute analysis ('Similar Fact Evidence'), cited in *John W.*

[86] [1998] 2 Cr App R 289.

[87] See *R* v *H* [1995] 2 AC 596, 611 (Lord Mackay), 613 (Lord Griffiths), 621 (Lord Mustill), and 626 (Lord Lloyd) (although note Lord Mackay's slightly more complex formulation at 603: 'the requirement then is for a particular relationship to exist between the allegation in issue and the allegations in evidence sought to be adduced as similar fact evidence'); *Randall*, [2004] 1 WLR 56, [2003] UKHL 69, [26] (Lord Steyn); and *O'Brien* v *Chief Constable of South Wales Police* [2005] 2 AC 534, [2005] UKHL 26, [31] (Lord Phillips). The Law Commission agreed with this reading of *P*: *Evidence in Criminal Proceedings: Previous Misconduct of a Defendant*, LCCP No 141 (London: HMSO, 1996), 32.

prejudicial effect: the idea which seems to be set out right at the start of passage quoted above. But in fact it was rare to find the Court of Appeal applying a pure balancing test as a means of deciding admissibility; reference to those sentences in *P* was usually accompanied by an assessment of how much similarity there was between one allegation, or conviction, and another, or of whether the evidence was evidence of mere propensity, or some such. And those other criteria were usually portrayed as doing most, if not all, of the work. *Bell* is an exception, where admissibility was justified because the similarities 'were such as to have forceful probative value considerably outweighing any question of any prejudice that there would be as a result of the jury hearing of the other allegations at the same time'.[88] The strength of the case—47 allegations of indecent assault by a number of different boys—perhaps explains why the Court of Appeal here felt comfortable with the language of balance. In *Harrison*, the Court made the rare move of accepting that the disputed evidence merely showed propensity, and portrayed *P* as making a 'fresh start', where the trial judge's assessment of the balance of competing considerations was key.[89] By way of contrast, the Court in *Thomas T* subordinated the balancing language to the older tests of non-coincidence and going beyond propensity: 'it is a precondition for the admission of similar fact evidence that the evidence strongly supports the charges faced by the defendant. If that precondition is not satisfied there is no balancing exercise to be carried out. That precondition was not met in the present case.'[90]

If *P* was not usually read as introducing a basic balancing test, what difference was it seen to make? It is not easy to say. In *Barney*, the Court of Appeal agreed with what seems to have been a widely held view: that '*P* follows *Boardman* as regards the degree of probative force required in similar fact evidence, but widens the manner in which the probative force can be established. It is not limited to cases where the offences display a striking similarity.'[91] The reference to *Boardman* allowed the Court to portray admissibility as still exceptional, requiring something more than 'mere propensity'. In *John Allen V*, however, *P* was depicted as having made more of a change; it 'diluted' the similar facts rule. The rule's 'now more broad-ranging and contextual nature undoubtedly offers judges a greater degree of latitude in assessing whether a combination of features, not striking in themselves, amount to a sufficient connection for the purposes of the rule'.[92] This reading of *P* helped to justify admissibility in a 'borderline' case, involving sexual assaults on two young girls in a domestic context.

As we have seen, one thing which can definitely be said about the law after *P* is that striking similarity was no longer needed. However, courts often felt that some degree of factual similarity was necessary. In *Kumar*,[93] D was convicted of two rapes involving different women. The Court of Appeal thought this a borderline case. It stressed the importance of ensuring 'that the prosecution case amounts to more than mere reliance on a number of accusations which have been

---

88 [2002] EWCA Crim 1719, [34].   89 [2004] EWCA Crim 1792, [34].
90 [2001] EWCA Crim 2915, [23].   91 [2005] EWCA Crim 1385, [21].
92 [2002] EWCA Crim 236, [43].   93 [2005] EWCA Crim 3549.

made'; the jury itself should be warned 'that it was not enough merely to rely upon the fact that the two had made allegations of rape, lest they fall into the error of thinking that because two have made such accusations there must be something in them'.[94] It was held that there was just enough similarity in the allegations that D, a mini-cab driver, had had non-consensual sex with two fares to justify cross-admissibility, but that lack of careful jury instruction made the convictions unsafe. In *Musquera*,[95] D was convicted of various sexual offences involving three young complainants. As to the law, the Court of Appeal considered that: 'While the decision in *DPP* v *P* has eliminated the necessity to identify a "striking" similarity, it is still necessary to invoke some identifiable common feature or features constituting a significant connection and going beyond mere propensity or coincidence.'[96] Here, the similarity was insufficient.

In these cases, then, the courts were looking for more than similarity of crime category; but precisely what extra element was required is hard to say. Beyond the sentence just quoted, the court in *Musquera* could add little, other than that there should be 'significant similarity' or some other relationship between the events. Given the vagueness here, it is hard to shake off the feeling that, despite Lord Mackays's hopes, in the wake of *P* admissibility remained something of a lottery. It is obviously not easy to distinguish *Musquera* from *P* itself, or from *John Allen V.* In *Massey*,[97] D was convicted of sexual assaults on three young men; the court distanced itself from *Musquera*, suggesting, somewhat disingenuously, that there the principal problem had been deficiencies in the summing up. The convictions were upheld.

A group of cases involving multiple allegations of indecent assaults by doctors provide a good illustration of the continuing unpredictability. In *Cowie*, the convictions were quashed on the grounds that the complaints were not cross-admissible.[98] *P*'s deference to *Boardman* was used to justify relying on statements in the latter case which emphasised the exceptional nature of admissibility.

> In our view we do not think that the nature of these allegations are such that, to use the words of Lord Salmon in *Boardman*, 'common sense makes it inexplicable on the basis of coincidence'. The number of complaints has to be assessed against the number of patients seen and also against the fact that the occasional misinterpretation or exaggeration by the patient is not a fanciful explanation for allegations of indecency in these circumstances.[99]

In the factually similar *Roy*,[100] however, the Court of Appeal considered that the recent decision in *P* meant that there could be no argument about cross-admissibility. The trial judge in *Haslam*[101] ruled that there was no cross-admissibility between a number of complaints against a psychiatrist; the only facts he did think could support each other were found on appeal—not without some justification, as one

---

[94] *Kumar*, [15], [22].   [95] [1999] Crim LR 857.   [96] *Musquera*, transcript p 9.
[97] [2001] EWCA Crim 2850.   [98] [2003] EWCA Crim 3522.   [99] *Cowie*, [27].
[100] [1992] Crim LR 185.
[101] [2004] EWCA Crim 1840. The trial judge's decision is a good example of how the concept of similarity could sometimes distort judgment: the judge thought the incidents similar because they were said to have taken place in the same room.

incident was consensual—to be insufficiently similar. *Carman*[102] lies somewhere between the extremes. The trial judge had not thought that all complaints of sexual assault by the doctor could be used to support each other, instead placing them in groups involving similar types of behaviour. The Court of Appeal remarked that some of the case law—referring to *Simpson*,[103] a case involving familial sexual assault—might have justified full cross-admissibility. In the event, though, it worried that the judge had not directed the jury sufficiently clearly that the allegations in one group could not be used to support those in another, and ended up quashing seven of the ten convictions—all of those where the behaviour was vaguely equivocal.

If *P* did not make admissibility decisions as predictable as Lord Mackay had hoped, it did not put paid to the older approaches to similar fact evidence either. After *P*, courts continued to rely on the categories approach, as well as on an interpretation of the admissibility rule as a ban on propensity reasoning. The categories approach could offer a way to engineer admissibility in cases where similarity was lacking. Thus, in *Buono*,[104] evidence that D had been driving dangerously shortly before his car crashed was used to prove that dangerous driving caused the crash, on the grounds that it rebutted the defence of accident. In *Baird*,[105] diary entries showing a sexual interest in boys were held admissible to rebut a defence of innocent association. And in *Simpson*,[106] cross-admissibility was justified by the idea of a 'course of conduct'—presumably a reference back to the old category of 'system'—a concept vague enough to justify admissibility in almost any case, certainly all of the doctor cases.

Reliance on a 'no propensity reasoning' rule was more common as a means of excluding, rather than admitting, evidence, especially if the evidence involved incriminating objects. While in *Furze*[107] the trial judge allowed evidence of dishonesty to prove conspiracy to defraud, on the grounds that it rebutted the defence of innocent association, the Court of Appeal held the evidence inadmissible, noting, among other things, that it only showed propensity. (In *Baird*,[108] however, priority went the other way, and the innocent association category was used to trump the argument that the diaries were merely evidence of inclination.) The defendant's interest in homosexual pornography was held inadmissible as pure propensity in the indecent assault case of *B(RA)*,[109] as was possession of child pornography in *Luke B*,[110] and the defendant's interest in young girls expressed in a 'poem' in *John R*.[111] Incriminating objects were not always held inadmissible, however. Despite the Court of Appeal's expression of the rule as a propensity based one in *Clarke*,[112] a robber's kit discovered in the defendant's car was held admissible because of its significance when added to other evidence of identification.

[102] [2004] EWCA Crim 540.   [103] (1994) 99 Cr App R 48.
[104] [2005] EWCA Crim 1313.   [105] (1993) 97 Cr App R 308.
[106] (1994) 99 Cr App R 48.   [107] [2003] EWCA Crim 2706.
[108] (1993) 97 Cr App R 308.   [109] [1997] 2 Cr App R 88.
[110] [2006] EWCA Crim 3231.   [111] CA 25 May 2000.
[112] [1995] 2 Cr App R 425.

Given the state of the law in the years following *P*, it is easy to see why the Law Commission concluded that '[i]t is hard for parties and courts to establish exactly what the law is in this area',[113] and that '[i]t is difficult for prosecutors to predict whether similar fact evidence can be adduced in a particular case; the defence does not know whether the prosecution's similar fact evidence will be admitted'.[114] It would be wrong, though, to use the decisions discussed here to paint a picture of complete arbitrariness. Although there was a degree of indeterminacy, and a relatively broad borderline where cases could go either way, many of the decisions roughly track the strength of the case; *Clarke*, for example, was certainly a better case to leave to the jury than *B(RA)*. But it is reasonably clear that the admissibility decisions were not determined by the rules; creative judges had so much choice between similarity, probative value, categories, forbidden reasoning, and other criteria that almost any decision could be justified. It is just that judges would usually not want to justify admissibility in weak cases.

5.6 *Randall*

Questions about propensity evidence reached the House of Lords four times between 1991 and 2005, dealing with issues such as how to deal with the possibility of collusion between witnesses,[115] the similar facts rule in civil cases,[116] and whether an allegation of criminal activity which had been prosecuted and resulted in acquittal could be used to support a new, similar allegation.[117] For present purposes, the most interesting of these decisions is *Randall*.[118]

Randall was not a case involving propensity evidence in the sense we have been focussing on in this chapter—where the prosecution seeks to admit such evidence to prove guilt, and the evidence must satisfy the common law admissibility test. *Randall* involved a dispute between co-defendants, Randall and Glean, charged with murder. As each blamed the other for the crime, both 'lost their shield' under section 1(3) of the Criminal Evidence Act 1898. This meant that the jury would be instructed to consider the defendants' criminal records as evidence of their credibility; the disputed question was whether the judge should also instruct the jury that they could consider Glean's record of violent crime as evidence of his propensity to violence. The House of Lords held that such an instruction was appropriate. What is interesting about *Randall* is the way in which Lord Bingham's judgment clearly embraces the relevance of the criminal record as evidence of violent propensity. *Randall* was not a case where the prosecution would have been able to rely on evidence of Glean's criminal record as evidence of murder. There was little similarity between the offences, and the evidence could

---

[113] Law Commission, *Evidence of Bad Character in Criminal Proceedings*, Law Com No 273, Cm 5257 (London: TSO, 2001), 50.

[114] Law Commission, LCCP No 141, 167.   [115] *R* v *H*, [1995] 2 AC 596.

[116] *O'Brien* v *Chief Constable of South Wales Police*, [2005] 2 AC 534, [2005] UKHL 26.

[117] *R* v *Z*, [2000] 2 AC 483.   [118] [2004] 1 WLR 56, [2003] UKHL 69.

not easily be fitted into a category. Any attempt to introduce the evidence might well have met with the response that this was evidence of 'mere propensity'. A dismissal of the evidence in these terms had sometimes been used in cases involving admissibility under the Criminal Evidence Act: 'There is a clear general principle, that, in general, evidence of propensity to commit a crime is not evidence that the man with that propensity committed the crime on the particular occasion.'[119] In *Randall*, however, Lord Bingham was not swayed by such unrealistic reasoning. The evidence was seen as relevant and admissible to show propensity. *Randall* was decided shortly before the 2003 Act came into force. Had legislative reform not intervened, it is an interesting question whether *Randall*'s openness about propensity reasoning would have had any impact on similar fact cases, where, as we have seen, even after *P* reference to 'forbidden reasoning' was still common. If the issue had returned to the House of Lords it might well have done, although it is possible that the analysis in *Randall* would have been considered to be confined to cases involving co-defendants where issues of relevance are sometimes seen differently.[120]

5.7 Conclusion

The discussion in this chapter has been largely expository. The various admissibility tests for propensity evidence found in the post-*Makin* case law have been described, partly so that they can be submitted to more critical scrutiny in the following chapter. Where I have been critical, this has partly been to draw attention to the fact that, as other writers have noted, the admissibility tests have not always worked on their own terms: for example, propensity reasoning has not been avoided, even by courts taking a 'forbidden reasoning' approach to admissibility. More generally, the history shows a tendency for high admissibility standards to be proclaimed but then abandoned in practice. Thus, the categories were expanded, and similarities were declared to be striking when they were not—most notably in *Boardman* itself.[121] When the rules were applied strictly, there was pressure to abandon them in order to admit probative evidence, as in the move away from striking similarity in *P* and later in identity cases in *John W*. While some might be critical of this drive towards lower standards,[122] another conclusion which might be drawn from this aspect of the history is that strict admissibility standards are simply unworkable.

In this chapter I have also tried to show how indeterminate the case law was, especially in the period between *P* and the introduction of the Criminal Justice Act 2003. This is a significant point. As we will see in Chapter 7, one criticism

---

[119] *Neale* (1977) 65 Cr App R 304, 307.
[120] See the discussion of 'broad' and 'narrow' views of *Randall* in *R v B(C)* [2004] 2 Cr App R 34, [2004] EWCA Crim 1254, [38].
[121] As Pattenden notes: 'Similar Fact Evidence', 465.
[122] See the discussion in the following chapter.

of the law under the CJA is that there are few clear rules and that admissibility of propensity evidence is unpredictable. There may be considerable truth in that criticism, but it would be wrong to presume that the law was clear before the CJA. As applied in the courts, it was anything but.

It might, though, be argued that the problems of the law were of form rather than substance, that the rules, despite their constant manipulation and indeterminacy, operated well enough in practice, with admissibility roughly tracking probative value. Hoffmann, writing shortly after *Boardman*, and reading that decision as one that allowed strongly probative evidence, suggested that 'there are virtually no cases which can be said in the light of *Boardman* to have been wrongly decided—a tribute to the power of common sense over the forms of legal reasoning'.[123] And Dennis has echoed this point, noting that there are few clear examples where very prejudicial propensity evidence of low probative value has been admitted.[124] This may well be true; it is hard to find reported cases where defendants have been unfairly disadvantaged by the rules on propensity evidence. But that, of course, is only half the story: defendants may well have been unfairly advantaged by the exclusion of propensity evidence which should have been admitted. Even on the brief review in this chapter, it is possible to point to cases where there can be little dispute that this has happened: *Harrison-Owen* is an obvious, if rather dated, example. And we simply have little idea what sort of evidence was being excluded by the courts under the propensity evidence rule. Because until recently the prosecution lacked appeal rights against admissibility decisions, a decision to exclude cogent propensity evidence could not be appealed, and so would rarely come to the attention of commentators.[125] At this stage, then, we are simply not in a position to say whether the Courts pre-CJA were generally getting things right. We will be in a better position to judge this when we have looked at the post-CJA case law.

---

[123] 'Similar Facts after *Boardman*', 204.

[124] I. H. Dennis, *The Law of Evidence* (2nd edn, London: Sweet & Maxwell, 2002), 624.

[125] One exception is an example used by McEwan: the case of Michael Maloney. 'Fear of causing excessive prejudice led Bathurst-Norman J. to insist that five accusations of rape made against Maloney by five different women be tried before separate juries, although the defence was consent in each case. The judge felt that he had to look for striking similarities between the incidents...In the event, each jury considered only one allegation of rape in isolation, and the defendant was acquitted by all but one.' J. McEwan, 'Law Commission Dodges the Nettles in Consultation Paper No. 141' [1997] *Crim LR* 93. See also the examples recounted at HC Debates 2 April 2003, Col 1024, and in J. R. Spencer, *Evidence of Bad Character* (Oxford: Hart Publishing, 2009), 4–5.

6

Understanding Propensity Evidence

In the previous chapter, we saw how the law governing the admissibility of propensity evidence developed in the period from *Makin*[1] to the introduction of the Criminal Justice Act 2003. The focus there was largely descriptive, although aspects of the law, in particular the malleability of the various admissibility tests, were evaluated. In this chapter, the analysis is more critical. Drawing on some of the cases discussed in the previous chapter as illustrative examples, I explore the inferential structure of propensity evidence: the reasoning process which links evidence of bad character to guilt. With this foundation in place, I move on to assess the various common law admissibility tests which featured in the previous chapter.

6.1 Patterns of Propensity Evidence

In Chapters 2 and 3, we examined the basic structure of the propensity inference. If D has previously committed a crime, that suggests he has a comparative propensity to offend (is more likely to offend than someone who has not committed a crime before). This makes it more likely that he is guilty. The discussion in the earlier chapters, however, kept things relatively simple, focussing on the case where D has a previous conviction. From the analysis of the case law in Chapter 5, it will be obvious that the facts of propensity cases vary considerably, frequently involving more complex factual patterns than a previous conviction and a new allegation of criminal activity.

Complex though the case law is, it is possible to group the cases into four main fact patterns—although we should be wary of seeing sharp distinctions between the different scenarios. In the simplest case, D has a previous conviction for a crime, and this previous conviction is used as evidence that he is guilty of the crime currently charged. The reasoning in this scenario is relatively simple: the previous conviction suggests that D has a high comparative propensity to commit the relevant crime, and therefore the previous conviction increases the probability of guilt (see Figure 6.1).

[1] [1894] AC 57.

Figure 6.1 The basic propensity inference from previous conviction (PC) to current crime (CC)

The reasoning process in this previous conviction model sheds light on the inferential process in other scenarios. Before moving on, it is worth noting that, while the clearest example involves a previous conviction, the reasoning process works in the same way even if we do not have an actual conviction as the basis for inference. A simple allegation that D has committed a crime can form the basis for a propensity inference, although that inference may be a weaker one than where an actual conviction is concerned.[2] If D has more than one previous conviction, then the propensity inference would normally be stronger. The strength of the inference might also be affected by other factors, such as the length of time between the previous conviction and current charge and facts about D which make reoffending less likely (see the discussion in Chapter 2).

The second scenario to consider is where, rather than having previous convictions, D is found in possession of incriminating articles. There is, for example, the robber's kit in *Clarke*,[3] the diary in *Baird*,[4] and the homosexual pornography in *B(RA)*[5] (see Figure 6.2). These cases are in fact similar to the previous conviction model; the differences between the scenarios are ones of degree (as noted above, an actual conviction is not a necessary element of the basic scenario).

With incriminating articles, the evidence of D's propensity may be less strong than in the previous conviction scenario. In *Clarke*, where a 'robbery kit' was found in the boot of Clarke's car, perhaps the most we can say is that D is associated with robbery rather than that he has committed robbery. This simply reduces the probability that he has robbed before, making the evidence weaker: in Figure 6.2 if the inference from IA to PC is weak, the propensity inference has less weight too. 'Incriminating articles', of course, is a wide and varied category. The diary entries in *Baird* showed a sexual interest in young boys. They did not show that Baird had ever actually assaulted young boys. As we saw in Chapter 4, however, there can be non-criminal bad character evidence. The propensity inference does not have to emanate from a previous crime. That too is just a difference in degree, not a fundamental difference in the way in which the reasoning process works. The evidence has a claim to relevance on the argument that those who write such diary entries are more likely to commit indecent assault than those who do not.

---

[2] I take a previous conviction to be the strongest and clearest case because the law gives convictions a special status. PACE, s 74(3) creates a rebuttable presumption that the defendant committed the convicted offence. Sometimes, however, previous convictions are challenged: for examples, see Chapter 7.

[3] [1995] 2 Cr App R 425.   [4] (1993) 97 Cr App R 308.   [5] [1997] 2 Cr App R 88.

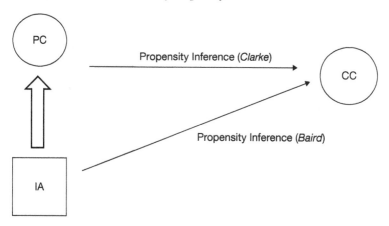

Figure 6.2 Propensity inference in case involving incriminating articles. The inference may be via a previous crime (PC) (a possibility in *Clarke*) or may proceed straight from the incriminating articles (IA) (as in *Baird*). In *Baird*, the propensity inference is along the lines that people who express fantasies about abusing children are more likely to do so than those who do not.

A third scenario is where several people accuse D of having committed similar crimes; *DPP* v *P*[6] and the doctor cases[7] are examples. Comparative propensity is again the key. As noted in relation to the first fact-pattern, a single allegation is evidence that D has committed a particular crime; it is therefore evidence of his comparative propensity to commit that crime, and can thus support a second allegation. But the evidence may gain strength in other ways. If there are multiple allegations, especially if they occur within a short space of time, that may well be evidence that D has a particularly high propensity to commit crime (see Figures 6.3 and 6.4). In the literature on similar facts, cases involving allegations are often depicted as employing very different reasoning to cases involving previous convictions and the like.[8] It is said that the probative value of the evidence results from the improbability of several complainants telling similar lies. That is true as far as it goes, but it is a mistake to think that this avoids a propensity inference. I explain why in more detail below.

It is possible for multiple allegations to be made by a single witness. We do not usually think of such a case as involving a propensity inference; intuitively there would be no gain, in terms of mutual support between counts, in trying the allegations together. But this is not because there is no propensity inference

[6] *DPP* v *P* [1991] 2 AC 447.
[7] *Cowie* [2003] EWCA Crim 3522; *Haslam* [2004] EWCA Crim 1840; *Roy* [1992] Crim LR 185; and *Carman* [2004] EWCA Crim 540.
[8] See, eg, Z. Cowen and P. B. Carter, 'The Admissibility of Evidence of Similar Facts: A Re-Examination' in *Essays on The Law of Evidence* (Oxford: Clarendon Press, 1956), 116; and *Musquera* [1999] Crim LR 857, with commentary by J. C. Smith.

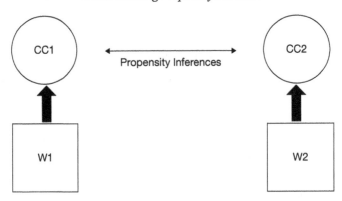

Figure 6.3 Propensity inferences (thin arrow) in a case involving two allegations (thick arrows) from different witnesses (W1 and W2). D is tried for both crimes concurrently. The allegations are mutually supportive in that to the extent that W1's allegation that D committed current crime 1 is credible, an inference can be drawn that D committed CC2, and vice versa. The inference from CC1 to CC2 replicates the basic model (Figure 6.1) where the inference is from PC to CC.

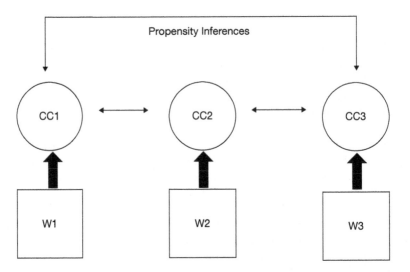

Figure 6.4 Propensity inferences in a case involving three allegations tried concurrently. Here, the case on each count is stronger than in Figure 6.3 as each gains force from two other allegations.

to be drawn, but because we will usually find the witness equally credible on all counts. Any shortfall in her credibility cannot be boosted via an allegation that suffers an equal shortfall in credibility. There are exceptions to this, however (Figure 6.5).[9]

---

[9] For a possible example, see *Maher* [1995] Crim LR 720.

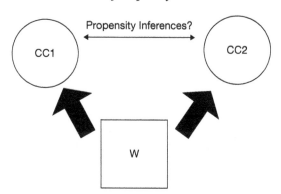

Figure 6.5 Same complainant propensity inferences. In a case where one witness alleges that D committed crimes on two occasions, we do not usually think in terms of a propensity inference. In the usual scenario, to the extent that W is a credible witness, she will be believed to a similar extent on both counts. She cannot corroborate herself. However, there may be some situations where a propensity inference between CC1 and CC2 is possible: if, for example, there were reasons to be especially sceptical of the allegation in relation to CC2 (perhaps W admits having been very drunk, and not remembering clearly what happened), a propensity inference from CC1 to CC2 would be possible. Also, if there was independent evidence to support CC1, a propensity inference could be drawn to CC2.

A final scenario is where D is associated with a suspicious pattern of events. *Smith*, where three of D's wives had drowned in the bath, is an example.[10] Another is *Makin*, where the Ds are associated with the dead bodies in the gardens of houses they have occupied. A less dramatic example is *Martin* v *Osborne*,[11] where D was convicted of operating a commercial vehicle without a licence. There was no direct evidence of him having been paid by his passengers, but the fact that he had made journeys between Ballarat and Melbourne on consecutive days, picking up and dropping off passengers en route, was sufficient to establish that he was operating for payment. These cases are similar to the cases involving multiple allegations. If one dead body is found in D's garden, that is suspicious; although there may be innocent explanations for it, it is still evidence of murder, rather like a single allegation of indecent assault made against a doctor.[12] The more bodies which are found, or the more allegations which are made, the more evidence there is that D has a propensity to commit sexual abuse or murder. The allegations,

---

[10] [1914–15] All ER 262. For a detailed account of the case, see J. Robins, *The Magnificent Spilsbury and the Case of the Brides in the Bath* (London: John Murray, 2010).

[11] (1936) 55 CLR 367.

[12] In a detailed analysis of the *Makin* decision, Cossins argues that the reasoning is 'circular': A. Cossins, 'The Legacy of the *Makin* Case 120 Years on: Legal Fictions, Circular Reasoning and Some Solutions' (2013) 35 *Sydney L Rev* 731. As the analysis here hopefully shows, this is false. This is not to deny Cossins's point that without evidence of cause of death (and given the possibility of death by disease), murder was a difficult charge to prove.

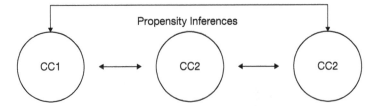

Figure 6.6 A suspicious pattern case, like *Smith*. The pattern of reasoning is very similar to that in Figure 6.4, except that there are no witnesses who make allegations to support each count. We should not make too much of that difference, though. In *Smith*, each incident is suspicious in itself, making it similar to an allegation of murder.

or the findings of the bodies, are mutually supportive (Figure 4). If none of the individual incidents is suspicious, their combination will not trigger an inference to guilt.

6.2 The Doctrine of Chances

As is well known, there is another way to think about cases such as *Smith* and *Makin*. In the United States, this way of thinking is termed the 'doctrine of chances';[13] in Australia, it is referred to as 'coincidence reasoning'.[14] The basic idea is that in *Smith* there are two explanations for the drownings: one is chance, or accident; the other is design, or murder. But the hypothesis that Smith was unlucky enough to have three wives drown in the bath by accident is sufficiently improbable that it can be rejected. We are thus left with the conclusion that Smith is a murderer. The reasoning here is rather like a process of hypothesis testing. If we want to know whether drug X cures disease Y, we compare X's performance to a placebo, where X and placebo are randomly distributed among Y-sufferers. If Y is relieved in more subjects who took X than who took a placebo, that does not necessarily mean that X is effective. The pattern may be due to chance. But, if the results are sufficiently unlikely to have occurred by chance, scientists may feel reasonably confident that X works. The usual scientific convention is that results will not be attributed to chance if the probability that they are due to chance is less than 0.05. In *Smith*, we seem intuitively to adopt something like this process. The three deaths being due to chance is so unlikely that we quickly reject that hypothesis and conclude that it is beyond reasonable doubt that they were murders.[15]

---

[13] See E. J. Imwinkelried, 'The Evolution of the Use of the Doctrine of Chances as Theory of Admissibility for Similar Fact Evidence' (1993) 22 *Anglo-Am L Rev* 73.

[14] See Evidence Act 1995 (Cth and NSW), s 98, which regulates the admissibility of 'coincidence' evidence; a separate provision, s 97, deals with 'tendency' evidence, although the admissibility test is expressed in the same terms.

[15] An argument found in the literature is that, taking *Makin* as an example, while the accumulation of bodies can show that the Makins were murderers, if we take one particular body, the accumulation cannot show that this one was murdered because the probability of accident in this

This pattern of reasoning is important for a number of reasons. As a matter of psychology, it is probably a better description of how people reason about a case such as *Smith* than is a process where each drowning is taken to be evidence of murder, each supporting the other by pointing to a propensity to murder by staged drowning. The intuitive process of reasoning in *Smith* is not intricate: we see a pattern and jump to the conclusion that there were three murders. Doctrine of chances, or 'coincidence' reasoning, is also said to be significant precisely because it avoids reasoning through propensity. The suggestion, then, is that it avoids 'forbidden reasoning', and so may be less problematic than other uses of character evidence.

A significant point about the doctrine of chances is that its scope of application is potentially quite wide. The parallel between the *Smith* model and the multiple allegations model (for example, the doctor cases) has already been drawn. We noted above that commentators sometimes talk about the improbability of similar lies, and courts too quite often rationalize such cases in terms of the doctrine of chances. A frequently quoted statement is that '[t]he rationale of similar fact evidence is that two or more people do not make up or mistakenly make similar allegations against the same person independently of each other';[16] each allegation is rather like finding another dead body in the garden. With sufficient allegations, we can reject the hypothesis of chance (ie that—ignoring the complicating factor of collusion—all the witnesses independently made up the allegations) and conclude that D has committed the crimes he is accused of committing. But we could also apply the doctrine of chances to the other models described above.[17] Indeed, it is sometimes claimed that the unlikelihood of coincidence is the foundation of all similar fact reasoning.[18] Where incriminating articles are concerned, it is

particular case remains the same as it was before we heard about the other bodies (see A. E. Acorn, 'Similar Fact Evidence and the Principle of Inductive Reasoning: Makin Sense' [1991] 11 OJLS 62, 81; and C. Tapper, 'Proof and Prejudice' in E. Campbell and L. Waller (eds), *Well and Truly Tried* (Sydney: Law Book Company, 1982). This also seems to be Cossins's point ('The Legacy of the *Makin* Case'). The reasoning appears to be along the lines that while tossing a coin and getting heads 20 times in a row is very unlikely, the probability of heads on each individual toss remains 0.5. This is a bad argument. The dead body we pick in *Makin* is not some randomly chosen death, but a body found on the premises of people who are very likely to be serial baby killers, where the probability of death by murder is far higher than that of death by accident. Similarly, in the coin analogy, if we conclude that the coin is biased or is being manipulated by the person tossing it, the probability of heads on a single throw is far higher than 0.5. Unfortunately, this confused analysis of the issue in *Makin* has now appeared in the case law: *Norris* [2009] EWCA Crim 2697; and discussion in M. Redmayne, 'Recognising Propensity' [2011] *Crim LR* 177. *Nicholson* [2012] 2 Cr App R 31, [2012] EWCA Crim 1568 revisits the *Norris* issue, but the discussion is so opaque it is hard to say how much of the reasoning in *Norris* is endorsed.

[16] *Ryder* (1994) 98 Cr App R 242, 250. See also *Brizzalari* [2004] EWCA Crim 310, [49]: 'where the prosecution witnesses are alleged to have made up their stories...the existence of common features may be more readily regarded as non-coincidental and therefore probative on the issue of lies than would be the case if identity were the issue. That is because the similar facts relied on are the making of similar allegations and not the events which are described in the allegations.'

[17] For other examples, see D. Hamer, 'The Structure and Strength of the Propensity Inference: Singularity, Linkage and the Other Evidence' (2003) 29 *Monash UL Rev* 137, 160.

[18] eg *Arp* [1988] 3 SCR 339, [44], [66], [72]. See also R. Nair, 'Weighing Similar Fact and Avoiding Prejudice' (1996) 112 *LQR* 262, 276–7.

often said that finding, for example, drug paraphernalia at the house of a person implicated in drug importation would be an odd coincidence if, as he claims, he was innocently involved.[19] It is then a small step to cases involving previous convictions: in *Dossett*, for example, a case where a previous conviction was used to support identification evidence, the trial judge asked the jury to consider 'the chances that Mr Ryan would mistakenly pick out from a line of nine males on an identification procedure the person who happened to have a previous conviction for robbery and ABH committed very close to the scene of the attack'.[20] The wide scope of doctrine of chances can be appreciated if we imagine that Smith had been convicted of two of the murders, whereupon it was discovered that he had previously been married to another woman who had died in the bath. The rejection of the chance hypothesis would still hold, and the conclusion of murder in the third case could still be reached without, it seems, propensity being involved, even in a case involving previous convictions.

It would, however, be wrong to conclude that propensity need play no role in similar fact cases. As a matter of intuitive psychology, the doctrine of chances model is most likely to be used by the fact-finder in a case like *Smith*. There, it is easy to think that there is no direct evidence that D has committed the crime, and that the only evidence is the improbability of three accidental drownings; additionally, that improbability is tiny. But even in *Makin*, there is a reasonable chance that the fact-finder will reason through propensity. The Makins were only charged with the murder of one child; the evidence of finding the other bodies was brought in to support that charge. The fact-finder might well have concluded that the evidence of the other bodies showed that the Makins were child killers, and then reasoned from this evidence of propensity to the conclusion that they had killed the victim in the actual case. Similarly, if Smith had been convicted of two of the deaths, there would then have been an obvious foundation for reasoning from that through propensity to a conclusion of murder in relation to the third death. And in cases involving multiple allegations, the fact-finder might well single out one complaint as especially compelling—perhaps because there is corroboration, or because the complainant seems very credible—and use this as a foundation for reasoning from propensity towards a conclusion of guilt in the other cases. As Hamer notes,[21] the potential reasoning processes are too fluid and unpredictable for it to be sensible to extend the doctrine of chances model much beyond cases like *Smith*.

There is a more fundamental reason to be sceptical of a non-propensity model of reasoning in similar fact cases. Assumptions about propensity play a role in all of the cases described above. The courts are quite fond of coincidence language, but when they describe the discovery of, say, drug paraphernalia as unlikely to be an innocent coincidence, they are not avoiding propensity. The coincidence is

---

[19] eg *Willis* (1979) unreported, quoted in *Peters* [1995] 2 Cr App R 77 at 81; *Lucas* [1995] Crim LR 400; *Groves* [1998] Crim LR 200; and *Yalman* [1998] 2 Cr App R 269.
[20] [2013] EWCA Crim 710, [33].
[21] Hamer, 'The Structure and Strength of the Propensity Inference'.

only suspicious because (on the assumption that drug use is more common among drug importers than among the general population) drug users have a propensity to import drugs. This is easy to see if we substitute some other coincidence: say that D shares a birthday with the drug courier he met at the airport. That would not be incriminating, because we do not assume that birth date is connected to drug dealing. In cases involving multiple allegations, the allegations only corroborate each other—they only prompt us to reject chance as an explanation—because we presume that someone who has, say, assaulted one woman has a propensity to assault others. Take away this connection and replace it with something anodyne, such as all the complainants having the same middle name, and there is no corroboration. The shared middle name might be immensely improbable—perhaps even more so than three accidental drownings—but we would tend to dismiss it as a strange but innocent coincidence because we cannot see any causal theory that would connect middle names to being a victim of crime.[22] Only if we thought that D might, for some strange reason, want to attack people with a particular middle name would it become significant; but that would just be because we would then have a propensity-based theory. Propensity, then, plays a role in 'probability of similar lies' cases. Unless we suppose that a person might have a propensity to repeat a certain type of behaviour, there will be no added value in the multiple allegations.[23]

From the foregoing, it should now be obvious that propensity plays a role in *Smith* itself. In *Smith*, we do not simply reject chance as an explanation. We conclude that design is more probable because Smith's having a propensity to murder by using a particular method is a more plausible explanation for the deaths than

[22] The improbability of coincidence can, though, prompt us to think hard about whether an odd psychological quirk might exist and thus might connect the crimes to a single perpetrator. For example, in *Sweeney* (CA 30 March 2000), D was charged with a series of burglaries. During more than one of these, the perpetrator had found a folder of the householder's photos and spread them out in order to look at them. On these facts, we are likely to conclude that the burglaries had the same perpetrator, one who takes a strange interest in the personal lives of his victims. A more difficult example is *Carroll* (1985) 19 A Crim R 410, where D was charged with the fetishistic murder of a young girl called Deidre. There was evidence that, around 10 years before the murder, he had suggested the same name for his own child. This may well be an innocent coincidence, and the appeal court was probably right to hold that this evidence should not have been admitted. But given the nature of the murder, one cannot rule out the possibility that the name had a particular significance for Carroll.

[23] This suggests why a comment sometimes made about the allegations in *Boardman* [1975] AC 421 is problematic. In *Boardman*, the complainants alleged that D had asked them to bugger him. The Court of Appeal thought that this detail—that Boardman wanted to play the 'passive' role—was significant, whereas the House of Lords was less impressed. Lord Cross, however, thought that it was the improbability of two false allegations sharing this detail that was significant: 'the point is not whether what the appellant is said to have suggested would be, as coming from a middle-aged active homosexual, in itself particularly unusual but whether it would be unlikely that two youths who were saying untruly that the appellant had made homosexual advances to them would have put such a suggestion into his mouth (460)'. The different perspectives, however, are just two sides of the same coin. Unless we think that a person would have a propensity to play the same role in different sexual encounters, then there is no corroboration to be had here. It may be true that this allegation is one that a youth would be unlikely to make up; but that just speaks to the credibility of the individual allegations, and does not mean that the repetition of this detail corroborates the accounts.

is chance. If we did not think that Smith, having drowned one wife, would be more likely than other people to drown another, then we would not see any significance in the pattern of deaths, just as we do not in the coincidences involving birthdays or middle names described above. There was perhaps a danger in using a medical hypothesis testing example to introduce doctrine of chances reasoning. It might suggest that there is a mechanism for rejecting chance as an explanation which concentrates simply on the improbability of chance. But the plausibility of alternative explanations should always play a role in our reasoning. If drug X is a homeopathic remedy, we would have no good reason to believe that it would be more effective than a placebo.[24] Even if the trial showed that it had an effect which was significant at the 0.05 level, we should be more reluctant to reject chance than if X was some drug for which where there was a pre-existing and reasonably plausible causal hypothesis as to why it should relieve Y. This was in part the problem in the case of Sally Clark.[25] Even assuming that the chances of two children dying of cot death were tiny, it was not safe to reject chance as an explanation for the deaths. The plausibility of the hypothesis that a mother would kill two of her children had to be assessed too.[26]

There may still be some differences between doctrine of chances reasoning and the basic type of propensity reasoning with which it is often contrasted. In the basic case D has a recent previous conviction for, say, burglary, and we start from an assumption that D has a propensity to commit burglary. In *Smith*, D's having a propensity to drown his wives is a hypothesis. While the hypothesis is confirmed when we reject chance, when we are deciding whether or not to do so it is not something we assume about Smith; it seems that all we have to do is to be prepared to posit it.

6.3 The Structure of the Propensity Inference: Comparative Propensity, Other Evidence, and Linkage

Having gained a clearer picture of the role of propensity in similar fact cases, we are now in a position to address other elements in the cases. Hamer has suggested that there are three principal sources of probative force in the cases: singularity, linkage, and other evidence.[27] His concept of singularity is covered by the key concept of comparative propensity, discussed above. In *Smith*, there is a high degree of singularity in the incidents: the drownings are similar to each other, and they seem to be a method of killing which very few people would use; likewise

---

[24] For a brief account, see B. Goldacre, *Bad Science* (London: Fourth Estate, 2008), ch 4.

[25] *Clark (Appeal Against Conviction No 2)* [2003] EWCA Crim 1020. See the discussion in Chapter 3.

[26] See A. P. Dawid, 'Bayes's Theorem and Weighing Evidence by Juries' in R. Swinburne (ed), *Bayes's Theorem* (Oxford: Oxford University Press, 2002), 75–8. Dawid suggests that the probability that a single child will be murdered in the first year of life is 0.00001.

[27] 'The Structure and Strength of the Propensity Inference'.

in *Straffen*. Where D is on trial for robbery, and he has a previous conviction for robbery, with no particular similarity in *modus operandi*, there is much less singularity; there is less again where he is on trial for theft and has a previous conviction for theft. But this is just to say that comparative propensity (the extent to which, if D has committed one crime, he is more likely than other people to commit a similar crime) varies between these examples. Apart from wanting to keep terminology simple, there is a slight advantage in referring to comparative propensity rather than singularity. The latter might suggest that a high degree of similarity is necessary for the propensity inference to work: it brings to mind the hallmark-type examples given in *Boardman* (graffito-writing burglars and the like).[28] But striking similarity is not a prerequisite for a propensity inference; even a previous conviction for theft might allow a propensity inference in a burglary case, albeit not a very strong one. Comparative propensity can also accommodate other factors, such as a tendency to commit crime with a particular co-offender or in a particular area.[29]

Linkage refers to the strength of the connection between D and the bad character evidence which forms the basis for the propensity inference.[30] Where D has a previous conviction for robbery, he is firmly linked to the bad character evidence; but where, as in *Clarke*,[31] incriminating items are found in his car, the link is not so strong. We cannot be sure that Clarke has committed a crime before, or even that he has planned to—the items might not be his (see Figure 6.7). This tends to weaken the propensity inference. Linkage also explains why the propensity inference is weaker in cases involving allegations rather than convictions.

Linkage also plays a role in cases where D is tried on more than one count. As shown in Figure 6.4, each allegation generates a propensity inference; the link between D and each count can vary. There might, for example, be eyewitness evidence of varying strength. Or the complainants might vary in terms of their credibility. An example of this can be found in the doctor cases, discussed in the previous chapter. Each allegation links D to a particular offence, but the link may be stronger or weaker, in that there may be more or less chance of the complainant being mistaken (or lying) about D's behaviour or sexual motivation. Thus, in *Carman*,[32] the Court of Appeal thought that allegations involving clitoral touching were stronger than ones involving the defendant pressing his groin against the patient during an examination; the latter behaviour was thought to be more likely to be innocent. The significance of linkage is that it will usually affect the strength of the propensity inference which can be drawn, because it makes us less sure that D has a comparative propensity to offend.

Linkage is a varied, but otherwise not particularly mysterious, factor in similar fact cases. The role of other evidence is even more straightforward. To return to

---

[28] See Chapter 5.
[29] This is well illustrated by *Dossett*, [2013] EWCA Crim 710, [18], where the prosecution argued that D had 'a propensity to commit robbery in conjunction with the co-accused and a propensity to attack older people in public places in that part of Basingstoke'.
[30] Hamer, 'The Structure and Strength of the Propensity Inference', 157.
[31] [1995] 2 Cr App R 425.   [32] [2004] EWCA Crim 540.

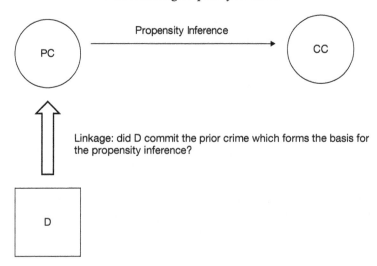

Figure 6.7 Linkage

the simplest case, where D is on trial for burglary and has a previous conviction for burglary, the amount of other evidence connecting him to the burglary for which he is on trial can vary. The more evidence there is, the stronger the case against him (see Figure 6.8).

This means that the propensity evidence needs to be less strong to justify a conviction. The other evidence does not affect the strength of the propensity inference; it is independent proof that the crime in question was committed. Contrast linkage, which does affect the strength of the propensity inference by making us less sure that D committed the misconduct which is the basis of the inference. Put another way, the other evidence speaks to sufficiency—the overall strength of the case against D—not admissibility. It is tempting to say, then, that the other evidence has nothing to do with propensity evidence, in the same way that the other evidence in a case has nothing to with any hearsay evidence which has been admitted. However, much thinking about propensity evidence presumes that the other evidence is connected to propensity and does affect admissibility. I explore this point below.

In a simple case, such as the one illustrated in Figures 6.7 and 6.8, linkage and other evidence operate independently. However, the relationship between the two factors is more complex in cases involving multiple counts tried together. Here, the same evidence provides both linkage and other evidence. In Figures 6.3 to 6.5, W1 alleges that D committed CC1, and W2 alleges that he committed CC2. Because propensity inferences are drawn from CC1 and CC2, linkage is a factor to bear in mind when considering the strength of propensity inference which can be drawn. The credibility of the allegation by each witness affects linkage. But the witness allegations can also be conceptualized as other evidence; even without a propensity inference from CC1, W2's allegation is evidence that CC2

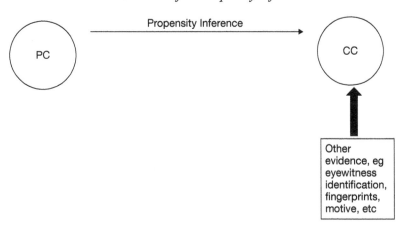

Figure 6.8 The role of the other evidence

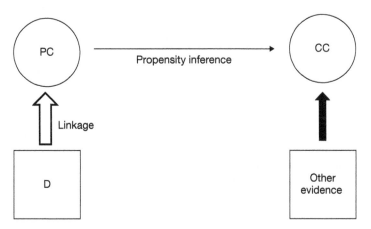

Figure 6.9 Interaction of factors. The stronger the propensity inference (which depends on both comparative propensity and linkage), the less other evidence needed to prove CC.

was committed. When the evidence between CC1 and CC2 is cross-admissible, the propensity inference from CC1 combines with the other evidence from W2 to make the case that CC2 was committed.

It should be obvious that the factors of comparative propensity, linkage, and other evidence interact. Where the propensity inference is strong (which usually depends on both linkage and the comparative propensity associated with the relevant misconduct), less other evidence will be needed to prove that D committed the crime charged (Figure 6.9).

Now that we have an idea of how propensity evidence works and of its relation to other factors, we can turn to a more complex issue which arose in the case law after *DPP* v *P*, concerning the way in which a jury should reason about propensity evidence in cases where identity is in issue. This will help to deepen our understanding of the way in which comparative propensity, linkage, and other evidence interact.

6.4 Identity Cases and the Sequence of Reasoning

In *McGranaghan*,[33] D was convicted of three burglary/rapes, committed within a two-year period in South West London and Surrey. There were connections between the crimes: the offender's sexual behaviour was similar; during two of the incidents he said that he could get 20 years for his behaviour; and each victim described the offender as having a particularly large penis and a Scottish accent. From this it may have been reasonable to conclude that the same person had committed all of the offences, and the prosecution certainly relied on this assumption. D spoke with a Scottish accent, and was picked out at identity parades by all three victims (although the identification procedures were not conducted well). There was also a small amount of circumstantial evidence connecting him to the crimes.

When *McGranaghan* came to the Court of Appeal, there was scientific evidence relating to blood type which made it unlikely that McGranaghan had committed one of the attacks. The same evidence provided some support for the contention that he had committed another of the attacks, but therefore undermined the theory that all had been committed by the same person. The Court of Appeal quashed all three convictions, in part because of the scientific evidence and in part for other reasons. In doing so, it made broader comments about the way in which juries should be instructed to approach evidence in similar cases. Only if the jury was sure that D had committed one of the crimes could it use that crime as propensity evidence that he had committed the others:

> An identification about which the jury are not sure cannot support another identification of which they are also not sure however similar the facts of the two offences may be. The similar facts go to show that the same man committed both offences not that the defendant was that man. There must be some evidence to make the jury sure that on at least one offence the defendant was that man.[34]

This has been described as a 'sequential' approach to identification in propensity cases.[35] Without a convincing case that D committed one of the crimes, the propensity inference cannot be engaged at all. But once it is accepted that D committed one of the crimes, the jury can proceed to consider another, combining a propensity inference from the first crime with any identity evidence connecting D to the other. And so on.

---

[33] [1995] 1 Cr App R 559. For a narrative account of the case, see B. Woffinden, *Hanratty: The Final Verdict* (London: MacMillan, 1999), appendix 1.
[34] *McGranaghan*, [1995] 1 Cr App R 559, 573.
[35] See R. Pattenden, 'Similar Fact Evidence and Proof of Identity' (1996) 112 *LQR* 446.

The Court of Appeal quickly backed away from the sequential approach, endorsing a 'pooling' approach in later cases, whereby the identity evidence on each count could be combined via the interconnecting propensity inference in order to prove that D committed one or more of the crimes, even if the jury could not be sure that he had committed one of them in isolation. *Downey* is an example of this approach.[36] Two petrol station robberies occurred within 15 minutes of each other. The petrol stations were three miles apart, and the robberies shared a similar technique. Here, there was a strong case that the crimes had been committed by the same person; they were 'welded together'.[37] Unsurprisingly, the Court of Appeal held that the identification evidence on the two counts could be combined in order to prove that D had committed the offences.

There is no doubt that the pooling approach is correct. This is obvious in *Downey*. If the crimes are 'welded' together, the identity evidence is mutually supportive just as if there were two witnesses to a single crime. Given that in *McGranaghan* the prosecution proceeded on the basis that the crimes had a single perpetrator, a pooling approach would in theory have been appropriate in that case too. But how far can this approach be taken? *Downey* and the later decision of *Barnes*[38] appear to confine pooling to cases where it is accepted that the same person committed all of the crimes, and the question is who committed them. But the work done by the propensity inference means that the pooling approach is not confined in this way. Figures 6.3 and 6.4 show how the propensity inference works in cases involving multiple counts. We approached those examples by thinking in terms of cases where identity is not in issue, but several complainants allege that D has, for example, indecently assaulted them (as in the doctor cases). D then denies the behaviour but does not deny having met the complainants. The structure of inference is exactly the same, however, where identity is in issue: figure 6.4 perfectly captures the basic inferential structure of a case like *McGranaghan*. In both situations, the complainants/witnesses are claiming that D assaulted them. Because a propensity inference flows between all counts, to the extent that W1 is credible we have evidence that D committed CC2 as well as CC1. And vice versa, with regard to W2. In this way, the evidence of W2 and W3 supports that of W1. In deciding whether D committed CC1, then, it is perfectly appropriate to pool the evidence relating to the other crimes.

John W[39] is a good illustration of this process (see Figure 6.10). D was tried for two attacks on women which bore some similarities, but it probably was not possible to conclude, merely on the basis of the details of the attacks, that the same person had committed both. Nevertheless, there was identification and circumstantial evidence linking D to both crimes. Although it is not clear whether the Court of Appeal endorsed pooling,[40] pooling would have been appropriate.

[36] [1995] 1 Cr App R 547.   [37] *Downey*, 552.   [38] [1995] 2 Cr App R 491.
[39] [1998] 2 Cr App R 289.
[40] The reasoning on this point is not very clear: see *John W* at 304–5. It seems that a pooling approach would have been allowed had the jury concluded, on the basis of the similarities, that both attacks were committed by the same person. Pattenden implies that a pooling approach is only possible on such a basis ('Similar Fact Evidence').

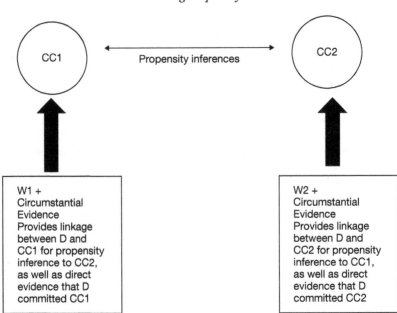

Figure 6.10 *John W*

If the jury was not convinced that D had committed CC1, it could use the evidence linking him to CC2 to show that there was some probability that he had a propensity to attack women, which might then persuade them of his guilt. And vice versa in respect of CC2. This is because linkage licenses a propensity inference. Note that in this scenario, linkage to CC2 supports a propensity inference towards CC1; the same evidence providing linkage is also other evidence, providing direct proof that D committed CC1.[41]

McGranaghan is certainly a disturbing case, so it is worth digressing slightly to say more about it. The crimes were sufficiently similar that, on the original evidence, it does seem reasonable to have concluded that they were all committed by the same person. In each case, McGranaghan was identified as the perpetrator by a witness. Yet the scientific evidence suggests that the crimes were not committed by the same person, and in particular that the two crimes where the attacker had said he could 'get 20 years' for his behaviour were committed by different people. Is *McGranaghan*, then, an illustration of the dangers of bad character evidence? It might be argued that we are too ready, on the basis of something like

---

[41] It should be noted that double-counting must be avoided. Evidence linking D to CC2 supports, via a propensity inference, the other evidence connecting D to CC1. This may convince the jury that D committed CC1. But when using a propensity inference from CC1 to support the other evidence connecting D to CC2, the propensity inference must not be boosted beyond being as strong as it would be before CC2 was used to support CC1. Otherwise, CC2 would be supporting itself. In terms of Figure 6.10, a way to put this would be that probative value can only travel along each arrow once.

the '20 years' comment, to conclude that the same person committed both crimes (a danger discussed in Chapter 3). My intuition—and I am aware that in voicing it, I may be illustrating the very danger just alluded to—is that this shared detail between the crimes is very significant, and that it is not easy to put it down to coincidence. One possibility is that the police manipulated one of the witnesses; another is that the scientific evidence is misleading. I find these more likely possibilities than that there were two people committing similar serious crimes, both telling their victims that they could 'get 20 years' for their attacks. No doubt this aspect of the case will remain a mystery. The other point to make about *McGranaghan* is that, as other commentators have noted, it may tell us as much about the dangers of eyewitness evidence as it does about the problems of propensity evidence.[42] In particular, we should be aware that while the evidence from the witnesses is mutually supportive, W2's and W3's identifications of McGranaghan may not add as much to the case against him as might first appear. This is not only because the identification procedures were not well conducted, but also because once McGranaghan has been identified by the first witness, it becomes reasonable to presume that if he is innocent he looks quite like the real culprit(s). And this becomes even more likely after a second identification. Thus, adding more identifications does not, on the whole, add as much to the case against him as adding another allegation does in the doctor cases, because new identifications confirm the prosecution theory (D is the culprit) and defence theory (D looks like the culprit) to an equal extent. In the final analysis, then, this feature of the case might lend some support to a sequential approach to propensity evidence on facts similar to those in *McGranaghan*.[43] A sequential approach would help to guard against the danger that the fact-finder will over-estimate the value of multiple identifications (although so might careful judicial instruction).

This is a convenient point to say something about collusion. Just as the identifications by the witnesses in *McGranaghan* can be explained by D's looking like the culprit, so multiple allegations can be explained by the complainants having put their heads together to concoct a story. To the extent that collusion is credible, the propensity inference is weaker because linkage is weaker (in the same way that any evidence that a complainant is lying weakens the inference). But unlike in *McGranaghan*, adding a new allegation may strengthen the case significantly, unless there is reason to think that the new complainant has colluded with the others.

Now that we have a basic understanding of the workings of the propensity inference, and its interaction with linkage and the other evidence, we can turn to another aspect of the analysis in Chapter 5, and assess the various admissibility tests developed by the courts prior to the introduction of the Criminal Justice Act 2003.

---

[42] Hamer, 'The Structure and Strength of the Propensity Inference', 171; and Pattenden, 'Similar Fact Evidence', 462–3.

[43] See the judgment, [1995] 1 Cr App R 559, at 574.

6.5 Categories

The categories approach which was developed in the early case law and endorsed in *Makin* continued to have some influence right up until the introduction of the 2003 Act, despite the fact that it had been sidelined by *Boardman*. We noted that one reason for the appeal of the test was that it seemed to provide judges with a reasonably determinate rule. Rather than making difficult judgments about probative value, judges could simply see if the case before them fitted a pre-established category. There is more to the appeal of the categories than this, though: the categories approach would not have had the longevity which it did had it not, at least sometimes, operated reasonably well by admitting probative bad character evidence. That it should have done so is, at first sight, puzzling. Taking the categories listed by Cross[44]—rebutting a defence of accident or involuntary conduct, rebutting the accused's plea of ignorance or mistake of fact; rebutting an innocent explanation of a particular act or of the possession of incriminating material; proving identity; and rebutting a defence of innocent association—one is prompted to ask: why should the fact that propensity evidence is being used for one of these purposes make any difference to its admissibility? The admissibility of other types of evidence, such as hearsay, eyewitness, or confession evidence, is not conditioned on a list of this sort. We should note, though, that most of the categories involve, in a loose sense, the rebuttal of a defence, and that the 'defences' generally involve D arguing that, while he is enmeshed in suspicious circumstances, he lacks criminal intent: they are 'confession and avoidance' defences. This suggests that there will be significant other evidence in the case.[45] In other words, the propensity evidence will have a limited and defined role to play and will not be asked to do too much work. The exception to this is the category 'proving identity'. In fact, Cross divides this category into two. In some cases, the propensity evidence will still be asked to play only a limited role, because it will back up testimonial evidence that D committed the crime. In other cases, the evidence will be asked to do more, but the examples given by Cross are of cases like *Straffen*,[46] where there is a very high comparative propensity; despite the relative lack of other evidence,[47] then, the propensity evidence is strong enough to do the work by itself.

The foregoing suggests why the categories approach works reasonably well. However, while it may help to ensure that, except in 'hallmark' cases like *Straffen*, propensity evidence is only asked to play a limited probative role, the categories approach is under-inclusive in this regard. Propensity evidence which does not

[44] R. Cross, *Evidence* (5th edn, London: Butterworths, 1979), 378–93.
[45] As astute commentators noted: see L. H. Hoffmann, 'Similar Facts after Boardman' (1975) 91 *LQR* 193, 201: the categories 'rather crudely...draw attention to the vital importance of the *other* evidence in the case'.
[46] [1952] 2 QB 911.
[47] In fact, the other evidence in *Straffen* was quite strong. Straffen was known to be in the (rural) area at the time, and he admitted having seen the victim, which put him in a limited pool of people who could have committed the crime.

fit into one of the categories may still be playing only a limited role because it is backed up by other evidence. Cross's category of proving identity illustrates the probative structure here: in the cases where propensity evidence is being used to support testimonial evidence of identity, the propensity evidence is playing a corroborative role rather than having to prove the issue by itself. But in Cross's list, this rather ad hoc category is limited to cases where identity is the issue, which means that if propensity evidence is used to prove some other fact it will be inadmissible even if there is supporting testimonial evidence. *Lewis* provides a good example.[48] There, when D denied indecent behaviour while drying his partner's children after a bath, propensity evidence was admissible because it fitted the category of rebutting an innocent explanation. The propensity evidence could not, though, be used to prove the allegation that on another occasion he had masturbated in front of the children, because there was no corresponding category—this despite the fact that there was supporting evidence from three witnesses. Once one grasps that the categories approach works, to the extent that it does, by limiting the probative demands placed on the propensity evidence, this makes no sense.

The categories approach as derived from *Makin* has few if any supporters in England and Wales today. Nevertheless, the view that propensity evidence might be admissible for some purposes but not for others has its defenders. For example, Amarasekara and Bagaric suggest that propensity evidence 'is most probative where the *actus reus* is not in dispute and the only fact in issue is the *mens rea* or identity'.[49] For Lippke, the class of case where propensity evidence has most value is narrower; he excludes identity cases.[50] While there is considerable confusion in the way in which these authors present their arguments, these approaches share a core of good sense with the categories approach, because they identify situations where there will usually be other evidence to support the charge. But, while this

---

[48] (1983) 76 Cr App R 33.

[49] K. Amarasekara and M. Bagaric, 'The Prejudice against Similar Fact Evidence' (2001) 5 *E & P* 71, 93.

[50] R. Lippke, 'Criminal Record, Character Evidence, and the Criminal Trial' (2008) 14 *Legal Theory* 167. (See also C. R. Williams, 'Approaches to Similar Fact Evidence: England and Australia' in P. Mirfield and R. Smith (eds), *Essays for Colin Tapper* (Oxford: Oxford University Press, 2003), 23, 39–40; and Cossins, 'The Legacy of the *Makin* Case'.) Lippke argues that knowing 'that the defendant is the kind of person who would commit the crime in question if given the opportunity tells us nothing about whether she is the person who committed the crime *in this case*. There may have been numerous individuals in the vicinity of the crime about whom it is true that they would have committed the crime if given the opportunity' (181–2). It is hard to see why the existence of other people with the same bad character means that the character evidence against D has no probative value. Would we say that the fact that another person in the area might look similar to D (or even the existence of an identical twin) negates the value of eyewitness evidence? These factors should simply be factored into an assessment of probative value, and in the case of character, comparative propensity achieves this. Of course, there may be cases with particular facts where things are more complicated: if there was a prison break on the night of the crime, putting many people with similar criminal records to D in the vicinity of the crime at the relevant time, this will mean that the case against D is less strong than it might otherwise be. One way to think about this would be to view the comparative propensity calculation as comparing D not with the general population, but with the specific population who had access to the crime scene.

sort of approach might offer a very rough rule of thumb, it is plainly inadequate, as the example of the masturbation incident in *Lewis* shows. Further, that these commentators do not agree on the breadth of the class where propensity evidence has a decent claim to be admitted points to the arbitrariness of such approaches.

6.6 Striking Similarity

In the standard history, *Boardman* replaced the categories approach with one based on striking similarity. Similarity seems to be a rough measure of probative value: the more similar two crimes are, the more likely it is that they were committed by the same person, or, in a case of multiple allegations, the more likely that they were committed at all. The qualifier 'striking' suggests that very high comparative propensity is necessary (recall the illustrative examples used in *Boardman*). In one sense, the shift to a focus on something like probative value is an improvement on the categories approach. But there is also a sense in which the striking similarity test is less helpful than the categories: viewed in the abstract, it does not manage to incorporate any measure of the strength of the other evidence. Given the vagueness of 'striking', this was perhaps not always a problem in practice. In a weak case, a judge might always say that similarity was insufficiently striking. But problems do emerge if we focus on reasonably strong cases. In the cases involving multiple allegations which led to pressure to revisit *Boardman*, there would often be little similarity beyond the level of crime category; yet the other evidence, in the form of allegations by victims, was reasonably strong—it would usually be enough by itself to justify letting each case go to the jury even if they were tried separately. And this is why in *P* Lord Mackay was keen to do away with the need for striking similarity. As we saw, though, in many cases after *P* there continued to be an emphasis on the need for some degree of similarity.

There are further difficulties with tests based on similarity and striking similarity. Similarity is an extremely vague concept. An elephant and Beethoven's ninth symphony are objects which are about as different as it is possible to imagine, yet they still have some degree of similarity in that they both inhabit our universe. Any two crimes will of course share far more similarity than this: theft and sexual assault are similar simply by virtue of being crimes and, given what we know about the generality of deviance, they are also linked at a less conventional level. In practice, of course, 'similarity' is not radically indeterminate. Like other context-sensitive words, a shared understanding of the context in which it is being used allows us to talk about similarity without too much difficulty.[51] When it comes to a similarity test for the admissibility of propensity evidence, we have already seen that a degree of vagueness has some advantage, because it allows a court to take the other evidence into account. At the same time, flexibility was

---

[51] See, eg, J. Stanley, 'Semantics in Context' in G. Preyer and G. Peter (eds), *Contextualism in Philosophy: Knowledge, Meaning, and Truth* (Oxford: Clarendon Press, 2005).

limited in practice: no judge would hold theft and sexual assault to be similar, nor even burglary and burglary. 'Similarity' appeared to require something more than similarity at the level of crime category. But viewed through the lens of comparative propensity, this is problematic. Because some crimes are rarer than others, they will have higher levels of comparative propensity. We might think that burglary is not similar enough to burglary to justify admissibility without some similarity in *modus operandi*; but why should murder, which presumably has a much higher comparative propensity, not be admissible to prove murder without links at the level of *modus operandi*? A good illustration of the problem here is Williams's response to *John W*,[52] in which, shortly after *P*, the Court of Appeal admitted propensity evidence to prove identity without requiring striking similarity. Williams's complaint is that both incidents 'involved sexual attacks which were in no way unusual'.[53] Thankfully, though, sexual attacks of the sort involved in *John W*, where a potential victim is grabbed in public, are quite rare. What Williams presumably means is that the offences were not unusual for sexual attacks. But why on earth should that be significant? The insistence that there be more similarity might make sense were the crime a rather more common one, such as shoplifting, but it is especially puzzling given that in *John W* there was other evidence connecting D to the attacks.

A further problem in taking crime category to be significant is that crimes vary in their specificity in terms of how they are drafted. The trend in the modern criminal law has been towards broadly defined offences, but there are exceptions, as well as some older, more particularistic offences which remain on the statute books. Assaulting a clergyman in the discharge of his duty is an example of the latter;[54] racially aggravated assault is an example of the former.[55] It may be that similarity-based analyses would admit that such crimes are sufficiently similar to each other to license admissibility. This concession, though, would surely raise more questions about why other crimes, such as the assaults in *John W*, should not be regarded as similar to each other. I shall return to this point in the discussion of general and specific propensity, below, where the criticism bites deeper.

The point made in the last two paragraphs is that if our starting point for thinking about similarity is crime categories, and we thus demand something more than similarity in offences as they are defined by the criminal law, admissibility will not track comparative propensity, which is the concept which should really be doing the work. There is another way in which the search for similarity can lead us away from comparative propensity. In *Carman*,[56] one of the cases involving allegations of sexual assault against a doctor, the trial judge had proceeded by

[52] [1998] 2 Cr App R 289.
[53] Williams, 'Approaches to Similar Fact Evidence', 39. See also Williams's earlier comments on *Armstrong* [1922] 2 KB 555: 'The evidence...showed no more than that the accused had a propensity for murder by poisoning. Such a propensity is not sufficiently unusual to render the evidence admissible.' C. R. Williams, 'The Problem of Similar Fact Evidence' (1979) 5 *Dalhousie LJ* 281, 335.
[54] Offences Against the Person Act 1861, s 36.
[55] Crime and Disorder Act 1998, s 29.
[56] [2004] EWCA Crim 540. Cf *Litchfield* (1994) 86 CCC (3d) 97.

placing the allegations in groups involving relatively similar forms of behaviour. Allegations of one type—such as the doctor pressing his groin against a patient during an examination—were held not to be admissible to support allegations of another type, such as inappropriate touching during a vaginal examination. It is not obvious that the similarities thought to be important here are in fact significant. The underlying propensity is one to sexually assault patients, and there is little reason why someone who sexually assaults their patients should be more likely to do it in one particular way than another; especially given that different patients will present different opportunities for the doctor's straying hands. The general point is that unless we think that there is a reason why a person should tend to use the same *modus operandi*, similarities in *modus operandi* will not be significant.[57] The emphasis on similarity can prompt us to focus on insignificant similarities; we saw some more general examples of this in the discussion of striking similarity in the previous chapter.

6.7 Forbidden Reasoning

If *Boardman* introduced a test of striking similarity, it also lent weight to a test that had played a role in the earlier law: the forbidden reasoning approach, which asked whether the bad character evidence was being used to prove propensity ('forbidden reasoning'), or whether it was being used for some other reason. This often overlapped with the categories approach, because by describing the evidence in terms of its probative purpose, such as the purpose of rebutting a defence, it could be made to look as if the evidence was being used to do something other than show that the defendant had a propensity to commit crime. The principal criticism of this approach emerged in the preceding chapter and in the earlier discussion in this one: the reasoning in similar fact cases nearly always involves reasoning through propensity. The reasoning can of course be redescribed in other terms, but this does not change the nature of the reasoning; and if the justification for singling out propensity reasoning is that jurors may give too much weight to propensity, then redescription of the reasoning process does not eliminate this danger. Worse still, jurors were often instructed to avoid propensity reasoning. Judicial instructions on the law of evidence are often criticized for asking jurors to perform 'mental gymnastics', but at least gymnastics are possible without suspension of the laws of physics. It was usually impossible for jurors to use the bad character evidence without relying on propensity; the law's implication of jurors in its own failure to understand the reasoning process involved in character evidence—or failure to be honest about it—is one of the sorrier episodes in the law of evidence.

It is true that not all bad character evidence involves propensity reasoning. There are fairly well-known examples where propensity reasoning plays no significant

---

[57] See also the point about *Boardman*, made at n 23 above.

role. One is provided by Williams: D is on trial for burgling two houses, and goods stolen from the first house are found left in the second.[58] Here, finding the goods makes it likely that whoever burgled the first house burgled the second, and so evidence connecting D to one burglary also links him to the second. Another example is where bad character evidence is used to prove knowledge: D's conviction for safe-cracking might show that he knows how to crack a safe.[59] But these fact patterns are quite unusual. It is also not obvious that the fact that there is a route to a conclusion of guilt which does not rely on propensity should make a difference to whether or not we admit or exclude the evidence[60]—there might still be some potential for prejudice here.

Apart from cases like the burglary example just considered, there are the doctrine of chances cases. We have seen that, while it is difficult to classify cases, some—*Smith* being the prime example—do seem to involve doctrine of chances reasoning. However, I argued above that propensity plays a role in doctrine of chances cases. Unless it is plausible that someone who murders one wife should want to murder other wives, then we will not conclude that he did. While propensity plays a different role here than it does in the simple case where D has a previous conviction, being posited as a hypothesis to be confirmed rather than an assumed starting point, this is probably not significant when it comes to deciding whether or not to admit the evidence. If the concern is that jurors will put too much weight on propensity, then this could lead to problems in a doctrine of chances scenario as much as in a case involving a previous conviction. A juror who thinks that someone who murders one wife is very likely to kill another will conclude that *Smith* is a triple murderer rather more quickly than someone who thinks that serial murders of wives are much less common.[61] In the same way, after throwing six on a dice five times in a row, you will be more likely to conclude that dice is biased if you drew it from a bag in which 10 per cent of the dice are known to be biased than if it is one just bought from a shop. That weighs against classifying cases like *Smith* as being ones which do not involve forbidden reasoning.

---

[58] 'Approaches to Similar Fact Evidence', 23.

[59] Cf R. B. Kuhns, 'The Propensity to Misunderstand the Character of Specific Acts Evidence' (1981) 66 *Iowa L Rev* 777, 790–1. Kuhns argues that there is a propensity inference involved in the knowledge example, because a propensity to retain knowledge is involved. This is obviously right, but seems to me to stretch the idea of propensity too far beyond paradigm cases of behaviour (would we want to say that identification evidence involves a propensity inference because it assumes that people have a propensity to look the same at T2 as they did at T1?).

[60] See A. A. S. Zuckerman, 'Similar Fact Evidence: The Unobservable Rule' (1987) 104 *LQR* 187, 191.

[61] There is a puzzle here. If you think that serial uxoricide is common, then comparative propensity is lower than if you think it rare. So why is the case against *Smith* more compelling in the former case? The answer lies in linkage. If Smith was not the only person who had the opportunity to kill his wives, then we might conclude that there had been three murders, but be less sure about attributing the murders to Smith—the more so if Smith lived in a town where bath-drowning murder was common. But in the actual case the strong linkage to Smith makes it implausible that anyone else committed the murders, so we conclude Smith is guilty and would do so even if he lived in a town where bath-drowning murder was common.

6.8 Probative Value Versus Prejudicial Effect

On one level, there can be no criticism of a test for admissibility of propensity evidence which weighs probative value against prejudicial effect. That evidence should not be admitted unless its probative value outweighs its prejudicial impact is surely a key principle of evidence law and could be said to be the basic admissibility test for any evidence. However, what is noticeable about the PV/PE test is how seldom it was used by judges. As we saw, after *P* very few judgments relied on the test by itself; the reasoning in the cases was nearly always dominated by one of the other admissibility tests. Some would argue that this is not surprising, because the PV/PE test is in fact flawed. The argument is that probative value and prejudicial effect are incommensurables which cannot be weighed against each other;[62] indeed, courts have sometimes made this point.[63]

At a theoretical level, this criticism of the PV/PE test is misplaced. Probative value and prejudicial effect may be rather different from each other, but once they are placed in the context of a common value, it is not hard to see how, in theory, they can be weighed against each other. The obvious common value which provides a framework here is the accuracy of fact-finding. We can ask: if this propensity evidence is introduced, is it likely, overall, to increase or decrease the accuracy of the verdict? Because propensity evidence often has some legitimate probative value, it can increase the accuracy of fact-finding. However, if the fact-finder is likely to give it far too much weight, be distracted by it, or convict the accused with little regard to the evidence, it might decrease fact-finding accuracy. It is true that, in practice, it may be difficult to apply this analysis to a particular piece of propensity evidence.[64] And while PV/PE can be said to be the governing principle of evidence law, it is notable that we tend not to use it as the test for admissibility of various problematic types of evidence such as eyewitness identifications, confessions, and hearsay. It may be, then, that in practice some more structured test is needed to govern the admissibility of propensity evidence. But if so, surely the way to structure the test is in terms of the key issues of comparative propensity, linkage, other evidence, and potential prejudice.

In addition to the difficulty of applying it in practice, there is a further reason why a test based on an assessment of probative value and prejudicial effect might not place the law on a rational basis. This is that judges—and indeed commentators—have not always proved very able at analysing the basic ingredient of probative value or relevance. Writing soon after *Boardman*, Hoffmann

---

[62] Zuckerman, 'Similar Fact Evidence', 196.

[63] In *R v T* (aka *R v M*) [2001] EWCA Crim 3014, at [72], the Court of Appeal 'recognis[ed] that there is an intellectual difficulty in balancing the probative force of the evidence against the prejudice that its commission would engender'.

[64] This was the Law Commission's principal criticism of PV/PE: *Evidence in Criminal Proceedings: Previous Misconduct of a Defendant*, LCCP No 141 (London: HMSO, 1996), 166–7; and *Evidence of Bad Character in Criminal Proceedings*, Law Com No 273, Cm 5257 (London: TSO, 2001), 50–1, 95.

hailed that decision as an 'intellectual breakthrough', because, as he read it, it emphasized that 'whether similar fact evidence was admissible or not depended simply and solely upon its probative strength, and whether it had sufficient strength was in each case a question of degree'.[65] But there are some rather odd views about relevance to be found in *Boardman*. Thus, Lord Hailsham suggested that 'when there is nothing to connect the accused with a particular crime except bad character or similar crimes committed in the past, the probative value of the evidence is nil and the evidence is rejected on that ground'. But '[w]hen there is some evidence connecting the accused with the crime, in the eyes of most people, guilt of similar offences in the past might well be considered to have probative value'.[66] And for Lord Salmon, in a burglary case evidence that D had a long series of convictions for burglary 'would show nothing from which a reasonable jury could infer anything except bad character and a disposition to burgle... [I]t could not reasonably be regarded as evidence that [D] was the burglar'.[67] In fact, Hoffmann himself, while emphasizing that relevance is the key to admissibility, seems to share these views about relevance. Commenting on *Ball*,[68] a case in which evidence that the defendants had previously committed incest was used to show that their present living arrangements—sharing a house where only one bedroom was in use—were not innocent, he suggested that the evidence was 'highly relevant because it dispelled any doubt'[69] as to the Balls' guilt. But what, he asks, if the police had found that two bedrooms were in use in the house? Then the bad character evidence would have been inadmissible: 'it was the evidence of the bedroom... which made the similar fact evidence sufficiently relevant to be admissible'.[70] This analysis of *Ball* has been very influential.[71]

On the face of it, these views about relevance are odd. As the courts now recognize, the burglary convictions referred to by Lord Salmon are probative of the fact that D has committed the present burglary. In the same way, that the Balls have previously committed incest is evidence that they are doing so now, in that it increases the probability that they are. It does not matter what other evidence there is in the case; the discovery that a single bedroom is in use does not affect the probative value of the bad character evidence. While there are situations where one piece of evidence affects the probative value of another[72]—evidence that D wears glasses is irrelevant until a witness states that the culprit wore glasses;

---

[65] 'Similar Facts after Boardman', 193.   [66] *Boardman* [1975] AC 421, 451.
[67] *Boardman* [1975] AC 421, 462. Other examples of this sort of thinking in the case law are *Thompson* [1918] AC 221 and *Kenyon* [2004] EWCA Crim 821, [19], [21].
[68] [1911] AC 47.   [69] 'Similar Facts after Boardman', 202.
[70] 'Similar Facts after Boardman', 202.
[71] See I. H. Dennis, *The Law of Evidence* (London: Sweet & Maxwell, 2007), 63–4 (cf 756); D. W. Elliott, 'The Young Person's Guide to Similar Fact Evidence—I' [1983] *Crim LR* 284, 295; and Williams, 'The Problem of Similar Fact Evidence', 303. See also D. K. Piragoff, *Similar Fact Evidence* (Toronto: Carswell, 1981), 144: 'the other evidence effect[s] the degree of relevancy of the inferential link flowing from the similar fact evidence to the fact in issue...'.
[72] A good general account of evidential interactions is D. Schum, 'Evidence and Inferences about Past Events: An Overview of Six Case Studies' in W. Twining and I. Hampsher-Monk (eds), *Evidence and Inference in History and Law: Interdisciplinary Dialogues* (Evanston, IL: Northwestern University Press, 2003), 22–6.

evidence that a witness has a motive to lie decreases the value of her evidence—the propensity evidence examples are not situations of this sort. Nevertheless, the view expressed by Hailsham, Salmon, and Hoffmann must have intuitive appeal. One explanation for this concerns the pragmatics of the word 'evidence'; we tend not to say that E is evidence for P where E's addition to our corpus of information will not leave E looking reasonably likely. So we do not say that the fact that I am about to step into an elevator is evidence that I will die in an elevator, nor that it is relevant to whether or not I will, even though it slightly increases the probability that I will die in an elevator.[73] But if we also had information that one of the elevator's cables was frayed, or that I had just been poisoned, we might do. Thus, in Lord Salmon's example, it is right that there is something odd about saying that D's previous convictions for burglary are evidence that he burgled my house last night when there is no other reason to suspect him; but we should not let pragmatics affect our views of what is and is not relevant. Any relevant evidence, no matter how small its probative value, has a claim to be admitted. Together, a number of slight pieces of evidence may add up to a convincing case. Saying that each is not evidence until it is placed alongside the others only obscures things.

One consequence of the way in which relevance was analysed in *Boardman*, and in other cases, was that a shift away from the categories tended to replicate the categories in a different guise. To say that previous convictions are irrelevant and therefore inadmissible when there is no other evidence to connect D to the crime charged is similar to saying that previous convictions are irrelevant until a category—such as accident, or innocent association—is activated.[74] This, then, is

[73] The elevator example is taken from P. Achinstein, *The Book of Evidence* (New York: Oxford University Press, 2001). Achinstein uses the example to illustrate a normative fact about evidence: on his theory, E is only evidence for H when it increases the probability of H above 0.5. A pragmatic interpretation of the phenomenon, which I find more convincing, is elaborated in P. Maher, 'Subjective and Objective Confirmation' (1996) 63 *Philosophy of Science* 149; cf P. Achinstein, 'Swimming in Evidence: A Reply to Maher' (1996) 63 *Philosophy of Science* 175. A slightly different argument against the probabilistic view of evidence on which I am relying is developed by Davis and Follette, who argue that evidence that D is having an extra-marital affair is irrelevant to the question of whether he murdered his wife unless there is a good amount of other evidence to support the claim. See D. Davis and W. Follette, 'Rethinking the Probative Value of Evidence: Base Rates, Intuitive Profiling, and the "Postdiction" of Behavior' (2002) 26 *Law & Human Behavior* 133 and 'Towards an Empirical Approach to Evidentiary Ruling' (2003) 27 *Law & Human Behavior* 661; cf R. D. Friedman and R. Park, 'Sometimes What Everybody Thinks They Know Is True' (2003) 27 *Law & Human Behavior* 629; and D. Kaye and J. Koehler, 'The Misquantification of Probative Value' (2003) 27 *Law & Human Behavior* 645. Davis and Follette's thinking seems to be influenced by the fact that when we measure the impact of evidence in terms of the finite scale between 0 and 1, its impact appears to be muted when we have a very small or very large starting point. For example, if men having extra-marital affairs are three times more likely to murder their wives than men who are not, a prior probability of guilt of 0.01 increases to 0.03 when we introduce this evidence, but a prior of 0.5 increases to 0.75, which looks to be a more significant increase. However, in both cases the odds are increased threefold, so the appearance of variation in probative value is something of an illusion. For clear illustrations, see G. Wells, 'Murder, Extramarital Affairs, and the Issue of Probative Value' (2003) 27 *Law & Human Behavior* 623.

[74] This merging of the categories and an analysis of probative value can be observed in various cases involving drug possession. For example, in *Willis*, discovery of heroin at the defendant's home '[i]n the ordinary way...would not have been relevant, but in this case...it became relevant because she was denying any knowledge of the heroin in her handbag and in her green case' ((1979), unreported, quoted in *Peters*, [1995] 2 Cr App R 77, at 81). In *Guney* [1998] 2 Cr App R 242 at 226,

a further reason why *Boardman* and *P*, while rethinking doctrine, often seemed to have little effect in practice.

While the foregoing identifies a common misunderstanding about probative value, we should not be too quick to criticize. Just as the categories approach works, insofar as it does, by incorporating a measure of the other evidence, so does the 'contextual' view of relevance found in the views described above. In this way, the contextual view might be said to help protect defendants from conviction on less than proof beyond reasonable doubt. As Hoffmann observes, discussing *Ball*, had there not been the evidence about a single bedroom being in use in the house, the bad character evidence 'would have to bear the whole weight of proving that an outwardly normal relationship was in fact incestuous'; 'it would no longer be a matter of using the similar fact evidence to dispel a mere doubt'.[75]

Still, there is something very odd here. In *Ball*, the similar fact evidence would only bear the whole weight if the judge let the case go to the jury, and surely a case where the only evidence of guilt is such previous behaviour is not strong enough to get that far. Consider another situation involving weak evidence. If the only evidence against D is a weak eyewitness identification, or that D had a motive to commit crime, we would withdraw the case from the jury; we would not hold the evidence inadmissible, or say that it is irrelevant, or that it is weaker than in a case where there is other evidence pointing to guilt. It is therefore strange that questions of relevance and sufficiency should be elided where propensity evidence is concerned. And while the contextual view of relevance is often harmless, it is not conducive to clear thinking about propensity evidence. If we want to make good admissibility decisions, it is surely preferable to separate questions of relevance and sufficiency, as well as questions about the probative value of the propensity evidence and of the other evidence.

6.9 Commentators

So far, we have examined the principal admissibility tests for propensity evidence used by the English courts prior to the introduction of the 2003 Act. While the case law was developing, there was of course considerable academic commentary on what was going on. Much of this literature tried to explain the case law, often suggesting that the cases, while seeming to use different admissibility tests, could in fact be reconciled with each other once the role of a particular factor was grasped. In this way, commentators largely endorsed what the courts were doing, if not their way of doing it—at least until the decision in *P*. In this section, I do not propose to review all of the academic literature on propensity evidence. The

the Court states that: 'The defendant's possession of a large sum of cash, or enjoyment of a wealthy lifestyle, does not, on its own, prove anything very much, and certainly not possession of drugs. If there is a little additional but highly tenuous evidence which links the defendant with drugs, cash or lifestyle evidence may remain valueless.'

[75] 'Similar Facts after Boardman', 202.

aim, rather, is to pick out and scrutinize some key themes from the commentary, especially that which emerged in the wake of *Boardman* and *P*. As throughout the chapter, the emphasis is on analysis of reasoning processes.

Commentators tended to realize that propensity reasoning played a larger role in the cases than the courts admitted.[76] Most were also critical of the categories as being too rigid an approach, and endorsed a shift towards focussing on a balance of probative value and prejudicial effect. At the same time, the idea of forbidden reasoning exerted a strong pull. Thus, in an influential essay written before *Boardman*, Cowen and Carter argue that PV/PE is the key to admissibility.[77] Nevertheless, they see considerable value in identifying cases where character evidence is relevant 'primarily via propensity' as opposed to other modes of reasoning. The reason for the distinction is that 'propensity relevance is dangerous because its probative value depends, and depends always, entirely upon the assumption that [D] has not mended his ways. That he may have done so is a possibility to which a lay trier of fact is often unwilling to give due regard.'[78] While this emphasis on propensity is criticized by Williams,[79] Williams does not entirely eschew the idea that propensity reasoning is especially problematic: 'the distinction between relevance other than via propensity and relevance via propensity separates in a rough and ready fashion classes of case where similar fact evidence is often admissible from classes of case where it is often inadmissible'.[80] We have already seen one reason to be cautious of this approach: propensity reasoning is ubiquitous, even playing a role in *Smith* (to take up Cowen and Carter's concern, the more we think Smith might have mended his ways, the less likely we are to conclude that he killed all of his wives). Commentators who highlight the dangers of propensity reasoning usually argue that some cases are exempt from it, with the bad character evidence therefore admissible,[81] but such arguments tend to be mistaken. An example is Cowen and Carter's contention that cases involving multiple allegations are non-propensity cases, because they involve reasoning based on the 'improbability of similar lies'.[82]

Even if there was a distinction to be drawn between allegations and convictions, it would lead to a problematic doctrine. Cowen and Carter note that in a case involving previous convictions or admitted misconduct, the evidence will be propensity evidence and so will probably be excluded, but if the evidence involves

---

[76] One of the most insightful analyses is Zuckerman, 'Similar Fact Evidence'. See also Piragoff, *Similar Fact Evidence*, esp ch 3; and P. Mirfield, 'Similar Facts—Makin Out?' (1987) 46 *CLJ* 83 (it is instructive that in 1987 Mirfield still thought it was worth basing an article on the argument that the law does not really regard reasoning from disposition as illegitimate).

[77] 'The Admissibility of Evidence of Similar Facts'.

[78] 'The Admissibility of Evidence of Similar Facts', 139.

[79] 'The Problem of Similar Fact Evidence', 288.

[80] 'The Problem of Similar Fact Evidence', 347.

[81] A slightly different approach is found in I. H. Dennis, *The Law of Evidence* (2nd edn, London: Sweet & Maxwell, 2002), 630. Dennis argues that the propensity/non-propensity distinction is significant as marking a distinction between cases where admissibility is subject to rule rather than discretion.

[82] 'The Admissibility of Evidence of Similar Facts', 116.

allegations of the same misconduct, it might be admitted under the 'improbability of lies' rationale, with propensity not being engaged. Thus, if D has three previous convictions for rape, they cannot be admitted on a charge of rape, but three allegations of rape could be. On this analysis, what is almost certainly the more powerful evidence (because of stronger linkage) is excluded. The authors' frankness in biting this bullet is admirable, but the conclusion they draw is a good example of the cost of attempting to impose categories on the case law. Faced with this example, Piragoff rightly concludes that 'any rule of admissibility based on a differentiation of reasoning is absurd'.[83] He too argues that a PV/PE test should dominate. But Piragoff's view is not that there is no distinction to be made between allegations and previous convictions; like others, he is taken in by the idea that a reasoning process based on 'objective improbability' rather than propensity can be applied to the former, but not the latter. Rather, Piragoff thinks that the difference should not be so significant in terms of admissibility. Piragoff actually endorses Cowen and Carter's 'possibility of change' argument as a reason to be suspicious of propensity evidence, but argues for admissibility in a case like *Ball* because, while this involves admitted conduct and therefore propensity, that the Balls have not changed is corroborated via the other evidence—the fact that only one bed was in use in their house.[84] This way of dealing with the supposed propensity problem has obvious difficulties. While using one piece of evidence to corroborate the inferential foundation of another does not necessarily involve circular reasoning, it does involve a pointless zero sum game. If we use the other evidence to confirm the existence of a continuing propensity, we are taking probative value from the other evidence. While the exercise might make the propensity evidence stronger, we will be left with the same amount of probative value overall, and if we do not realize this we risk double-counting the evidence. The simpler way to proceed is to let each piece of evidence do its own work. It is of course possible that the Balls have changed, but, as we saw in Chapter 4, this is already taken into account in the concept of comparative propensity. We presume that they are more likely than other people to commit incest, not that they necessarily will. If, for some reason, one wants to give the Balls the benefit of the doubt by presuming that they have changed—and this may be how Cowen and Carter and Piragoff see things—then we are simply presuming that they no longer have a comparative propensity to commit incest, and the evidence of their prior relationship will be irrelevant. The case will then depend entirely on the evidence of the single bed being in use, and is probably too weak to go to the jury. We can, as before, use the other evidence to confirm a continuing tendency, but, as just explained, that will not make the case any stronger overall.

Piragoff's suspicion of propensity reasoning also emerges in another way. For him, a bare previous conviction shows no more than 'dispositional capacity'—that D is capable of committing the crime—and this is of minimal probative value.[85] For Piragoff, it is dispositional capacity at which the first, exclusionary, limb of

---

[83] *Similar Fact Evidence*, 95.   [84] *Similar Fact Evidence*, 137–45.
[85] *Similar Fact Evidence*, ch 4.

Lord Herschell's statement in *Makin* is aimed. But, if 'evidence can be probative beyond merely showing general dispositional capacity, or can show dispositional capacity in such a specific manner, etc. in relation to the offence charged,
and sufficiently so, the evidence may be admitted'.[86] Williams expresses a similar
idea: 'Evidence which shows no more than that the accused possesses a general
propensity towards a certain class of criminal activity is, of course, inadmissible.
However, if propensity can be rendered more specific by virtue of the fact that
the crime charged and the similar fact evidence each have as their object the same
individual, the evidence may be admitted.'[87] The idea here has been reasonably
influential: a distinction can be drawn between general and specific propensity,
with reasoning only being forbidden when it relies on the former.[88] Similarity
between crimes or allegations will result in specific propensity and admissibility.
The general/specific distinction might then make sense of much of the case law;
in particular, the cases which are often used to argue that propensity reasoning
has been endorsed by the courts can now be reconciled with Herschell's *dictum*.
Straffen had a very specific propensity to murder young girls in a particular way;
Ball had a propensity, not just to commit incest, but to commit it with this particular sister.[89] This argument obviously escapes the criticism, rehearsed above,
that nearly all cases do involve propensity reasoning.

Another point in favour of a distinction between types of propensity is that,
broadly speaking, the more specific the propensity, the higher the probative value.
However, there are many problems with this way of thinking about admissibility. For one thing, we have seen that there are more variables in play than the
probative value of the character evidence. In particular, the strength of the other
evidence might justify a case which involves relatively weak propensity evidence
going to the jury. When Harrison-Owen is found in another person's house, and
claims that his presence there is involuntary, why should the jury not be told that

---

[86] *Similar Fact Evidence*, 107. Piragoff continues: 'For example, in *Paradis v R.* [[1934] SCR
165], the evidence of prior attempts to burn the building in question not only showed dispositional
capacity to destroy property, but also particularized such to the specific building which was the
subject-matter of the offence charged.'

[87] 'The Problem of Similar Fact Evidence', 302.

[88] For an early version of this argument, see J. Stone, 'The Rule of Exclusion of Similar Fact
Evidence: England' (1933) 46 *Harvard L Rev* 954.

[89] Williams makes this distinction in respect of *Ball* (see 'The Problem of Similar Fact Evidence',
303), as does Piragoff (*Similar Fact Evidence*, 139). As well as being influential among commentators, the idea of a distinction between general and specific propensity also has some support in the
case law. In some cases, the courts have said that evidence showing mere propensity or disposition
is not admissible: 'mere propensity to commit crimes is not sufficient. There must therefore be
some identifiable connection of character or other circumstances between the two alleged offences'
(*Osmanioglu* [2002] EWCA Crim 930, [20]); evidence would be admissible if it 'would tend to
show, not a general propensity, but a systematic technique of dishonesty' (*Docherty v Reddy* [1977]
ICR 365; see also *Chopra* [2007] 1 Cr App R 16, [2006] EWCA Crim 2133, [20], interpreting the
common law as requiring more than mere propensity). Juries were sometimes instructed not to rely
on evidence of mere propensity (eg *Gibbs, Ponder and Davis* [2004] EWCA Crim 3431, [32]; and
Brizzalari [2004] EWCA Crim 310, [51]). But most often such statements seemed to be little more
than a gloss on other tests, or accompanied a reference to one of the categories that would allow
evidence of mere propensity to be redescribed in other terms (eg *Thompson* [1918] AC 221, 232; and
Michael F [2003] EWCA Crim 1151, [9]).

he has previous convictions for burglary?[90] Another problem is that the distinction between general and specific propensity does not track probative value very well. The distinction seems to be drawn at the level of crime category: propensity to burgle is a general propensity, propensity to burgle houses in a particular way, such as by gaining entry on a pretext, might be a specific propensity. But as we saw when examining striking similarity, the comparative propensities associated with various crimes vary, as does the specificity with which crimes are defined. If we decided to make burglary committed by entering premises on a pretext or child murder into a specific offence, would that make a difference to admissibility? Should it? A further problem is that it is not clear why we should want to draw a distinction between general and specific propensity in the first place. Do we have grounds to think that the former is more prejudicial than the latter? If the jury can overestimate the strength of general propensity, surely it can overestimate specific propensity too. The general/specific distinction draws an arbitrary line between permissible and impermissible inferences.

Perhaps the most sophisticated attempt to draw a distinction between general and specific propensity is developed by Acorn.[91] As her arguments might appear to avoid the criticisms above, they deserve some attention. Unlike many commentators, Acorn does not welcome a shift towards a PV/PE rule; for her, *Makin* should be defended as a ban on evidence which engages a particular type of reasoning. Acorn's example of forbidden reasoning involves a premise of 'universal constancy of human action': 'all people who act in a certain way in the past, act that way now and will continue so to act'.[92] This premise could be combined with the fact that D has a conviction for, say, theft, to give the conclusion that D is guilty of the theft charged. This problematic reasoning template is contrasted with one which can be applied to *Makin*—'all babies found in the Makin's garden were murdered by the Makins'[93]—as well as a third, intermediate, kind of reasoning which involves a generalization such as 'all parents who frequently sexually assault their children are likely to continue to do so' and the conclusion 'this accused is likely to be guilty of the sexual assault of his daughter'.[94] The intermediate reasoning may be acceptable if there is empirical warrant for the generalization. But the premise of universal constancy of human action underlying the first inferential pattern is too strong to be warranted. This would presumably mean that a single previous conviction for a crime such as burglary should not be relied on in a propensity argument relating to guilt.[95]

There are difficulties with Acorn's argument. The premise of universal constancy is presented in stark form and does not countenance any possibility of

---

[90] *Harrison-Owen* (1951) 35 Cr App R 108. [91] 'Similar Fact Evidence'.

[92] 'Similar Fact Evidence', 65.

[93] 'Similar Fact Evidence', 66. Acorn argues that *Straffen* also fits this template: all young girls killed by strangulation when S is in the vicinity, whose bodies are unconcealed and were not sexually assaulted were killed by S (73).

[94] 'Similar Fact Evidence', 66–7.

[95] As an example, Acorn cites *Clermont* [1986] 2 SCR 131, where a previous rape conviction was used to prove rape.

change; it is obviously false. But nothing this strong and implausible is needed to reason from a burglary conviction to guilt. All we have to do is say that D is more likely to burgle than someone without a conviction, and that this makes his guilt more likely. As we saw in Chapter 2, there is empirical support for this proposition, providing, in Acorn's terms, inferential warrant. And while this inference does not prove guilt by itself, it could be combined with other evidence to make a convincing case. As for the reasoning Acorn associates with *Makin*, an obvious question is how we arrive at the premise 'all babies found in the Makins' garden were murdered by the Makins'. We have seen that propensity does play a role even in the doctrine of chances version of the reasoning that leads to this conclusion. The *Makin* reasoning, then, is not so different from the other arguments identified by Acorn. Acorn does appear to acknowledge that an assumption about propensity plays a role in *Makin*, but she contends that 'the nature of the evidence in the *Makin* case supports that assumption'.[96] It is not clear what is meant here, but it may be that Acorn is attracted by something like Piragoff's problematic 'confirmation of propensity' argument.

One clear theme in the literature, then, is a suspicion of propensity inferences, or of a particular type of propensity inference. Another common assumption is that there should be a demanding admissibility test.[97] This is probably an element in Acorn's analysis: in her first two patterns of reasoning the desire seems to be to reach a categorical conclusion, one with no element of uncertainty, and the analysis proceeds as though the propensity evidence will have to do all of the work. In a similar vein, Mirfield sees value in the striking similarity test because it indicates that 'a high degree of probative force is required',[98] and criticizes a test of 'positive probative value' because it does not.[99] The 'erosion' of *Boardman* by *P* is bemoaned by Tapper,[100] who calls the reasoning in the latter case 'cursory and unconvincing'.[101] Dennis criticizes the Law Commission for proposing a test under which evidence with merely 'substantial' probative value would be admissible.[102] One does not have to look far to see why this sort of statement should be made. Many commentators are convinced that bad character evidence is especially dangerous. Thus, Cowen and Carter claim that evidence which is 'relevant via propensity tends to be objectionable because its real probative value is often far less than the probative value a lay tribunal of fact will attribute to it'.[103] Both

---

[96] 'Similar Fact Evidence', 72.

[97] There are exceptions: Zuckerman, 'Similar Fact Evidence'; and J. McEwan, 'Law Commission Dodges the Nettles in Consultation Paper No. 141' [1997] *Crim LR* 93. Spencer also approves of wider admissibility: see J. R. Spencer, *Evidence of Bad Character* (2nd edn, Oxford: Hart Publishing, 2009), 9–16. Spencer was an adviser to the Auld report, which called for significant relaxation of the rules: R. E. Auld, *Review of the Criminal Courts of England and Wales: Report* (London: Lord Chancellor's Department, 2001).

[98] 'Similar Facts—Makin Out?', 90.   [99] 'Similar Facts—Makin Out?', 93.

[100] C. Tapper, 'The Erosion of *Boardman v DPP*' *New LJ* 11 August 1995, 1223, and 18 August 1995, 1263. See also C. Tapper, *Cross and Tapper on Evidence* (9th edn, London: Butterworths, 1999), 359, where *P* is criticized for not emphasizing a high standard of admissibility.

[101] C. Tapper, 'Dissimilar Views of Similar Facts' (1995) 111 *LQR* 381, 384.

[102] I. H. Dennis, *The Law of Evidence* (2nd edn, London: Sweet & Maxwell, 2002), 638.

[103] 'The Admissibility of Evidence of Similar Facts', 120.

Allan and Palmer quote Murphy J's comments in *Perry* with approval: 'the admission of similar fact evidence "immediately conjures up a highly suspicious prejudicial atmosphere in which the presumption of innocence tends to be replaced with a presumption of guilt"'.[104] Williams suggests that 'there is... always the danger that the jury will adopt a simplistic line of reasoning to the effect that since the accused is prone to the commission of crimes similar to the one presently charged, he or she must on this occasion be guilty'.[105] It is important to understand the literature on bad character in the light of these assumptions about its prejudicial nature. And they are indeed assumptions: statements of this sort rarely refer to any good evidence which shows that jurors give too much weight to bad character evidence,[106] and I have argued in Chapter 3 that there is in fact very little evidence that jurors will do.

6.10 Conclusion

In this chapter, I have explored the reasoning process in similar fact cases, showing how the comparative propensity model works in the scenarios which frequently arise in the case law, noting the importance of other evidence and linkage as well as comparative propensity itself. I have then analysed the common law tests, measuring them against this normative model, to give a better idea of their strengths and weaknesses, and to explain why certain developments in the case law, such as a move towards an emphasis on probative value in *Boardman* and *P*, did not necessarily progress things. The focus then turned to certain common themes in the literature on propensity evidence, in particular the assumptions which are made about reasoning processes. I have suggested that the proper way to think about bad character evidence has often been misunderstood in both the case law and the literature: a good example of this is the claim that 'similar lies' cases do not involve a propensity inference. There has also been a marked tendency to elide what are, in other areas of the law, distinct issues of admissibility and sufficiency, as in the way in which the role of the other evidence was subsumed by the categories and integrated in judgments of 'contextual relevance'.

A common argument in the literature has been that Lord Herschell's formulation of the exclusionary rule in *Makin* is not without value. The argument depends on what Piragoff refers to as 'differentiation of reasoning', ie the claim

---

[104] The quotation is from A. Palmer, 'The Scope of the Similar Fact Rule' (1994) 16 *Adelaide L Rev* 161, 171, who is quoting *Perry* (1982) 44 ALR 449, 460. T. R. S. Allan endorses the *Perry* passage in 'Some Favourite Fallacies about Similar Facts (1988) 8 *Legal Studies* 35, 36.

[105] Williams, 'Approaches to Similar Fact Evidence', 22.

[106] Andrews and Hirst (J. A. Andrews and M. Hirst, *Andrews and Hirst on Criminal Evidence* (4th edn, London: Sweet & Maxwell, 2001), 408) do try to back up the claim that juries are considered to be 'particularly susceptible' to prejudice. But the evidence they cite, including the fact that 'jurors sometimes show obvious signs of relief or satisfaction when they learn that a defendant they have just convicted has previous convictions for similar offences', and *Bills* [1995] 2 Cr App R 643, where a jury tried to change its verdict on hearing of previous convictions, are perfectly compatible with propensity evidence simply being given its proper weight.

that different uses of character evidence involve different forms of reasoning, some of which (typically propensity, or 'general propensity' inferences) should be regarded with suspicion, if not disallowed completely. This sort of analysis has very little to be said for it. Propensity inferences are more or less ubiquitous, playing a role even in doctrine of chances reasoning; even if this were not true, a policy of treating propensity inferences differently would fail to accord significance to the role played by the other evidence.

Even when no attempt is made to defend Lord Herschell's *dictum*, much of the literature on propensity evidence presumes that there is considerable good sense in the accumulated case law. I am sceptical. Especially if one is not convinced of the need to treat propensity evidence with extreme caution—an assumed need which has driven much of the case law and commentary—then the case law prior to the 2003 Act offers little sound guidance on admissibility. In my view, the lessons to be drawn from the pre-2003 case law are largely negative: this is not the way to do things. Ultimately, none of the approaches taken by the courts worked well in all scenarios. It is therefore no surprise that, as we saw in the previous chapter, courts ended up picking and choosing from a multitude of tests. There are even few words of wisdom to take from the case law, because judicial pronouncements on propensity evidence were so often muddled.[107] To the extent that more constructive lessons can be drawn from the cases, they tend to rely on using the cases as illustrations of the operation of the propensity inference and its interaction with other factors. A good example is *McGranaghan*, which does seem to teach us something about the role played by identification evidence in propensity cases.

---

[107] See Hamer, 'The Structure and Strength of the Propensity Inference', at 150: 'the law reports are replete with ... misunderstandings about the operation and probative value of the propensity inference'.

7

Propensity Evidence under the Criminal Justice Act 2003

This chapter takes up the story of the admissibility of propensity evidence in England and Wales where it was left at the end of Chapter 5: with the introduction of the Criminal Justice Act 2003. The CJA was intended to enlarge the admissibility of propensity evidence against defendants, and it has done just that. The purpose of this chapter and the next one is both to provide a picture of the current state of play under the CJA—what are now the limits to admissibility?—and, drawing on the analysis in Chapters 2 and 6, to give a critical assessment of how the courts have dealt with the new regime.

7.1 The CJA Scheme in Outline

Section 101(1) of the CJA provides that evidence of a defendant's bad character is only admissible if it passes through one of seven specified gateways. In this chapter, the focus is on gateway (d): 'it is relevant to an important matter in issue between the defendant and the prosecution'. Although they are not considered in the present chapter, it is worth noting the other significant gateways:

(c) it is important explanatory evidence

...

(e) it has substantial probative value in relation to an issue between the defendant and a co-defendant

(f) it is evidence to correct a false impression given by the defendant

(g) the defendant has made an attack on another person's character.

The section continues:

101 (3) The court must not admit evidence under subsection (1)(d) or (g) if, on an application by the defendant to exclude it, it appears to the court that the admission of the evidence would have such an adverse effect on the fairness of the proceedings that the court ought not to admit it.

(4) On an application to exclude the evidence under subsection (3) the court must have regard, in particular, to the length of time between the matters to which that evidence relates and the matters which form the subject matter of the offence charged.

Section 103 provides important interpretation of gateway (d), specifying that the matters in issue[1] between the defendant and prosecution include 'the question whether the defendant has a propensity to commit offences of the kind with which he is charged, except where his having such a propensity makes it no more likely that he is guilty of the offence', as well as 'the question whether the defendant has a propensity to be untruthful, except where it is not suggested that the defendant's case is untruthful in any respect'. Under the terminology employed in this book, evidence showing that a defendant has a propensity to be untruthful is not 'propensity evidence', thus evidence of a propensity to be untruthful admitted through gateway (d) is not considered in this chapter, but is covered in Chapter 9, which deals with credibility evidence.

Section 103 continues by detailing ways in which a propensity to commit the current crime can be proved. When 'the question whether the defendant has a propensity to commit offences of the kind with which he is charged' is deemed to be an important matter in issue, the defendant's propensity:

103 (2) ...may (without prejudice to any other way of doing so) be established by evidence that he has been convicted of—
  (a) an offence of the same description as the one with which he is charged, or
  (b) an offence of the same category as the one with which he is charged.
 (3) Subsection (2) does not apply in the case of a particular defendant if the court is satisfied, by reason of the length of time since the conviction or for any other reason, that it would be unjust for it to apply in his case.
 (4) For the purposes of subsection (2)—
  (a) two offences are of the same description as each other if the statement of the offence in a written charge or indictment would, in each case, be in the same terms;
  (b) two offences are of the same category as each other if they belong to the same category of offences prescribed for the purposes of this section by an order made by the Secretary of State.[2]

Two categories of offences have been specified by the Secretary of State under 103(4)(b): a property offences category, which includes theft, robbery, burglary, taking vehicles without consent, and such like; and a category covering underage sex offences.[3] But in practice, not much has turned on whether offences are of the same category, or even of the same description. Being of the same category or description as the current charge has been held to be neither necessary nor sufficient for the admissibility of a previous conviction.[4] Thus, a previous conviction for assault occasioning actual bodily harm can be used to prove that the defendant has a propensity to commit an offence of grievous bodily harm,[5] even

---

[1] The qualification 'important' does not appear in s 103. This point has not yet been taken up in the case law on propensity evidence, although it does play a role in relation to credibility evidence in *Campbell* [2007] 2 Cr App R 28, [2007] EWCA Crim 1472, [30].

[2] Section 103(5) provides that 'a category prescribed by an order under subsection (4)(b) must consist of offences of the same type'. 'Type' is not further defined.

[3] Criminal Justice Act 2003 (Categories of Offences) Order 2004, SI 2004/3346.

[4] *Hanson and Others* [2005] 2 Cr App R 21, [2005] EWCA Crim 824, [8].

[5] See, eg, *Awaritefe* [2007] EWCA Crim 706; and *Wehbe* [2011] EWCA Crim 978.

though these offences are neither of the same category nor of the same description. At the same time, the courts discriminate between offences placed in the same category: they are, for example, wary of using theft to prove robbery.[6] Even when offences are of the same description, admissibility is not guaranteed: variation in the facts may be significant, as may the lapse of time since the conviction. Simply put, the courts apply the same test to all previous convictions, considering both similarity and staleness. The two categories which have been created therefore play little if any role in admissibility decisions, and this may well be why the Secretary of State has issued no further category orders.[7] The upshot of this is that the complexities of section 103(2) to (4) can be ignored.

Section 103 focusses on previous convictions, but gateway (d) is wider than this. Section 101, which contains gateway (d), refers to 'evidence of a defendant's bad character'. This is defined in section 98 as 'evidence of, or of a disposition towards, misconduct'; 'misconduct' is further defined in section 112(1) as 'the commission of an offence or other reprehensible behaviour'. As has been pointed out, 'reprehensible behaviour' is not the most transparent way of defining the concept around which the bad character provisions of the Act revolve.[8] Unsurprisingly, there is now a small case law[9] on what is, and is not, reprehensible. However, especially for the purposes of gateway (d), very little turns on this. The decision in *Manister* shows why.[10] D, aged 39, had been convicted of the indecent assault of a 13-year-old girl. The prosecution introduced evidence that a few years before, when aged 34, D had had a consensual sexual relationship with a 16-year-old girl, and also that he had made a suggestive comment to the complainant's 15-year-old sister. There was no suggestion that D had 'groomed' his previous young girlfriend, nor that her parents had disapproved. The Court of Appeal held that these incidents did not constitute 'reprehensible' behaviour. But this merely meant that admissibility did not have to be justified under the CJA provisions; instead, it could be considered under ordinary principles of evidence. The Court held that the evidence was relevant and therefore admissible at common law, and not subject to exclusion under section 78 of the Police and Criminal Evidence Act 1984 (PACE).[11] If the prior conduct had been classified

---

[6] *Tully and Wood* [2006] EWCA Crim 2270.

[7] According to Spencer, the creation of a category of violent offences was rumoured to have been considered, but nothing seems to have come of this. J. Spencer, *Evidence of Bad Character* (2nd edn, Oxford: Hart Publishing, 2009), 79.

[8] R. Munday, 'What Constitutes "Other Reprehensible Behaviour" under the Bad Character Provisions of the Criminal Justice Act 2003?' [2005] *Crim LR* 24; and J. Goudkamp, 'Bad Character Evidence and Reprehensible Behaviour' (2008) 12 *E & P* 116.

[9] See Goudkamp, 'Bad Character Evidence'; Spencer, *Evidence of Bad Character*, ch 2.

[10] *Weir and Others (Manister)* [2006] 1 Cr App R 19, [2005] EWCA Crim 2866. Cf *Fox* [2009] EWCA Crim 653.

[11] PACE, s 78 provides that: 'In any proceedings the court may refuse to allow evidence on which the prosecution proposes to rely to be given if it appears to the court that, having regard to all the circumstances, including the circumstances in which the evidence was obtained, the admission of the evidence would have such an adverse effect on the fairness of the proceedings that the court ought not to admit it.'

as 'reprehensible', the ultimate decision would doubtless have been the same: it would have been relevant to a matter in issue between prosecution and defence, ie whether D had a sexual interest in young girls. If it was not subject to exclusion under section 78, it is doubtful that it would have been excluded under the exclusionary test in section 101(3) of the CJA.[12] Thus, as the Court of Appeal put it in its later decision in *Smith*, whether relevant evidence is evidence of bad character as defined in the CJA 'makes no difference as [it is] admissible anyway'.[13]

Enough has now been said to sketch the basic scheme for admissibility under the CJA 2003. To summarize: evidence of prior misconduct is admissible as propensity evidence if it is relevant to an important matter in issue between the defendant and the prosecution, and this may include the question of whether the defendant has a propensity to commit the offence charged. While such evidence will often take the form of previous convictions or allegations of criminal behaviour, it need not. Propensity evidence, however, is subject to exclusion if admitting it would make the proceedings unfair. To gain a better idea of how this scheme works in practice, we now need to engage more closely with the case law.

7.2 Propensity under the CJA: The Basics

From what has been said in the previous section, it is understandable why, when the CJA was first introduced, it was not obvious that it would make much difference to the admissibility of propensity evidence. The basic admissibility test just described is very similar to the one usually taken to have been established by *DPP v P*:[14] propensity evidence can be admitted if it is more probative than prejudicial. However, we saw in Chapter 5 that, at least in the Court of Appeal, *P* rarely was applied as a basic PV/PE test. Instead, courts would pick and choose from a variety of common law tests in order to assess admissibility. At the very least, then, the CJA might be said to establish the *P* test more clearly than *P* ever did. However, even that might not have led to a dramatic change in the practice of the courts. One reason why *P* did not make a clean sweep was that courts took strange views of relevance: there was a tendency to view propensity evidence as only being relevant when, for example, one of the 'categories' was engaged. It might have been predicted, then, that under the CJA things would have continued as usual, with courts applying the categories and forbidden reasoning tests under the guise of an

---

[12] Goudkamp, 'Bad Character Evidence', 124, notes that there is a difference between s 78 and s 101(3): the latter provides that the court 'must' exclude the evidence, whereas the otherwise similar wording of s 78 only says 'may'. But this is surely not a significant difference. For it to be so, a court considering s 78 would have to hold that evidence should be admitted even though it ought not to be: see *O'Dowd* [2009] 2 Cr App R 16, [2009] EWCA Crim 905, [29]; and *Tirnaveanu* [2007] 2 Cr App r 23, [2007] EWCA Crim 1239 [28]. Cf *Hanson*, [2005] 2 Cr App R 21, [2005] EWCA Crim 824, [10]; and *Highton and Others* [2006] 1 Cr App R 7, [2005] EWCA Crim 1985, [13].

[13] *Edwards and Rowlands and Others (Smith)* [2006] 2 Cr App R 4, [2005] EWCA Crim 3244, [83]. See also *Mullings* [2011] 2 Cr App R 2, [2010] EWCA Crim 2820.

[14] [1991] 2 AC 447.

analysis of relevance. By and large, this has not occurred.[15] One reason for this is probably that the CJA states clearly that evidence of misconduct is admissible to show propensity. While, as noted above, much of section 103 of the CJA is now not significant in practice, subsection (2) is a clear prompt to judges that previous convictions show propensity.

The pre-CJA case of *Derek Charles L*[16] is a good illustration of the effect the CJA has had on judicial reasoning. As we have just seen, in *Manister,*[17] the Court of Appeal held that evidence of a consensual relationship with a young girl was relevant and admissible on a charge of indecent assault on another young girl. In *L*, D was charged with sexual assault of his daughters. The Court of Appeal held that evidence that D, in his 40s, had had a consensual sexual relationship with a girl aged between 16 and 18 was clearly inadmissible. While the decision was made with reference to *P*—'evidence that goes to mere propensity is not evidence that can go before the jury...what is required is something substantially more than that'[18]—it is clear that the Court of Appeal struggled to see the relevance of the evidence:

[The trial judge's direction] is a direction that where a man has demonstrated in the past that he has sexual interest in the fondling of a girl's breasts, that that in some way is indicative of the fact that he might well fondle indecently against her wishes and while she is asleep the breasts of his daughter. We think one only has to express that consideration for the obvious fallacy in it to be apparent.[19]

Contrast the statement in *Manister* that the evidence there 'was capable of demonstrating a sexual interest in early or mid-teenage girls'.[20] The point is not that the decision in *Manister* is a better one than that in *L*, merely that these two cases, decided just two years apart, show the profound effect on judicial thinking which the CJA has had. After the Act, judges see the relevance of previous behaviour differently.

---

[15] The impact of the old ways of reasoning is examined in more detail in the next chapter.
[16] [2003] EWCA Crim 1755.   [17] [2006] 1 Cr App R 19, [2005] EWCA Crim 2866.
[18] *R v L*, [2003] EWCA Crim 1755, [11].   [19] *R v L*, [16].
[20] [2006] 1 Cr App R 19, [2005] EWCA Crim 2866, [95]. *L* does raise a question mark over the decision in *Manister*, where the Court said 'we have no doubt that evidence of the relationship was admissible at common law'. *L* might just be distinguishable, but the case does suggest that this statement is wrong if it is intended to refer to the pre-CJA position. This may be significant, even if the statement is intended to refer to the present common law, ie rules for admissibility of evidence of previous behaviour not covered by the CJA. CJA, s 99 abolishes the 'common law rules governing the admissibility of evidence of bad character in criminal proceedings'. If 'evidence of bad character' is interpreted as only applying to misconduct/reprehensible behaviour as defined in the Act, then *L* still stands, because *L*'s consensual relationship was probably not reprehensible. On the other hand, it is arguable that s 99 abolishes the common law rules on 'evidence of bad character' as that phrase was understood at common law, ie as extending to the evidence in *L*, because *L* accepted that *DPP v P* applied. CJA, s 98 does, as we have seen, define 'bad character' for the purposes of the Act, but it is not entirely clear that the definition applies to s 99 (and hence restricts the field of abolition to rules relating to reprehensible behaviour), because the definition in s 98 applies to 'references...to evidence of a person's "bad character"', while the reference in s 99 is to 'rules governing the admissibility of evidence of bad character'.

When the CJA came into effect, the Court of Appeal made a habit of combining various appeals raising issues relating to the bad character provisions. This enabled it quickly to make several general statements about the new law. The Court made it clear that admissibility decisions were a matter of judicial discretion, and further that they were fact sensitive; it would therefore be reluctant to interfere with a decision, unless the trial judge had been unreasonable in the *Wednesbury* sense.[21] The CJA was also depicted as having made a significant change to the law:

The 2003 Act completely reverses the pre-existing general rule. Evidence of bad character is now admissible if it satisfies certain criteria and the approach is no longer one of inadmissibility subject to exceptions... If the evidence of a defendant's bad character is relevant to an important issue between the prosecution and the defence... then, unless there is an application to exclude the evidence, it is admissible. Leave is not required. So the pre-existing one stage test which balanced probative value against prejudicial effect is obsolete.[22]

While a few of the early decisions referred to *DPP* v *P*, reference to pre-CJA cases has been sparse, and has generally been discouraged.[23] This is fortunate. I suggested in Chapter 6 that there is little of value in the pre-CJA case law, and in this chapter I have already noted that there was a danger that old and muddled ways of thinking about relevance would survive the Act. The Court of Appeal has been wise to start afresh.[24]

In *Hanson*,[25] the first of the combined appeals, the Court of Appeal set out the general approach to propensity evidence. Its observations remain important:

There is no minimum number of events necessary to demonstrate... propensity. The fewer the number of convictions the weaker is likely to be the evidence of propensity. A single previous conviction for an offence of the same description or category will often not show propensity. But it may do so where, for example, it shows a tendency to unusual behaviour or where its circumstances demonstrate probative force in relation to the offence charged (compare *Director of Public Prosecutions v P*...). Child sexual abuse or fire setting are comparatively clear examples of such unusual behaviour but we attempt no exhaustive list. Circumstances demonstrating probative force are not confined to those sharing striking similarity. So, a single conviction for shoplifting, will not, without more, be admissible to show propensity to steal. But if the modus operandi has significant features shared by the offence charged it may show propensity.

When considering what is just under s.103(3), and the fairness of the proceedings under s.101(3), the judge may, among other factors, take into consideration the degree of similarity between the previous conviction and the offence charged, albeit they are both within the same description or prescribed category. For example, theft and assault occasioning actual bodily harm may each embrace a wide spectrum of conduct. This does not

[21] *Hanson*, [2005] 2 Cr App R 21, [2005] EWCA Crim 824, [15].
[22] *Manister*, [2006] 1 Cr App R 19, [2005] EWCA Crim 2866, [35]. *Chopra* [2007] 1 Cr App R 16, [2006] EWCA Crim 2133, [12], refers to the CJA as a 'sea change'.
[23] *Chopra*, [2007] 1 Cr App R 16, [2006] EWCA Crim 2133, [12]–[23]; *Saleem* [2007] EWCA Crim 1923, [22]; and *Woodhead* [2011] EWCA Crim 472, [22].
[24] Cf the approach of the Northern Ireland Court of Appeal in *Kearney* [2014] NICA 21.
[25] [2005] 2 Cr App R 21, [2005] EWCA Crim 824.

however mean that what used to be referred to as striking similarity must be shown before convictions become admissible. The judge may also take into consideration the respective gravity of the past and present offences. He or she must always consider the strength of the prosecution case. If there is no or very little other evidence against a defendant, it is unlikely to be just to admit his previous convictions, whatever they are.

...Old convictions, with no special feature shared with the offence charged, are likely seriously to affect the fairness of proceedings adversely, unless, despite their age, it can properly be said that they show a continuing propensity.[26]

The Court also noted the importance of carefully instructing the jury.

This passage does a decent job of outlining key features of the concept of comparative propensity. The number of previous convictions is important, as is their gravity—which usually tracks the extent to which they exhibit rare, and thus more probative, behaviour. The age of previous convictions is significant, as well as their similarity to the current charge and details of *modus operandi*. The Court also pointed to the significance of the other evidence, by warning against bolstering a weak case. While various criticisms might be made of the decision—such as that it overemphasizes differences between crimes of a similar type[27]—*Hanson* made a promising start to placing the law on a more rational footing.

Further progress in understanding the position under the CJA can only be gained by exploring the voluminous case law which followed *Hanson*. The Court of Appeal has warned against reading too much into admissibility decisions, which can often be fact-specific.[28] We should therefore avoid treating the cases simplistically, as showing, for example, that previous conviction X can be used to prove Y. There are potentially many significant variables in each case. Before moving on to consider these variables, it is useful to consider two cases which the Court of Appeal has identified as falling near the admissibility borderline. These give a general feel for the current state of play in respect of propensity evidence.

In *McMinn*,[29] D was convicted of affray and ABH, charges arising out of an incident of street violence. A previous conviction for ABH, gained two and a half years earlier when D was aged 15, was placed before the jury. The incident involved a fight in the school playground—although presumably a relatively serious one if it led to prosecution. The Court of Appeal observed that many judges would not have admitted the conviction, and counselled caution 'in the admission of a single instance of this kind'.[30] The case against D was otherwise reasonably strong, in that it would probably have gone to the jury even without the previous conviction: there was witness identification/recognition evidence. The second case is *McDonald*,[31] where D was convicted of assault and handling stolen goods—although on the latter count the initial charge had been robbery. Convictions for assault and robbery were admitted by the trial judge, the

---

[26] [2005] 2 Cr App R 21, [2005] EWCA Crim 824, [9]–[11].

[27] See at [27]: 'convictions for handling and aggravated vehicle taking, although within the theft category, do not, in our judgment, show, without more pertinent information, propensity to burgle as indicted or to steal.'

[28] *Renda and Others* [2006] 1 Cr App R 24, [2005] EWCA Crim 2826, [3].

[29] [2007] EWCA Crim 3024.   [30] *McMinn*, [10].   [31] [2007] EWCA Crim 1194.

convictions being from six and nine years earlier, when D was in his mid to late teens. In the current case, there was no dispute that D was at the scene of crime with other youths and had been in possession of the stolen mobile phone shortly after the incident. The Court of Appeal did not express an opinion as to whether the judge had gone beyond his discretion, but did comment that this was a 'finely balanced decision',[32] especially in light of the lapse of time since the prior crimes. It found the conviction unsafe because the trial judge had mistakenly instructed the jury that the previous conviction was relevant to credibility.

7.3 Constituting Propensity

7.3.1 Time-lapse

Sections 101(4) and103(3) explicitly draw attention to the length of time between previous conviction and current charge, and the two decisions just described suggest, as does *Hanson*, that this is a factor which the courts take into account. This is welcome: as we saw in Chapter 2, the criminological literature shows that the risk of reoffending declines with age,[33] and a rough rule of thumb is that a minor conviction loses probative value after ten years without further offending. Passage of time is especially important where young offenders are concerned.[34] Offending is most common in the mid to late teens, after which offending rates tend to decline quickly. Thus, a gap of a few years after an offence committed at age 17 is rather more significant than the same gap after an offence committed in the late 20s. This is one reason why the Court of Appeal was right to see *McMinn* and *McDonald* as borderline decisions. In *McDonald*, however, it might have gone further and held that a six-year gap with no convictions rendered the previous convictions more or less irrelevant.

Various other decisions emphasize the significance of time-lapse. *R* v *M*[35] is an example: D was tried for offences involving the use of a sawn-off shotgun. This was quite a weak case, and the Court of Appeal held that a previous conviction for possessing a sawn-off shotgun some 20 years earlier should not have been admitted to show propensity. A 22-year gap was considered a reason to be sceptical about admitting convictions for violence on a charge of violence in *Lafayette*.[36]

---

[32] *McDonald*, [30].

[33] See, eg, A. Piquero, D. Farrington, and A. Blumstein, *Key Issues in Criminal Career Research: New Analyses of the Cambridge Study in Delinquent Development* (Cambridge: Cambridge University Press, 2007), ch 4.

[34] CJA, s 108 is also relevant here. It provides that where D is aged 21 or over, and the previous conviction relates to an offence committed when under the age of 14, the conviction will be inadmissible, unless both offences are indictable only, or the court concludes that the interests of justice require admissibility. This section will probably only rarely apply, although the courts have been prepared to take it as a 'steer' in cases which fall outside its terms: *Assani* [2008] EWCA Crim 2563; and *B* [2008] EWCA Crim 1850.

[35] [2006] EWCA Crim 3408. The case is also reported as *Murphy*.

[36] [2008] EWCA Crim 3238. See also *McGarvie* [2011] EWCA Crim 1414, discussed further below.

The previous convictions in *Awaritefe*[37] were for assault occasioning actual bodily harm (two convictions) and assaulting a police officer; they were admitted on charges of GBH with intent and wounding. The ABH convictions had been gained about ten years before, when D was aged 19. While suggesting that this fell somewhere near the borderline, the Court of Appeal was not prepared to rule that admitting the convictions had been wrong. But in *R v TB*,[38] less serious offending at an even younger age was viewed more charitably. A rather more hard-headed attitude is seen in *Miller*,[39] a case involving an 8-year-old conviction for a sexual offence gained when D was 16:

A conviction while a young person might be the consequence of immaturity; time will tell whether the offender does change and avoids offending when an adult. But that does not alter the proposition that such a prior conviction may be evidence of propensity.[40]

Ultimately, it will be for the jury to decide whether such a conviction should be taken to be evidence of propensity, and the staleness of the offence should be brought to the jury's attention.[41] But the decision in *Miller* is rather too dismissive of the argument that isolated convictions gained at a young age show little, something which judges are in a better position to understand than jurors.

A difficult question about time-lapse is whether time spent in prison should count as part of the time elapsed since the previous conviction, or whether, on the not entirely convincing theory that D does not have the opportunity to offend in prison, it is only time outside prison that counts. The trial judge in *Benabbou* took the latter view.[42] Given that there are no rigid rules on time-lapse, and because longer custodial periods will tend to reflect a more serious—and hence more significant—offence, there is probably little need to decide which view is correct.[43]

If passage of time is significant, the courts recognize that it needs to be set against the seriousness of the conviction in question. On trial for murder in 2005, the defendant in *Glen* had his previous conviction for murder—committed in 1989 when he was aged 17—admitted against him, and the Court of Appeal saw no problem here.[44] The courts also seem to consider that a propensity to commit certain sexual offences is less affected by the passage of time than are other propensities—this is one explanation for the decision in *Miller*, noted above. In *Cox*,[45]

[37] [2007] EWCA Crim 706.
[38] [2010] EWCA Crim 1983: 'to say that a single offence of vehicle taking at age 14 is evidence of a propensity to steal cars at the age of 18 is a bold submission' (at [15]).
[39] [2010] EWCA Crim 1578.
[40] *Miller*, [18]. Cf *Assani*, [2008] EWCA Crim 2563, [15]: 'On the issue of a propensity for violence, the lapse of time and the age of the person at the time of the earlier incident are highly relevant considerations.'
[41] See *Lafayette* [2008] EWCA Crim 3238, [40].
[42] [2012] EWCA Crim 1256, [19]. The Court of Appeal may also have taken this view in *Campbell* [2006] EWCA Crim 1305, [14].
[43] There is some evidence that time spent in custody delays reoffending rather than reducing its chances: prison does not shorten a criminal career. See J. F. Macleod, P. G. Grove, and D. P. Farrington, *Explaining Criminal Careers: Implications for Justice Policy* (Oxford: Oxford University Press, 2012), 220.
[44] *Glenn and Wright* [2006] EWCA Crim 3236.　　[45] [2007] EWCA Crim 3365.

D was convicted of indecent assault on a 13-year-old girl. Previous convictions from 1981 for sexual offences against girls of a similar age were admitted against him. *M*—the case involving the sawn-off shotgun—was distinguished: 'There is, it seems to us, some force in the proposition...that a defendant's sexual mores and motivations are not necessarily affected by the passage of time.'[46] The Court continued, in a passage which, like *Manister*, shows how comfortable judges now can be with the idea of propensity: 'In the end...we ask ourselves whether the fact that this defendant had, many years ago, demonstrated a sexual interest in a pubescent girl of 12 made it more likely that he had committed the offence which was now charged. In ordinary common sense, the answer to that is, unhesitatingly, yes it did.'[47]

Several other cases treat sexual offences the same way. In *Sully*,[48] previous convictions from 1968 and 1974 were adduced, although factual similarity may have played a role here: all incidents involved touching young girls' bottoms. In *Woodhouse*,[49] an 11-year-old previous caution was admitted; again, there was some similarity in the facts. The defendant in *R* v *A*[50] was convicted of various sexual offences committed against his daughter in the 1980s and early 1990s; the bad character evidence related to sexual material with an incestuous theme stored on the defendant's computer between 2005 and 2008. The Court of Appeal 'readily accept[ed] that in many cases a gap in time of this duration, coupled with this order of events, might militate against admitting evidence of bad character. However, incestuous rape in particular is no ordinary offence. It can only be committed by an abnormal offender against a very limited number of victims and usually for a relatively short period of time.'[51] But there are limits to the admissibility of other instances of sexual misconduct; an allegation of sexual misconduct was held to have been improperly admitted in *B*: 'It would be dangerous, in our view, for a jury to conclude on the facts of this case that the then 38 year old appellant male had a propensity for sexual activity with a child because of what he (allegedly) did when he was aged 14 with a 9 year old member of his extended family.'[52] Given D's age at the time, this seems right. A more surprising decision is *McGarvie*, where the Court of Appeal held that the trial judge had been wrong to admit 18- and 33-year-old convictions for sexual offences on a charge of sexual assault.[53]

In these cases, the Court of Appeal is making assumptions about the psychology of sexual offenders. And these assumptions are not obviously correct: is a propensity towards incest abnormal in a way a propensity towards, say, GBH is not?

---

[46] *Cox*, [28]. See also *R* v *B* [2011] EWCA Crim 1630; and *Morgan* [2009] EWCA Crim 2705.

[47] *Cox*, [29].   [48] [2007] EWCA Crim 3512.

[49] [2009] EWCA Crim 498.   [50] [2009] EWCA Crim 513.

[51] *R* v *A*, [20]. The echoes of *Thompson* [1918] AC 221 are obvious. Note the emphasis put on 'this order of events', the implication being that later convictions are less apt to show propensity than previous convictions. Given that offending tends to decline with age, if anything the opposite is the case. See also *R* v *B* [2011] EWCA Crim 1630, for a case with very similar facts: the defendant's interest in abusive pornography in later life was again held to have been properly admitted.

[52] *Richard William B* [2008] EWCA Crim 1850, [17].

[53] [2011] EWCA Crim 1414. Cf *Baker* [2012] EWCA Crim 1801.

Are sexual offenders less likely to desist than other offenders? It is probably not helpful to label certain offenders as abnormal. Sexual offending is a form of deviance like any other. Most sexual offenders do not specialize in sexual offending, in that they also have a propensity to commit non-sexual crimes, and risk factors for sexual offending are similar to those for other crimes.[54] Nevertheless, there is some evidence of specialism within sexual offending itself, so it is possible that incest offenders form a distinct subgroup.[55] More significantly, though, the Court of Appeal appears to be right to put less weight on time-lapse in cases involving sexual offences. Several studies of sexual recidivism emphasize the need for long follow-up periods in order to capture all new offences committed by a study cohort, in contrast to some other types of offending.[56] This seems to be especially true of those convicted of sexual crimes against children, who have been said to pose a 'significant risk for reoffending throughout their li[ves]'.[57]

7.3.2 Single act propensity

From the cases discussed so far, it will be obvious that propensity can sometimes be constituted by a single instance of misconduct—what Munday usefully terms 'single act propensity'.[58] Given the statement in *Hanson* that '[a] single previous conviction for an offence of the same description or category will often not show propensity',[59] it is not surprising that the pros and cons of single act propensity have often been argued on appeal. In *Long*,[60] the Court of Appeal seems to have considered that the statement in *Hanson* meant that a single recent previous

---

[54] D. Andrews and J. Bonta, *The Psychology of Criminal Conduct* (5th edn, Albany, NY: LexisNexis, 2010), 478–82.

[55] See K. Soothill, B. Francis, B. Sanderson, and E. Ackerley, 'Sex Offenders: Specialists, Generalists, or Both? A 32 Year Criminological Study' (2000) 40 *Brit J Criminol* 56. The finding of very low recidivism rates for intra-familial sex offenders also suggests that they may be a distinct group: R. Hood, S. Shute, M. Feilzer, and A. Wilcox, 'Sex Offenders Emerging from Long-Term Imprisonment: A Study of Their Long-Term Reconviction Rates and of Parole Board Members' Judgements of their Risk' (2002) 42 *Brit J Criminol* 371. See further A. Cossins, 'The Behaviour of Serial Child Sex Offenders: Implications for the Prosecution of Child Sex Offences in Joint Trials' (2011) 35 *Melbourne UL Rev* 822.

[56] See K. Soothill and T. Gibbens, 'Recidivism of Sexual Offenders: A Reappraisal' (1978) 18 *Brit J Criminol* 267, 273, who note that with property offenders a follow up period of three to five years would be expected to capture 80 to 90 per cent of reoffending, but that in their study of serious underage sex offenders, 'only half of those eventually reconvicted had done so within 5 years'. See also J. Cann, L. Falshaw, and C. Friendship, 'Sexual Offenders Discharged from Prison in England and Wales: A 21-year Reconviction Study' (2004) 9 *Legal and Criminological Psychology* 1, who suggest that the long-term persistence of risk in sex offenders is not confined to those who target young victims.

[57] R. Hanson, R. Steffy, and R. Gauthier, 'Long-Term Recidivism of Child Molesters' (1993) 61 *J Consulting and Clinical Psychology* 646, 650. For a similar conclusion, see R. Prentky, R. Lee, R. Knight, and D. Cerce, 'Recidivism Rates among Child Molesters and Rapists: A Methodological Analysis' (1997) 21 *Law & Human Behavior* 635. See also R. Hanson, 'Age and Sexual Recidivism: A Comparison of Rapists and Child Molesters', *Public Safety Canada Research Report 2001–01*, at <http://www.publicsafety.gc.ca/cnt/rsrcs/pblctns/sxl-rcdvsm-cmprsn/index-eng.aspx>.

[58] R. Munday, 'Single-Act Propensity' (2010) 74 *J Crim L* 127.

[59] [2005] 2 Cr App R 21, [2005] EWCA Crim 824, [9].   [60] [2006] EWCA Crim 578.

conviction for robbery could not be used to prove robbery, but this is probably the high-point of arguments against single act propensity: it stands in stark contrast to the decision in *McMinn*, discussed earlier.[61] As we saw in Chapter 2, most offenders are convicted only once, so it is right to view a single conviction for a minor offence as having little probative value. In Chapter 4, we also saw that this point might be mirrored by a moral argument that a first offence should be viewed as a lapse.

Like the age of a previous conviction, the fact that there is only a single previous conviction is merely one variable among many. For example, if, as in *Woodhouse*,[62] the previous instance involves a sexual offence, that will count in favour of admissibility. Similarity on the facts is also deemed significant; in *Bernasconi*, 'both incidents involved unusual behaviour, namely the production of an imitation weapon for apparently no obvious reason. The mere fact, therefore, that the previous conviction related to a single occasion did not prevent it from demonstrating a propensity.'[63] *Johnson*[64] involved a series of burglaries of country houses and commercial premises. One of the defendants, Nicholls, had a single previous conviction for theft from a skip. The Court of Appeal considered this properly admitted: 'The bad character evidence established the commission of an acquisitive offence of dishonesty with [one of the co-defendants] within the timespan of the alleged conspiracy and dangerous driving away from the scene.'[65] In the light of other case law, the best defence of this decision is that the propensity to offend with a particular person outbalanced the fact that this was a single conviction for a much less serious crime.[66]

7.3.3 Specific propensity

The fact that previous convictions—or a single conviction—establish propensity does not mean that they establish a propensity to commit the currently charged

---

[61] See further *Brown* [2012] EWCA Crim 773, [24].   [62] [2009] EWCA Crim 3512.
[63] [2006] EWCA Crim 1052, [8].
[64] [2009] 2 Cr App R 7, [2009] EWCA Crim 649.   [65] *Johnson*, [34].
[66] A propensity to commit offences with a specific other person is highlighted in one of the JSB's exemplar jury directions. See Judicial Studies Board, *Crown Court Bench Book: Directing the Jury* (2010), (available at: <http://www.judiciary.gov.uk/publications-and-reports/judicial-college/crown-court-bench-book-directing-the-jury>), 208; see also *Hookway* [2011] EWCA Crim 1989; and *Dossett* [2023] EWCA Crim 710. Criminological research does support the view that co-offending is an important dynamic. Young offenders are more likely to commit offences with others, and peers probably play a significant role in introducing first-time offenders to crime. Most offenders engage in both solo and co-offending, although there is some evidence of a tendency towards one or other offending pattern. (See Piquero et al, *Key Issues in Criminal Career Research*, ch 8.) The research does not address the really pertinent question: whether there is a propensity to commit offences with a specific other person, but it does seem likely that such a propensity exists, if only because random choice of co-offender is unlikely. However, two fact patterns should be distinguished: (i) A and B have offended together in the past; evidence that A committed crime X with another person is evidence that B was that other person. (ii) A and B have offended together in the past. They admit being together at the relevant time, but deny committing offence X; their past co-offences are used as evidence that they did. Here, the co-offending dynamic probably adds little to the individual propensities that will be revealed by A's and B's individual criminal histories.

offence. Whatever the truth of the general theory of crime,[67] the courts tend not to see connections between different types of crime: a tendency to commit sexual offences is not considered to be evidence of a propensity to violence.[68] *Tully and Wood*[69] is a significant decision on this point. The defendants were tried for robbery. They both had long criminal records, including a number of convictions for property offences. The trial judge admitted all of these convictions. On appeal, it was held that only previous convictions for robbery should have been admitted:

The judge was wrong to hold, in effect, that a propensity to obtain other people's property by one means or another made it more likely that these appellants would have committed this offence... The whole thrust of the guidance in *Hanson* is that the court should only admit convictions which have some probative force by reason of their similarity to the offence charged. To allow the Crown to prove a propensity to obtain other people's property by some means or another is, in our view, to allow them to cast far too wide a net. Such evidence has limited probative value and has a potentially prejudicial and harmful effect... There are a great many people who have a propensity to acquire other people's property by one means or another. On the other hand, previous convictions for robbery would be much more probative and a conviction for robbing somebody using a knife to reinforce a threat of violence would increase the probative effect.[70]

The element of use or threat of violence that is present in robbery is doubtless what worries the Court here. But in concentrating on the robbery convictions, the Court failed to address another problem. Wood was aged 25 at the time of the offence, and his robbery convictions were gained when he was aged 15 to 16; Tully's robbery offences were also somewhat stale. This, in fact, was what had persuaded the trial judge to put the whole record in.

The Court of Appeal is not always as sensitive to the distinctions between offences as it was in *Tully and Wood*. Gourde was convicted of attempted murder, his previous convictions for robbery, possessing cannabis, arson, and affray being admitted against him as propensity evidence.[71] In the context of a balanced direction to the jury, this was held to be perfectly proper: 'We note in passing that two of the convictions were for violent offences: robbery and affray. In the circumstances of this case, those convictions could be used for the purpose identified by the judge.'[72] Here, a propensity to commit violence is seen to generalize in a way that a propensity to obtain other people's property does not.

When it comes to drugs offences, the Court of Appeal has sometimes seen propensity as specific to a type of drug. So, in *Rooney*,[73] offences of supplying cannabis

---

[67] M. R. Gottfredson and T. Hirschi, *A General Theory of Crime* (Stanford: Stanford University Press, 1990).

[68] See *Leaver* [2006] EWCA Crim 2988.   [69] [2006] EWCA Crim 2270.

[70] *Tully and Wood*, [26]–[27]. See also *Urushadze* [2008] EWCA Crim 2498 (six previous convictions for shoplifting not admissible on a charge of robbery); and cf *Johnson*, [2009] 2 Cr App R 7, [2009] EWCA Crim 649.

[71] *Gourde* [2009] EWCA Crim 1803.

[72] *Gourde*, [34]. See also *R v T and Others* [2010] EWCA Crim 148, where the Court of Appeal was not impressed by the argument that previous convictions for robbery did not show a propensity to violence.

[73] [2007] EWCA Crim 3475.

and ecstasy were not thought to be relevant to a charge of possessing cocaine with intent to supply—although the fact that the previous offences were connected, and so were close to being a single act, played some role in this decision. In *Beverley*,[74] a conviction relating to supply of cannabis was held irrelevant to large-scale importation of cocaine. But in *Belogun*,[75] *Beverley* was distinguished and a conviction for possessing cannabis with intent to supply was considered relevant to supply of crack and heroin: the reason seems to be that there was an intervening conviction involving crack.[76] Finally, in *Adams*,[77] D, whose defence involved the claim that he had purchased a large quantity of class A drugs in order to kill himself, was charged with possessing heroin with intent to supply; previous convictions—which, as in *Rooney*, were really a single transaction—for possessing cannabis, amphetamine, and ecstasy with intent to supply were admitted against him. With very little argument, the Court of Appeal accepted the propriety of this.

The tendency in many of the decisions discussed so far is to view propensity quite narrowly. On occasion, this seems to be taken to an extreme. In *Crawford*, the trial judge described the propensity as being 'to approach lone females in the street and to grab their handbags as they wear them on their shoulders and tug it from them and flee'.[78] Surely it is the propensity to commit street robbery which is significant, rather than these details of the incidents, which put one in mind of the contortions judges sometimes went through to find 'striking similarity' under *Boardman*.[79] Better decisions have emphasized more general propensities which underlie specific instances of misconduct. For example, in *Leaver*,[80] D was charged with rape. The Court of Appeal had no issue with the trial judge's instruction to the jury that D's previous conviction for indecent exposure was relevant to whether he was 'the sort of person who is prepared to degrade and insult a woman for his own sexual gratification'.[81] A more dubious decision is *Burton*,[82] where D was charged with arson. Evidence was admitted that he had previously threatened to burn down his ex-girlfriend's father's house, had once assaulted a girl by holding a lighter close to her face, and when questioned about an offence of dishonesty had told the police that he had burned the relevant chequebook. This miscellany was found to show a 'propensity to deal with fire in an inappropriate way'.[83] Perhaps there is something to this theory, but equally this may be an example of gerrymandering propensity from random similarities.

---

[74] [2006] EWCA Crim 1287.   [75] [2008] EWCA Crim 2006.

[76] In this, and some of the other cases discussed in this section, it may be possible to detect a principle of 'putting in the whole CV'. A conviction that would be judged irrelevant were it to stand in isolation might be admitted if it is part of a long and varied history of offending. Obviously, *Tully and Wood* goes against this possible trend.

[77] [2006] EWCA Crim 2013.

[78] *Freeman and Crawford* [2009] 1 Cr App R 11, [2008] EWCA Crim 1863, [14].

[79] [1975] AC 421.   [80] [2006] EWCA Crim 2988.

[81] *Leaver*, [31]. There may sometimes be a problem in over-generalizing, however. In *Miller*, [2010] EWCA Crim 1578, a significant similarity between two sexual offences was held to be 'abuse of power', a notion vague enough to cover much offending. In *Miller* itself, it is hard to see how it established a link between rape of a member of D's household and D's earlier involvement in a gang rape of an acquaintance.

[82] [2008] EWCA Crim 376.   [83] *Burton*, [16].

7.3.4 Non-criminal propensity evidence

We have already seen, with the decision in *Manister*,[84] that non-criminal conduct can raise admissibility issues. 'Non-criminal bad character evidence' was discussed in Chapter 4, where the emphasis was on moral issues. Here, the focus is on the underlying question of relevance. In the pre-CJA case *R v L*,[85] the Court of Appeal thought that the defendant's entirely legal sexual relationship with a much younger girl was not relevant to the question of whether he had engaged in non-consensual sexual conduct with his daughters. But in *Manister*, a similar relationship was considered to show the defendant's sexual interest in young girls, which was then taken to be relevant to the non-consensual conduct which was charged. The pre-CJA decision in *Dolan*[86] raises similar questions about the relationship between legal and illegal conduct. Dolan was on trial for the murder of his infant son, who had died from a fractured spine thought to have been caused by shaking. The prosecution led evidence of the defendant's short temper and violent conduct towards inanimate objects—he had, for example, smashed up the shower and his own car when they did not work. The Court of Appeal concluded that this evidence should not have been admitted: it was irrelevant.

In the post-CJA case of *Osborne*,[87] evidence was led to show that D would behave aggressively—although not violently—when he stopped taking medication for his schizophrenia. The Court of Appeal considered that this was possibly even less relevant than the evidence in *Dolan*.[88] *Saleem*[89] raises more complex issues. D was convicted of causing GBH with intent; the attack had been pre-planned, and D was alleged to have filmed it on his mobile phone. The admissibility issue concerned material found on D's computer: photographs showing the injuries suffered by victims of violent assaults—which, in the absence of clear proof that they were taken by D, were probably best seen as 'showing an interest in violent images'[90]—as well as rap lyrics downloaded from the internet. One of the lyrics had been modified by D: 'Im gon make history, 1stly dey gon call me mister an dey gon say I dissed ya, I hav 2 b carfull hu I talk 2 becos ur bird wil be da listner, 2ndly February 24th my birth day im gon make it ur worst day, 3rdly do I have 2 have u layin in emergency 2 have dem stitch ya?' The attack on V had taken place on D's birthday. The Court of Appeal held that this evidence had been rightly admitted, but it was cautious about saying that the evidence showed a propensity towards violence:

We agree with the view taken by the judge. Neither the violent images nor the rap lyrics were evidence of propensity to commit the offence with which the appellant was charged.

---

[84] [2006] 1 Cr App R 19, [2005] EWCA Crim 2866. [85] [2003] EWCA Crim 1755.
[86] [2003] EWCA Crim 1859. [87] [2007] EWCA Crim 481.
[88] *Osborne*, [36]. Another good example is *Mckenzie* [2008] RTR 22, [2008] EWCA Crim 758, where evidence from D's driving instructor as to his driving habits was used to prove death by dangerous driving. The Court of Appeal rightly held that this should not have been admitted.
[89] [2007] EWCA Crim 1923. [90] *Saleem*, [37].

This evidence showed an interest in violent images and in something violent happening on his birthday, but not a propensity to commit violence. As the appellant accepted presence in the vicinity, they were relevant to showing that presence was not innocent, given the interests shown by the violent images and the rap lyrics.[91]

This is the first sign we have come across that old ways of thinking about propensity have survived the Act—a theme explored in more detail in the following chapter. No doubt it is in part the difficulty of the relevance problem that encouraged the trial and appellate judges to avoid saying that an interest in violence translates to participation in violence. But the violent material could only show that D's presence in the park was not innocent—ie that he had participated in the attack[92]—if it showed a propensity to participate in violence. Otherwise, the evidence would be no more relevant than evidence showing an interest in sex would be relevant to a charge of rape.

Is the evidence in these cases relevant? Should it be admitted? It is not always easy to separate questions of relevance from other issues in these scenarios. As the quotation from *Dolan* suggests, one worry is that admitting such evidence could lead to a wide-ranging enquiry into a person's life—a boundless moral or psychological audit. If we put this concern to one side, it is easier to focus on relevance. Dolan's behaviour was certainly quite extreme—taking a hammer to his own car—and it is easy to speculate that there is a connection between the lack of self-control displayed in the context of inanimate objects and lack of self-control when faced with a screaming baby. Gottfredson and Hirschi's general theory of crime, after all, is really a general theory of lack of self-control that does not confine itself to crime.[93] And relevance is a low standard: all we need do is suppose that those who smash up malfunctioning cars are more likely than other people to respond violently to human beings. Nevertheless, there is much speculation here, and given the moral significance of violence towards another human being, as well as the conclusions about the fragility of character traits drawn in Chapter 2, it is a bit of a stretch to make a propensity argument. A similar response to *Osborne* is appropriate—especially as Osborne's behaviour seems to have gone no further than shouting at other people.

The relevance argument in *Saleem* might seem to raise much-debated questions about the connection between violent images and violent conduct.[94] But the material in question was not just rap music and portrayals of violence. The

---

[91] *Saleem*, [37].

[92] Going along just to watch is not a crime, unless the participants took encouragement from D's presence: *Clarkson* [1971] 3 All ER 344.

[93] See Gottfredson and Hirschi, *A General Theory of Crime*, esp ch 5; and E. Goode, 'Out of Control? An Introduction to the General Theory of Crime' in E. Goode (ed), *Out of Control: Assessing the General Theory of Crime* (Stanford: Stanford University Press, 2008).

[94] See A. Dennis, 'Poetic (In)Justice: Rap Music Lyrics as Art, Life, and Criminal Evidence' (2007) 31 *Columbia J L & Arts* 1. In *Callum* [2010] EWCA Crim 1325, this was even the subject of expert evidence.

birthday reference meant that the lyric read more like an actual threat. While still written in the register of fantasy, it was more open to a sinister interpretation than a self-penned violent lyric might otherwise be. In propensity terms, D was more likely to use violence on his birthday than someone who had not written those words. But without the mention of the birthday—or without the attack taking place on D's birthday—the case for admissibility would have been weak. As for the photos, these were not fictitious images, but images of the victims of real attacks. That made a good case for a propensity argument.

Manister and *L* also raise complex issues. In *Manister*, the Court of Appeal treated the evidence of D's previous sexual relationship with a 16-year-old girl as relevant 'to the issue of whether the appellant had a sexual interest in [the complainant, a 13 year old girl]. It was capable of demonstrating a sexual interest in early or mid-teenage girls, much younger than the appellant.'[95] In other words, the Court was treating it rather like the coin collector example discussed in Chapter 4: Manister did not have a propensity to commit sexual assault, but, if he did sexually assault someone, he was more likely than other people to pick a young victim. This seems to be the right approach, and avoids the more contentious argument that men who get into relationships with teenage girls have a propensity to commit sexual assault. While *L* involved the added complexity of incest, the same argument probably works there. Nevertheless, in *Manister*, the Court was making a more controversial assumption, for unless the evidence showed that Manister's sexual interests extended to girls, like the complainant, below the age of consent and as young as 13, it was irrelevant. This is a more difficult question and deserved careful analysis.

Finally, *R* v *D, P and U*[96] did not involve non-criminal evidence, but does raise similar issues about inferring one type of behaviour from another, and echoes the argument in *Manister*. Various defendants charged with child abuse had evidence of possession of (illegal) child pornography admitted against them. 'It is obvious,' the Court of Appeal said, 'that it does not necessarily follow that a person who enjoys viewing [child pornography] will act out in real life the kind of activity which is depicted in [it] by abusing children. It follows that the evidence of possession of such photographs is not evidence that the defendant has demonstrated a practice of committing offences of sexual abuse or assault.'[97] Instead, the Court secured relevance by the argument that the evidence simply showed a sexual interest in young children, which made 'it more likely that the allegation of the child complainant is true, rather than having coincidentally been made against someone who does not have that interest.'[98] But a sexual interest in young children surely is an interest in having sex with them. If it is a pure fantasy interest then

---

[95] [2006] 1 Cr App R 19, [2005] EWCA Crim 2866, [95]. As the trial judge put it: '[i]t is something that you can take into account in deciding whether he might have been attracted to [A]. It does not mean that he would have behaved as she says that he behaved; that is assaulting her sexually. To state the obvious, you can be attracted to someone without assaulting them' (at [96]).
[96] [2012] 1 Cr App R 8, [2011] EWCA Crim 1474.   [97] *R* v *D, P and U*, [6].
[98] *R* v *D, P and U*, [6].

it cannot be relevant.[99] No doubt the Court was right to admit the evidence, but as in *Saleem* it avoided analysing the evidence carefully by using the language of coincidence.

The cases analysed in this section involve difficult questions. The inferences involved require careful thought. While there are few signs that we are heading down the sort of slippery slope discussed in Chapter 4—where the trial becomes an investigation of every aspect of a person's life[100]—the courts do not always give the relevance questions the attention they deserve, a theme to which I return in Chapter 8.

7.4 Excluding Relevant Propensity Evidence

Section 101(3) of the Criminal Justice Act 2003 provides that:

The court must not admit evidence under subsection (1)(d) or (g) if, on an application by the defendant to exclude it, it appears to the court that the admission of the evidence would have such an adverse effect on the fairness of the proceedings that the court ought not to admit it.

This has been described as establishing a 'broad discretion',[101] one which the judge should bear in mind even if the defendant makes no formal application.[102]

Section 101(4) explicitly draws the court's attention to the question of time-lapse when considering 101(3).[103] Time-lapse was discussed above, because it makes more sense to view it as an aspect of propensity, and therefore part of the initial judgment of probative value, rather than as only going to the issue of fairness.[104] Ignoring time-lapse, then, in what circumstances do the courts consider admitting bad character as evidence of propensity to be unfair?

---

[99] The Court concludes with the typical fudge of a coincidence argument: '[i]n ordinary language to show that he has a sexual interest in children does make it more likely that the allegation of the child complainant is true, rather than having coincidentally been made against someone who does not have that interest' (ibid., [7]). Coincidences, however, are irrelevant without propensity: see the discussion in Chapter 6.

[100] *Kane* [2013] EWCA Crim 1487 may be the worst example of prosecution abuse of propensity evidence. Unable to produce evidence of Kane's suspected offending, the prosecution relied on evidence of his association with criminals. The Court of Appeal held that this should not have been admitted.

[101] *Edwards and Rowlands*, [2006] 2 Cr App R 4, [2005] EWCA Crim 3244, [82]. As Tapper points out, technically this is not a discretion because the words 'must not' leave the court no choice (C. Tapper, 'The Law of Evidence and the Rule of Law' (2009) 68 *CLJ* 67). However, the language of s 101(3) obviously establishes a 'standard' rather than a 'rule', and the broad evaluative nature of the judgment involved in its application grants the judge considerable leeway.

[102] *Manister*, [2006] 1 Cr App R 19, [2005] EWCA Crim 2866, [38].

[103] As does s 103(3).

[104] Although sometimes fairness will be engaged by time-lapse, as the Court of Appeal noted in *McKenzie* [2008] RTR 22, [2008] EWCA Crim 758, [25]: 'It has also to be borne in mind that if the allegations of prior misconduct have not given rise to any previous investigation, the evidence is liable to be stale and incomplete. The defendant may also be prejudiced in trying to meet it, for lapse of time and inability to pinpoint details (eg of time and place) may result in such allegations being hard to repel and the jury may be left thinking that there is no smoke without fire.'

As long as the bad character evidence is found to establish a relevant propensity, and the jury is warned not to give it too much weight, a court will be unlikely to hold that admitting bad character evidence is unfair. The bad character evidence will be prejudicial, in the sense that it increases D's chance of conviction, but will probably not be seen as being unfairly prejudicial.[105] When courts seem to hold otherwise, invoking section 101(3) to justify the exclusion of bad character evidence, it is usually because they have doubts about whether the evidence does establish propensity.[106] *Benabbou*[107] is something of an exception to this general trend: a previous conviction for rape was held to be 'technically admissible' to prove sexual assault and assault by penetration. But because the previous conviction involved a different (though more serious) factual scenario, the Court thought that probative value was weak,[108] and that the conviction 'must have had a highly prejudicial effect on the fairness of the trial'.[109] Another option, taken in *Baker*,[110] would have been to inform the jury of the rape conviction, but not the facts.

Defendants who want to avoid having bad character introduced therefore do best to concentrate their fire on the initial question of whether the evidence shows a relevant propensity. In *Hanson*, the Court of Appeal did offer defendants a further exclusionary argument: the prosecution should not use propensity evidence to bolster a weak case. This criterion might be seen as part of section 101(3)'s fairness evaluation. It is not surprising to find the case law littered with defence claims that the prosecution is propping up a flimsy case by dragging up the defendant's past. But in the appeal courts, such arguments appear to have little chance of success. While this in itself gives some insight into how the courts approach the issue, there is little explicit appellate guidance on when a case might be seen as being too weak to be supported by propensity evidence. The Court of Appeal has rejected the argument that a case is too frail when it depends on a single eyewitness,[111] and in *Burton*[112] a conviction for arson was upheld where without the propensity evidence the case was flimsy, resting on D's having a possible motive, having left the property around the time the fire started, and the absence of evidence of an accidental cause of fire.[113] While it has been argued that propensity evidence should only be used where the prosecution is able to make out a case to answer without it,[114] the courts do not seem to have taken this line.[115]

---

[105] See *De Vos* [2006] EWCA Crim 1688, [30].

[106] See, eg, *Tully and Wood*, [2006] EWCA Crim 2270; and *Clements* [2009] EWCA Crim 2726.

[107] [2012] EWCA Crim 1256.

[108] The previous offence involved grabbing the victim in the street and driving her away; the current charges involved opportunistic sexual attacks committed in people's houses. It is hard to see why these differences were thought to be significant: surely someone who would participate in the very serious previous rape would have a tendency to commit less serious assaults too.

[109] *Benabbou*, [23].   [110] [2012] EWCA Crim 1801.

[111] *Miller*, [2010] EWCA Crim 1578.   [112] [2008] EWCA Crim 376.

[113] But nor was there any evidence that the fire had been started deliberately.

[114] R. Munday, '"Round up the Usual Suspects!" Or What Have We to Fear from Part 11 of the Criminal Justice Act 2003' (2005) 169 *JP* 328.

[115] See *Shrimpton* [2007] EWCA Crim 3346, [21]. There must be considerable doubt whether *Burton* would have gone to the jury without the propensity evidence.

This must be right, because propensity evidence can sometimes be powerful. Any rule restricting propensity evidence to supporting a case already strong enough to justify a conviction would have thwarted Straffen's[116] conviction for the murder of Linda Bowyer—in the absence of the propensity evidence, all that incriminated Straffen was his presence in the area around the time the crime was committed. Reflection on the *Straffen* example in fact suggests that *Hanson's* warning about bolstering a weak case is misleading. Strong propensity evidence can convert the frailest case into a convincing one. *Hanson's* concern is best understood as being that judges should be careful to make sure that the propensity evidence is not being asked to bear more weight than it can carry, in other words, that when combined with the other evidence the case as a whole is strong enough to prove guilt beyond reasonable doubt. This is a question of sufficiency, of whether the case is strong enough to go to the jury.

The general picture, then, is that arguments based on fairness cut little ice in the vast majority of cases.[117] Occasionally, though, section 101(3) is significant. Reasoning prejudice and moral prejudice are not the only dangers involved in introducing evidence of the defendant's bad character. If there is any dispute about the bad character evidence, considerable time and effort may have to be put into deciding whether the defendant did indeed commit the prior wrongdoing. While the defendant may only be charged with one offence, he may end up having to respond to multiple allegations. Bloated by 'satellite litigation', the trial may take far longer than it would otherwise do, and the jury's focus be deflected from the real issues.

O'Dowd[118] is the paradigmatic example of these problems. O'Dowd was tried for a number of offences arising from an incident in which he was said to have falsely imprisoned and raped the complainant. The Crown, 'perhaps mindful of the difficulties in prosecuting rape cases, considered it needed the evidence of…three bad character complainants. It did so because it considered the appellant was masterly at manipulating vulnerable women such as SS, a drug addict, and defending himself by reviling them in a way which, but for the evidence of similar allegations by others and similar defences, might well cast doubt on her allegations.'[119] Of the three similar incidents, spanning a period of 22 years, one had resulted in an acquittal (in respect of which D had later been prosecuted for forgery), one had led to a conviction, and the third involved a prosecution which had been stayed for abuse of process when the complainant revealed that she was aware of O'Dowd's history. O'Dowd was a belligerent character. Unwilling to concede anything, he disputed the correctness of the previous conviction and

---

[116] *Straffen* [1952] 2 QB 911.

[117] The empirical research on the operation of the CJA did find that trial judges often excluded evidence on grounds of unfairness. Without more detail, it is impossible to know whether this means that s 101(3) does play a significant role in practice, or whether these decisions were merely ways of holding that the evidence did not establish a significant propensity. Morgan Harris Burrows LLP, *Research into the Impact of Bad Character Provisions on the Courts*, Ministry of Justice Research Series 5/09 (London: Ministry of Justice, 2009), 25.

[118] [2009] 2 Cr App R 16, [2009] EWCA Crim 905.   [119] *O'Dowd*, [57].

at one point sacked his defence team, choosing to defend himself. For these and other reasons, the trial ended up lasting six and a half months. Nearly 40 per cent of the days on which evidence was heard involved bad character evidence, as did 148 pages of the judge's 434 page summing up. O'Dowd's conviction was quashed on appeal. The admission of the bad character evidence rendered the trial 'unnecessarily and unduly complex', and, together with other interruptions to the trial, had made it 'very difficult for the jury to keep its eye on the ball'.[120]

The Court of Appeal was in no doubt that things had got out of hand in *O'Dowd*. Yet given the difficulties of proving rape and the power of the evidence once all the incidents were seen alongside each other, it is evident why the prosecution took the course it did. The appeal judgment does offer some constructive comments: the judge should have considered asking the prosecution to pick the most compelling of the three allegations and to introduce evidence relating only to that one. The judge might also have used section 74(3) of PACE to facilitate proof of the disputed previous conviction.[121] This provision creates a rebuttable presumption that the defendant committed the offence underlying the previous conviction. No doubt mindful of the Court of Appeal's criticisms in *O'Dowd*, the trial judge in *R* v *C*[122] invoked section 74(3) together with the overriding objective in the Criminal Procedure Rules[123] in order to thwart the defendant's claim that he had been wrongfully convicted on a previous occasion. The trial judge's view was that: 'A second jury is not the appropriate tribunal to determine the correctness of an earlier conviction and so there must be compelling grounds for satellite litigation...A defendant's interests are protected generally by the appellate process; if a defendant has fresh evidence, then that evidence should be considered by an appellate court and not by a jury.'[124] The practical implication was that the defendant would not be allowed to cross-examine prosecution witnesses called to establish the facts of the earlier conviction. This time, the Court of Appeal thought that the judge had gone too far. While the defendant bore an evidential burden, he could not be prevented from questioning prosecution witnesses. But in order to guard against satellite litigation, the prosecution might initially rely on the presumption, and decide what witnesses to call to bolster it once the defence had made its case for mistaken conviction.

Evidence law has long been concerned with managing the issues in contention at trial. Every issue can be disputed, and a potentially endless chain of claim and counterclaim can quickly spiral out of control. This has led to doctrines such as the collateral finality rule.[125] No doubt the CJA's new admissibility threshold for

---

[120] *O'Dowd*, [83]–[84].

[121] *O'Dowd*, [71]. Section 74(3) provides that conviction for an offence is proof of its commission 'unless the contrary is proved'.

[122] [2011] 1 Cr App R 17, [2010] EWCA Crim 2971.

[123] The overriding objective set by rule 1.1 is to try cases justly, which includes dealing with them efficiently and expeditiously.

[124] *R* v *C*, [7].

[125] See, eg, P. Roberts and A. Zuckerman, *Criminal Evidence* (2nd edn, Oxford: Oxford University Press, 2010), 351–63.

propensity evidence is susceptible to creating protracted disputes around issues of marginal relevance, eating up trial resources and distracting the jury. Nevertheless, we should be wary of thinking that propensity evidence is always a sideshow to the main event. As the discussion of comparative propensity in Chapter 2 showed, propensity evidence can be powerful, even in the absence of the sort of 'striking similarity' seen in cases such as *Straffen*. That a person has previously committed a serious violent or sexual offence tells us a lot about them, and may turn an otherwise weak case into a strong one. An allegation of this sort can be well worth spending time on. Perhaps the prosecution went too far in *O'Dowd*, but the stakes were high and it is not obvious that its strategy went beyond what is acceptable, nor that it left the jury unable to cope.

7.5 Warning the Jury

In *Hanson*, the Court of Appeal emphasized the importance of directing the jury carefully on the relevance of bad character evidence. This is a familiar development. The law of evidence in England and Wales is coming to rely less on strict rules of inadmissibility. This does not mean that the law is no longer concerned that the jury will put too much weight on particular types of evidence; rather, such fears are now represented in the judicial directions which are given to juries.[126] Where inferences from silence are concerned, judicial warning has even been identified as a necessity by the European Court of Human Rights,[127] and if part of the standard warning on inferences from silence is omitted, a defendant will have good grounds for appeal. An indication of the importance of jury guidance in the modern criminal trial is the Judicial Studies Board's Crown Court Bench Book, *Directing the Jury*, which now runs to nearly 400 pages, most of which cover issues of evidence and procedure.[128] There has been some concern that this has inculcated a 'tick box' culture, where judges insulate themselves from criticism by reciting boilerplate warnings with little concern as to whether the jury really understands them or whether they fit the facts of the instant case. There is also concern that in some areas—inferences from silence again being a good example—directions have become too complex and show too little respect for the jury's common sense.[129] Consequently, the latest version of the Bench Book has moved away from giving standard warnings, instead presenting illustrative

[126] See Roberts and Zuckerman, *Criminal Evidence*, 676–93.
[127] *Condron* v *United Kingdom* (2001) 31 EHRR 1; and *Beckles* v *United Kingdom* (2003) 36 EHRR 13.
[128] Judicial Studies Board, *Crown Court Bench Book: Directing the Jury* (2010), available at: <http://www.judiciary.gov.uk/publications-and-reports/judicial-college/crown-court-bench-book-directing-the-jury>.
[129] These criticisms are particularly associated with Lord Phillips, who conveyed them during his tenure as Lord Chief Justice. See his judgment in *Campbell* [2007] 2 Cr App R 28, [2007] EWCA Crim 1472, [19]–[43], and 'Trusting the Jury', Criminal Bar Association Kalisher Lecture, 23 October 2007.

examples which require some reworking by the trial judge.[130] In many areas, though, there remains a standard list of points to be covered.

Hanson outlined the warning requirement for propensity evidence as follows:

the judge in summing-up should warn the jury clearly against placing undue reliance on previous convictions. Evidence of bad character cannot be used simply to bolster a weak case, or to prejudice the minds of a jury against a defendant. In particular, the jury should be directed; that they should not conclude that the defendant is guilty or untruthful merely because he has these convictions; that, although the convictions may show a propensity, this does not mean that he has committed this offence or been untruthful in this case; that whether they in fact show a propensity is for them to decide; that they must take into account what the defendant has said about his previous convictions; and that, although they are entitled, if they find propensity as shown, to take this into account when determining guilt, propensity is only one relevant factor and they must assess its significance in the light of all the other evidence in the case.[131]

That there is no 'rigid formula' to be followed was emphasized in *Edwards*, but 'what the summing-up must contain is a clear warning to the jury against placing undue reliance on previous convictions',[132] together with an explanation of what the evidence has been introduced to prove. Failure to give a proper warning may well render a conviction unsafe.

7.6 Conclusion: Assessing Gateway (d)

The propensity limb of gateway (d) is the lynchpin of the Criminal Justice Act's scheme for the admissibility of bad character evidence against defendants. In the appeal courts, it has brought about a significant change in the law and in judicial thinking. In the vast majority of cases discussed in this chapter, the bad character evidence would not have been admitted as propensity evidence before the CJA came into force. The new provisions have legitimated the use of propensity evidence: not only is it seen as relevant where it was not before, it is also not seen as being prejudicial where it was before. It is obviously harder to know what is going on in the trial courts, but what research there is confirms the picture of profound change. Whereas before the CJA evidence of the defendant's bad character was most often introduced by the prosecution as evidence of credibility,[133] now it usually gains admission as evidence of propensity.[134] Whatever one thinks about the

---

[130] For discussion of this policy, see the *Crown Court Bench Book*, v–ix. A 'companion' to the bench book was later published, listing in simpler form issues which need to be considered when directing the jury: *Crown Court Bench Book Companion* (2012), available at: <http://www.judiciary. gov.uk/publications/crown-court-bench-book-directing-the-jury-2/>.

[131] *Hanson*, [2005] 2 Cr App R 21, [2005] EWCA Crim 824, [18].

[132] *Edwards* [2006] 1 Cr App R 3, [2005] EWCA Crim 1813, [3].

[133] M. Zander and P. Henderson, *Crown Court Study* (London: HMSO, 1993), 119.

[134] See Morgan Harris Burrows, *Research into the Impact of Bad Character Provisions*, 14, 22–3. Gateway (d) was the route through which bad character evidence was admitted in 86 per cent of cases where it was admitted, and it appears that very few of these cases involved the credibility limb of (d).

wisdom of admitting more bad character evidence, it must surely be conceded that there is something positive here. By expanding the use of propensity evidence, the CJA has inaugurated a more honest approach: juries are less likely to be faced with complex, and frequently ridiculous, instructions to the effect that bad character evidence reflects on credibility but not on propensity (see further Chapter 9). On the theme of transparency, it is also apparent that judges are now more open about propensity, often clearly labelling bad character evidence as propensity evidence rather than using the double-speak of the categories or forbidden reasoning, as they used to do.[135]

Beyond this, assessing gateway (d) is not a straightforward task. There is no simple way of summarizing exactly what the gateway allows, nor is there agreement on the background policy question of when propensity evidence should be admitted. In previous chapters, I have argued that propensity evidence can have considerable probative force and that there is little reason to think that admitting it is prejudicial. I assess gateway (d) from this perspective.

While the headline in any assessment of gateway (d) is that more propensity evidence is now admissible, we are still a long way from a regime of automatic admissibility. The CJA's admissibility scheme remains dominated by crime similarity. A previous conviction for a violent offence will not be introduced as evidence that D committed a property offence, despite the fact that it would be relevant: offenders tend to be generalists, thus those who commit assault are also more likely to steal than the average person. This is not to argue that the CJA should go further. Offenders also specialize—they are 'specialized generalists' as it was put in Chapter 2—so by concentrating on crime similarity the courts are tending to admit the most probative previous convictions. While it might be justified in inferential terms, going further than this would be fairly radical, and might well give the jury the impression that the prosecution was simply trying to blacken the defendant's name—a strategy which could backfire.

Similarity is not the only dimension on which the probative value of propensity evidence should be judged: time-lapse, offence seriousness, and the number of convictions are also relevant. Overall, the courts have done well by identifying these criteria and taking them into account in most cases. While convictions for sexual offences appear to get special treatment—often being admitted when very stale—there is some empirical justification for this practice.

If the courts have identified the relevant factors underlying propensity inferences, this does not mean that they are drawing the admissibility threshold in the right place. Some decisions are open to criticism for setting too low a standard. *McMinn* is the most prominent example,[136] where a single conviction for ABH gained at the age of 15 was used to prove a new charge of ABH. If *McMinn* is a precedent, then the admissibility threshold is quite low, and once beyond the most common property offences there is little chance of excluding a conviction

---

[135] See Chapters 5 and 6.
[136] [2007] EWCA Crim 3024. See also *Johnson*, [2009] 2 Cr App R 7, [2009] EWCA Crim 649, where theft from a skip was used to prove burglary.

for a similar offence—the cautionary comments about 'single act propensity' in *Hanson* having been overridden. Certainly, *McMinn* and some other decisions can be criticized for paying insufficient attention to the young age at which a previous conviction was gained—although this is not a factor to which the courts are universally insensitive.

If *McMinn* is a precedent, that is. A prominent feature of the CJA bad character jurisprudence is that the Court of Appeal has tried to limit the extent to which a rigid case law accumulates. Trial judges are granted considerable discretion, with their admissibility decisions only reviewable for *Wednesbury* unreasonableness, and the Court emphasizes the factual particularity of each case. In *McMinn* itself, the Court cautioned against admitting 'a single instance of this kind',[137] even while upholding the trial judge's decision to do so. This brings us to some of the central questions about the 2003 Act. In reviewing the case law, I have highlighted various instances where there is a degree of inconsistency between decisions. And it is not possible to describe the current admissibility threshold with much precision—the best that can be done is to note that the courts take a variety of factors into account. The application of gateway (d) is obviously not an example of rule-based decision-making. This state of affairs has its critics, notably Tapper, who argues that the way in which the appeal courts approach bad character evidence is inimical to the rule of law, and Schauer, who claims that evidence law should generally be rule-based.[138] The question, then, is whether there is something problematic in gateway (d) and the untidy jurisprudence that has developed around it. Can we do better?

The bad character provisions of the CJA have generated a large amount of case law. As in any area of law, there are bound to be some decisions which are out of kilter with the vast majority, and which are probably best regarded as mistaken. *Long*,[139] an early decision decrying the use of single act propensity, is an example. The criticism of the CJA jurisprudence has to be understood as being aimed at something more significant than the occasional *Long*: a general lack of consistency and predictability in the case law. The chaos, however, should not be exaggerated. Readers of this chapter should have a reasonable idea of when bad character evidence is prone to be admitted. Anyone with a previous conviction for a similar offence—where similarity is understood in terms of broad categories, such as sexual, violent, and property offending—is at risk. We can go a little beyond this by noting that factors such as seriousness and time-lapse play a role, but for non-serious offending confident prediction is admittedly difficult. There is a large grey area surrounding cases like *McMinn*, where admissibility might go either way.

---

[137] [2007] EWCA Crim 3024, [10].
[138] Tapper, 'The Law of Evidence'; and F. Schauer, 'In Defense of Rule-Based Evidence Law—and Epistemology Too' (2008) 5 *Episteme* 295. See also F. Schauer, 'On the Supposed Jury-Dependence of Evidence Law' (2006) 155 *U Penn L Rev* 165; and cf M. Damaška, 'The Jury and the Law of Evidence: Real and Imagined Interconnections' (2006) 5 *Law, Probability & Risk* 255. A good general discussion of discretion in evidence law is Roberts and Zuckerman, *Criminal Evidence*, 25–30.
[139] [2006] EWCA Crim 578.

The clarity and predictability of the propensity evidence rule prior to the CJA should not be exaggerated either. In Chapter 5, we saw that, after the House of Lords decision in *DPP* v *P* in 1991, judges tended to pick and choose among a range of admissibility rules, making it hard to say just when propensity evidence would be admitted (and even before *P*, the various rules were hardly crystal clear). Indeed, it may well be that today's admissibility practice is no less determinate than its predecessor. The admissibility threshold is certainly lower, applying to previous convictions for less serious crimes and with fewer connecting similarities: in other words, a larger pool of cases. It is no surprise, therefore, that more cases should fall into the grey zone of arguable admissibility. But whatever the truth of this rough comparison, it is significant that the Court of Appeal has taken a rather hands-off approach to the new regime, emphasizing the trial judge's discretion. Again, though, this is not a complete break with the past. While in *Boardman* Lord Cross held that the application of the propensity rule involved a question of law, not discretion,[140] in the wake of *DPP* v *P* the Court of Appeal quite often referred to the admissibility decision as discretionary,[141] a nod to the inevitable degree of judgment involved in its application. The Court also noted the need to give due deference to the trial judge's decision.[142] But the application of the *Wednesbury* standard of review to the new legislation has certainly gone some way beyond this: the Court of Appeal is much less interventionist than it was. There are relatively few cases where it has held propensity evidence to be wrongly admitted under the CJA.

Comparisons with the old law only take us so far. After all, some will claim that the rot set in before the CJA, with *DPP* v *P* and its vague balancing test. The real questions are about the costs of having a vague admissibility rule, and whether it would be possible to have a more precise one. Propensity evidence does not stand in isolation. The modern history of evidence law in various jurisdictions has involved a shift towards governing admissibility through judicial discretion, with strict rules being watered down and remoulded to include increasingly wide areas of judgment.[143] This trend is not welcomed by all.[144] Many of the criticisms form part of the familiar case against drafting norms as standards

---

[140] [1975] AC 421, 457.

[141] *Allen* [2002] EWCA Crim 2886, [18]; *Kenyon* [2004] EWCA Crim 821, [17]; and *Harrison* [2004] EWCA Crim 1792, [34].

[142] *Cowie* [2003] EWCA Crim [27] 3522; and *Barney* [2005] EWCA Crim 1385, [14]–[15]. In the latter, the Court of Appeal, while not interfering with the trial judge's decision to admit the evidence, noted that other trial judges would have decided the issue differently—an observation which has become quite common under the CJA.

[143] For example, The Federal Rules of Evidence, introduced in 1975 in the United States, are generally seen as a decisive step away from rigid rules. See J. Waltz, 'Judicial Discretion in the Admission of Evidence under the Federal Rules of Evidence' (1985) 79 *Northwestern UL Rev* 1097; and T. Mengler, 'The Theory of Discretion in the Federal Rules of Evidence' (1989) 74 *Iowa L Rev* 413. In Canada, the hearsay rule has been relaxed, and admissibility of hearsay is now governed by the 'principled approach' which requires a direct enquiry into the factors justifying admissibility. See D. Paciocco and L. Stuesser, *The Law of Evidence* (5th edn, Toronto: Irwin Law, 2008).

[144] See the sources cited in n 138 above; and E. Swift, 'One Hundred Years of Evidence Law Reform: Thayer's Triumph' (2000) 88 *California L Rev* 2437.

rather than as rules.[145] The application of standards is more difficult to review on appeal, thus giving more power to first-instance decision-makers. Partly as a consequence, standards are less predictable, create inconsistency, and leave scope for judicial bias. By encouraging appeals, standards may also be costly in terms of resources.[146] There are stock responses to these points: predictability is less important in procedural law than in many areas of substantive law; because strict rules tend to be over- and under-inclusive with regard to their rationales, they too create inconsistencies; bias can be controlled to an extent by asking judges to give reasons. The experience with the CJA probably bears out the concern that standards create more appeals, but this may be an acceptable cost of more individualized and contextualized decision-making. This last point is important. In evidence law, the case for admitting evidence is frequently made in terms of probative value. Probative value is very hard to capture in anything like a strict rule. That is one of the lessons of the history of the propensity evidence rule recounted in Chapter 5. The tighter versions of the rule—based on the categories, forbidden reasoning, or striking similarity—were problematic in part because they did not reflect probative value, and that is one reason why the law moved on to give us *DPP* v *P*'s vaguer balancing test and now the loose framework which is the CJA and its case law.

Looking closely at the arguments made by those who press for a rule-based evidence law, the key concern appears to be that certain types of evidence resist unbiased evaluation, either by the fact-finder or by the judge playing the screening role.[147] In the current context, this argument is as much against the admissibility of character evidence as it is against discretion. But if, as argued here, bad character evidence is usually not prejudicial, then we do not need to tie the hands of judges to prevent their biases running away with them. Even if one is simply the sort of person who prefers rules to standards, it is hard to imagine a rule-based regime which would admit evidence in roughly the situations that gateway (d) does. The complex interplay of the different factors determining relevance is the stumbling block. For example, a rule holding that previous convictions more than ten years old should not be admitted has its attractions, but it would fall foul of the situation where there was considerable factual similarity between an 11-year-old conviction and the current charge, or where the conviction involved a serious sexual offence. It is likely that with character evidence rules can only be formulated if they eschew an attempt to track probative value—as did the old rules, such as the categories approach.

If we want to admit bad character evidence in roughly the situations which gateway (d) does—and this seems to me to be a sensible policy—then we probably

---

[145] See, eg, P. Schlag, 'Rules and Standards' (1985) 33 *UCLA L Rev* 379; and F. Schauer, *Thinking Like a Lawyer: A New Introduction to Legal Reasoning* (Cambridge, MA: Harvard University Press, 2009), ch 10.

[146] Tapper, 'The Law of Evidence', 72, suggests that in Canada the adoption of the 'principled' approach to hearsay has caused considerable litigation.

[147] See Swift, 'One Hundred Years of Evidence Law Reform'; and Schauer, 'In Defense of Rule-Based Evidence Law'.

have to accept that we will not have rule-based decision-making. Cases like *McMinn* may be more or less inevitable once we choose something like gateway (d); if we want broader admissibility than the common law, we should not be too critical of them. That said, there is something to the complaint that the Court of Appeal has gone too far in leaving trial judges to their own devices. It did not have to adopt a *Wednesbury* standard of review.[148] There is a bizarre quality to the *McMinn* strategy of cautioning against the use of single act propensity even while allowing it, as if the Court is denying the precedential quality of its own decisions. But judges and prosecutors will draw lessons from *McMinn*, and the likely outcome is that the admissibility threshold will be driven ever lower. The early decisions such as *Hanson* were a welcome attempt to give general guidance on the new legislation. With several years' more experience, revisiting them in new guideline judgments would be worthwhile.

[148] No doubt the Court of Appeal's hands-off policy was partly an attempt to discourage appeals, and to allow them to be dealt with quickly when they did occur. The Court of Appeal is notoriously over-worked, so perhaps there is a sense in which it had to adopt light touch review—especially as the equally complex and contentious hearsay provisions of the CJA were introduced at the same time. But it is also possible that a more interventionist policy would have allowed it to lay down clearer guidelines for admissibility, which would in time have given trial judges sufficient guidance that the flood of appeals would have abated.

8

Propensity, Coincidence, and Acquitted Misconduct

In the previous chapter, we saw that under the Criminal Justice Act 2003 the courts have by and large been comfortable with the idea of using bad character evidence to show propensity—in marked contrast to the situation prior to the Act. In this chapter, the assessment is slightly more negative. The reasoning underlying the use of propensity evidence continues to be misunderstood. While sometimes the confusion is harmless, at other times it can be prejudicial to defendants.

One of the questions analysed here is how courts understand propensity evidence. As we saw in Chapters 5 and 6, prior to the CJA propensity evidence was often described in non-propensity terms. This still occurs, and can be problematic because it may mean that the evidence does not get the scrutiny it deserves. Especially troublesome in the case law has been the distinction between propensity and coincidence reasoning. This chapter also considers the use of acquitted misconduct to prove guilt. Here, there are questions of principle—what weight should be given to the fact that an allegation of criminal activity was prosecuted and resulted in acquittal?—but questions about the way in which inference is understood continue to be pertinent.

8.1 Simple Misclassification

Prior to the CJA, the categories approach and the fear of 'forbidden' reasoning often led courts to deny that evidence was propensity evidence when it plainly was. It is not surprising that lawyers have sometimes used these old ways of thinking when making arguments under the new Act. To their credit, the courts have often seen through these claims. For instance, in *Wilkinson*,[1] D was charged with sexual offences against children; several previous convictions for similar offences were admitted against him. On appeal, the defence drew on the categories argument which had been successful in the pre-CJA case of *Lewis*:[2] given that the defence was a complete denial (rather than, for example, an attempt to give an

---

[1] [2006] EWCA Crim 1332.   [2] (1983) 76 Cr App R 33.

innocent explanation for admitted behaviour), the defendant's propensity was irrelevant. The Court of Appeal responded astutely:

We are not able to accept that submission. The relevant propensity is a propensity to do what it is alleged occurred—that is a sexual offence against a girl. It cannot, in our judgment, make any difference to the question of admissibility whether the appellant denies any physical contact with the girl or whether he admits some lesser physical contact. In our judgment, the question of propensity is as important—it is no more and no less important—if the defence is a complete denial of contact as in a situation where it is admitted that some sexual contact occurred but not that which is alleged in the charge.[3]

In the burglary case of *Johnson*, the trial judge had ruled that previous convictions were not propensity evidence, but were relevant to whether the defendants would participate in a conspiracy to burgle. The Court of Appeal saw through this, properly labelling the convictions propensity evidence.[4]

However, the courts are not always so perceptive. In *Saleem*,[5] a case discussed in Chapter 7, the Court of Appeal explicitly denied that the photographs and rap lyrics were evidence of a propensity to participate in violence, holding instead that they were relevant to show that D's presence was not innocent. Of course, the evidence could only show that presence was not innocent if the evidence showed a propensity to participate in violence. Here, the mistake is problematic. *Hanson* holds that questions of propensity should be analysed carefully, with two initial questions being: '[d]oes the history of conviction(s) establish a propensity to commit offences of the kind charged?'; and '[d]oes that propensity make it more likely that the defendant committed the offence charged?'.[6] Obviously, this sort of analysis should also apply where the bad character evidence does not involve previous convictions. In *Saleem*, the question of whether the photographs and lyrics established a propensity to violence was one which deserved careful consideration. But it did not receive it, and this seems to be because the Court of Appeal relied on the conveniently vague argument that the material went to rebut innocent presence. It pursued a similar strategy in *R v D, P, and U*,[7] where the question was whether possession of child pornography could be used to prove child abuse.

Saleem is not an isolated example. There are various other cases where the court has claimed that propensity evidence is not propensity evidence, but that it is, for example, evidence of identity or that it rebuts a claim of coincidence.[8] In most of these cases, the confusion does not seem to have been harmful—issues

---

[3] *Wilkinson*, [17].   [4] [2009] 2 Cr App R 7, [2009] EWCA Crim 649 [15], [19].
[5] [2007] EWCA Crim 1923.   [6] [2005] 2 Cr App R 21, [2005] EWCA Crim 824, [7].
[7] [2012] 1 Cr App R 8, [2011] EWCA Crim 1474, [6].
[8] See, eg, *Simmerson* [2006] EWCA Crim 2636; *Miller* [2009] EWCA Crim 2890; *Jordan* [2009] EWCA Crim 953; *Tirnaveanu* [2007] 2 Cr App R 23, [2007] EWCA Crim 1239; and *Vo* [2013] EWCA Crim 2292. *O'Leary* [2013] EWCA Crim 1371 contains the very strange argument that, when two allegations of fraud were tried together, 'the evidence was relied upon not for its capacity to establish propensity to commit offences of fraud or theft but for its capacity to demonstrate that [the complainants] Mrs Werner and Mr Knight had been deliberately selected because they were vulnerable' [12].

such as the age of convictions have been considered. But in *Kamara*,[9] the classification of previous convictions as rebutting a defence of innocent association seems to have led the Court of Appeal to close its eyes to the defence argument that single act propensity was not sufficient. And in *Laurusevicius*,[10] the Court of Appeal's inability to recognize propensity evidence actually led to it ruling a previous conviction inadmissible. D put forward an innocent explanation for the evidence connecting him to a burglary. The Court of Appeal was persuaded that a previous burglary conviction was not propensity evidence, but 'went to rebut a defence which produced, if it were true, a coincidence',[11] finding the coincidence insufficiently compelling to justify admissibility.

A more subtle version of the problem arose in *Isichei*, where D was convicted of ABH and robbery.[12] The attacker had approached the victim saying he wanted 'his coke back'; D had a previous conviction, from six years before, for being involved in the importation of cocaine. Here, it is true that the evidence was not being used as propensity evidence in the usual sense: the claim was not that people who import cocaine have a propensity to assault and rob. As the Court of Appeal put it, it was evidence 'of identification through the medium of a connecting factor so as to place Isichei in a discrete category of persons interested in cocaine'.[13] But that does not mean that propensity was irrelevant, for only if we think that those who are involved in importing cocaine will have a propensity to be involved with the drug six years later will we think that the evidence suggests that *Isichei* falls into the 'interested in cocaine' category. For this reason, D's propensity *was* an important matter in issue between prosecution and defence, and admissibility should have followed the scheme of section 103(1)(a) and its case law.[14] It is too easy to fall into the pattern of thinking that the cocaine link 'cannot be a coincidence', but where a transient feature is concerned it may well be—just as if the attacker had worn a red scarf and there was evidence that D had worn one six years earlier. The time-lapse in *Isichei* should have been given due consideration, both by the court and by the jury.

8.2 Propensity, Pooling, and Cross-Admissibility

In the previous chapter, the discussion concentrated on relatively simple scenarios involving propensity evidence: D is charged with a crime and previous convictions, or other items of incriminating evidence, are introduced as propensity evidence. But, as we saw in Chapter 6, more complex scenarios can also arise where D disputes the facts said to give rise to the propensity inference. This may be because, for example, the propensity inference depends on an untried allegation of misconduct, or because D is charged with more than one crime and the evidence

---

[9] [2011] EWCA Crim 1146.
[10] [2008] EWCA Crim 3020. In the event, however, D's conviction was upheld.
[11] *Laurusevicius*, [17].   [12] [2006] EWCA Crim 1815.   [13] *Isichei*, [32].
[14] Cf I. H. Dennis, *The Law of Evidence* (5th edn, London: Sweet & Maxwell, 2013), 827.

is treated as cross-admissible between the counts. In dealing with these more complex fact patterns, the Court of Appeal has made a number of errors. A failure to recognize and understand propensity inferences underlies many of them.

The Court of Appeal got off to a good start with its decision in *Chopra*.[15] D, a dentist, was charged with three counts of indecent assault. The evidence was treated as cross-admissible between the counts, and D was convicted on two of them.[16] This, then, was a classic case of multiple allegations where, as explained in Chapter 6, the allegations are mutually supportive via propensity inferences. The Court held that the evidence was propensity evidence:

> Of course, where propensity is advanced by way of multiple complaints, none of which has yet been proved, and whether they are proved or not is the question which the jury must answer, that is a different case from the case where propensity is advanced through proof of a previous conviction which may be incapable of contradiction. However, the 2003 Act governs all evidence of bad character, not only conclusive or undisputable evidence.[17]

As for the question of when evidence on one count could be treated as cross-admissible on another, the Court held that the test is now a basic one of relevance.[18]

Doubts were first expressed about *Chopra*'s classification of cross-admissible counts as propensity evidence in *Wallace*.[19] D was tried for offences connected to four robberies. There were similarities between the robberies, and there was some evidence connecting D to each of them, such as a carrier bag with his fingerprint found at one of the scenes of crime. The evidence was treated as cross-admissible, and D was convicted on all counts. In the Court of Appeal it was doubted whether, when considering one count, evidence on the other counts was properly classified as bad character evidence: 'Although technically within the definition of "bad character", the purpose of the admission of the evidence was not to prove that the appellant was of bad character in the sense that that expression is commonly understood. Once before the jury the evidence was relevant for what it tended to prove, namely that when viewed as a whole the appellant was guilty of each of the offences.'[20] The significance of this is that: 'No "bad character" direction to the jury would have been necessary. Indeed no reference to "bad character" in the commonly understood sense of the words would have been necessary at all. The case should, and no doubt would, have been summed up just as it was, as a case that depended on circumstantial evidence.'[21]

---

[15] [2007] 1 Cr App R 16, [2006] EWCA Crim 2133.

[16] The acquittal related to a count where the complaint was not spontaneous, but arose after patients were contacted.

[17] *Chopra*, [15].

[18] *Chopra*, [16]. The Court went on to say: 'By way of example we mention, as the Court did in *Hanson*, that it may well be that one kind of assault will fail to be capable of establishing propensity to commit a different kind of assault' (at [24]).

[19] [2007] 2 Cr App R 30, [2007] EWCA Crim 1760.   [20] *Wallace*, [39].

[21] *Wallace*, [44].

The *Wallace* approach was taken up and extended in *McAllister*.[22] Here, the Court of Appeal, dealing with an interlocutory appeal, held that evidence relating to a robbery in Scotland of which D had been acquitted could not be used as evidence that he had committed the currently charged robbery, committed in Leeds. On its facts, this may have been a reasonable decision: opening up questions about the previous acquittal might have bogged the trial down in complex satellite issues.[23] It is the way in which the Court of Appeal analysed the relevance of the previous conviction which is problematic. It held that the acquittal evidence was not propensity evidence:

We emphasise that point because from time to time in the submissions both before the judge and before us we detect an error which is not uncommon, namely a confusion between those cases in which it is sought to adduce evidence of the commission of other offences because it shows a propensity and those in which it is sought to adduce such evidence because it strengthens other evidence tending to establish guilt.[24]

The Court went on to explain that while *Hanson*—a case involving previous convictions—was properly seen as a propensity case, *Chopra* was not:

Rather, it is a case in which the prosecution sought to adduce the evidence of all the complaints to make good its reliance on "the unlikelihood of coincidence"...*Chopra* demonstrates the danger of attaching a wrong label to a case. If *Chopra* is categorised as a case of propensity, then the necessary *Hanson*-type directions would have to be given. But it is not. It is merely a case, as we have said, in which a complaint in relation to one allegation strengthened the cogency of the evidence in relation to the other offences. A true propensity case requires the prosecution to prove the defendant's guilt of another offence (which may or may not be the subject of another conviction). Once the jury is satisfied that a defendant is guilty of that other offence (or disreputable conduct), it may deploy that conclusion as tending to show he is more likely to have committed the offence on the indictment. But that is not the position either in *Wallace*, or in *Chopra*, in which the jury was required to look at all the evidence and then reach a conclusion in relation to each particular offence.[25]

To clarify the terminology, we might say that, for the Court of Appeal, there are propensity cases (ones like *Hanson*), and 'coincidence' cases, like *Chopra*. This

---

[22] [2009] 1 Cr App R 10, [2008] EWCA Crim 1544. See also *Freeman and Crawford* [2009] 1 Cr App R 11, [2008] EWCA Crim 1863.

[23] See *McAllister* at [32]–[33], and discussion in Chapter 7.

[24] *McAllister*, [13]. The Court continued: 'Asking a jury to look at evidence relating to a number of allegations as a whole in order to cast light on the evidence relating to an individual offence is not asking a jury to consider a propensity to commit an offence; on the contrary, it is merely asking the jury to recognise that the evidence in relation to a particular offence on an indictment may appear stronger and more compelling when all the evidence, including evidence relating to other offences is looked at as a whole. In other words, the evidence is adduced not as evidence of a propensity, but rather to explain and augment other evidence of guilt' [14].

[25] *McAllister*, [19]–[21].

reflects the Australian terminology,[26] and is also the way in which the Judicial Studies Board has put things.[27]

As well as drawing a distinction between types of bad character evidence, in the passage just quoted the Court equates propensity with facts proved beyond reasonable doubt. Only when the jury is sure that the defendant has committed other misconduct can it draw a propensity inference. Consequently, these questions of classification have come to have an impact on the probative structure of the trial. As the Judicial Studies Board Bench Book puts it: '[a] propensity to commit an offence is also relevant to guilt on other counts but, before the propensity can be utilised by the jury, it must be proved. Only if the jury is sure that the evidence of A is true can they conclude that the defendant had a propensity to commit the kind of offence alleged by complainant B.'[28] In this way, the Court in *McAllister* allowed that evidence relating to the acquittal might be used as propensity evidence: 'If the jury had concluded that the defendant had committed the [acquitted] robbery, it would also amount to evidence of a propensity, in the trial for the Leeds robbery.'[29] The courts and the JSB give no justification for this way of thinking, and the 'sure' requirement as the basis for a propensity inference is not a logical necessity. In terms of the analysis in Chapter 6, the degree to which it is proved that D committed the crime from which a propensity inference is drawn is a question of linkage. The weaker the linkage, the weaker the propensity inference. But a weak inference can still be worth drawing.

This requirement of being sure that D committed a crime before drawing a propensity inference takes us back to another issue considered in Chapter 6. We saw there that in the pre-CJA case law a distinction could be drawn between a 'sequential' and a 'pooling' approach to cases involving more than one count. In *McGranaghan*,[30] the Court of Appeal held that, in cases where identity is in issue, a sequential approach should be taken. Only if the jury was sure that D had committed one of the crimes could it use evidence linking him to that crime, via a propensity inference, as proof that he had committed another one of the crimes he was charged with. But *McGranaghan* was quickly confined to its facts. Faced with a case where it was obvious that two crimes had been committed by the same person, the Court of Appeal allowed that the evidence connecting D to each crime could be 'pooled', or combined.[31] The case law, though, never seemed to address

---

[26] See Evidence Act 1995 (Cth and NSW), s 98, which regulates the admissibility of 'coincidence' evidence; a separate provision, s 97, deals with 'tendency' evidence, although the admissibility test is expressed in the same terms.

[27] Judicial Studies Board, *Crown Court Bench Book: Directing the Jury* (2010), 202.

[28] *Crown Court Bench Book*, 204.

[29] [2009] 1 Cr App R 10, [2008] EWCA Crim 1544, [27]. What is not clear is whether the Court thought that evidence relating to the Scottish robbery could be used at all—ie either as propensity evidence or as evidence strengthening the other evidence—unless the jury was sure D had committed it. At [31], it comments, seemingly as a general observation, that '[t]he jury would have to conclude that the Scottish jury was wrong before it deployed the evidence in relation to Leeds'. In truth, the evidence was only relevant on the basis of propensity, and was relevant as long as the jury thought that the evidence relating to the Scottish robbery was more compatible with guilt than innocence.

[30] [1995] 1 Cr App R 559.

[31] *Downey* [1995] 1 Cr App R 547. See also *Barnes* [1995] 2 Cr App R 491.

directly the question of whether pooling could also be used in cases where a jury was not sure that two crimes were committed by the same person, and in her insightful article Pattenden did not suggest that the sequential approach should go that far.[32] As for cases where the disputed issue was not identity, there was no suggestion that a sequential approach should be taken in cases involving multiple allegations—like *P*[33]—or suspicious patterns—like *Smith*[34] and *Makin*.[35]

In the light of the recent Court of Appeal decisions described here, the situation seems to be that, as a matter of definition, propensity evidence requires a sequential approach (because propensity inferences are only possible where the jury is sure that D has committed other misconduct). As for non-propensity ('coincidence' cases), a sequential approach is not required in the same definitional way. But, as we have just seen, prior to the CJA it may have been required in identity cases where it was not accepted that all of the crimes had been committed by the same person. There are signs that this is the position under the CJA. In *Wallace*, the Court of Appeal accepted the propriety of pooling, but it also seems to have presumed that the robberies were all committed by the same group of men, and the prosecution probably predicated its argument for pooling on that assumption.[36] The JSB directions, which appear to be based on the scenario in *Wallace*, also imply that an important first step in a pooling case is to decide whether all of the offences were committed by the same person or people.[37]

In some cases under the CJA, the Court of Appeal has been tempted to extend the sequential approach beyond identification cases. In *Norris*,[38] a classic suspicious pattern case in which a nurse was charged with murdering several elderly patients by injecting them with insulin, the Court of Appeal seemed to take a sequential approach: a conclusion in case A could only be used in relation to another case if the jury was certain that D had caused the death in case A. In *Lowe*, the Court went so far as to endorse the *Lucas* lies direction in relation to a case involving multiple allegations:

> In formulating this approach we have drawn a ready parallel between it and the approach to evidence as to lies, that is, the *Lucas* Direction. Just as the latter imposes a two stage consideration (are you sure that he did lie? If so, why did he lie—were the reasons consistent with guilt or were they or may they have been innocent?), we have here in a case not involving previous convictions, a need to make a finding as to the fact of the incident alleged before proceeding to a further stage of assessment of significance in accordance with the burden and standard of proof.[39]

---

[32] R. Pattenden, 'Similar Fact Evidence and Proof of Identity' (1996) 112 *LQR* 446.

[33] *DPP* v *P* [1991] 2 AC 447.   [34] (1915) 11 Cr App R 229.

[35] *Makin* v *AG for New South Wales* [1894] AC 57.

[36] [2007] 2 Cr App R 30, [2007] EWCA Crim 1760, [17], [37].

[37] *Crown Court Bench Book*, 208. The instruction at [207], which envisages pooling, probably takes it for granted that the offences were committed by the same people.

[38] [2009] EWCA Crim 2697. The discussion is not completely clear as to whether the sequential approach was only adopted in relation to one of the counts, where the evidence against D was stronger (that count being used as a 'foundation' for the others), or if it allowed pooling between the less well-evidenced counts once a decision on the first count was made.

[39] [2007] EWCA Crim 3047, [22]. The reference is to *Lucas* [1981] QB 720.

Similar approaches were taken in *R* v *Z*[40] and *R* v *S*.[41] The implications of this extension of the sequential approach are radical indeed. Think of the classic example of *Smith*,[42] the brides in the bath case. Directing the jury that it had to consider each case separately, and only use the evidence in relation to bride A to support the case concerning B or C if it was sure that D had murdered A would more or less ensure Smith's acquittal. On the particular facts of some of these cases, perhaps there is a case for a sequential approach—a point to which I return below. But these judgments give little indication that the rulings are to be so confined.

Luckily, the Court of Appeal has spotted the problem. In the joined appeals of *Freeman and Crawford*, the Court singled out the decision in *S* as being 'too restrictive'.[43] 'Whilst the jury must be reminded that it has to reach a verdict on each count separately, it is entitled, in determining guilt in respect of any count, to have regard to the evidence in regard to any other count, or any other bad character evidence if that evidence is admissible and relevant…'[44] However, this still leaves unanswered questions. *Freeman* involved allegations of sexual assaults on children, and to that extent a pooling approach is unremarkable. But *Crawford* involved street robberies, and identification was in issue. It is not clear whether the Court accepted—or the prosecution was arguing on the basis that—the crimes had been committed by the same person.[45] It may be, then, that the Court of Appeal was extending a pooling approach to identification cases where it is not accepted that all crimes were committed by the same person: this is in tension with some authorities, both pre- and post-CJA. It is not the approach taken in the JSB directions.

8.3 Problems with the Propensity/Coincidence Distinction

We have seen that cases involving more than one count raise a number of connected issues, and that the law currently offers few clear answers. Which cases are properly regarded as propensity cases? What instruction should be given to the jury as regards the dangers of propensity reasoning? When is a pooling approach appropriate? As regards the first question, it should be obvious from the analysis in Chapter 6 that all of the cases discussed in this section involve propensity in some way or other. There seems to be a consensus, however, that cases such as *Wallace*—which involved multiple counts of robbery and evidence of moderate strength connecting D to each of them—are not propensity cases.[46] Ormerod

---

[40] [2009] 1 Cr App R 34, [2009] EWCA Crim 20.
[41] [2008] EWCA Crim 544. See also *R* v *T* [2008] EWCA Crim 484, [26]. Here, the *Lowe* approach was said not to be a 'rigid formula'. However, the absence of a direction to consider the evidence of three uncharged complaints separately was a factor in allowing the appeal.
[42] (1915) 11 Cr App R 229.
[43] [2009] 1 Cr App R 11, [2008] EWCA Crim 1863, [20].
[44] [2009] 1 Cr App R 11, [2008] EWCA Crim 1863, [20].
[45] It is doubtful that it would have been appropriate to do so.
[46] See J. R. Spencer, *Evidence of Bad Character* (2nd edn, Oxford: Hart Publishing, 2009), 89; I. H. Dennis, *The Law of Evidence* (5th edn, London: Sweet & Maxwell, 2013), 827–8; and P. Roberts and A. Zuckerman, *Criminal Evidence* (2nd edn, Oxford: Oxford University Press, 2010), 628.

and Furston go so far as to say that: 'In a case such as *Wallace*, there is no sensible way in which partial evidence of identity can be said to be evidence demonstrating W's propensity to rob.'[47] 'Demonstrating' is a tricky word, as it is susceptible to be read as meaning 'showing beyond doubt'. Read in this way, Ormerod and Furston's claim is a truism. But on those terms an eyewitness description which vaguely fits D cannot be said to be evidence demonstrating identity; yet surely it is evidence *of* identity, and admissible as relevant to identity. In the same way, evidence that D committed one of the robberies is evidence of propensity, and admissible as relevant to propensity. To the extent that the evidence is credible, it suggests that D has a propensity to commit robbery. It is perfectly natural to refer to this as propensity evidence, and nothing in the CJA suggests that this way of thinking is inappropriate. Questions of language apart, when we look at the logic of inference the role of the evidence in the example depends on propensity: unless people who commit robbery have a tendency to commit other robberies, evidence that D committed robbery A is not relevant to whether he committed robbery B. Describing the evidence as coincidence evidence does not make propensity disappear. It is only a suspicious, as opposed to innocent, coincidence that D should be connected to more than one robbery if robbers have a propensity to rob.

However, whatever the underlying logic, it must be acknowledged that in *McAllister*[48] the Court of Appeal had practical reasons for classifying, in the way it did, some evidence as propensity evidence and some evidence as coincidence evidence. Its concern was that *Hanson* directions were being used in cases, such as *Chopra*, which they fitted poorly. And there is something to this concern. According to *Hanson*, the jury should be warned:

that they should not conclude that the defendant is guilty or untruthful merely because he has these convictions; that, although the convictions may show a propensity, this does not mean that he has committed this offence...and that, although they are entitled, if they find propensity as shown, to take this into account when determining guilt, propensity is only one relevant factor and they must assess its significance in the light of all the other evidence in the case.[49]

It is not that easy to see how these warnings could be applied to a case involving multiple allegations. For a case like *Chopra*, the JSB's Bench Book suggests a direction along the following lines:

The fact that these three little girls have made similar but otherwise unconnected complaints about the defendant's behaviour makes it more likely that each of those complaints is true. In that sense, the evidence of each of the three complainants is capable of lending support to the others...the closer the similarities between the complaints the less likely it is that they can be explained away as coincidence.[50]

---

[47] R. Fortson and D. Ormerod, 'Bad Character Evidence and Cross-Admissibility' [2009] *Crim LR* 313, 326.
[48] [2009] 1 Cr App R 10, [2008] EWCA Crim 1544.
[49] [2005] 2 Cr App R 21, [2005] EWCA Crim 824, [18].
[50] *Crown Court Bench Book*, 205–6.

I shall refer to this as a 'coincidence' direction.

There is, then, something to be said for the Court of Appeal's approach to the classification question. However, it is not without problems. There are risks involved in obscuring the role of propensity in bad character cases. Even if we take the propensity/coincidence distinction to be purely conventional, as simply a way of dealing with the problem of jury directions in cases involving multiple allegations or suspicious patterns, the terminology risks causing confusion in other cases. We saw examples of this above, and more follow below. With care, this problem could be avoided, but there are further issues. Where propensity is identified as the basis for admissibility, courts are prompted to look carefully at whether propensity is established, and the jury can also be asked to focus on this. The question of time-lapse between one instance of misconduct and another is the most obvious critical issue, as it was in *Isichei*.[51] In many cases involving multiple allegations, there will be no significant time-lapse. In *Wallace* and *Crawford*, for example, the robberies charged together had occurred close together in time. But suppose a case involving allegations of sexual assaults on children, where a recent allegation is charged alongside a much older one. With no undisputed misconduct, this case would fall under the coincidence model. The question of continuing propensity would be important here: unless one thinks that someone who sexually assaults children will have a propensity to do so many years later, then the two allegations will not support each other. The coincidence model risks obscuring this. And just as it is clumsy to give a *Hanson* direction in a case like *Chopra*, it is not immediately obvious how to incorporate *Hanson* warnings in the sort of circumstantial evidence direction advocated by the Court of Appeal. We should also note that a previous allegation from many years before might not be charged and tried alongside the recent one, but merely used as evidence to corroborate the recent charge.

One way in which a court might be tempted to respond to these issues would be to classify the older allegation as propensity evidence. This would trigger an appropriate direction; but it would also change the probative structure of the trial. As we have seen, the position seems to be that evidence can only be used as propensity evidence if the jury is sure that the alleged misconduct occurred. But coincidence evidence can be pooled, and used to support other allegations even if the misconduct is not proved. So classification is not just a question of terminology and judicial instructions: if evidence is classified as propensity evidence, it makes it harder for the prosecution to prove its case. While the decision in *R v Z*[52] is not necessarily an example of the repercussions of classificatory decisions, it does show the impact which the pooling/sequential issue can have. The prosecution sought to support the charged allegation of historic rape with a similar and uncharged allegation. The Court of Appeal ruled that the jury should have been instructed not to take the uncharged allegation into account unless it was sure

[51] [2006] EWCA Crim 1815.   [52] [2009] 1 Cr App R 34, [2009] EWCA Crim 20.

that it was true. On the facts of the case, this was effectively to rule the allegation inadmissible, weakening the prosecution case.[53]

A further problem with the coincidence/propensity distinction is that, by associating different judicial instructions with different evidential scenarios, it may complicate things for both judges and juries. As the Court of Appeal noted in *McAllister*, the previous acquittal would have become propensity evidence, rather than coincidence evidence, if the jury had concluded that D had committed that crime. A *Hanson* instruction would then have been appropriate. But presumably a coincidence direction would have been needed as well, to cover the eventuality that the jury did not find that count proved, but merely suspicious. In cases involving multiple allegations, one allegation may stand out as being far more convincing than others. Then it may be appropriate to direct the jury to concentrate on that count first, and a *Hanson* direction will be needed. But if the judge is unsure whether the jury will, or should, take this approach rather than a coincidence approach whereby it treats each allegation as mutually supportive, then separate directions to cover each eventuality will be needed.

Perhaps the problems noted so far are largely practical ones which could be overcome with care. But there will always be something puzzling about having a system whereby *Hanson* directions are required in some cases, but not in others. Presumably, a *Hanson* warning is thought appropriate because of concern that juries will over-value propensity, and jump to conclusions on the basis of it. But over-valuing propensity is also a danger in coincidence cases. As we saw in Chapter 6, assumptions about propensity are involved even in classic 'coincidence' cases such as *Smith*. The more you think that someone who kills one wife is likely to kill another, the more quickly you will come to a conclusion that Smith is a multiple murderer. It is true that in a case where there is no dispute that D has committed other misconduct there may be particular dangers. In such a case, there may be a danger of 'moral prejudice': the jury may have fewer qualms about convicting D, and may convict when not convinced beyond reasonable doubt. But this possibility exists in any case of multiple allegations where it is possible that the jury will reach a conclusion on one count before others. Further, rightly or wrongly, *Hanson* does not really target the danger of moral prejudice.

The current approach, then, which requires different directions in what are really very similar scenarios, is problematic for a number of reasons. Admittedly, finding a good way of warning a jury about the dangers of propensity in a case where there is no proved misconduct is not simple, and it may be that the Court of Appeal's solution—distinguishing between propensity and coincidence cases—is the best that can be done (although there is a strong case for adopting less confusing terminology, such as proved and unproved propensity). But it is surely worth thinking hard about whether a single direction could provide

---

[53] In the event, this was not critical, as the Court of Appeal had already ruled the allegation inadmissible as hearsay.

a model for all cases, or at least, for the sake of consistency, whether a warning about undue reliance on propensity could be worked into the coincidence direction.[54]

8.4 Pooling

The questions about classification and jury directions considered above are connected to the distinction between sequential and pooling approaches. As we have seen, the current position appears to be that pooling is permissible in cases involving multiple allegations or suspicious patterns, but that in cases involving identity, pooling may only be permissible where it is accepted that two or more crimes were all committed by the same person or people.

There is, however, no good reason for distinguishing between identity cases and other cases, because, as should be apparent from the analysis in Chapter 6, all cases have the same logical structure. In a case with multiple allegations, each allegation is evidence that D committed that particular crime; it is also, therefore, evidence that he has a propensity to commit that type of crime, and it is this evidence of propensity which supports the other allegations. In a case like *Wallace*, where D is charged with several robberies and there is some evidence to link him to each one, evidence linking him to one robbery is evidence that he committed that particular crime; it is also, therefore, evidence that he has a propensity to commit that type of crime, and it is this evidence of propensity which supports evidence linking him to the other robberies.[55]

Pooling, then, is always appropriate as a matter of inferential logic. But this does not mean that it is always wrong to direct the jury that it should be sure about the truth of one allegation before using it as the basis for a propensity inference. We saw above that in *Lowe* the Court of Appeal used an analogy with the *Lucas* direction on lies, holding that no inference should be drawn from one allegation unless the jury was sure of its truth. On the facts, there was some reason to take this approach. *Lowe* is an example of 'same complainant propensity'. C alleged that D had raped her, and this allegation was the subject of the trial. But during the trial C also gave evidence that D had been violent towards her on other occasions. In this situation, one allegation cannot usually be taken to support another, because the same person is testifying to both, and there is usually no reason to think that D has more reason to lie, or be mistaken, about one event

[54] For a suggested instruction, see M. Redmayne, 'Recognising Propensity' [2011] *Crim LR* 177, 192.

[55] *John W* [1998] 2 Cr App R 289, discussed in Chapter 6, is a good example of a case where pooling would be a correct approach where some evidence linked D to two crimes, but it was not obvious that both had been committed by the same person. The Court of Appeal judgment is not very clear on the question of whether it allowed pooling, but on balance it seems to imply that it was appropriate: see esp at 305.

than another (see Figure 6.5 in Chapter 6).[56] Because the jury should therefore believe C to the same extent in relation to both events, a direction that jurors could not find D guilty of the rape unless they thought he had committed the other misconduct made some sense.[57]

8.5 Double-Counting

The most serious problem arising from a failure to recognize propensity where it exists is that a defendant may be prejudiced by having the same inference drawn against him from the same evidence twice, under different guises. An example is found in the current JSB bench book, which gives an example of a specimen direction in a case where D is tried on one count for a crime committed against C, and the prosecution call evidence from two other women, A and B, to show that D had behaved in a similar way towards them.[58] The direction suggests that the evidence of A and B can be used in two ways. First, as coincidence evidence: 'the prosecution contends that it is no coincidence that all three of these witnesses describe similar conduct...you are entitled to regard the evidence of each witness as supportive of the others'. Second, the evidence can be used as propensity evidence: 'the fact that the defendant possessed such a tendency makes it more likely that he behaved towards [C] as she says'.[59] The clear implication is that the evidence can be used in both of these ways; it is not a question of either or.[60] These supposedly different inferences involve the same propensity inference described in different ways. It would be prejudicial to the defendant to draw them cumulatively.

This double-counting error has occurred in some cases.[61] Upholding the trial judge's decision to admit previous convictions in *Pope*,[62] a robbery case involving disputed identification evidence, the Court of Appeal commented that the bad character evidence fell into both the categories of coincidence and propensity: 'It showed that he had a tendency to steal people's property and to be prepared to use force to do so. It also strengthened the identification made by Charlene...The judge was entitled to take the view that the evidence should be admitted because

---

[56] There are exceptions. If C was very drunk at the time of one of the incidents, but was sober at the time of the other, then the jury might use a propensity inference from the sober incident to resolve doubts about the accuracy of C's memory in relation to the drunk incident. See further D. Hamer, 'The Structure and Strength of the Propensity Inference: Singularity, Linkage and the Other Evidence' (2003) 29 *Monash L Rev* 137, 178.

[57] As far as one can tell from the report, there was no independent evidence to support C's account of the previous violent incidents. There was, however, one separate incident about which her daughter gave evidence, and the *Lucas* approach would not have been necessary here.

[58] *Crown Court Bench Book*, 179.   [59] *Crown Court Bench Book*, 179.

[60] For the same mistake, see Z. Cowen and P. B. Carter, 'The Admissibility of Evidence of Similar Facts: A Re-Examination' in *Essays on the Law of Evidence* (Oxford: Oxford University Press, 1956), 118.

[61] See also *Benabbou* [2012] EWCA Crim 1256, [12], where the trial judge seems to have made the double-counting mistake. The conviction was quashed by the Court of Appeal on other grounds.

[62] [2010] EWCA Crim 2113.

it served a double purpose.'[63] In *Dossett*,[64] D denied participating in a robbery. The trial judge had instructed the jury that his previous convictions were relevant both to the correctness of an eyewitness identification ('what are the chances that Mr Ryan would mistakenly pick out from a line of nine males on an identification procedure the person who happened to have a previous conviction for robbery and ABH committed very close to the scene of the attack'),[65] and to show that D had a propensity to violence. The Court of Appeal endorsed this double-counting approach. While in *R* v *N(H)*,[66] the Court observed that it would be rare to ask the jury to draw both a propensity and a coincidence inference, this remark was aimed at non-conviction evidence (the scenario in the JSB direction). '[I]t is not so unusual,' the Court remarked, 'for the jury to consider the effect of a relevant *previous conviction* as demonstrating a relevant propensity *and* the unlikelihood that similar but independent complaints are, as between themselves, coincidental or malicious.'[67] It may be that it is not unusual, but it is both wrong and prejudicial to the defendant. This is where a failure to understand propensity reasoning leads.

8.6 Acquitted Misconduct Evidence

In the pre-CJA case of *R* v *Z*,[68] D was on trial for rape. He had been tried for rape on four previous occasions, but had only been convicted once. The lower courts found that the evidence passed the—then relatively strict—test for admissibility of propensity evidence, but thought that the decision in *Sambasivam*[69] precluded them from admitting it. The House of Lords allowed the prosecution's appeal, holding that all four previous complainants could be called to give evidence. This is controversial, and in some jurisdictions the law blocks such a strategy.[70] One argument is that the use of acquitted misconduct offends the 'principle that in criminal proceedings a person should not have to defend himself twice against the same allegation of criminal wrongdoing'.[71] The arguments for such a principle, however, are not strong. Putting to one side, as contentious in themselves, the exceptions to the double jeopardy principle which now exist in England and Wales,[72] there are still situations where a defendant may have to defend himself more than once on the same charge. The Court of Appeal can order a retrial after quashing a conviction, and if a jury is hung there may also be a new trial. It is true that in these situations there is no finalized verdict, but, as long as the argument

---

[63] *Pope*, [20]–[21].   [64] [2013] EWCA Crim 710.   [65] *Dossett*, [33].
[66] [2011] EWCA Crim 730.   [67] *R* v *N(H)*, [31], original emphasis.
[68] [2000] 2 AC 483.
[69] *Sambasivam* v *Public Prosecutor, Malaya* [1950] AC 458.
[70] Notably Canada: see *Grdic* [1985] 1 SCR 810; and *Arp* [1998] 3 SCR 339.
[71] H. Stewart, 'Issue Estoppel and Similar Facts' (2008) 53 CLQ 382, 397. See also *Arp*, [78].
[72] Criminal Procedure and Investigations Act 1996, s 54; and Criminal Justice Act 2003, Pt 10. See generally A. Ashworth and M. Redmayne, *The Criminal Process* (4th edn, Oxford: Oxford University Press, 2010), 397–402.

rests, as it seems to, on the basic vexation of having to respond time and again to the same claim, this is of little significance. An acquitted defendant can also face a civil claim for conduct of which he has been acquitted. While this situation does not involve a second criminal charge, this too is not significant if the objection is vexation.

A different argument is that a verdict of not guilty should be taken to establish innocence, and that the state should be bound by this.[73] Viewed as a matter of logic, this is not a tenable position to take. A not-guilty verdict is a finding that the case was not proved beyond reasonable doubt, so is perfectly compatible with the fact-finder having thought guilt very likely. As a matter of political morality, the argument for not questioning acquittals may have more going for it. But we need to be clear that in the *Z* situation D is not put in jeopardy of conviction for the offences of which he has been acquitted,[74] and the serial acquittal of a serial rapist is quite a high price to pay for a principle whereby the state is never allowed so much as to imply that an acquitted person is guilty.[75] If the argument is meant to be based on the presumption of innocence, then it struggles to explain why allegations of misconduct which were never prosecuted can be admitted, but acquitted misconduct cannot.

A further worry might be that the criminal justice system will undermine itself by producing inconsistent verdicts.[76] The key point in a case like *Z*, however, is that we have new evidence which was not available to the original juries. The juries which acquitted Z may have been perfectly right to do so given the evidence before them. But with hindsight enhanced by our ability to see the bigger picture—five independent complainants alleging that Z raped them—we are in a very different evidential situation.[77]

[73] See *Grdic*, [1985] 1 SCR 810, [35]. Duff et al argue for a similar principle: A. Duff, L. Farmer, S. Marshall, and V. Tadros, *The Trial on Trial: Volume 3: Towards A Normative Theory of the Criminal Trial* (Oxford: Hart Publishing, 2007), 216–18.

[74] In immediate jeopardy, at least. It is possible that once a conviction is secured on the new charge, this could be used as the basis for quashing the original acquittal under the exception to the double jeopardy rule introduced by the CJA 2003, and then as part of the evidence to convict D in a new trial. But if this is objectionable it is because of underlying objections to making exceptions to double jeopardy, and not because acquitted misconduct is admissible on the new charge.

[75] Of course, it would be unsatisfactory if the state routinely slandered the acquitted by alleging their guilt. Few people have the time or resources to use the law to clear their name. But in the *Z* situation D does have a chance to rebut the allegations, usually with the benefit of legal aid.

[76] Mahoney makes much of this point, arguing that if one uses allegation A as part of the evidence on allegation B, it would be inconsistent to convict on B without becoming convinced beyond reasonable doubt that A is true (R. Mahoney, 'Acquittals as Similar Fact Evidence: Another View' (2003) 47 *CLQ* 265). As a matter of logic, this is wrong. To use the sort of analogy relied on by Mahoney, if ten witnesses all implicate D, that may well add up to a convincing case. But the conclusion that D's guilt is proved beyond reasonable doubt does not require one to conclude that it is beyond reasonable doubt that none of the witnesses is lying or even mistaken. Witness X's evidence may point towards guilt, even though one has reservations about it, and those reservations need not disappear once D is believed to be guilty. Similarly, even if, as the result of a medical trial, one concludes that drug Y causes vomiting, while one can revisit the cases of vomiting in the cohort who took Y armed with good evidence that Y was the cause, it remains possible that an individual case of vomiting was not caused by Y.

[77] See P. Roberts, 'Acquitted Misconduct Evidence and Double Jeopardy Principles: From *Sambasivam* to *Z*' [2000] *Crim LR* 952, 958–9. Roberts puts the point slightly differently, arguing

There are, then, no strong reasons of principle to conclude that using acquitted misconduct evidence to prove guilt is automatically unfair. But in *Z*, the House of Lords did not rule out the possibility that the use of such evidence would be unfair in an individual case: it stressed that admissibility was subject to the fairness discretion in section 78 of PACE. Lord Hobhouse commented that:

Fairness requires that the jury hear all relevant evidence. It also requires that the defendant shall not without sufficient reason be required more than once to rebut the same factual allegations. In principle a case supported by probative similar fact evidence is a sufficient reason. However, in exercising his discretion under section 78, the judge must take into account the position of both the prosecution and the defendant. If the fairness of the trial will be compromised by the non-exclusion of the similar fact evidence, the evidence should be excluded although otherwise admissible...Any prejudice to the defendant arising from having to deal a second time with evidence proving facts which were in issue at an earlier trial is simply another factor to be put into the balance. The fact that the previous trial ended in an acquittal is a relevant factor in striking this balance but is no more than that.[78]

Under the CJA, section 101(3) provides a similar framework for exclusion.

Z is still good law, and several post-CJA cases have involved acquitted misconduct evidence. However, as we have seen, admissibility standards for propensity evidence are very different now. The argument for admissibility in *Z* was strong partly because at the time it took fairly compelling propensity evidence (in *Z*, four previous allegations of rape) to engage the 'similar fact' exception to the rule excluding bad character evidence, and Lord Hobhouse's reference to 'sufficient reason' has to be read in light of that. But today a single previous conviction for a similar offence has a claim to be admitted. Consequently, there are cases where single instances of acquitted misconduct are introduced as propensity evidence.[79] How far might this be pushed? Take *McMinn*,[80] one of the cases identified in the previous chapter as lying at the admissibility threshold. If McMinn had been acquitted of causing ABH in the playground spat, could the complainant have been called to give evidence at McMinn's trial for the new offence of ABH? This may be less bizarre than it first sounds. Had the previous allegation not been prosecuted, it would be just that, an allegation, with a claim to be admitted just like other allegations of misconduct. Significantly, section 109 of the CJA provides that for the purposes of the CJA character provisions, a reference to the relevance and probative value of evidence is a reference to relevance and probative value on the assumption that the evidence is true.[81] Acquitted misconduct therefore has to

---

that the meaning of the original evidence changes when seen in the context of the bigger picture. Although I doubt anything hangs on it in this part of the discussion, I am cautious about this interpretation: the evidence in the original trial is worth exactly what it always was, we simply have more evidence.

[78] [2000] 2 AC 483, 510.
[79] *Loughman* [2007] EWCA Crim 1912; and *Boulton* [2007] EWCA Crim 942.
[80] [2007] EWCA Crim 3024.
[81] Subject to s 109(2): 'a court need not assume that the evidence is true if it appears on the basis of any material before the court...that no court or jury could reasonably find it to be true'.

be treated as having the same evidential value as convicted misconduct.[82] If evidence of questionable value is to be excluded, it is the fairness discretion in section 101(3) which will have to do the work. Because 101(3) does not refer to relevance or probative value, section 109 has no hold over it, so the judgment of fairness can take into account the weaker nature of the evidence as well as the added complexity it will impose on the trial.[83] This offers a way out in an acquitted misconduct version of *McMinn*.

In the background to the *McMinn* scenario is a question about whether the fact of acquittal is significant when it comes to directing the jury about the weight to place on acquitted misconduct evidence. Evidence law usually regards an acquittal as mere opinion, and therefore irrelevant.[84] There are exceptions. In *Cooke*,[85] D was permitted to introduce evidence of the acquittal, in a separate trial, of his alleged co-conspirators. The reason was that all had been interviewed by the same police officer, and the acquittals suggested that the jury had not believed the officer's testimony about their confessions. The situation where the prosecution introduce evidence of acquitted misconduct under gateway (d) is less clear. Sometimes, the Court of Appeal has taken the irrelevance approach. In *Hamidi*,[86] the prosecution introduced evidence of D's previous involvement in VAT fraud to help prove a new charge of VAT fraud. The previous incident had led to an appeal to the VAT tribunal, which concluded that Hamidi had been an innocent dupe in a fraud perpetrated by others. Given that this finding was made on the balance of probabilities, there is reason to give it more weight than an acquittal in a criminal trial. The defence, however, was permitted to say little about the tribunal's conclusion, other than that Hamidi had not been prosecuted, but that 'civil proceedings got underway and that eventually the restraint order was discharged and the frozen funds released'.[87] The Court of Appeal thought this quite proper:

> The Judge declined to admit evidence of the tribunal's finding on the ground that it was irrelevant. We agree with him. The tribunal's finding was not part of the evidential picture but the judgment of the tribunal upon the evidence. We recognise that in circumstances such as these trial Judges may permit the earlier decision to be adduced in evidence. We have had to consider whether there is a ground in legal principle for admission of such evidence or that the rules of evidence are relaxed by way of instinctive concession to the

---

[82] This is not quite so strange when seen in the wider evidence law context. Questions about the credibility of witnesses have traditionally been left to the jury: see *Galbraith* [1981] 1 WLR 1039 and discussion in Ashworth and Redmayne, *The Criminal Process*, 340–2. Section 109 also reflects the pre-CJA position which ignored questions about possible contamination of propensity evidence when deciding admissibility: *R v H* [1995] 2 AC 596.

[83] However, *Edwards and Rowlands* [2006] 2 Cr App R 4, [2005] EWCA Crim 3244 does throw some doubt on this strategy. Discussing the application of s 101(3) and s 78 the Court noted that while the judge 'will have regard to the potential weight of [the] evidence it is not his job to usurp the jury's function of deciding what evidence is accepted and what rejected. But obviously if, for example, it is inherently incredible that would be likely to be a strong factor against admitting it... The judge's job is to police the gateway not to embark on the jury's job of evaluating the evidence' (at [82]). Cf *Assani* [2008] EWCA Crim 2563, [16], where lack of a conviction is considered a factor affecting probative value.

[84] *Hui Chi Min v R* [1991] 1 AC 34, 42–4.   [85] (1986) 84 Cr App R 286.

[86] [2010] EWCA Crim 66.   [87] *Hamidi*, [39].

defence. The latter would appear to be the basis for admission of the evidence quoted from the summing up above. We are satisfied that the decision of the tribunal was inadmissible on the issue which the jury was required to determine because its decision and its reasoning was irrelevant. It was open to the appellant to meet the evidence as he had before the tribunal by deploying such evidence, explanations and arguments as might be necessary to undermine the prosecution's assertion of propensity. The admission of the underlying evidence without the finding of the tribunal did not, as we see it, generate any unfairness. The jury received a strong direction to the effect that first they had to be sure of propensity and second that if they were sure they should not afford it undue weight. It was a matter for them to weigh up the evidence for themselves.[88]

On other occasions, however, the 'instinctive concession to the defence' wins the day. In *Mustapha*,[89] D's previous acquittal, which appears to have come about because the jury was not convinced by police testimony, was 'a significant and important part' of the defence case. 'The acquittal was not just a fact "to be taken into account" it was a very significant fact for the jury to consider in Mustapha's favour.'[90] Not only should the judge have explained this clearly to the jury, the Court of Appeal went so far as to conclude that the evidence should have been excluded under section 101(3) on grounds of prejudice.[91] Similarly, in *Boulton*,[92] the Court of Appeal considered that the jury should have been told not that the acquittal was irrelevant, but that it meant that original jury had not been convinced by the original complainant. In contrast, in *Robinson*,[93] a case not involving gateway (d), D argued that he should have been allowed to tell the jury that he had been acquitted of two minor instances of sexual misconduct mentioned during his trial for other instances of sexual misconduct against the same complainant. The aim was to cast doubt on the complainant's credibility. The Court of Appeal rejected the argument, finding that the *Cooke* exception did not apply.[94]

There may be reason to treat acquitted misconduct evidence admitted under gateway (d) differently from acquittals which defendants wish to introduce, in cases like *Cooke* and *Robinson*, to cast doubt on an element of the case against them. Once acquitted misconduct is introduced, the jury may well speculate as to whether it was prosecuted, and if so what happened, and if not why not. Telling the jury about the acquittal may be the best way to quell speculation. In the *Robinson* scenario, speculation is less likely (although one suspects that the main reason why courts are reluctant to allow defendants to introduce evidence about acquittals of their own accord is that this would apply in a much wider range of cases). As to whether the new jury should be told to give any weight to the fact of

---

[88] *Hamidi*, [39].   [89] [2007] EWCA Crim 1702.

[90] *Mustapha*, [39]. There is a parallel here with *Cooke* (1986) 84 Cr App R 286.

[91] *Mustapha*, [47], [33]. This conclusion owes something to the fact that the Court thought that even if the previous allegation of possessing a firearm was true, it was of little relevance to the present case because it was not clear which of the principal's accomplices had handed him the gun. This evaluation seems to ignore the joint enterprise context: even if Mustapha had not been the one to hand over the gun, he had become involved in a joint enterprise involving a firearm.

[92] [2007] EWCA Crim 942, [42].   [93] [2011] EWCA Crim 916.

[94] It is not clear that a court has the power to exclude defence evidence on these grounds. See discussion in *Phillips* [2012] 1 Cr App R 25, [2011] EWCA Crim 2935.

acquittal, no doubt the feeling that D has been put on the back foot, as it were, by the introduction of the acquitted misconduct makes the idea of making a concession to the defence attractive. It is true that the new jury will often have enough evidence to make its own decision: the prosecution is rightly warned that if it wants to introduce acquitted misconduct evidence, it needs to be in a position to put before the court all of the evidence called at the previous trial.[95] But pointing the jury to the fact of the acquittal may be a convenient way to alert it to think carefully about the weight to put on the bad character evidence.[96]

To summarize, then, acquitted misconduct evidence is admissible. When of minimal value it might be excluded under CJA, section 101(3), but, *contra Hamidi*, there is good reason to tell the jury about the previous failure to convict or find liable, and to instruct the jury to put some weight on this. There is, however, a serious complication to the treatment of acquitted misconduct under the CJA. The passage from *Hamidi*, quoted above, ends with the observation that '[t]he jury received a strong direction to the effect that first they had to be sure of propensity'. This means that, unless the jury was convinced beyond reasonable doubt that D had committed the previous crime, it could not use it as the basis for a propensity inference. As we have seen, this is a standard part of the propensity landscape. Propensity inferences can only be drawn from behaviour proved to the criminal standard. As noted above, there is no need for this stricture. Weak linkage weakens, but does not bar, a propensity inference. While guilt must be proved beyond reasonable doubt, no other facts, apart from those essential to a finding of guilt, need be.[97]

The requirement of being sure before drawing a propensity inference has implications for the use of acquitted misconduct to prove guilt. If the jury has to be sure that D committed the crime he was acquitted of, then the introduction of a previous acquittal will often make little sense. Taking *Hamidi* as an example, the jury would have to be convinced that D committed the earlier fraud, even though the VAT tribunal thought he was unlikely to have done. It is hard to believe that the jury could have attained the requisite level of certainty, especially if told to put some weight on the earlier verdict. In other cases, single previous acquittals for rape have been introduced to prove a new charge of rape, without, it seems,

---

[95] *Loughman*, [2007] EWCA Crim 1912.

[96] It is still puzzling that in *Mustapha* the Court of Appeal was so emphatic that the acquittal was very significant, but was less so in *Boulton*. This also echoes non-gateway (d) case law where failure to believe police officers appears to be seen as more significant than failure to believe complainants of sexual offences. The best explanation may be that a jury's failure to be convinced by police testimony is much rarer, and therefore more significant, than a failure to believe a sexual offence complainant. In the non-gateway (d) situation, there may also be something to the argument that police officers, as regular witnesses, are better able to learn from their mistakes and cover up weaknesses in their testimony the second time around.

[97] A useful discussion is D. Hamer, 'The Continuing Saga of the *Chamberlain* Direction: Untangling the Cables and Chains of Criminal Proof' (1997) 23 *Monash UL Rev* 43. Despite not being a logical requirement, directions telling the jury to be sure of a particular fact before drawing an inference from it are now relatively common in English law, often imposed in areas where the courts are slightly nervous about a type of evidence, an inference from the defendant's silence being a good example: see M. Redmayne, 'Analysing Evidence Case Law' in P. Roberts and

any new evidence to boost them.[98] Knowing that the earlier jury acquitted, how can the new jury be convinced beyond reasonable doubt that D really was guilty? The answer might seem obvious. As noted above, with previous acquittals there is a hindsight factor. The fact that there is a new allegation against D makes it more likely that he was guilty of the previous crime, because a propensity inference can be drawn from the allegation.[99] But if, as the courts insist, a propensity inference can only be drawn from proved allegations, this cannot help.[100] Once the new crime is proved beyond reasonable doubt, it is too late for the old allegation—now buttressed by the new one—to add anything. There are therefore two linked problems here. The earlier argument for the use of previous acquittals made the point that in using an acquittal to prove guilt on a new charge, the criminal justice system would not be producing inconsistent verdicts. But the way in which the courts handle propensity evidence means that this is no longer true: unless new evidence is introduced to cast doubt on the old charge, the new jury is being asked to reject the previous jury's finding on the basis of the same evidence which that jury heard. The second problem is that it is hard to see how the new jury can be convinced that D committed the earlier crime when the previous jury acquitted and there is no new evidence. Asking the jury to consider the previous acquittal when deliberating on the new charge therefore verges on bad faith.

If the requirement of being sure that D committed the previous crime before drawing a propensity inference from it was dropped, this logical stalemate would evaporate. The 'sure' requirement does not appear to have applied to acquitted misconduct before the CJA,[101] so it is puzzling that the courts have decided that it is necessary. Even if a case can be made for it, the courts should not have simply presumed that the *Z* framework for admissibility could be transposed unaltered to the new law without realizing the implications of both the sure requirement and the new lower admissibility threshold.

Might the coincidence model offer a way out of this problem? Perhaps. The jury might reason that two allegations of, say, rape are unlikely to be made against D if they are untrue. In *McAllister*,[102] D was charged with an armed robbery which took place in Leeds. The prosecution sought to introduce evidence that D had been acquitted of a different armed robbery, committed some three days later in Banff, Scotland.[103] The trial judge accepted that this would be appropriate

---

M. Redmayne (eds), *Innovations in Evidence and Proof: Integrating Theory, Research and Teaching* (Oxford: Hart Publishing, 2007).

[98] *Loughman* [2007] EWCA Crim 1912; and *Boulton* [2007] EWCA Crim 942.

[99] See *Hamidi* [2010] EWCA Crim 66, [36]: '[t]he decision of the tribunal was not capable of binding the jury. The jury heard additional evidence of the appellant's further involvement in [the new fraud]'.

[100] At this point, my quibble with Roberts, sketched in n 77 above, becomes more significant.

[101] See *Barney* [2005] EWCA Crim 1385. While the Court of Appeal does not address the issue, it seems that neither it nor the trial judge thought that a 'sure' direction was needed.

[102] [2009] 1 Cr App R 10, [2008] EWCA Crim 1544.

[103] With the added complication that the Scottish verdict was 'not proven'.

under the coincidence model: 'was it a mere coincidence he was present in both Banff and then Leeds at the time of two similar shot-gun robberies?'[104] On an interlocutory appeal, the Court of Appeal allowed the legitimacy of this type of argument, but nevertheless seemed to think that the new jury would have to be sure of the defendant's guilt before reasoning from coincidence: 'The jury would have to conclude that the Scottish jury was wrong before it deployed the evidence in relation to Leeds.'[105] This is odd: under the CJA pretty much the whole point of the coincidence model is that it avoids the need for a preliminary finding that D definitely committed some previous bad act. Nevertheless, there is reason to be cautious about using a coincidence direction in a case like *McAllister*. It does not really beggar belief that an innocent person should be visiting two towns when armed robberies take place. But spurred on by the coincidence argument, there is a risk that the jury will think that there is no smoke without fire, and not look carefully into the evidence on the acquitted charge. This may well have been the Court of Appeal's ultimate, and appropriate, concern. It held that the facts of the Banff robbery should not be put before the jury, because the jury would need to consider the evidence on the acquitted charge in detail, leading to complex satellite litigation.

In the previous chapter, problems related to complexity and satellite litigation caused by introducing bad character evidence were noted. *McAllister* suggests that there is a connection between the conditions imposed by courts on the use of acquitted allegations and the ensuing complexity of the trial. If the jury needs to be sure that D committed the previous crime, there is greater need for a trial within a trial to resolve the issue. Still, taking a more relaxed approach would not make the satellite litigation problem disappear. The evidence which was called at the previous trial exists, and if the jury is to evaluate the likelihood that D committed the acquitted crime, there is an argument for hearing it—although without the need to be sure of D's guilt on that charge it would be more reasonable to impose restrictions on the evidence to be called. In *McAllister*, the Banff allegation involved reasonably complicated circumstantial evidence, and it would have been difficult to avoid a protracted rehearing of the issues. In some cases, though, such as the rape cases where previous acquittals have been introduced without apparent difficulty,[106] the previous case may hang on the testimony of a single complainant, making a resurrection of the acquitted charge much more feasible.

8.7 Conclusion

Before the Criminal Justice Act 2003 came into force, it was common for judges who admitted propensity evidence to deny that that was what they were doing. Even after the decision in *DPP* v *P*, approaches based on 'forbidden reasoning'

---

[104] *McAllister* [2009] 1 Cr App R 10, [2008] EWCA Crim 1544, [26].
[105] *McAllister*, [31].
[106] *Loughman* [2007] EWCA Crim 1912; and *Boulton* [2007] EWCA Crim 942.

and the categories still had considerable influence. The story told in Chapter 7 shows how things have changed. In the vast majority of cases, judges are now happy to embrace the idea of propensity. This sea change could not have been predicted with confidence: denial and doublethink might have continued, but by and large they have not. In terms of intellectual honesty, this can only be a good thing. In this chapter, however, the appraisal has been rather more negative. Especially where multiple allegations are concerned, courts are not always so good at recognizing propensity. The problems should not be exaggerated: the confused thinking analysed here often does little harm. But the danger is that once muddled analysis becomes entrenched, it will lead to more serious errors. In particular, questions of time-lapse will not get the attention they deserve, and the problem of double-counting—where the same inference is drawn twice under different guises to prove the same issue—will become common. Defendants are treated unfairly when lawyers fail to understand how to reason with bad character evidence.

When it comes to the requirement that the jury be sure that misconduct occurred before drawing an inference from it, defendants benefit. But the sure approach has little to recommend it. It can be switched on and off by describing the same evidence as propensity or coincidence evidence. If taken seriously, it means that cases involving acquitted misconduct ask juries to do what is more or less impossible—to be sure that the acquitted misconduct occurred before drawing an inference from it. I have explained that the sure requirement is not a logical one. In some contexts, the courts recognize this. In *Robinson*,[107] a case involving co-defendants, D1 introduced evidence about D2's violent disposition under gateway (e) of the CJA. Unsurprisingly, D2 argued that no inference could be drawn against him from this evidence unless the jury was sure that the wrongful behaviour had occurred. The Court of Appeal made short shrift of this argument:

> It is trite law that a jury only have to be sure that the ingredients of the offence have been proved. The jury do that after considering all the relevant evidence. There is no requirement for the jury to be sure about any particular piece of evidence (unless, without that piece, the ingredients of the offence would not have been proved).[108]

Things would be much better if the courts brought this elementary insight to bear on gateway (d). It would then be less tempting to describe propensity evidence as coincidence evidence as a way of avoiding the sure requirement, and we might all have a better view of what is going on when bad character evidence is used to prove guilt.

---

[107] [2006] 1 Cr App R 32, [2005] EWCA Crim 3233.   [108] *Robinson*, [85].

9

Character and Credibility

The most obvious use to which evidence of a defendant's bad character can be put is to show a propensity to commit crime—the topic of most of the book to this point. But common law jurisdictions have long permitted evidence of bad character to be used as evidence of the defendant's lack of credibility. In fact, before the Criminal Justice Act 2003 came into force, bad character evidence was much more often introduced as evidence of a defendant's lack of credibility than as evidence of propensity.[1] Although this situation has now been reversed,[2] the CJA has retained the credibility use of bad character. Indeed, while the wide propensity gateway now makes credibility evidence less important, the Act actually expands the situations in which credibility evidence can be admitted.

Prior to the CJA, credibility evidence was governed by section 1(f)(ii) of the Criminal Evidence Act 1898. This allowed a defendant's bad character to be introduced in cross-examination where 'the nature or conduct of [D's] defence is such as to involve imputations on the character of the prosecutor or the witnesses for the prosecution, or the deceased victim of the alleged crime'. This was 'tit for tat': admissibility depended on whether D made an attack of his own on the character of a witness. But the courts imposed important restrictions on section 1(f)(ii). Bad character was admitted under this provision as evidence of D's credibility, not his propensity, and the rule in *Butterwasser* meant that tit for tat was only unleashed if D himself testified,[3] because only then was his credibility thought to be in issue.

The CJA retains tit for tat: gateway (g) of section 101 allows evidence of D's bad character to be admitted 'if the defendant has made an attack on another person's character'. Unlike section 1(f)(ii), section 101 is not restricted to the introduction of evidence in cross-examination, therefore *Butterwasser* no longer applies. Section 106 explains that D attacks another person's character if:

(a) he adduces evidence attacking the other person's character,
(b) he ... asks questions in cross-examination that are intended to elicit such evidence, or are likely to do so, or

[1] M. Zander and P. Henderson, *Crown Court Study* (London: HMSO, 1993), 119.
[2] Morgan Harris Burrows LLP, *Research Into the Impact of Bad Character Provisions in the Courts* (London: Ministry of Justice, 2009), 14, 22–3.
[3] *Butterwasser* [1948] 1 KB 4.

(c) evidence is given of an imputation about the other person made by the defendant—
    (i) on being questioned under caution, before charge, about the offence with which he is charged, or
    (ii) on being charged with the offence or officially informed that he might be prosecuted for it.

Also significant is gateway (d), which has a credibility limb as well as the propensity limb examined in detail in Chapters 7 and 8. Gateway (d) allows evidence of the accused's bad character to be introduced if 'it is relevant to an important matter in issue between the defendant and the prosecution'. Section 103 explains that the matters in issue between the defendant and the prosecution include 'the question whether the defendant has a propensity to be untruthful, except where it is not suggested that the defendant's case is untruthful in any respect'.[4] These provisions are the subject of this chapter.

9.1 Crime and Credibility

There is a certain ambiguity in references to the defendant's credibility. An account put forward by a defendant may lack credibility because it is implausible. And the account may appear especially implausible because of the defendant's criminal record, as when a defendant with previous convictions for burglary explains his presence in the garden of a burgled house by saying he was looking for some privacy because he needed to urinate. This is not the sense in which credibility is used here, nor is it the law's rationale for admitting previous convictions under gateway (g) and the credibility limb of gateway (d). Here, the focus is on the defendant's credibility in the sense of his veracity, his 'propensity to be untruthful' as section 103 puts it.

When bad character evidence is introduced as evidence of a defendant's lack of credibility, it will almost always involve previous convictions. A key assumption, then, is that there is a connection between criminality—or certain types of criminality—and credibility. Is this plausible? It might initially seem that it is not: everybody lies. One well-known study found members of the public recording an average of two lies told each day.[5] We lie because lying can make things easier for us, or because we want to present ourselves as better than we are.[6] These motivations are obviously present where a person is charged with a crime they have in fact committed. Not only are we all prone to lie, we all have good reason to put that propensity to work to escape conviction.

While there is much truth in the foregoing, the fact that we all lie does not mean that some of us are not more prone to lie than others. In fact, the distribution of lying among the population appears to be heavily skewed, with a

---

[4] CJA, s 103(1)(b).
[5] B. M. De Paulo et al, 'Lying in Everyday Life' (1996) 70 *J Personality & Soc Psychol* 979.
[6] See, generally, T. R. Levine, R. K. Kim, and L. M. Hamel, 'People Lie for a Reason: Three Experiments Documenting the Principle of Veracity' (2010) 27 *Communication Research Reports* 271; A. Vrij, *Detecting Lies and Deceit: Pitfalls and Opportunities* (2nd edn, Oxford: Wiley-Blackwell, 2008), ch 2; and R. Feldman, *Liar: The Truth About Lying* (London: Virgin Books, 2010).

small proportion of people responsible for a large proportion of lies.[7] Nor does the existence of a strong motivation, such as the avoidance of conviction, mean that interpersonal differences in propensity to lie will have no impact on our choices. A high proportion of suspects confess to the police, and an even higher proportion plead guilty.[8] It is true that many of these will do so for reasons other than their qualms about lying: because the case against them is strong,[9] or because they expect lenient treatment by not contesting guilt. Still, this does not mean that honesty, or lack of it, plays no role in defendants' decisions. It is therefore worth considering whether the credibility-crime link is plausible.

The psychological research considered in Chapter 2 suggests that, while situational influences are important in explaining behaviour, stable personality traits do exist. Might honesty be one such trait? One of the best-known studies in personality psychology, a study which did much to support the claims of situationism, suggests not. Hartshorne and May found that the honesty of individual children varied significantly from one situation to another: children who would cheat on an academic test would not cheat at sport.[10] However, there is considerable dispute over the interpretation of these findings,[11] and the existence of interpersonal variation in the frequency of lying casts some doubt on the situationist account.[12] More recent research does support the theory that honesty is a robust, cross-situational trait. One study goes so far as to claim that a personality trait akin to honesty might be added to the 'big five' personality factors—the primary units of modern trait theory.[13] If this is right, we might expect this personality trait to be correlated with criminality. Criminological research supports this contention. As we have seen, offenders tend to be generalists rather than specialists, and have a tendency to commit a wide range of anti-social behaviours, not just those which are criminalized. 'Offending is one element of a larger syndrome of anti-social behaviour that arises in childhood and tends to persist into adulthood with numerous different behavioural manifestations.'[14] Research on

---

[7] K. B. Serota, T. R. Levine, and F. J. Boster, 'The Prevalence of Lying in America: Three Studies of Self-Reported Lies' (2010) 36 *Human Communications Research* 2. See also D. A. Kashy and B. M. DePaulo, 'Who Lies?' (1996) 70 *J Personality & Soc Psychol* 1037.

[8] More than 60 per cent of suspects make at least a partial admission: see C. Clarke and R. Milne, *National Evaluation of the PEACE Investigative Interviewing Course* (London: Home Office, 2001), 33. See also M. McConville, *Corroboration and Confessions: The Impact of a Rule Requiring that No Conviction Can be Sustained on the Basis of Confession Evidence Alone* (London: HMSO, 1993), 32–3. Unsurprisingly, confessions are strongly correlated with guilty pleas: see McConville, *Corroboration and Confessions*. Around 80 per cent of defendants in the Crown Court plead guilty: see A. Ashworth and M. Redmayne, *The Criminal Process* (Oxford: Oxford University Press, 2010), 294.

[9] See G. Gudjonsson, *The Psychology of Interrogations and Confessions: A Handbook* (Chichester: Wiley, 2003), 153.

[10] H. Hartshorne and M. A. May, *Studies in the Nature of Character: 1. Studies in Deceit* (New York: Macmillan, 1928).

[11] R. V. Burton, 'Generality of Honesty Reconsidered' (1963) 70 *Psychol Rev* 481.

[12] See Serota et al, 'The Prevalence of Lying in America'; and Kashy and DePaulo, 'Who Lies?'.

[13] M. C. Ashton, K. Lee, and C. Son, 'Honesty as the Sixth Factor of Personality: Correlations with Machivellianism, Primary Psychopathy, and Social Adroitness' (2000) 14 *Eur J Personality* 359.

[14] D. Farrington, 'Human Development and Criminal Careers' in M. Maguire, R. Morgan, and R. Reiner (eds), *Oxford Handbook of Criminology* (Oxford: Oxford University Press, 1997), 380.

schoolchildren points to a correlation between deviancy and honesty.[15] There is now a fairly large literature on academic dishonesty—no doubt because it is easy for academics to study, there being convenient access to a large pool of research subjects. The research finds individual differences among students in terms of their propensity to cheat, and also suggests links with other forms of deviance.[16] It is therefore plausible to suppose that offenders have a comparative propensity to lie. The law on the credibility uses of bad character will be assessed on the basis of this assumption.

9.2 Gateway (d): Propensity to be Untruthful

Gateway (d) is potentially very radical. Section 103 stipulates that, unless the prosecution accepts that the defendant's case is truthful (which might be the case if, for example, the dispute at trial is solely about questions of law, such as whether D's action was reasonable), D's propensity to be untruthful is in issue. While the difference in wording between section 101(d)—which refers to *important* matters in issue—and section 103—which refers simply to matters in issue—leaves some wriggle room, once the credibility-crime link is accepted (and the courts have long accepted it), gateway (d) potentially allows D's previous convictions to be introduced in any criminal trial where there is a dispute of fact. The courts, however, have not interpreted gateway (d) in this way. This is not surprising, both because of the breadth of other gateways, which ensures that much character evidence gets admitted anyway, and because such automatic admissibility would have been a profound change from past practice.

In *Hanson*,[17] the first significant appeal involving the CJA's character provisions, the Court of Appeal moved to narrow gateway (d) by limiting the type of conviction that could pass through it:

As to propensity to untruthfulness, this, as it seems to us, is not the same as propensity to dishonesty. It is to be assumed, bearing in mind the frequency with which the words honest and dishonest appear in the criminal law, that Parliament deliberately chose the word 'untruthful' to convey a different meaning, reflecting a defendant's account of his behaviour, or lies told when committing an offence. Previous convictions, whether for

---

[15] D. Farrington, 'Juvenile Delinquency' in J. C. Coleman (ed), *The School Years: Current Issues in the Socialization of Young People* (London: Routledge, 1992), 128–30.
[16] J. K. Cochran et al, 'Academic Dishonesty and Low Self Control: An Empirical Test of a General Theory of Crime' (1998) 19 *Deviant Behavior* 227; K. L. Blankenship and B. E. Whitley, 'Relation of General Deviance to Academic Dishonesty' (2000) 10 *Ethics and Behavior* 1; A. U. Bolin, 'Self-Control, Perceived Opportunity, and Attitudes as Predictors of Academic Dishonesty' (2004) 138 *J Psychol* 101; B. E. Whitley, 'Factors Associated with Cheating among College Students: A Review' (1998) 39 *Research in Higher Education* 235; S. E. Newstead, A. Franklyn-Stokes, and P. Armstead, 'Individual Differences in Student Cheating' (1996) 88 *J Educational Psychol* 229; and S. Etter, J. J. Cramer, and S. Finn, 'Origins of Academic Dishonesty: Ethical Orientations and Personality Factors Associated with Attitudes about Cheating with Information Technology' (2006) 39 *J Research on Technology in Education* 133.
[17] *Hanson and Others* [2005] 2 Cr App R 21, [2005] EWCA Crim 824.

offences of dishonesty or otherwise, are therefore only likely to be capable of showing a propensity to be untruthful where, in the present case, truthfulness is an issue and, in the earlier case, either there was a plea of not guilty and the defendant gave an account, on arrest, in interview, or in evidence, which the jury must have disbelieved, or the way in which the offence was committed shows a propensity for untruthfulness, for example, by the making of false representations.[18]

In early decisions on gateway (d), convictions for benefit fraud[19] and obtaining by deception[20] were said to demonstrate a propensity to be untruthful. In *Alobaydi*, the defendant, on trial for rape, had previous convictions for burglary and violence admitted against him via gateway (d), because he had pleaded not guilty at the earlier trial.[21] This, then, was how the gateway (d) worked under *Hanson*.

Gateway (d) was quickly narrowed further. In *Campbell*, the Court of Appeal stated that:

The question of whether a defendant has a propensity for being untruthful will not normally be capable of being described as an *important* matter in issue between the defendant and the prosecution. A propensity for untruthfulness will not, of itself, go very far to establishing the commission of a criminal offence. To suggest that a propensity for untruthfulness makes it more likely that a defendant has lied to the jury is not likely to help them. If they apply common sense they will conclude that a defendant who has committed a criminal offence may well be prepared to lie about it, even if he has not shown a propensity for lying whereas a defendant who has not committed the offence charged will be likely to tell the truth, even if he has shown a propensity for telling lies. In short, whether or not a defendant is telling the truth to the jury is likely to depend simply on whether or not he committed the offence charged. The jury should focus on the latter question rather than on whether or not he has a propensity for telling lies... For these reasons, the only circumstance in which there is likely to be an *important* issue as to whether a defendant has a propensity to tell lies is where telling lies is an element of the offence charged. Even then, the propensity to tell lies is only likely to be significant if the lying is in the context of committing criminal offences, in which case the evidence is likely to be admissible under s.103(1)(a) [the propensity limb of gateway (d)].[22]

Campbell more or less kills off the credibility limb of gateway (d). After *Campbell*, there are very few cases where the Court of Appeal has approved of evidence led to show a propensity to be untruthful.[23] In *Belogun*,[24] the issue between prosecution and defence was whether D's defence of duress was truthful. The prosecution had been allowed to call evidence that D had a previous conviction for perverting the course of justice: he had forged a document in order to get himself out of trouble

---

[18] *Hanson*, [13].

[19] *Edwards and Others* [2006] 1 Cr App R 3, [2005] EWCA Crim 1813, [33].

[20] *Highton and Others* [2006] 1 Cr App R 7, [2005] EWCA Crim 1985, [57]; and *Ellis* [2010] EWCA Crim 163.

[21] [2007] EWCA Crim 145.   [22] [2007] 2 Cr App R 28, [2007] EWCA Crim 1472.

[23] Apart from *Belogun*, the only other example I am aware of is *Jarvis* [2008] EWCA Crim 488. The decision is not very clear, but the Court of Appeal considered that the evidence showed a propensity to be untruthful. This, however, was a case where the evidence was admissible, if at all, as propensity evidence (albeit propensity to commit offences of dishonesty).

[24] [2008] EWCA Crim 2006.

after missing meetings with his probation officer. Noting *Campbell*'s restrictive view of gateway (d), the Court commented:

> it is a truism that each case has to be looked at on its own facts. In this case the prosecution did not seek to introduce evidence of other offences of dishonesty committed by this appellant, in particular theft. They sought to introduce the evidence of perverting the course of justice for a specific reason. In the case which the jury was trying, the sole issue was whether the defence of duress put forward by the appellant was a truthful and valid defence. His past conviction related to a fabricated attempt made by him to deceive a court so as to get himself out of trouble for his failure to comply with a court order. In this context the judge was perfectly entitled to regard that conviction as relevant to an important matter in issue between the parties.[25]

In truth, *Belogun* is not easily reconciled with *Campbell*. *Campbell*'s argument is that all guilty defendants have a strong motivation to lie which swamps any pre-existing propensity. That Belogun had previously lied to save himself is neither here nor there. As *Campbell* notes, where evidence of a propensity to be untruthful really is relevant, it can be admitted under the propensity limb of gateway (d): in *Belogun*, the prosecution would then have had to argue that the conviction showed that D had a propensity to lie to get himself out of trouble. The banality of that claim may suggest why the prosecution did not make it; it also demonstrates why, if *Campbell* is right, *Belogun* is a bad decision.

But is *Campbell* right? The decision received poor reviews from the commentators: 'flawed reasoning';[26] 'obviously incorrect';[27] 'dubious logic'.[28] One reason why *Campbell* is controversial is that it has far-reaching implications, because the argument that the guilty will tend to lie and the innocent tell the truth, irrespective of their propensity to be honest, would seem to apply to all credibility uses of character evidence, including tit for tat and the credibility use of good character evidence. As we will see, *Campbell* has in fact been confined to gateway (d). The decision is sufficiently radical that it might well have been rethought even within those narrow confines were it not for two factors. First, the liberal admissibility of bad character evidence under the propensity limb of gateway (d) and under the new tit for tat provision means that the propensity to be untruthful gateway is rarely worth fighting over. Second, *Campbell* was a decision of a Court of Appeal led by Lord Phillips, then Lord Chief Justice and soon to be the senior Law Lord and thence President of the Supreme Court.

Campbell is right, more or less. As I noted above, in the criminal trial there are strong situational pressures on defendants. These certainly mean that the innocent will tell the truth, at least about the central issue in the trial.[29] And the guilty

---

[25] *Belogun*, [23].   [26] A. Keane, 'Flawed Reasoning' (2008) 158 *NLJ* 168.
[27] J. R. Spencer, *Evidence of Bad Character* (2nd edn, Oxford: Hart Publishing, 2009), 94.
[28] A. J. Roberts, 'Case Comment (*R v Lafayette*)' [2009] *Crim LR* 809, 810.
[29] The innocent may well lie about peripheral matters, eg they may lie about presence at the scene of crime. But it is unlikely that propensity to lie has much influence here, because the lie is caused by a situational factor (avoiding conviction). Further, the fact-finder is likely to be focussed on the big question—is D lying when he denies guilt—not less central ones.

have a strong motivation to lie. Where *Campbell* might be criticized is in focus-sing on the situation during a contested trial and thus not considering the factors which influence whether D ever gets to testify in court. Many guilty defend-ants do tell the truth, in that they plead guilty, a decision influenced by previous choices as to whether or not to confess to the police.[30] It may be that those with a disposition to lie are less likely to confess and to plead guilty. However, the sen-tence discount, which offers a significantly reduced sentence to those who plead guilty, provides a strong motivation for the guilty to plead guilty. It is therefore likely that the estimated probability of acquittal, rather than propensity to be untruthful, is the most significant factor in the decision to plead guilty. It thus seems right to say that the situational pressures on defendants mean that whether D has a propensity to be untruthful will not be a very significant issue in most trials. *Hanson*'s innovations—restricting the relevant evidence to offences involv-ing deception and convictions after not-guilty pleas—make little difference to this argument. Because offenders tend to be generalists, the idea of a group of offenders who have a particular tendency to be untruthful does not really hold up. And if situational factors dominate the decision on plea, little can be read into an earlier not-guilty plea.

There is a further reason why a defendant's propensity to be untruthful is of little significance. We are assuming that a credibility-crime link is plausible. As Richard Friedman points out,[31] if the offender is guilty, then the credibility-crime link means that he has a propensity to be untruthful, whether or not he has pre-vious convictions. To think otherwise involves reasoning along the following lines: 'I thought that if D had committed theft, he wouldn't lie about it, but I changed my mind when I discovered he had a previous conviction for forgery.' If D is innocent, then, as already noted, he is unlikely to lie about the central issue, however much he normally lies.

There are counter-arguments to the foregoing. One is that practised liars may be better at lying than ingénues, or that some people simply have a talent for lying.[32] There may be something to that, but if it is this argument which is relied on it needs to be put to the jury in those terms, and it never has been.[33] A better argument looks back to the discussion in Chapter 4, where it was suggested that a first offence might be regarded as a lapse rather than as a serious commitment to offending (this issue is taken up again in Chapter 11). This was largely a moral claim, based on von Hirsch's account of mitigation in sentencing, but there may also be some empirical truth in it. Many offending careers are short-lived aberra-tions in the teenage years. And where propensity to commit crime is concerned,

---

[30] See points made in 8 above.
[31] R. D. Friedman, 'Character Impeachment Evidence: Psycho-Bayesian [!?] Analysis and a Proposed Overhaul' (1991) 38 *UCLA L Rev* 637.
[32] See A. Vrij and S. Mann, 'Good Liars' (2010) 38 *J Psychiatry & Law* 77; and C. F. Bond and B. M. DePaulo, 'Individual Differences in Judging Deception: Accuracy and Bias' (2008) 134 *Psychol Bull* 477.
[33] Nor would this account for the current law, which allows bad character evidence to be intro-duced under (g) even if D does not testify.

the courts have shown some sympathy for the argument that a single conviction for a not very serious offence signifies little.[34] If a defendant has no previous convictions, perhaps he deserves the benefit of the doubt, ie the presumption that he would admit it if he was guilty. In light of this, the reasoning in the previous paragraph can be reframed to make it more plausible: 'I thought that if D had committed theft, and it was his first offence, he might well admit it; but when I discovered that he had a previous conviction for burglary, I thought it was more likely that he would lie.'

There seems to me to be something quite attractive about the argument that first-time offenders deserve the benefit of the doubt when it comes to their credibility, echoing as it does a reluctance to use single convictions as evidence of propensity to offend. (As with propensity to offend, of course, it is not obvious where we should draw the limits: replace 'theft' with 'rape' in the quotation which ends the previous paragraph and the chain of reasoning is rather less appealing.) Even so, the justification for introducing previous convictions as evidence of a propensity to be untruthful is hardly strong. Fact-finders are faced with a defendant denying guilt in court, and they are likely to recognize that guilty defendants have very strong reasons to lie in this situation. Lack of credibility is surely the default assumption.[35] If we want to prompt the jury to recognize that certain offenders may be more likely to confess and plead guilty than others, the way to do this is to allow those with no previous convictions to signal this fact. This is in fact what we do through the good character direction. Where a defendant has no previous convictions, he is entitled to a direction that he is a person of good character, and the judge should note that this is relevant to both his propensity to offend and his credibility (see Chapter 10).[36] One of the arguments against *Campbell* is that its logic—the guilty lie and the innocent tell the truth—applies equally to the good character direction, and that it would be shocking if we were to abandon the direction.[37] There is some truth in that. As noted above, *Campbell* may be too focussed on the situation at trial, whereas it needs to be remembered that defendants appear at trial only because of their prior choices: 'if he was guilty, he would have pleaded guilty' may be a sensible line of thought; 'if he was guilty, he would admit it at trial' is not. But *Campbell* and the good character direction can coexist. If we start from the assumption that the guilty are likely to lie, then the good character direction reminds us that there may be an exception to that. On the other hand, if we start from the assumption that the guilty will plead guilty, and therefore treat defendants' claims of innocence at trial as worthy of belief, it

---

[34] See *Hanson*, [2005] 2 Cr App R 21, [2005] EWCA Crim 824, and discussion in Chapter 7.

[35] See D. Pritchard, 'Testimony' in A. Duff et al (eds), *The Trial on Trial: Volume One: Truth and Due Process* (Oxford: Hart Publishing, 2004). See also T. R. Levine, R. K. Kim, and J. P. Blair, '(In)accuracy at Detecting True and False Confessions and Denials: An Initial Test of a Projected Motive Model of Veracity Judgments' (2010) 36 *Human Communication Research* 82.

[36] *Vye* [1993] 1 WLR 471.

[37] See Keane, 'Flawed Reasoning'. Not everyone is so wedded to the good character direction: cf P. Roberts and A. Zuckerman, *Criminal Evidence* (2nd edn, Oxford: Oxford University Press, 2010), 638.

might make sense to introduce previous convictions as evidence of a propensity to be untruthful, but to abandon good character directions. The former situation seems far more likely to reflect the fact-finder's assumptions.[38]

It might be argued that there is little harm in letting the prosecution argue that D's previous convictions reflect on his credibility. But the fact remains that even if jurors do think that guilty defendants are likely to have admitted guilt, previous convictions have little bearing on credibility. The credibility-crime link only means that offenders are more likely to lie than other people, not that there is a vast difference between them. And previous offender or not, guilty people have very strong motivations to lie when accused of crimes they think they can get away with. A comparative propensity to lie is unlikely to have much effect on people's choices when it comes to admitting guilt. That we give those without previous convictions a small benefit of the doubt via the good character direction does nothing to undermine this basic position. If, in spite of this, we admit previous convictions on an issue on which they have little probative value, they may be misused by the jury, most probably because credibility gets confused with propensity. After all, the consensus of the jury research is that limiting instructions—use the evidence for purpose X not obvious purpose Y—have little effect.[39] So, *Campbell* gets it more or less right.

This section has spent considerable time teasing out the implications of introducing evidence of a propensity to be untruthful. The conclusion is that the Court of Appeal was right to dismantle the credibility limb of gateway (d). It might be questioned whether it was worth giving so much space to a provision which, even before its demise, was of little significance. The reason for doing so is that it is important to have a clear view of the relevance of previous convictions as evidence of credibility, and *Campbell* is a convenient foil for teasing out the arguments. The rights and wrongs of *Campbell* are, by and large, the rights and wrongs of any practice of introducing previous convictions on the issue of a defendant's credibility.

9.3 Gateway (g): Tit for Tat

Section 101's gateway (g) allows evidence of a defendant's bad character to be admitted 'if the defendant has made an attack on another person's character'. An attack may be made by introducing evidence, through cross-examination, or by allegations made by D during police interview. Section 106 explains further:

(2) In subsection (1) 'evidence attacking the other person's character' means evidence to the effect that the other person—

---

[38] For some evidence in support, see Levine et al, '(In)accuracy'.
[39] See M. J. Saks, 'What Do Jury Experiments Tell Us about How Juries (Should) Make Decisions?' (1997) 6 *S Cal Interdisciplinary LJ* 1, 36, 50.

(a) has committed an offence (whether a different offence from the one with which the defendant is charged or the same one), or

(b) has behaved, or is disposed to behave, in a reprehensible way;

and 'imputation about the other person' means an assertion to that effect.

In *Hanson*, the Court of Appeal suggested that the case law prior to the CJA would provide useful guidance on when an attack had been made.[40] Under the old law, an 'emphatic denial' of the prosecution case would not trigger tit for tat,[41] even if the implication was that witnesses were lying. But going further, and explicitly suggesting lies, probably would. An allegation that the police had fabricated evidence would usually lead to the introduction of D's previous convictions, and the Court of Appeal has implied that it still will.[42] Introducing evidence of a person's criminal behaviour—most obviously, previous convictions—is an attack. So in *Singh*,[43] alleging that the complainant was smoking crack was an attack, as was the claim in *Lewis* that the complainant was masturbating in a public toilet (the crime of sexual activity in a public toilet).[44] More controversially, in *Lamaletie*, D's claim that he was acting in self-defence triggered gateway (g): 'Lamaletie had in interview alleged not simply that Mr Yadessa struck the first blow but that he "was attacking me everywhere": even the allegation that he had started the fight would probably be an allegation of reprehensible conduct, but Lamaletie in any event went further.'[45] On this logic, a claim of duress, or provocation, might well amount to an attack.

A graphic illustration of the operation of gateway (g) is *Ball*.[46] Ball was tried on two counts of rape. In police interview, he claimed consent and 'told the police that most of the men in the local public house had had sexual intercourse with the complainant. He criticized the complainant's sexual promiscuity in very disparaging terms. She was easy. "She's a bag really, you know what I mean, a slag".'[47] Ball was to regret these comments. The prosecution introduced them as evidence of his attitude towards the complainant, to show, among other things, that he would have regarded her refusal to consent as 'meaningless'.[48] The judge then allowed evidence of Ball's previous convictions to be introduced, because evidence had been given that he had made imputations about another person's character. The Court of Appeal thought this perfectly proper.[49]

---

[40] [2005] 2 Cr App R 21, [2005] EWCA Crim 824, [14].   [41] *Rouse* [1904] 1 KB 104.

[42] See *R* v *M* [2006] EWCA Crim 3408, [19].   [43] *Singh* [2007] EWCA Crim 2140.

[44] *Lewis* [2007] EWCA Crim 3030.   [45] *Lamaletie* [2008] EWCA Crim 314, [8].

[46] *Renda and Others (Ball)* [2006] 1 Cr App R 24, [2005] EWCA Crim 2826.

[47] *Ball*, [33].   [48] *Ball*, [37].

[49] This raises questions about the justice of using D's comments in the police station as a trigger for the admissibility of his previous convictions. At trial, D will usually have been warned by counsel of the consequences of attacking another person's character. While Ball would have been offered legal advice before interview, even if he had taken this up it is unlikely that his adviser would have alerted him to the risks of criticizing others (although perhaps now this should be standard practice); he would, however, have been cautioned that anything he said might be used against him. Whether lack of warning is a problem may depend on the cogency of the underlying justification for tit for tat. If admitting D's record really is necessary to put the fact-finder in the full picture, then perhaps there is nothing objectionable here, just as if D had told an exculpatory story and the

Before the CJA, evidence introduced under the tit for tat rationale was evidence of the defendant's credibility and could not be used to show propensity to offend. Given acceptance of the credibility-crime link, this meant that previous convictions for any crime could be introduced: there was no need for a *Hanson*-like connection to deceptive conduct. The rationale for admitting evidence through gateway (g) will be explored in detail below, but in broad terms the justification is still made in terms of credibility: 'The purpose of gateway G is to enable the jury to know from what sort of source allegations against a witness...have come...persons of bad character may of course tell the truth and often do, but it is ordinary human experience that their word may be worth less than that of those who have led exemplary lives.'[50] The courts have followed the old law in not applying the restrictions of *Hanson*, and certainly not the locked door of *Campbell*, to gateway (g). In *George*, the defendant's complaint that convictions for violence, burglary, and drugs offences should not have been admitted through (g) was rejected: '*Hanson* teaches that where evidence is adduced to establish a propensity, a distinction between offences of dishonesty and evidence of untruthfulness must be maintained. No such distinction arises where the evidence is adduced to show the character of the source of an accusation, pursuant to section 101(g).'[51]

One criticism of the old law was that juries were asked to perform 'mental gymnastics' by using a previous conviction for, say, GBH, as evidence of a defendant's lack of credibility, but not as evidence of propensity to violence. With more bad character evidence admitted under the propensity limb of gateway (d), this is less of a problem, but the Court of Appeal has in any case held that once evidence is admitted through gateway (g), it can be used for any purpose to which it is relevant.[52] Thus, evidence admitted through (g) may be used to show that D has a propensity to commit the type of offence with which he is charged. This does not mean, however, that juries are never asked to make fine distinctions. In *Singh*, D was on trial for robbery, and his allegation that the complainant smoked crack triggered the admissibility of his convictions for disorder, assaults on policemen, criminal damage, and drink-driving as evidence of his credibility. The trial judge instructed the jury as follows:

You now know that the defendant, on whose behalf those allegations were put to [the complaint] has a number of criminal convictions...If you think it right, you may take his bad character into account in deciding whether or not the defendant's evidence to you from the witness box was truthful. A person with a bad character may be less likely to tell the truth, but it does not follow that he is incapable of doing so. You may weigh his convictions in the balance in deciding whether you believe his evidence to you yesterday and first thing today. But it is for you to decide to what extent, if at all, his character helps you

---

prosecution showed that he had told a similar story in the past when accused of other crimes. But if the justification for tit for tat is dubious, lack of warning may add to its problematic nature.

[50] *Singh* [2007] EWCA Crim 2140, [8].
[51] *George* [2006] EWCA Crim 1652, [30]. See also *Lewis* [2007] EWCA Crim 3030, [13]–[14].
[52] *Highton and Others* [2006] 1 Cr App R 7, [2005] EWCA Crim 1985, [10]; and *Campbell* [2007] 2 Cr App R 28, [2007] EWCA Crim 1472, [25].

when judging his evidence. Bear in mind, as I have said, that his bad character cannot by itself prove that he is guilty. It would therefore be wrong to jump to the conclusion that he is guilty just because he has a bad character. The defence point out that on all occasions in the past he has pleaded guilty, and incidentally, none of the offences of which he has previously been convicted are offences of dishonesty; but you may take them into account in the way that I've just described if you think it right; but it's a matter for you to judge.[53]

The Court of Appeal thought that this was the proper approach. In *Lamaletie*, the response to D's claim of self-defence was to introduce his six previous convictions for violence. The jury was instructed that these were relevant 'in one regard and one regard only': to D's credibility.[54] While the Court of Appeal thought that in this case the convictions probably could have been used as propensity evidence,[55] it has approved similar directions in other cases.[56] Thus, one of the most embarrassing aspects of the old law lingers on, despite the Court of Appeal having as good as admitted that juries ignore such instructions.[57]

   Lamaletie also illustrates another feature of the law. While Ball's attack on the complainant's character may have been gratuitous—'she's a bag'—*Lamaletie* was simply putting forward his defence that the complainant had attacked him first. This defence carried a very high price. Before the CJA was introduced, the courts had on occasion toyed with a 'no-stymie' principle, whereby tit for tat would not occur if D's attack on another person was essential to his defence.[58] But while it was agreed that there was a discretion to block recourse to tit for tat where it would be unfair, this discretion was rarely exercised. The Law Commission's proposals included a no-stymie principle, whereby D would not 'lose his shield' if he introduced 'evidence that has to do with the alleged facts of the case'.[59] This would have protected Lamaletie, but probably not Ball. The provision did not make it into the CJA. The CJA does contain a fairness discretion, however, and this specifically applies to gateway (g). Under section 101(3), the court should not admit evidence of D's bad character if it 'would have such an adverse effect on the fairness of the proceedings that the court ought not to admit it'. We saw in Chapter 7 that 101(3) is rarely used in cases involving gateway (d), and the same is true of (g). If *Lamaletie* was not a case for section 101(3), few cases are.[60]

---

[53]   [2007] EWCA Crim 2140, [11].
[54]   [2008] EWCA Crim 314, [7]. The judge went so far as to remark: '[o]ne linking factor is, there is clearly a link that there has been a history of Mr Lamaletie being untruthful in relation to offences of violence. But you are not asked to regard it as to anything other than going to his credit, whether he has been truthful about what has happened or not' (at [7]).
[55]   *Lamaletie*, [13]. The trial judge had been worried by the absence of details about the offences, a concern the Court of Appeal thought misplaced.
[56]   *Lafayette* [2008] EWCA Crim 3238.
[57]   *Renda (Razaq)* [2006] 1 Cr App R 24, [2005] EWCA Crim 2826, [82].
[58]   See Roberts and Zuckerman, *Criminal Evidence*, 642–6; and P. Mirfield, 'The Argument from Consistency for Overruling *Selvey*' (1991) 50 *CLJ* 490.
[59]   Law Commission, *Evidence of Bad Character in Criminal Proceedings*, Law Com No 273, Cm 5257 (London: TSO, 2001), 97–8, 214–17.
[60]   For an exceptional decision holding that evidence admitted under (g) should have been excluded on fairness grounds, see *Benabbou* [2012] EWCA Crim 1256. Cf *Peter Edmund W* [2011] EWCA Crim 472.

One more aspect of the gateway (g) case law deserves to be mentioned. In Chapter 7, we saw that when it comes to evidence of propensity to offend, the courts have been quite sensitive to time-lapse. Old convictions will generally not be admitted, unless they are for serious offences or sexual offences. This is as it should be. Section 101(4) prompts judges to think about time-lapse when considering an application to exclude evidence under section 101(3).[61] Yet here judges treat gateway (d) and (g) differently: while time-lapse is seen as eroding propensity to offend, it is rarely seen as diminishing lack of credibility. *Lewis* illustrates this point.[62] After an incident in a public toilet, Lewis was charged with sexual activity with a child. The prosecution application to introduce a 1985 conviction for gross indecency—also involving a public toilet—was turned down because this was 'a single conviction 21 years earlier'.[63] But when Lewis attacked the complainant's character—his story was that a false allegation had been made because he told the boy off for masturbating in the toilet—the conviction came in. 'I take into account the lapse of time,' stated the trial judge, 'but it does seem to me, to be only fair to both sides, prosecution as well as defence, that if this allegation is to be made, the jury should know something about the person making that allegation.'[64] Instructing the jury, the judge explained: 'You may take [the conviction] into account in deciding whether or not the Defendant's evidence to you was truthful when he says that it was H, not him, who was involved in sexual behaviour...You are not allowed to say that the Defendant is more likely to be guilty of this offence because he has that conviction in 1985.'[65] The Court of Appeal approved of all this, and this is not an isolated instance. Various other cases suggest that time-lapse has little, if any, bearing on the use of previous convictions to show lack of credibility.[66]

This is odd. If propensity to offend fades with time, surely propensity to lie, which is presumed to be connected to offending, does too. Perhaps it is arguable that propensity to lie is some deeper and less changeable character trait. The extremes may wear off, while the underlying anti-social attitudes remain. If D has an old previous conviction for violence, we might think him no longer very likely to be violent, but still prone to be aggressive. This explanation faces the obstacle that we are talking about *comparative* propensity. It is perfectly plausible that a tendency to extreme behaviour, such as being very violent, fades more quickly than a tendency to less extreme behaviour. Ten years on, however, while a person's violent nature may be much diminished, there is probably still a comparative propensity to be violent—to be more prone to violence than other people—for the very reason that extreme behaviour is rare among the comparator class (those

---

[61] 'In an application to exclude evidence under subsection (3) the court must have regard, in particular, to the length of time between the matters to which that evidence relates and the matters which form the subject of the offence charged.'

[62] [2007] EWCA Crim 3030.   [63] *Lewis*, [8].   [64] *Lewis*, [10].

[65] *Lewis*, [16].

[66] *Edwards* [2006] 2 Cr App r 4, [2005] EWCA Crim 3244; *Highton* [2006] 1 Cr App R 7, [2005] EWCA Crim 1985, [52]; and *R v PD* [2012] EWCA Crim 2163. *R v C* [2011] EWCA Crim 939 allows the possibility of excluding stale evidence under (g), but rejects it in the actual case.

without convictions for violence). The courts understand this, which is why, where propensity evidence is concerned, they will admit a 20-year-old conviction for murder, but not for theft. The failure to apply this reasoning to credibility evidence is puzzling.

9.4 Tit for Tat: A Practice in Search of a Rationale

As the previous section makes clear, there is much about gateway (g) which needs justifying. A defendant might have a 20-year-old conviction for violence admitted against him simply for alleging self-defence, with the scant protection that the jury would be told that the conviction only reflects on his credibility. How do the courts justify gateway (g)?

A starting point is the demise of *Butterwasser*. A defendant is no longer insulated from tit for tat by staying out of the witness box. This may tell us something about the notion of credibility deployed by gateway (g), but it also deserves analysis in its own right because the position under the CJA is controversial.[67] Lord Goddard presented the decision in *Butterwasser* as a matter of logic: 'there is no authority, and I do not see on what principle it could be said, that if a man does not go into the box and put his own character in issue, he can have evidence given against him of previous bad character when all that he has done is to attack the witnesses for the prosecution. The reason is that by attacking the witnesses for the prosecution and suggesting they are unreliable, he is not putting his character in issue; he is putting their character in issue.'[68] Things become rather less convincing, however, when Lord Goddard goes on to explain why things change when D testifies: 'the reason why, if he gives evidence, he can be cross-examined if he has attacked the witnesses for the prosecution is that the statute says he can'.[69] A better explanation, of course, would be that D does put his character in issue by testifying. He takes the oath and implicitly asks the jury to believe him.[70] There is, then, a sense in which his credibility is in issue. How different, though, is the situation where D does not testify? Here, D does not take the oath, but will still be putting forward some sort of defence through his lawyer. Roberts and Zuckerman argue that in this situation, if D attacks a prosecution witness, his credibility is not in issue: 'Defence counsel is saying to the jury, for example, "don't believe this witness because she is a criminal and has previous convictions to prove it", not "don't believe this witness because my client...asks you not to". The accused electing not to testify is merely putting the prosecution to proof, no matter what

---

[67] See Roberts and Zuckerman, *Criminal Evidence*, 645–6.   [68] [1948] 1 KB 4, 7.
[69] *Butterwasser*, 7.
[70] A broadly Gricean point: see H. P. Grice, 'Logic and Conversation' in *Studies in the Ways of Words* (Cambridge MA: Harvard, 1989). 'Try to make your contribution one that is true' is one of Grice's 'maxims of quality' for verbal communication. Of course, the trial is a sceptical context where observers are less likely to take D's assertions to be true than in everyday conversation: see Pritchard, 'Testimony'.

his counsel might say to prosecution witnesses in order to test their evidence in cross-examination.'[71]

Roberts and Zuckerman are partly right. If I see you reading a Wikipedia article on quantum physics and say 'be careful, Wikipedia is full of errors, and here is an authoritative study to prove it', then I am not putting my credibility in issue as to the truth of the article, because I am not claiming that this particular article does contain errors. Counsel's pointing to W's previous convictions can be seen in the same way. But there are complications. First, not all examples of tit for tat follow this structure. In *Singh* and *Lewis*, particular allegations relating to the complainant's behaviour at the time of the alleged offence are made. Even focussing on the Roberts and Zuckerman example, it is not necessarily true that D's credibility is not in issue. D is disputing the witness's evidence, and this will usually be about a matter on which he has personal knowledge. If the witness said, for example, 'I saw D hit V', then by saying 'don't believe W', or even 'here are reasons to be cautious about W's evidence', D is implying that he did not hit V. Indeed, just by pleading not guilty D is making a claim that he did not commit the offence, so his credibility—would he have admitted the offence if he was guilty?—is in issue. It is true that the not-guilty plea can be seen as merely 'putting the prosecution to proof' rather than as putting forward any positive claim to innocence. No oath is administered at the time of plea. And if the prosecution case is based on a series of witnesses with track records for lying, then perhaps it is a weak case and D does not deserve to be convicted. Nevertheless, what matters is how the fact-finder understands D's plea and the arguments put forward at trial, and surely these are seen as claims to 'actual innocence', not just legal innocence. If jurors did think that by pleading not guilty defendants were saying no more than 'I'm not claiming I didn't do it, just that the prosecution can't prove that I did', then no doubt the conviction rate would be rather higher than it is. And no doubt if a defendant did want to disambiguate his case in this way, a court would be content to shield him from tit for tat.

It is therefore difficult to defend *Butterwasser* on the grounds that a defendant who does not testify does not put his credibility in issue. But part of Lord Goddard's argument does ring true: 'by attacking the witnesses for the prosecution and suggesting they are unreliable, he is not putting his character in issue; he is putting their character in issue'. What is puzzling about tit for tat is that an attack on another person, whether put through D's lawyer or through D's own testimony, acts as a trigger, as if the fact-finder suddenly has a reason to be interested in D's credibility when she did not before. Even in *Singh* and *Lewis*, where D makes a specific allegation, it is not really correct to say that D puts his credibility in issue by doing so. His credibility was in issue when he denied the charge. The most that can be said is that he extends the number of issues over which there is a dispute.

The difficulties faced by the courts in justifying gateway (g) are heightened by the need to distinguish the practice under (g), where any previous conviction may be admitted, from that under (d), where *Hanson* and *Campbell* hold that most, if not all, previous convictions are irrelevant. In *George*, it was said that:

Hanson teaches that where evidence is adduced to establish a propensity, a distinction between offences of dishonesty and evidence of untruthfulness must be maintained. No such distinction arises where the evidence is adduced to show the character of the source of an accusation, pursuant to section 101(1)(g).[72]

The Judicial Studies Board Benchbook sidelines *Hanson* and *Campbell* by distinguishing propensity to be untruthful from 'general creditworthiness as a witness'.[73] The distinction would appear to be between a general propensity to lie, and a more specific propensity to commit, for example, fraud. That, of course, ignores *Campbell*'s argument about the irrelevance of a propensity to lie in a situation involving strong situational pressures.

Singh and *Lewis* go a little further in providing a rationale for (g):

In our view the existence of a criminal conviction in the past may well be relevant to a Defendant's credibility, even if that conviction resulted from a plea of guilty. Such a Defendant is not a person of previous good character. In any event, when the jury are having to assess the credibility of two conflicting witnesses, it will often not be right or fair that a Defendant can blacken the name of the prosecution witness while presenting himself as having an unsullied character, at least by implication.[74]

The second argument was effectively encapsulated in the proposition that the appellant's convictions were irrelevant to his credibility. We do not think that they were. They may not have been such as to demonstrate a track record for untruthfulness. They would not have been independently admissible under gateway D if there had not been the attack on the credibility of the complainant that there was. But the attack on the complaint had been made. The relevance of the attack was that if it was true it provided a reason why the complainant should be disbelieved. When the jury was assessing the evidence of the two main parties to this trial it was judging the complainant's credibility against that of the accused. The attack having been made, it was entitled to have regard to the source from which came the accusations which might affect the jury's judgment of the complainant...We think that it is perfectly plain that, once admitted under gateway G, bad character evidence does go to the credibility of the witness in question. That accords with common experience. It is, among other things, the obverse of the reason why a defendant is entitled to plead his own good character in support of his claim that he should be believed.[75]

While in *Lewis* the trial judge had directed the jury that D's lack of credibility was relevant specifically to whether his allegation that the complainant was masturbating was true, *Singh* sensibly rejects this restrictive approach.[76]

---

[72] *George* [2006] EWCA Crim 1652, [30].
[73] Judicial Studies Board, *Crown Court Bench Book: Directing the Jury* (2010), 182.
[74] *Lewis* [2007] EWCA Crim 3030, [14].   [75] *Singh* [2007] EWCA Crim 2140, [10].
[76] 'It would be wholly artificial to say that this information about the appellant went to whether he was to be believed in what he said about the complainant being a user of crack cocaine and not to whether he was believed in what he said about how the complainant came to be parted from his chain and his mobile phone' (*Singh*, [10]). See also *R* v *C* [2011] EWCA Crim 939, [24]: '[a]lthough

One justification for tit for tat given in *Lewis* is that by attacking the complainant, D 'at least by implication' presented himself as a person of good character. In some situations, that may be a good reason for informing the jury about a defendant's previous convictions. In particular, if D introduces evidence about a complainant's or witness's previous convictions, a jury may reason that, given that the courts allow previous convictions to be introduced, if D had any relevant ones it would be told about them.[77] This 'implied assertion' analysis is less convincing in cases such as *Lewis* and *Singh*, where D does not bring up anyone else's previous convictions. Why, by saying 'the complainant was smoking crack', is D presenting himself as being of good character?

A different argument is made in *Singh*: the jury needs to know the source from which the accusation came. D is taken to be saying something along the lines of 'don't believe C, he smokes crack'. If we accept that offending is relevant to credibility, what remains puzzling is why the jury needs to have information with which to assess D's credibility only when he makes such an accusation, and not when he simply denies that he mugged the complainant. Why does the fact-finder need information about the source of an accusation, but not of a denial? A more promising argument is suggested in *Lewis*: that the jury has to assess the credibility of two conflicting witnesses. It has information about the credibility of one, so it is only fair that it should also have information about the other. This sounds more sensible, but the precise basis for the argument needs to be determined. Sometimes, one can only make a comparative assessment. If I am trying to work out which car to buy, and am given a figure for the fuel consumption of one of the cars I am considering, that is not much help to me, because I do not have much idea what counts as good or bad fuel consumption. But if I have that information about all of the cars on my list, it is easy to work out which is best. That cannot be the analogy with tit for tat. If the fact-finder thinks criminality is connected to lying, she will understand the significance of information about the complainant's bad character. If she does not, then no harm is done by D's attack on W and there is no justification for introducing evidence of D's bad character in response. No doubt the fact-finder would like more information in order to judge who is more likely to be telling the truth, just as if I do know what counts as good fuel consumption I would want such information about all of the cars. One nearly always wants more relevant information, but that does not explain why D's allegation

---

character is adduced initially for the purpose of allowing the jury to determine whether the particular attack is true, it will inevitably affect the jury's assessment of D's credibility as a whole'.

[77] See S. Seabrooke, 'Closing the Credibility Gap: A New Approach to Section 1(f)(ii) of the Criminal Evidence Act 1898' [1987] *Crim LR* 231. Seabrooke expresses some doubt about this rationale, and the extent to which he endorses it is not entirely clear. This way of thinking about tit for tat seems to have influenced the Law Commission, for whom it was the main rationale for the doctrine: *Evidence of Bad Character*, 149–51. Even if one accepts that by attacking a prosecution witness D is making an implied assertion that he has no previous convictions, there still needs to be an explanation of why this triggers admissibility, ie why D's record becomes relevant when it was not before. If the jury might begin the trial thinking that D had no previous convictions, surely the argument from not misleading the jury would justify revealing D's record from the word go.

triggers admissibility of his own record, rather than his record going in as soon as he disputes the prosecution case. This is particularly so in cases like *Lewis* and *Singh*, which are credibility contests from the word go.

A more promising way of explaining the trigger aspect of tit for tat is that D changes the nature of the credibility contest by bringing up aspects of another person's moral character.[78] What started off as a dispute to be judged on the basis of ordinary criteria, such as plausibility, coherence, and demeanour, has become a moral contest. If D wants to have things that way, he bears the consequences. That seems to be the best version of the comparative credibility argument. But if it is to provide a rationale for tit for tat, it needs to be restricted to cases where it really applies. *Lewis* and *Singh* are not such cases. Here, D is making an allegation against C, and does not appear to be arguing that C lacks moral credibility—the wrongdoing is merely part of his defence story. What is more, the complainants deny the allegations, which means that the claim of wrongdoing simply cannot play a role in the jury's assessment of their credibility. 'I don't believe C's denial that he smokes crack because he smokes crack' is not a sensible line of reasoning. Better examples of the moral contest account of gateway (g) are cases where D brings up a prosecution witness's previous convictions, thus using facts extraneous to the case to turn it into a moral contest.[79]

One question, of course, is why defendants should be allowed to turn a trial into a moral contest in the first place. Might the courts not exert more control over defendants' attacks on prosecution witnesses? Under section 100 of the CJA, the character of non-defendants is admissible if it is 'of substantial importance in the context of the case as a whole'—a relatively high admissibility threshold. This provision does imply that courts might be able to prevent gratuitous attacks, making cases where there is a good reason to invoke gateway (g) rare. A problem, however, is that there is an asymmetry between defendants and witnesses when it comes to the relevance of bad character. If situational pressures, together with the fact that guilty defendants are, by definition, offenders, and thus assumed to have a greater than average propensity to lie, mean that defendants' previous convictions have little probative purchase on their credibility, the same is not true of witnesses. Witnesses' choices are not determined by pressure to avoid conviction. There may then be good reason for defendants to bring up the records of witnesses, to show that they are not the trustworthy people they might otherwise appear to be.[80]

---

[78] A. Zuckerman, *The Principles of Criminal Evidence* (Oxford: Clarendon Press, 1989), 271–3; cf the more cautious analysis in Roberts and Zuckerman, *Criminal Evidence*, 644.

[79] Not every use of previous convictions works in this way. If D introduces evidence that someone else has previous convictions in order to bolster a claim that they, not D, committed the crime, this is propensity evidence, not a claim to moral credit (cf the prosecution's introduction of D's record to show propensity to offend). Pointing to an allegation that a police officer has fabricated evidence in another case, to show that they may have planted evidence in the current case, is more borderline.

[80] See Friedman, 'Character Impeachment Evidence'.

9.5 Deterring Defendants

The discussion of tit for tat up until this point may seem rather naïve. The most obvious reason for the practice is that it exists to deter defendants from making attacks on prosecution witnesses. In *Selvey*, the House of Lords worried that if it accepted the no stymie principle, 'there would be no limit to the amount of mud which could be thrown against an unshielded prosecutor while the accused could still crouch behind his own shield'.[81] While this may be part of the underlying rationale for tit for tat, it is rarely voiced by the courts and does not feature in the post-CJA jurisprudence. So it is important, and not simply naïve, to scrutinize those justifications which are put forward. It is hardly surprising that deterrence is not explicitly argued in the case law. It implies that the courts try to prevent defendants putting forward relevant defences. Why on earth would we want to deter *Lamaletie* from putting forward a defence of self-defence? Even in *Ball*, where the attack on the complainant might be thought to be gratuitous—genuine mud-slinging—deterrence is a flimsy rationale, for defendants at interview are unlikely to know what the consequences of such claims will be.

It has occasionally been questioned whether tit for tat is compatible with Article 6 of the ECHR, which guarantees the right to a fair trial. When scrutinizing the CJA, the Joint Committee on Human Rights raised the argument that tit for tat undermines the defendant's right to defend himself.[82] The point has received judicial attention. The Criminal Procedure (Scotland) Act 1995 allows a defendant, in certain circumstances, to introduce evidence about a complainant's sexual history in a sexual offence trial. But doing so may trigger admissibility of the defendant's previous convictions for sexual offences.[83] The Privy Council, hearing a challenge to this provision as a devolution issue, held that this was compatible with Article 6.[84] Lord Brown's response to the appellant's argument that the provision penalized him for running a perfectly proper defence was that:

the accused has no fundamental right to keep his past convictions from the jury. There is nothing intrinsically unfair or inappropriate in putting these into evidence and, indeed, in doing so not merely on the limited basis that they go only to the accused's credibility (the fiction which to my mind disfigured the administration of criminal justice in England and Wales for far too long...) but on the wider ground that they bear also on the accused's propensity to commit offences of the kind with which he is charged.[85]

This is true, but does not meet the defendant's argument that he was being penalized for defending himself. If he did not adduce evidence of the complainant's sexual history, his previous convictions would not go in (Scots law has little scope for introducing propensity evidence). A response to this argument might

---

[81] *Selvey* v *DPP* [1970] AC 304, 355.
[82] Joint Committee on Human Rights, *Second Report 2002–03: Criminal Justice Bill*, HL paper 40 2002–03, [23]. The Committee dropped this objection when section 101(3) was pointed out.
[83] Section 275A.   [84] *DS* v *HM Advocate* [2007] UKPC 36.   [85] *DS*, [103].

be that the introduction of D's record is a necessary reaction to the sexual history. If D testifies in his own defence, he cannot complain that he has to undergo cross-examination—something which he would avoid if he did not testify. He should not be able to give a one-sided account, and while some defendants may be deterred from testifying by the prospect of cross-examination, this is not unfair. But it would be much harder to justify a set of rules whereby D could avoid cross-examination as long as he did not, for example, dispute the truth of a confession. The lack of rational connection between trigger and response would make this look like deterrence pure and simple. This therefore brings us back to the puzzles of tit for tat: why is the revelation of D's record thought to be a suitable response to the introduction of sexual history? According to Lord Rodger:

> The jury are entitled to have regard to these factors when determining whether the Crown has proved its case against the accused. Section 275A would provide an element of parity or balance in the treatment of the two sides by giving the jury an opportunity, when considering their verdict, to have regard also to what the accused had done on other occasions.[86]

Talk of balance and parity is not enlightening. D's record does not help the jury to understand the complainant's sexual history. So why should D lose a protection—even an underserved one—just because he relies on sexual history evidence? No doubt for many there is an intuitive feeling that tit for tat, whether involving credibility or propensity, is fitting. We enjoy poetic justice and the simple equity of an eye for an eye. Criminal trials, however, should involve more than the 'justice of the playground',[87] so the intuitive sense that there is something right about tit for tat is not enough. Yet we seem to lack any compelling justification for the practice.

9.6 Conclusion

Tit for tat under the Scottish rape shield legislation is in one respect easier to defend than gateway (g). The defendant's previous convictions for sexual offences are clearly relevant to the question of whether he committed the current offence. Any justification of gateway (g), however, needs to address an issue which has so far been left in the background: the *Campbell* objection. D's previous convictions have little relevance to his credibility in court because the situational factors are such strong determinants of whether D lies or tells the truth. In addition, if D is guilty, then the credibility-crime link means that he has a propensity to lie. As we saw above, outside the gateway (d) context the courts have simply ignored *Campbell* without ever assessing the argument it makes.

---

[86] *DS*, [85].

[87] P. Roberts, 'All the Usual Suspects: A Critical Appraisal of Law Commission Consultation Paper No 141' [1997] *Crim LR* 75, 91.

The two best arguments in favour of credibility tit for tat are the implied assertion argument and the moral contest argument. But both of these rationales need some sort of response to *Campbell*. It is hard to see what the response might be, unless we switch the focus to propensity. If, by pointing out that another witness has previous convictions, D implies that he has none, that may mislead the jury. The jury may think that D has no previous convictions which would make him more likely to commit the crime, when in fact he has. And sometimes the moral contest will be a propensity battle: 'look at his previous convictions, he is more likely to have committed the crime than me'. It is not obvious, though, that gateway (d) is needed to deal with these eventualities. If D has previous convictions which demonstrate his propensity to commit crime, they can be admitted as normal under gateway (d). And there is also gateway (f): 'evidence to correct a false impression given by the defendant'.

It makes little sense to use previous convictions to demonstrate a defendant's lack of credibility. The Court of Appeal in *Campbell* was right to disable the credibility limb of gateway (d). To the extent that some defendants are more likely than others to plead guilty because they have a low propensity to lie, the good character direction can be used as a signal. The continued use of tit for tat under gateway (g) is indefensible. This provision attaches a price to legitimate defences, a price which sometimes involves the revelation of stale convictions. Juries are asked to make fine distinctions between credibility and propensity, distinctions which we have little reason to believe they will make. The justifications for tit for tat are for the most part risible. We would be far better off without gateway (g).

10

Good Character

This short chapter examines the law on the evidential significance of the defendant's good character. The discussion of good character contextualizes some of the earlier discussion of bad character evidence and helps to set the stage for the discussion of character in sentencing in Chapter 11, where we find that evidence about the defendant's good character plays a significant mitigating role.

10.1 The Importance of Good Character

Defendants are entitled to lead evidence of their own good character: they may call character witnesses and attest to their own lifestyle and good deeds.[1] The old rule, that defendants could only call character evidence by way of evidence of general reputation rather than evidence about specific instances of behaviour, is no longer followed.[2] Leading evidence of good character, however, may be a risky strategy if the defendant has previous convictions. Section 101(1)(f) of the Criminal Justice Act 2003 provides that the prosecution is permitted to introduce evidence of the defendant's bad character in order to 'correct a false impression given by the defendant'. Under the old law, character was held to be 'indivisible': a defendant charged with a sexual offence who attested to his good conduct towards women could trigger introduction of previous convictions for property offences.[3] This will no longer necessarily be the case, because 'evidence is admissible under section 101(1)(f) only if it goes no further than is necessary to correct the false impression'.[4] This is a welcome concession to defendants. Even though, as we have seen, propensity to crime appears to be general, and thus previous convictions for property offences are evidence of a propensity to commit sexual crime, a defendant's claims about his treatment of women is not—and would surely not be taken to be—an assertion of a complete lack of previous convictions. Further, as the

---

[1] See, eg, *Olu, Wilson and Brooks* [2011] 1 Cr App R 33, [2010] EWCA Crim 2975, [60]. For a good example of the sort of things character witnesses can say ('a man of great integrity'; offending would be 'out of character'), see 'Character witness says husband of former News International chief Executive is "capable of being completely daft"', *The Guardian*, 7 April 2014 (<http://www.theguardian.com/uk-news/2014/apr/07/charlie-brooks-drank-fairy-liquid-hacking-trial>).

[2] *Del-Valle* [2004] EWCA Crim 1013, [11]. Cf *Rowton* (1865) 169 ER 1497.

[3] *Winfield* [1939] 4 All ER 164.

[4] CJA, s 105(6). See *Somanathan (Weir)* [2006] 1 Cr App R 19, [2005] EWCA Crim 2866.

property offence convictions would not be admissible under section 101(1)(d), it does not seem fair to admit them under (f). Things would be different if the defendant made a more general claim about his good character.

Even if a defendant does not call evidence of his good character, the judge is obliged to instruct the jury on it if the defendant lacks significant previous convictions. This judicial duty was affirmed by the Court of Appeal and House of Lords in the 1990s,[5] and the 2003 Act does not expressly alter it.[6] The good character direction has two limbs: a credibility limb and a propensity limb, although the former does not have to be given if the defendant has not testified and is not relying on anything said in police interview. A 'standard' direction is suggested in the Bench Book:

You have heard that the defendant is a man in his middle years with no previous convictions. Good character is not a defence to the charges but it is relevant to your consideration of the case in two ways. First, the defendant has given evidence. His good character is a positive feature of the defendant which you should take into account when considering whether you accept what he told you. Secondly, the fact that the defendant has not offended in the past may make it less likely that he acted as is now alleged against him.

It has been submitted on behalf of the defendant that for the first time in his life he has been accused of a crime of dishonesty. He is not the sort of man who would be likely to cast his good character aside in this way. That is a matter to which you should pay particular attention.

However, the judgements what weight should be given to the defendant's good character and the extent to which it assists on the facts of this particular case are for you to make. In making that assessment you are entitled to take account of everything you have heard about him.[7]

The good character direction is taken very seriously by the Court of Appeal: failure to give a direction, or a sufficiently emphatic direction, is frequently a successful ground of appeal. Telling the jury that the defendant is entitled to present himself as being of good character is insufficient: the direction should be presented as coming from the court rather than simply from the defendant.[8] Further, especially under the credibility limb, there is a mandatory element to the direction: telling the jury that good character is 'something that perhaps you can take into account' is 'unacceptably diffident by reference to the JSB Direction, viz "it is a factor which you should take into account"'.[9] At the same time, as the JSB Direction suggests, as long as the jury takes the good character evidence into account—which presumably means considers it—the jury can give it what weight it sees fit.[10]

---

[5] *Vye* (1993) 97 Cr App R 134; and *Aziz* [1996] 1 AC 41.
[6] But see *Doncaster* [2008] EWCA Crim 5, [42].
[7] Judicial Studies Board, *Crown Court Bench Book: Directing the Jury* (2010), 164.
[8] *Dillon* [2013] EWCA Crim 122; *Gbajabiamila* [2011] EWCA Crim 734; *Yee-Mon* [2011] EWCA Crim 1069; and *Moustakim* [2008] EWCA Crim 3096.
[9] *R* v *GJB* [2011] EWCA Crim 867, 21.
[10] There is some tension here, because 'take into account' is most obviously read as 'give weight to', and the comment in *R* v *M (CP)* [2009] 2 Cr App R 3, [2009] EWCA Crim 158, [15] that ' there is no room for a jury to disagree as to the propriety of using the good character of the defendant in his favour' might seem to support that reading. But *M (CP)* probably only establishes that if the

This much is relatively straightforward. The main complexity concerns the question of just when a defendant is entitled to a good character direction: what if he has minor, or stale, convictions? What if he has convictions for offences very different from the one now charged? What if the prosecution, or a co-defendant, alleges that D has committed a crime which did not result in conviction? What if D claims that an earlier conviction is false? What if, at trial, D admits to involvement in some illicit behaviour, but denies the most serious charge against him? In *Gray*,[11] D was charged with murder. He admitted using some violence in the course of the altercation which led to the murder, but denied being involved in the actual killing. D had a fairly recent previous conviction for driving while drunk, with no licence or insurance. The Court of Appeal held that in cases involving minor or stale convictions judges have a discretion to give a good character direction, and that where a previous conviction 'can only be regarded as irrelevant or of no significance in relation to the offence charged, that discretion ought to be exercised in favour of treating the defendant as of good character'.[12] This discretion should have been exercised in the defendant's favour in *Gray*. As for wrongdoing admitted by the defendant during the trial, the underlying principle is that the good character direction should be modified rather than withheld. This is the approach the trial judge should have taken in *Gray* (a full credibility, but modified propensity direction), but the Court did recognize a 'narrowly circumscribed residual discretion to withhold a good character direction in whole, or presumably in part, where it would make no sense, or would be meaningless or absurd or an insult to common sense, to do otherwise'.[13] However, it was emphasized that examples of the proper exercise of this discretion were hard to come by;[14] even in a case where D admitted serious wrongdoing such as manslaughter, but denied murder, a modified direction would be appropriate, because of the significance of the intention to do serious bodily harm or to kill in the case of murder.[15]

At first, this practice of giving a good character direction in a case where D has admitted violent behaviour seems very odd. If D had a previous conviction for an offence of violence and was on trial for a much more serious offence of violence, he would be unlikely to benefit from a good character direction; indeed, he might well have the conviction admitted as propensity evidence under the CJA's gateway (d). There is no logical difference between this situation and the one where D admits some of the less serious parts of the wrongdoing with which he is charged. The practice does make more sense, though, when we bear in mind that when

judge concludes that D's convictions are too stale to take into account, the jury should not disagree and treat D as being of bad character. But then it is presumably up to the jury what, if any, weight to place on D's good character. It would be very unusual if a rule of evidence required the jury to give weight to a particular item of evidence.

[11] [2004] 2 Cr App R 30, [2004] EWCA Crim 1074.   [12] *Gray*, [57].
[13] *Gray*, [57].
[14] The Court noted the examples of *Zoppola-Barrazza* [1994] Crim LR 833, where D admitted smuggling gold to avoid paying taxes, but denied importing cocaine, and *Shaw* [2002] 1 Cr App R 10, [2001] UKPC 26, where D admitted selling cocaine and being a member of an armed group which had set out to inflict revenge on the victim.
[15] This example originates in *Vye*, (1993) 97 Cr App R 134.

a previous conviction is introduced as propensity evidence, the jury is given a warning against putting too much weight on it. Indeed, this seems to have been part of the Court of Appeal's thinking in *Gray*: the jury might have been asked to contrast the admitted wrongdoing with the much more serious assault which formed the basis of the murder charge.[16]

Further intricacies of the good character direction can be gleaned from recent cases. In *R* v *D*,[17] D was charged with raping his wife. He admitted using violence against her during the course of the marriage, but the Court of Appeal held that his lack of previous convictions for sexual offences was significant: this should have resulted in a modified good character direction emphasizing that it 'was less likely that he would have committed the offences of rape'.[18] Despite its assessment of the case as a strong one, the Court quashed the defendant's convictions. *R* v *D* pushes good character jurisprudence into absurdity: at most the jury should have been asked, as in *Gray*, not to put too much weight on the admitted bad character. But even this would have been dubious on the facts: as the prosecution pointed out, their case was that the purpose of the rapes—as is surely true of much marital rape—was humiliation and 'punishment', rather than sexual gratification. The admitted violence was evidence against D, not evidence in his favour.

How should a judge deal with disputed bad character evidence? This was the issue in *Olu, Wilson, and Brooks*.[19] D was on trial for being involved in a stabbing. Olu had a caution for possessing an offensive weapon (a knife), but argued that he had accepted the caution to avoid further detention in the police station rather than because he was guilty. The correct approach in this situation, the Court of Appeal held, was to give a conditional good character direction, asking the jury to take good character into account if they found that Olu had not committed the offence underlying the caution.

How defensible are the rules on evidence of a defendant's good character? Much of the groundwork for answering this question has been done in previous chapters. Good character evidence has a useful role to play in the criminal trial. If, as seems likely, jurors draw assumptions about a defendant's criminal record, or simply assume that the defendant has a criminal record, then the good character direction helps to put jurors straight. Empirical evidence, from Lloyd-Bostock's studies, suggests that good character evidence has a modest, but positive, effect compared to a base condition of no information about character.[20] As we have seen, the good character direction has two limbs: a credibility limb and a propensity limb. In Chapter 9, it was suggested that evidence of lack of credibility should

---

[16] [2004] 2 Cr App R 30, [2004] EWCA Crim 1074, [64].

[17] [2012] 1 Cr App R 33, [2012] EWCA Crim 19.

[18] At [16]. See also *Garnham* [2008] EWCA Crim 266, where a similar approach is taken to a defendant on trial for a sexual offence who had previous convictions for non-sexual offences. No doubt these cases reflect the rather dubious assumption that sex crimes are different from other crimes: see discussion in Chapters 2 and 7.

[19] [2011] 1 Cr App R 33, [2010] EWCA Crim 2975.

[20] See discussion in Chapter 3. See also M. Lupfer et al, 'Presenting Favorable and Unfavorable Character Evidence to Juries' (1986) 10 *Law & Psychol Rev* 60.

generally not be admitted where defendants are concerned, but that using a lack of previous convictions as evidence of the defendant's credibility might nevertheless be defensible. The argument was that the good character direction reflected the thought that first-time offenders might be more likely to plead guilty, as well as the assumption that fact-finders will tend to think that defendants' claims of innocence should be treated sceptically. This would even justify a good character direction in a case such as *Gray*, where the defendant admits some wrongdoing, but denies the most serious charge.

In *Doncaster*,[21] the Court of Appeal noted that while the CJA does not alter the rules on good character evidence, it may still have an impact on them. If more bad character evidence is admitted, then, especially in cases where this does not involve convictions, judges may be inclined to give modified good character directions. This may be defensible in terms of an analogy with the protective part of a bad character direction. But there is another way in which the CJA may call for some rethinking of good character jurisprudence. In Chapter 9, we saw that the CJA has undone *Butterwasser*:[22] defendants can no longer escape the 'tit for tat' rule by not testifying. The new thinking—which stands up to analysis—is that defendants are taken to be making a claim to innocence by pleading not guilty, and that where they put forward a positive defence they are claiming that the defence is true. While I argued that there are good reasons to get rid of tit for tat, as long as it stays then it is incoherent to allow the prosecution to introduce evidence supposedly reflecting on the defendant's credibility under gateway (f) when he does not testify, but not to give the credibility limb of the good character direction when there is no testimony from D. In cases where D does not testify or rely on any statement in interview, the good character direction should still encompass his credibility in the sense of the credibility of his defence as a whole.

10.2 Conclusion

Good character evidence does not come without costs: modified directions and conditional directions certainly add to the complexity of the trial and provide fertile ground for appeals. And sometimes, as in *R* v *D*, the Court of Appeal goes too far in trying to give the defendant the benefit of the doubt. The Court certainly takes good character seriously, which may well reflect an understanding, gained through trial experience, of how such evidence can play an important role in rebutting the jury's assumptions about defendants. Like bad character, good character does not make the judge's task any easier, but that is not to say that taking it seriously is not, for the most part, worthwhile.

---

[21] [2008] EWCA Crim 5, [42].　　　[22] [1948] 1 KB 4.

11

Punishing Character

Sentencing is the domain of criminal justice where the defendant's previous, and likely future, behaviour has most impact. Previous convictions are widely seen as relevant to sentence: recidivists are sentenced more harshly in all common law jurisdictions. In England and Wales, as in other jurisdictions, there are special sentencing regimes for 'dangerous' offenders, based on the assumption that some offenders are, on the basis of their criminal history, especially likely to commit further serious offences. In parallel with the law of evidence, it is not only previous convictions which are relevant to sentencing. Pleas in mitigation often range quite widely over the defendant's character,[1] and the pre-sentence report, if ordered, will include information on such factors as the defendant's attitude to the offence, any anti-social or discriminatory attitudes connected to the offence, and education, training, and employment.[2]

Just as with the law of evidence, the basic questions to be addressed here are whether the reliance on the defendant's character is justified when it comes to determining sentence. While for many it is intuitively obvious that there should be a recidivist premium—meaning that repeat offenders should be sentenced more harshly—some have questioned whether this practice can be justified, and the precise impact that criminal history should have is controversial. There are similar questions about character-based mitigation: why might the offender's good record of employment, for example, be relevant to sentence? Does it reflect on culpability, or is the offender being sentenced on his character? If so, is that appropriate, or does it impinge on what, according to Tonry, is the 'fundamental principle that people are punished for what they have done ... not for who or what they are'?[3] When it comes to the sentencing of 'dangerous' offenders, issues arise which were touched on in Chapter 4. Is it problematic to sentence people on the basis of a judgment about what their future choices will be? And if we conclude that special sentencing regimes for the dangerous are acceptable, do we then have

---

[1] See J. Shapland, *Between Conviction and Sentence: The Process of Mitigation* (London: Routledge, 1981).

[2] See the example of a pre-sentence report appended to National Offender Management Service, Probation Circular 12/2007: Pre-Sentence Reports.

[3] M. Tonry, 'The Questionable Relevance of Previous Convictions to Punishments for Later Crimes' in J. V. Roberts and A. von Hirsch (eds), *Previous Convictions at Sentencing: Theoretical and Applied Perspectives* (Oxford: Hart Publishing, 2010).

any resources to object to the pre-emptive detention of non-offenders who are judged to be dangerous?

One of the claims made in this chapter and the next is that arguments about the role of character in sentencing have some parallels with debates about using character to prove guilt: there is benefit to be had in discussing one in light of the other. But there are also considerable differences between the two uses of character evidence. Where character is used in the process of guilt determination, the typical argument is that D's previous convictions make it more likely that he committed the current offence. This, as we saw, is an argument from comparative propensity. When it comes to sentencing, the most obvious parallel is with 'dangerous offenders', where the argument for longer sentences is usually based on the value of incapacitation given the risk of further serious offending. The judgments of risk in this context, however, are rather more frail than in the guilt determination domain. When we are assessing the likelihood of guilt, it does not matter that, when judged simply on the basis of the previous conviction, the defendant is not very likely to have committed another crime: it is comparative propensity which matters, and we usually have other evidence to support the claim that D committed the current offence. But if we are to assess whether an offender who has twice been convicted of GBH is likely to reoffend, the criminal record—and perhaps other aspects of character—is all we have to go on.

In more standard sentencing contexts, where D is sentenced more harshly than he otherwise would be because of a long record of not very serious offences, there might be an argument from deterrence—D needs a longer sentence because he is not easily deterred—or it might be contended that the prior convictions make the current offence more serious on the basis that D is more culpable. These arguments have little in common with the use of previous convictions in the evidential context. Perhaps the closest example is a case where criminal record is used to prove *mens rea*, as where D admits physical contact with V, but denies a sexual or violent motivation.[4] But there the argument is typically that the criminal record helps to show that D's conduct was not innocent, whereas in sentencing, the argument for increased culpability accepts that the conduct was not innocent, but claims that D is more culpable because the record shows, say, a deeper commitment to offending (whether this claim is plausible is assessed below).

This chapter starts by looking more closely at some of the ways in which criminal record and other forms of character evidence impact on sentencing in England and Wales, before moving on to justificatory arguments. The focus in this chapter is on the ordinary case; issues of dangerousness and incapacitation are taken up in the following chapter.

---

[4] See, eg, *Lewis* (1983) 76 Cr App R 33.

11.1 The Impact of Character on Sentencing

Sentencing decisions in England and Wales are governed by a mixture of statute, guidelines issued by the Sentencing Council and its predecessors, and decisions of the Court of Appeal. But all this leaves considerable discretion to sentencers. Offences created by statute have a maximum sentence, but this is usually far higher than what might be expected in an ordinary case. The statutory sentencing framework sets out broad principles. Section 142 of the Criminal Justice Act 2003, for example, states that the purposes of sentencing are punishment, crime reduction, reform and rehabilitation, public protection, and reparation. Section 143 instructs sentencers on how to determine offence seriousness: 'in considering the seriousness of any offence, the court must consider the offender's culpability in committing the offence and any harm which the offence caused, was intended to cause or might foreseeably have caused'. Most relevant for our purposes is section 143(2):

In considering the seriousness of an offence ('the current offence') committed by an offender who has one or more previous convictions, the court must treat each previous offence as an aggravating factor if (in the case of that conviction) the court considers that it can be so treated having regard, in particular, to—

(a) the nature of the offence to which the conviction relates and its relevance to the current offence, and
(b) the time that has elapsed since the conviction.

While this initially appears to be a clear statement that previous offending aggravates the seriousness of the current offence, it is not clear-cut: it would be open to judges, for example, to consider that previous convictions can rarely be treated as aggravating a current offence (perhaps only where the same victim has been targeted). However the provision is interpreted by judges, it is notable that it echoes some of the factors we find in the character evidence provisions of the 2003 Act: time-lapse is thought to be significant, and the reference to relevance presumably indicates that previous offences are considered to be more of an aggravating factor when the offences are closer in kind to the current offence.

Sentencing discretion is most confined where there is a guideline for the offence being sentenced. Courts are under a duty to follow guidelines published by the Sentencing Council, unless it would be against the interests of justice to do so.[5] Guidelines have a fairly standard format: they identify a starting point and a sentencing range.[6] The starting point is identified simply by looking at the facts of

---

[5] Coroners and Justice Act 2009, s 125. This does leave judges a lot of discretion, because the primary duty is to sentence within the broad offence range, not the much narrower category range (on categories, see below). For general discussion, see A. Ashworth, 'The Struggle for Supremacy in Sentencing' and J. V. Roberts, 'Complying with Sentencing Guidelines: Latest Findings from the Crown Court Sentencing Survey' in A. Ashworth and J. V. Roberts (eds), *Sentencing Guidelines: Exploring the English Model* (Oxford: Oxford University Press, 2013).

[6] For various examples, see <http://sentencingcouncil.judiciary.gov.uk/guidelines/guidelines-to-download.htm>.

the case; aggravating and mitigating factors may then raise or lower the sentence. Under the Sentencing Council guideline for domestic burglary, for example, the offence is split into three categories of seriousness: greater harm and higher culpability (category 1); greater harm and lower culpability or lesser harm and higher culpability (category 2); and lesser harm and lower culpability (category 3).[7] The harm and culpability ratings are assessed by referring to a list of factors such as: significant loss, occupier at home (greater harm); and significant degree of planning, weapon carried (greater culpability). Once the sentencer has decided on category, the guideline gives the relevant starting point and range. Thus, category 1 has a starting point of three years' custody and a range from two to six years; category 2 starts at one year's custody with a range from a high level community order to two years' custody; category 3's starting point is a high level community order and the range is from a low level community order to 26 weeks' custody. To decide the point in the range at which the sentence should fall, the sentencer consults the list of aggravating and mitigating factors. Some of these relate to the offence (for example, child at home, offence committed at night), but others are personal. Personal aggravating factors include previous convictions, while among the personal mitigating factors are: 'no previous convictions or no relevant/recent convictions'; remorse; 'good character and/or exemplary conduct'; and steps taken to address addiction or offending behaviour. In a category 2 case, then, an offender with previous convictions might receive a sentence above the one-year starting point, while an offender with no record and other evidence of good character might escape custody altogether. Significant elements in this guideline (repeated in other recent Sentencing Council guidelines) are that the absence of previous convictions is a mitigating factor (rather than just a neutral one), and that good character is a factor to be considered over and above the absence of previous convictions.

Turning to the case law, the first thing to note is that, since section 143(2) of the CJA 2003 was introduced, the Court of Appeal has not discussed it in terms of broad principle, but only in the context of its impact on individual appeals.[8] Some older decisions suggested that previous convictions were not an aggravating factor (although their absence might mitigate): 'no prisoner is to be sentenced for the offences which he has committed in the past and for which he has already been punished'.[9] It is doubtful, however, whether such strictures had much effect on day-to-day sentencing practice.[10] Post 2003, the Court of Appeal has certainly taken the position that previous convictions do aggravate offence seriousness. In

[7] Sentencing Council, *Burglary Offences: Definitive Guideline* (London: Sentencing Council, 2011), 8–9.
[8] See A. Ashworth, *Sentencing and Criminal Justice* (5th edn, Cambridge: Cambridge University Press, 2010), 218.
[9] *Queen* (1981) 3 Cr App R (S) 245, 246.
[10] See J. V. Roberts, *Punishing Persistent Offenders: Exploring Community and Offender Perspectives* (Oxford: Oxford University Press, 2008), 102–4; and E. Baker and A. Ashworth, 'The Role of Previous Convictions in England and Wales' in Roberts and von Hirsch, *Previous Convictions at Sentencing*.

Khaleel, the Court observed that: 'In the evaluation of seriousness consideration must be given to every previous conviction in accordance with the provisions in s.143(2) of the 2003 Act...Murder committed by a man at large on licence following conviction for manslaughter on an earlier occasion in virtually identical circumstances of violence may be assessed as an offence of particularly high seriousness.'[11] The defendant in *Lunkulu* was sentenced for manslaughter and kidnapping. He had a long criminal record, 'of particular relevance...were convictions for violent offences'.[12] The Court thought that while a 12-year sentence was an appropriate starting point in this case, the previous convictions justified a sentence of 14 years.[13] These two cases emphasize the similarity between previous and current offences, but non-similar offences are also sometimes held to aggravate. In *Morrison*,[14] D was sentenced for possessing a prohibited firearm. Among his previous convictions were another firearm offence and supply of heroin and cocaine. Even with the assumption that the drug dealing was not the reason for possessing the gun in the present case, the Court of Appeal thought that the trial judge had been right to treat the drug offence as an aggravating factor under section 143(2).

We saw above that the Sentencing Council guidelines acknowledge that a lack of previous convictions can be a mitigating factor. This is not an innovation: good character, in the sense of both a clean record and extra-legal evidence of good behaviour and having made positive social contributions, has long been considered to mitigate. A recent example is *O'Bryan*,[15] where the Court of Appeal held that participants in a relatively sophisticated armed robbery 'were each entitled to pray in aid their positive good character...Neither had any relevant previous convictions, but, over and above that, both had dedicated considerable time and energy to their communities which, prior to this offence, held them in considerable regard.' This was said to be 'very considerable mitigation'.[16]

Statute, guidelines, and case law, then, hold good and bad character to be factors which affect sentence. The empirical evidence confirms that these are significant factors in sentencing in the trial courts. The Crown Court Survey is based on short forms filled out by all sentencers after sentence is passed.[17] Respondents are asked about the number of previous convictions taken into account, and also about other aggravating and mitigating factors. The 2012 survey found that previous convictions frequently impacted on sentence, with around 30 per cent of offenders having one to three convictions considered to be relevant.[18] Having

---

[11] [2013] 1 Cr App R (S) 122, [2012] EWCA Crim 2035, [14].
[12] [2011] 1 Cr App R (S) 119, [2010] EWCA Crim 2463, [9].   [13] *Lunkulu*, [18].
[14] [2013] 1 Cr App R (S) 35, [2012] EWCA Crim 1255.
[15] [2013] 2 Cr App R (S) 16, [2012] EWCA Crim 2661.   [16] *O'Bryan*, [26]–[27].
[17] On some of the limitations of the survey, see N. Padfield, 'Exploring the Success of Sentencing Guidelines' in Ashworth and Roberts, *Sentencing Guidelines*, 44–5.
[18] Sentencing Council, *Crown Court Sentencing Survey 2012* (London: Sentencing Council, 2012), 22. An exception is sexual offences, where significantly fewer offenders had convictions taken into account. This may be because in these cases sentencers think that only sexual offences are relevant, whereas for other offences a more promiscuous conception of relevance is used.

at least one previous conviction taken into account substantially increased the chance of being sentenced to immediate custody.[19] The difference was especially prominent in some offences: for driving offences, 22 per cent of offenders with no previous convictions taken into account were sentenced to immediate custody, compared to 52 per cent of those with one to three such convictions.[20] But the detailed picture tends to be one of diminishing aggravation. With the exception of sexual offences and arson/criminal damage, 'where an offender already had at least one relevant and recent previous conviction, any further ones taken into account by the judge had less of an impact on the likelihood of being sentenced to immediate custody'.[21] Despite the language of section 143(2), then, the courts do not 'treat each previous offence as an aggravating factor', but only, by and large, the first few relevant convictions.[22] As for good character, this was explored through a tally of mitigating factors recorded by judges. In this context, good character should refer to something beyond the absence of previous convictions, previous convictions having been the subject of a previous part of the questionnaire.[23] There was some mitigation in the majority of cases.[24] 'Good character/exemplary conduct' and 'offence out of character' were common mitigating factors, affecting about 20 per cent of sentences where mitigating factors were present. Remorse, which is arguably connected to good character, featured in around 30 per cent of cases involving mitigation.[25]

Other studies confirm the importance of character in sentencing decisions. Hough, Jacobson, and Millie studied sentencing decisions shortly before the introduction of the 2003 Act, with a focus on factors leading to custodial sentences.[26] In cases at the custody threshold, personal mitigation (factors relating to the offender rather than the offence, and often, although not exclusively, character-based) was found to be the most significant factor in tipping a decision away from custody, while criminal history was often a determining factor in taking cases in the other direction.[27] The authors concluded that:

The emphasis on the personal undoubtedly makes the sentencing process a highly subjective one, in which the individual sentence... has to assess the incentives and capabilities of

---

[19] *Crown Court Sentencing Survey 2012*, 23.
[20] There is other evidence that the impact of previous convictions may be offence-specific. The Court of Appeal has suggested that previous convictions may have more impact in burglary cases (*Saw* [2009] 2 Cr App R (S) 54, [2009] EWCA Crim 1), and Roberts and Pisa-Sánchez found them to have a more significant impact in theft: J. V. Roberts and J. Pisa-Sánchez, 'Previous Convictions at Sentencing: Exploring Empirical Trends in the Crown Court' [2014] *Crim LR* 575.
[21] *Crown Court Sentencing Survey 2012*.
[22] See further Roberts and Pisa-Sánchez, 'Previous Convictions at Sentencing'.
[23] The report is slightly ambiguous here. It notes that 'lack of previous convictions' has been excluded from the mitigation scores, having been covered in a previous section, but in that section it is in fact lack of previous convictions *taken into account* which is probed, so it is possible that respondents took lack of any previous convictions to be evidence of good character (*Crown Court Sentencing Survey 2012*, 29).
[24] *Crown Court Sentencing Survey 2012*, 29.
[25] *Crown Court Sentencing Survey 2012*, 31.
[26] M. Hough, J. Jacobson, and A. Millie, *The Decision to Imprison: Sentencing and the Prison Population* (London: Prison Reform Trust, 2003). For earlier research, see, eg, C. Flood-Page and A. Mackie, *Sentencing Practice: An Examination of Decisions in Magistrates' Courts and the Crown Court in the Mid-1990's* (London: Home Office, 1998), 74.
[27] Hough et al, *The Decision to Imprison*, 37.

the offender and his or her attitudes towards the offence and offending, such as the presence or absence of remorse and the determination to stop offending. These assessments feed judgements about responsibility and culpability.[28]

Jacobson and Hough examined the role of personal mitigation in Crown Court sentencing post 2003, through observation of and interviews with sentencers. Again, such mitigation was found to play a significant role in sentencing decisions and to be a key factor in pulling cases back from custody.[29] Good character and remorse were among the most commonly cited aspects of personal mitigation.[30] 'It is clear that the severity of a sentence tends to be reduced,' the authors observed, 'if an offender has no previous convictions at all, or—to a lesser extent—if he has few or no *relevant* previous convictions, or if he has not offended in recent years.'[31]

11.2 Should Character Influence Sentence?

As the previous section shows, character has a very significant impact on sentences awarded in England and Wales. Good character mitigates, bad character aggravates, and this can make the difference between a custodial and non-custodial sentence. But is this justifiable? The issues here are complex. To simplify them I shall focus, to start with, on previous convictions and their absence. More will be said about other types of character evidence later. The next difficulty is that normative questions about sentencing can only be addressed against the backdrop of a theory of sentencing, and therefore punishment theory comes into play—a notoriously contested area. While I regard retributivism as an important aspect of punishment—punishment expresses censure—I doubt that retributive reasons alone can justify a system of punishment which involves hard treatment: crime reduction must be part of the justification for punishment.[32] While some theorists restrict the role of crime reduction to the general justifying aim of punishment, excluding it from principles of distribution such as decisions about sentence,[33] I do not rule out basing sentencing decisions on reductionist concerns.[34]

---

[28] Hough et al, *The Decision to Imprison*, 41.
[29] J. Jacobson and M. Hough, *Mitigation: The Role of Personal Factors in Sentencing* (London: Prison Reform Trust, 2007), 13–14.
[30] Jacobson and Hough, *Mitigation*, 15.   [31] Jacobson and Hough, *Mitigation*, 31.
[32] See D. Husak, 'Why Punish the Deserving?' in *The Philosophy of Criminal Law: Selected Essays* (Oxford: Oxford University Press, 2010); J. Gardner, 'Introduction' in H. L. A. Hart, *Punishment and Responsibility: Essays in the Philosophy of Law* (Oxford: Oxford University Press, 2008), xxxi; and T. M. Scanlon, 'Giving Desert Its Due' (2013) 16 *Philosophical Explorations* 1.
[33] See T. Brooks, *Punishment* (London: Routledge, 2012), ch 5.
[34] This is not the place to develop a detailed theory of punishment. As should be evident, while seeing retribution as part of the justification for state punishment, other concerns, such as deterrence and incapacitation, seem to me to play a role in justifying the institution of state punishment and in determining sentences. For resources which I have found helpful in thinking about punishment, see Husak, 'Why Punish the Deserving?'; Gardner, 'Introduction'; ; Scanlon, 'Giving Desert

If crime reduction is relevant to sentencing, then it might seem that a recidivist premium could be justified fairly simply, in terms of deterrence and/or incapacitation. It might be thought that enhanced sentences for repeat offenders will discourage recidivism (deterrence), or keep the most prolific offenders off the streets (incapacitation). But this is in fact doubtful.[35] While there is good reason to think that having a system of crime enforcement in place reduces crime, it appears that sanction severity has no effect on crime levels. Increased sentences do not work through general deterrence,[36] and as for individual deterrence: 'the majority of studies have found that incarceration has either no effect or undesirable effects on subsequent offending'.[37] The question of the crime-reducing effects of incapacitation is complex.[38] While offenders who are imprisoned cannot commit crime (if crime committed in prison is discounted), enhanced sentences for repeat offenders will not necessarily reduce offending. As we saw in Chapter 2, most criminal careers are short, with offenders dropping out of crime after one or two offences. Incapacitation serves no purpose if it targets an offender who would desist even if not imprisoned. With an offender who would otherwise reoffend, there may be replacement effects—intuitively plausible with crimes such as drug-dealing or crimes committed in groups—where someone else commits the crimes which would have been committed by the imprisoned offender.[39] Nor will incapacitation work if it simply delays reoffending—as some evidence suggests it does—rather than shortening the offending career.[40] There is also the issue that even without a recidivist premium many offenders are imprisoned and therefore incapacitated. For such offenders, extending the sentence to reflect criminal record may only have a marginal effect on crime rates. Because of these and other issues, interpreting the empirical evidence on incapacitation is not easy. The research suggests that

Its Due'; M. T. Cahill, 'Punishment Pluralism' in M. D. White (ed), *Retributivism: Essays on Theory and Policy* (Oxford: Oxford University Press, 2011); M. Berman, 'Two Types of Retributivism' in R. A. Duff and S. Green (eds), *The Philosophical Foundations of Criminal Law* (Oxford: Oxford University Press, 2011); and V. Tadros, *The Ends of Harm: The Moral Foundations of Criminal Law* (Oxford: Oxford University Press, 2011), chs 1–5.

[35] A good review of the empirical evidence is A. Bottoms and A. von Hirsch, 'The Crime-Preventive Impact of Penal Sanctions' in P. Cane and H. M. Kritzer (eds), *The Oxford Handbook of Empirical Legal Research* (Oxford: Oxford University Press, 2010). See also L. Kazemian, 'Assessing the Impact of a Recidivist Sentencing Premium' in Roberts and von Hirsch, *Previous Convictions at Sentencing*.

[36] See A. N. Doob and C. M. Webster, 'Sentencing Severity and Crime: Accepting the Null Hypothesis' (2003) 30 *Crime & Justice* 143. For more recent, and slightly more nuanced, reviews, see D. S. Nagin, 'Deterrence: A Review of the Evidence by a Criminologist for Economists' (2013) 5 *Ann Rev Econ* 83; and D. S. Nagin, 'Deterrence in the Twenty-First Century' (2013) 42 *Crime & Justice* 199.

[37] Kazemian, 'Assessing the Impact', 240. See also D. S. Nagin, F. T. Cullen, and C. L. Jonson, 'Imprisonment and Reoffending' (2009) 38 *Crime & Justice* 115; and D. S. Nagin and G. M. Snodgrass, 'The Effect of Incarceration on Re-Offending: Evidence from a Natural Experiment in Pennsylvania' (2013) 29 *J Quant Criminol* 601.

[38] See generally F. E. Zimring and G. Hawkins, *Incapacitation: Penal Confinement and the Restraint of Crime* (New York: Oxford University Press, 1995); and A. R. Piquero and A. Blumstein, 'Does Incapacitation Reduce Crime?' (2007) 23 *J Quant Criminol* 267.

[39] See Zimring and Hawkins, *Incapacitation*, ch 3.

[40] See J. F. MacLeod, P. G. Grove, and D. P. Farrington, *Explaining Criminal Careers: Implications for Justice Policy* (Oxford: Oxford University Press, 2012), 220.

policies of 'selective incapacitation', which aim to target the most prolific offenders, face problems in identifying those offenders.[41] As for strategies of imprisoning more people (relevant because, as we have seen, criminal record can take an offender over the custody threshold), or increasing sentence length, there is some evidence that incapacitation reduces crime, but researchers caution against pursuing incapacitation as a policy because the costs outweigh the benefits.[42] 'Home Office estimates... suggest that the prison population would need to increase by around 15 per cent for a reduction in crime of 1 per cent.'[43] If a policy of incapacitation targeted the most dangerous offenders—those thought likely to commit serious violent and sexual offences—then, perhaps, the cost-benefit analysis would go the other way. I explore the policy of incapacitating the dangerous in Chapter 12. The focus for now is on a recidivist premium which applies to all offences, and here the case for incapacitation does not seem to be made out. Nor should we expect enhanced sentences to deter. For this reason, in what follows I concentrate on whether the recidivist premium can be justified from within a largely retributive framework. For those who are more optimistic about incapacitation, the discussion is still relevant to cases which fall well below the custody threshold, where the recidivist premium may increase the level of fine or lead to a more burdensome community penalty. Optimists can also reflect back on the case for a general recidivist premium after considering the issues raised in Chapter 12.

The question, then, is whether the recidivist sentencing premium can be justified on retributive grounds. It might seem that it cannot be. If offenders are to be sentenced on the basis of offence seriousness, where seriousness reflects culpability and harm caused, it is not obvious that a tenth offence is any more serious than a first offence. Unsurprisingly, then, some retributivists argue that criminal record is simply irrelevant to sentence.[44] That stance obviously rubs against practice and

---

[41] See Bottoms and von Hirsch, 'Crime-Preventive Impact', 114–17; and A. R. Piquero and A. Blumstein, 'Does Incapacitation Reduce Crime?' (2007) 23 *J Quant Criminol* 267, 276.

[42] See W. Spelman, 'Jobs or Jails? The Crime Drop in Texas' (2005) 24 *J Policy & Management* 133; and H. Wermink, R. Apel, P. Nieuwbeerta, and A. J. Blokland, 'The Incapacitation Effect of First-Time Imprisonment: A Matched Sample Comparison' (2013) 29 *J Quant Criminol* 579. Cf A. Barbarino and G. Mastrobuoni, 'The Incapacitation Effect of Incarceration: Evidence from Several Italian Collective Pardons' (2014) 6 *Am Econ J: Econ Policy* 1. Vollaard found a very significant selective incapacitation effect for a policy of selective incapacitation in the Netherlands, but cautions against generalizing this result to other countries because of the comparatively low imprisonment rate in the Netherlands at the time of the research. If sentencers started from a higher baseline (as they would do in England and Wales), it is doubtful that there would be such a marked impact: B. Vollaard, 'Preventing Crime through Selective Incapacitation' (2012) 123 *Econ J* 262. See further A. A. J. Blokland and D. S. Nagin, 'Estimating the Effects of Imprisonment: Intended and Unintended Consequences of Incarceration' in M. Malsch and M. Duker (eds), *Incapacitation: Trends and New Perspectives* (Farnham: Ashgate, 2012).

[43] *Making Punishments Work: Report of a Review of the Sentencing Framework in England and Wales* ('The Halliday Report') (London: Home Office, 2001), 1.66. The report continues: 'If efforts were targeted at particular groups of offenders, for instance those with drug problems who commit more offences per year, per offender, a 1% reduction in crime would require a smaller (7%) increase in the prison population.'

[44] See, eg, G. Fletcher, *Rethinking Criminal Law* (New York: Oxford University Press, 1978), 459–66; and M. Bagaric, 'Double Punishment and Punishing Character: The Unfairness of Prior Convictions' (2000) 19 *Criminal Justice Ethics* 10.

widely shared intuition: sentencers, policy-makers, the public, and even offenders themselves think that repeat offenders do deserve harsher sentences.[45] Sometimes, of course, we are right to ignore received wisdom if theory does not support it. But we should be sure of our theory first, and several writers have attempted to reconcile the relevance of criminal record to a recidivist sentencing framework. Prominent among these is von Hirsch, whose theory of progressive loss of mitigation was discussed briefly in Chapter 4 and provides a suitable starting point for the present discussion.[46]

A sentence should never be increased, according to von Hirsch, on the ground that the offender has offended before. Repetition does not aggravate. To argue that the offender should be punished for showing defiance by continually ignoring the law's message is to adopt an argument which should have no place in a liberal criminal justice system.[47] But this does not mean that the absence of previous convictions should not mitigate, and lead to a lower sentence. In von Hirsch's scheme, then, there is progressive loss of mitigation: a first offender will receive a lower sentence than the one the judge would otherwise think appropriate. A second offence might still receive some mitigation, though not as much. The third or fourth[48] offence might then be sentenced at the normal level—the initial mitigation having been lost—but from that point on sentencing will be 'flat rate' instead of increasing in line with the number of convictions accumulated. The explanation for this approach is that an offender should be treated as a moral agent, capable of responding to censure, but should also be seen as fallible. The initial discount reflects the notion of a lapse: 'a transgression (even a fairly serious one) should be judged less stringently when it occurs against a background of prior compliance... [E]ven an ordinarily well-behaved person can have his or her inhibitions fail in a moment of weakness, wilfulness, or aggression.'[49] Reducing the sentence shows a 'limited tolerance for human frailty'.[50] The discount also reflects an assumption about how the offender should respond to censure: he should do so by making an effort of will to desist. The 'reduced penal response' recognizes the offender's 'assumed capacity to make an effort of will to desist from further

---

[45] See the survey evidence reported in Roberts, *Punishing Persistent Offenders*, chs 7–8.

[46] Von Hirsch has elaborated his views on progressive loss of mitigation on several occasions. Here, I rely largely on A. von Hirsch, 'Proportionality and Progressive Loss of Mitigation' in Roberts and von Hirsch, *Previous Convictions at Sentencing*. His first, and most detailed, elaboration of the progressive loss of mitigation theory was 'Desert and Previous Convictions in Sentencing' (1981) 65 *Minnesota L Rev* 591. See also A. von Hirsch, 'The Discount Approach: Progressive Loss of Mitigation' in A. von Hirsch, A. Ashworth, and J. Roberts (eds), *Principled Sentencing: Readings on Theory and Policy* (Oxford: Hart Publishing, 2009); and A. von Hirsch and A. Ashworth, *Proportionate Sentencing: Exploring the Principles* (Oxford: Oxford University Press, 2005), 148–55. For endorsement of the progressive loss of mitigation approach, see R. A. Duff, *Punishment, Communication, and Community* (Oxford: Oxford University Press, 2001), 167–70.

[47] See A. von Hirsch, 'Record-Enhanced Sentencing in England and Wales' (2002) 4 *Punishment & Society* 443; and Fletcher, *Rethinking Criminal Law*, 463–6.

[48] There is no easy way to specify the number of convictions at which mitigation is lost. Three-four is the suggestion in von Hirsch and Ashworth, *Proportionate Sentencing*, 149.

[49] Von Hirsch, 'Proportionality', 2.

[50] Von Hirsch and Ashworth, *Proportionate Sentencing*, 151.

offending'.[51] The thinking seems to be that the full force of the criminal law is not needed where there is an expectation that the offender will desist of his own motivation. This reflects the reality of recidivism: most offenders do desist after one or two convictions.[52]

For von Hirsch, then, there are two reasons for mitigation. We should provide limited tolerance for lapses and respect the offender's ability to attend to censure. Why, though, should we show tolerance for lapses (the first reason for mitigating)? Von Hirsch denies that the mitigation reflects offender culpability, but that denial seems to be motivated by wanting to distinguish progressive loss of mitigation from theories of first-offender discounts (such as one he espoused previously[53]) which rely on 'degree of intent, consciousness of wrongdoing, or the like'.[54] So, if A and B commit the same offence, and B has committed a similar offence before, the argument that B 'should know better by now' is ruled out as a reason for differential treatment. Talk of A's losing his customary self-control or acting in a 'moment of weakness, wilfulness or aggression'[55] suggests that the thinking may be that A responded to strong situational pressure—surely a culpability factor. Or perhaps the very fact that an act is uncharacteristic renders it less culpable. But it is hard to see what non-culpability-based reasons there could be for treating A more leniently, apart from the fact that he is more likely to respond to censure, which von Hirsch identifies as a distinct argument for mitigation. It seems, then, that von Hirsch's theory is partly based on culpability.

I am sympathetic to von Hirsch's theory of progressive loss of mitigation, and in what follows I explore it and point to problems in alternative accounts. Having raised the possibility that the 'tolerance' reason for mitigation is in fact a culpability factor, a useful starting point for thinking more deeply about progressive loss of mitigation is Lee's critique of the theory.[56] Lee sees von Hirsch's argument as character-based: first-time offenders should be considered to be basically good people who have lapsed rather than people who are more firmly committed to crime. Their acts are 'out of character'. Lee's concern about this is that:

If one's criminal record serves only the evidentiary function of revealing one's true character, then the significance of conviction and punishment becomes merely incidental. In other words, if there were a better way of getting at the question of offenders' characters, then we would not need to pay attention to criminal records at all. And there is no reason to think that a conviction record is a better measure of character traits than, say, family background, education, work history and relationship to community. [57]

---

[51] Von Hirsch, 'Proportionality', 10.   [52] See discussion in Chapter 2.

[53] See A. von Hirsch, *Doing Justice: The Choice of Punishments* (Boston, MA: Northeastern University Press, 1976), 85.

[54] Von Hirsch, 'Proportionality', 11.

[55] Von Hirsch, 'Proportionality', 2. Note also the reference to 'pressures and temptations' in A. von Hirsch, *Past or Future Crimes: Deservedness and Dangerousness in the Sentencing of Criminals* (Manchester: Manchester University Press, 1986), 85. In this work, von Hirsch is also explicit that tolerance is a matter of desert, not of mercy (at 84).

[56] Y. Lee, 'Repeat Offenders and the Question of Desert' in Roberts and von Hirsch, *Previous Convictions at Sentencing*.

[57] Lee, 'Repeat Offenders', 53.

The fear that the sentencing process is on a slippery slope if it comes to focus on character is a common one. If we start to sentence on character—which, however benign it first looks, may be what progressive loss of mitigation is doing—then, in Walker's colourful phrase, we take a 'leap into a bog without boundaries'.[58] Recall also Tonry's claim that it is a fundamental principle that offenders are sentenced for what they have done, not who they are.[59] Beyond the rhetoric lurk difficult questions. Might character actually be an appropriate object of punishment? Or might character in fact be so closely tied to culpability that in punishing character we are punishing for culpability?

11.3 Character and Criminal Liability

There is in fact an ongoing debate among criminal law theorists as to whether and in what ways character plays a role in criminal responsibility. 'Character theorists' vary in the accounts they give. For Bayles, '[b]lame and punishment are not directly for acts but for character traits'.[60] This is a fairly extreme view, for it suggests that the criminal law has little need to be interested in criminal conduct and that it could, instead, focus on bad or dangerous character.[61] But while this problem makes character theory look dubious, there are reasons to think that character does play a role in grounding criminal responsibility. While criminal conduct is thought to be essential to punishment, ultimately we punish people, not conduct. Some notion of character may play a role in forging the link between offenders and their conduct: it is because conduct is a product of a person's ongoing agency that it is fair to hold the person responsible for her conduct.[62] This suggests that what the philosophical literature refers to as 'attribution' may be a significant factor in determining responsibility.[63] In cases where agency is disrupted—hypnotism or brainwashing would be extreme examples—it may not be appropriate to attribute conduct to the agent.

---

[58] N. Walker, *Sentencing: Theory, Law and Practice* (London: Butterworths, 1985), 45.

[59] 'The Questionable Relevance of Previous Convictions'.

[60] M. D. Bayles, 'Character, Purpose, and Criminal Responsibility' (1982) 1 *Law & Phil* 5, 7. See also K. Huigens, 'Virtue and Inculpation' (1995) 108 *Harvard L Rev* 1423. For more modest accounts, which still give a significant role to character, see N. Lacey, *State Punishment: Political Principles and Community Values* (London: Routledge, 1988), ch 3; and L. Reznik, *Evil or Ill? Justifying the Insanity Defence* (London: Routledge, 1997), ch 11.

[61] Horder, for example, criticizes Bayles for elevating the character theory 'from a theory about criminal culpability into a theory of criminal liability'. J. Horder, 'Criminal Culpability: The Possibility of a General Theory' (1993) 12 *Law & Phil* 193, 206. Sher also criticizes this implication of the 'Humean view' of character and responsibility: G. Sher, *In Praise of Blame* (New York: Oxford University Press, 2006), ch 2.

[62] Sher, *In Praise of Blame*, 33.

[63] See G. Watson, 'Two Faces of Responsibility' in his *Agency and Answerability: Selected Essays* (Oxford: Oxford University Press, 2004); A. M. Smith, 'Responsibility for Attitudes: Activity and Passivity in Mental Life' (2005) 115 *Ethics* 236; and T. M. Scanlon, *What We Owe to Each Other* (Harvard: Harvard University Press, 1998), 277–94. This approach is criticized in N. Levy, 'The Good, the Bad and the Blameworthy' (2005) 1 *Ethics & Social Philosophy* 2.

The more moderate versions of character theory in criminal law build on these insights. They accept that criminal responsibility should be based on conduct, but see a role for character in raising questions about the way in which conduct reflects on the agent. Thus, for Duff, the 'element of truth' in character theory is that 'the actions for which a person is convicted and punished must be "hers" in that they must be appropriately related to attitudes or motives that are necessary aspects of her continuing identity as a person'.[64] In suggesting that action which is out of character might not be an appropriate target of criminal responsibility, however, the character theorist faces another criticism. If D, a person of hitherto good character, unexpectedly commits a crime, is the implication that he is not responsible for this out-of-character action? Duff's answer is that criminal action generally constitutes criminal character: 'an act of theft is not merely strong evidence of the distinct and underlying character-trait, but partly constitutive of the particular kind of dishonesty that concerns the law'.[65] A single act, then, suffices for criminal liability. In some circumstances, however, we may have reason to doubt that an action is properly attributed to the agent, as perhaps in a case of extreme emotional disturbance.

Tadros, the most sophisticated proponent of character theory, takes a similar view.[66] For him, an agent is not responsible for actions which are out of character. Rather than relying heavily on Duff's argument that criminal actions constitute criminal character, Tadros suggests that what is required to tie conduct to character is 'acceptance', a concept he cashes out in fairly minimal terms. That a person's 'action was motivated by an inclination that she does not commonly have is not sufficient to undermine the claim that her action was reflective of her persistent self', for 'her lack of desire or ability to control that motivation' may be enough to make it hers.[67] For Tadros, what might dissociate an agent from her conduct is involuntary—or perhaps on occasion voluntary[68]—intoxication, and provocation.[69] The role of character in grounding criminal responsibility, then, tends to be confined to cases of radical disruption of agency.

Returning to the questions raised at the end of the preceding section, the argument that we should punish for character is unattractive. But to say that character plays a role in grounding criminal responsibility is not to say that we punish for character, any more than the claim that capacity plays a role in shaping criminal responsibility means that we punish for capacity. Character plays a legitimate role in culpability assessments because, when we punish a person, we want to know that the conduct for which we are punishing him is attributable to him in a meaningful way, that it genuinely reflects his evaluative judgments.[70] However, in the

---

[64] R. A. Duff, 'Choice, Character, and Criminal Liability' (1993) 12 *Law & Phil* 345, 378.

[65] Duff, 'Choice, Character, and Criminal Liability', 379.

[66] V. Tadros, *Criminal Responsibility* (Oxford: Oxford University Press, 2005), esp ch 2.

[67] Tadros, *Criminal Responsibility*, 52–3.   [68] Tadros, *Criminal Responsibility*, 303 n 17.

[69] Tadros, *Criminal Responsibility*, 294–306.

[70] I take this phrase from Smith, 'Responsibility for Attitudes'. Smith's gloss is helpful: such judgments are 'not necessarily consciously held propositional beliefs, but rather tendencies to regard certain things as having evaluative significance. These judgments, taken together, make up the basic

more convincing accounts, character only plays a significant role where there is the possibility of a major disruption of agency. In sentencing practice and in theories such as progressive loss of mitigation, character appears to play a much larger role. The simple fact that a person acted in an uncharacteristic manner may be enough to mitigate sentence. It might, therefore, seem that character theories of criminal responsibility cannot support the widespread use of character evidence in mitigating and aggravating sentence.

This conclusion would, however, be too quick. When it comes to questions of criminal responsibility, the criminal law operates in fairly black and white terms. The defendant is responsible for his conduct or he is not.[71] Sentencing decisions grade culpability: given that the defendant has been found criminally responsible, just how culpable was the act? This would seem to allow a role for less major disruptions of agency. The character theory of criminal responsibility has many critics, but a notable feature of the literature is that even while damning it, the critics often allow that character may play a role in sentencing.[72] Tadros himself takes this line: while the simple fact that an act was out of character will not negate criminal responsibility, 'we may not think as badly of [D] if his wrongful action is out of character, and that may have an impact on the level of punishment deserved'.[73] None of the literature, however, explains why an uncharacteristic action is less culpable than one which is fully in character.

11.4 Character, Culpability, and Sentencing

The argument that good character reduces culpability flows fairly readily from the arguments in the previous section. For the purposes of the criminal law it may be reasonable to treat questions of attributability as all or nothing in the vast majority of cases. But there is no reason why we cannot think of attribution as a question of degree when it comes to sentencing: conduct may be tied more or less closely to the agent's evaluative judgments—more or less expressive

---

evaluative framework through which we view the world. They comprise the things we care about or regard as important or significant. "Judgments" in this sense do not always arise from conscious choices or decisions, and they need not be consciously recognized by the person who holds them. Indeed, these judgments are often things we discover about ourselves through our responses to questions or to situations' (251–2).

[71] This, of course, is a slight exaggeration. English law recognizes the partial defences of provocation and diminished responsibility, and the gradations of *mens rea* fine-tune culpability. However, even if some or all of these doctrines are thought of in terms of attribution, the end result of the trial is a bivalent decision: guilty or not guilty, and there still seems to be considerable room for further fine-tuning. For the argument that current law operates in terms which are too black and white, see D. Husak, '"Broad" Culpability and the Retributivist Dream' (2012) 9 *Ohio State LJ* 450; and D. O. Brink and D. K. Nelkin, 'Fairness and the Architecture of Responsibility' in D. Shoemaker (ed), *Oxford Studies in Agency and Responsibility: Volume 1* (Oxford: Oxford University Press, 2013).

[72] See, eg, Horder, 'Criminal Culpability', 207; and J. Gardner, 'The Gist of Excuses' (1998) 1 *Buffalo Crim L Rev* 575, 578.

[73] *Criminal Responsibility*, 296.

of his character, we might say.[74] When D, who has spent many years as an active member of a criminal gang, beats up V who is threatening to testify against D's associates, we might think that D would find it hard to distance himself from this action even if it was his first act of violence. The action speaks to D's long-term commitment to furthering the aims of the criminal gang. It would be different if D was involved in an act of violence while leading an otherwise blameless life; while he would find it difficult to dissociate himself from the act completely, the act would be less closely tied to his values and motivations than in the former case. This framework might also explain why premeditation increases culpability: actions which we have thought long and hard about are often more closely tied to us than those we commit impulsively.[75] The theory of progressive loss of mitigation finds support in this account: it is easier for D to distance himself from an initial crime than a second one, and a second one than a third one. The idea of actions which are more or less closely tied to our evaluative judgments therefore helps to explain the notion of lapse relied on by von Hirsch.

While this explanation of the role of character in mitigating wrongdoing has some appeal, I am not sure that it is convincing. It is essentially an argument about culpability: out-of-character actions are less blameworthy than those which are in character. Against this view, Sher contends that 'the amount of blame that someone deserves when he behaves badly depends not on how typical of him the bad behaviour is but simply on how bad it is'.[76] It might be claimed that Sher is confusing different dimensions of blameworthiness. Attributability is one dimension, but the extent to which an act was intentional and the degree of harm caused are other dimensions, which also need to be considered. So perhaps the amount of blame a person deserves depends not just on how bad the conduct was (in the sense of how harmful and how intentional it was), but also on how typical the act was. That is a possibility, and it helps to preserve the notion of a lapse as something which is less culpable. But this view may trade on ambiguity in the idea of a lapse. To say that something was a lapse can imply that it was done unintentionally rather than that it was out of character. To think more carefully about this issue, then, we need to focus on an example where D commits a crime—a minor assault, say—intentionally. Is D less blameworthy for the assault because he acted out of character? The answer to that question may depend on getting a clear sense of what blameworthy means—no easy matter.[77] But one distinction might be helpful in thinking about this question. For present purposes, blameworthiness might be distinguished from culpability, where culpability involves a question such as 'how serious a breach of the norms underlying the criminal law was this',

---

[74] This may be Watson's view: '[i]f I dance clumsily, it is inescapably true of me that I was (on that occasion) a clumsy dancer. But if what I do flows from my values and ends, there is a stronger sense in which my activities are inescapably my own: I am committed to them' ('Two Faces of Responsibility', 270).

[75] The *Crown Court Sentencing Survey*, 23, found 'lack of premeditation' and 'unplanned' to be common mitigating factors in robbery and homicide.

[76] Sher, *In Praise of Blame*, 29.

[77] For a variety of perspectives, see D. J. Coates and N. A. Tognazzini (eds), *Blame: Its Nature and Norms* (New York: Oxford University Press, 2013).

while blameworthiness involves questions about the appropriate response to the person who committed the breach. It seems to me that the intentional assault is no less culpable because it was a lapse, in the sense of being out of character.[78] There is another possibility, though, which was briefly noted earlier. The idea of 'lapse' may refer to the fact that D offended because of situational pressures. He is generally well-behaved, but he committed the assault because V provoked him, or the theft because it was just too tempting when his employer left the safe unlocked on the day he needed to repay a debt. Situational pressures may be relevant to culpability. If this is right, however, situational pressures will be relevant whether or not D has a good character.[79] Perhaps good character has some value as evidence of whether D offended because of situational pressure or because of his own propensity, but using it in this way would at least be problematic. As we saw in Chapter 2, it is not easy to distinguish the personal from the situational,[80] and we should also be wary of a doctrine which would allow those with good character, but not others, to claim situational pressures in mitigation.

The argument that good character is an index of culpability in the sentencing context is therefore not very convincing. This, however, is not the end of the story. The arguments to this point suggest that von Hirsch's first argument for progressive loss of mitigation—tolerance for a lapse—is weak (lapses are not less culpable, and it is hard to make sense of the lapse argument unless it is culpability-based). But the second reason for progressive loss of mitigation relates to blameworthiness. The 'reduced penal response' recognizes the offender's 'assumed capacity to make an effort of will to desist from further offending'.[81] And here the question of whether an act was in character may be far more significant. To the extent that an act is out of character, we may think it appropriate to reduce the amount of censure directed at the offender, especially because censure is usually expressed through hard treatment, something which we should not impose lightly. If the

---

[78] Von Hirsch does make much of the fact that lapse is an everyday moral notion, and this might be thought to support the argument that lapse is related to culpability. In everyday life, the argument would go, we do not have the institution of punishment, so if we treat lapses more leniently this must be because of culpability factors rather than blameworthiness factors. However, many theorists think that practices of blaming in everyday life are tied up with the reactive attitudes or the impairment of relationships (for the latter view, see T. M. Scanlon, *Moral Dimensions: Permissibility, Meaning, Blame* (Harvard: Harvard University Press, 2008), ch 4). By terming something a lapse, then, it is possible that we are saying that our reactive attitudes should be tempered, or that we should not hold a relationship to be as damaged as we might otherwise do. There are, of course, other theories of blame which may not have the resources to explain lapses in this manner (eg Sher, *In Praise of Blame*, ch 6). But the aforementioned phenomena are certainly common enough to account for the everyday notion of lapse without tying it to culpability. Note, too, that it is an exaggeration to say that everyday life does not involve punishment (see L. Zaibert, *Punishment and Retribution* (Dartmouth: Ashgate, 2006)).

[79] In the *Crown Court Sentencing Survey*, at 23, provocation is recorded as a mitigating factor in assault cases in addition to 'offence out of character', which suggests that it operates independently.

[80] See in particular C. B. Miller, *Character and Moral Psychology* (Oxford: Oxford University Press, 2014), 158–70. I suspect that any attempt to work out a situational theory of lapse will collapse into the question of how typical certain behaviour is for a person, the account criticized above.

[81] 'Proportionality', 10.

offence was a lapse, the offender is more likely to make a serious effort to desist and there is less need for the full amount of censure.

If character is relevant to sentencing because it informs a judgment about whether the offender is likely to respond appropriately to censure, might it aggravate as well as mitigate?[82] The obvious thought is that the more offences on the offender's record, the more need for harsher censure in order to get through to the offender. This argument might be rationalized in terms of individual deterrence, but I suggested above that deterrence-based arguments do not support the recidivist premium. A more refined version of the argument would suggest that, if progressive mitigation works by taking an optimistic view of the offender and his chances of responding to censure—a view which becomes less and less realistic as the criminal record grows—then continued offending should lead us to take an increasingly pessimistic view. While we should always treat an offender as a moral agent and not give up on the possibility that he will change, we can accept that that possibility becomes less and less likely the more he offends. That is a reasonable argument, but it might not be very significant in practice. Once we think that an offence is broadly in character (after, say, two or three offences) we withdraw mitigation, and, all else being equal, sentence at the normal level—the level dictated by the seriousness of the offence. Further offences might increase our confidence that offending is in character and that the offender lacks the moral resources to change, but this would presumably make an increasingly small difference. Once mitigation has been used up, there might be modest aggravation for one or two subsequent offences, but after that sentencing should revert to a 'flat rate' model, where previous convictions make no difference.

11.5 Leaping into the Bog?

Earlier, we noted Lee's concern that if the sentencing process is focussed on character, then there seems no reason to privilege criminal record as evidence of character: why not introduce evidence of such things as 'family background, education, work history and relationship to community'? Even if we are not directly punishing offenders for their character, but simply trying to gauge the extent to which conduct is out of character, Lee's worry remains. It is, indeed, one which emerges time and again in the literature on the character theory of criminal responsibility. If character is relevant to culpability, will the trial and sentencing process become a full moral audit of the defendant's life?

To be more specific, here is an illustration of how the problem arises. Suppose Dave has been convicted of racially aggravated common assault: during an argument about a parking space, he pushed V and shouted a racist insult before walking off. When considering mitigation, the court notes that this is Dave's first offence

---

[82] Von Hirsch denies that repeated offending aggravates (see, eg, 'Desert', 613–16). His argument is that the consequence would be that sentences would become wildly disproportionate. But this does not rule out some aggravation.

and gives a lower sentence than it would otherwise do, on the grounds that D has a good chance of responding appropriately to censure because the offence is out of character. When reviewing the criminological literature in Chapter 2, I noted that 'offending is one element of a larger syndrome of anti-social behaviour that arises in childhood and tends to persist into adulthood with numerous different behavioural manifestations'.[83] This suggests that the prosecution might respond to the defence claim of mitigation by introducing evidence of Dave's anti-social (but non-criminal) behaviour. Evidence, perhaps, that Dave often turns up late to work, is rude to colleagues, keeps his neighbours awake at night by playing loud music, and uses racist language when talking to his friends. This, the prosecution could argue, shows that Dave's offence is in fact in character. Therefore, Dave should not receive mitigation, even though this is his first conviction.

There are various ways in which one might try to argue against this step down the slippery slope towards the sentencing process becoming a full moral audit. Roberts simply asserts that only previous convictions (or their absence) should be used to judge whether an offence is out of character, but what is needed is an argument.[84] A sophisticated one has been made by Duff. 'A disposition to engage in non-criminal conduct,' he suggests, 'is not yet a disposition to break the law.'[85] Duff does allow that non-criminal behaviour might allow us to predict that a person will break the law, but 'that would be to predict... not merely a further manifestation of a character-trait which she already and fully has, but rather a development of her character into criminality. It is by and only by her actions that she constitutes herself as a thief or as a fraud, and constitutes her character as criminally dishonest.'[86] Duff goes on to note that his overall argument for the distinctiveness of criminal character depends on the assumption that there is a significant difference between criminal and non-criminal conduct.[87]

Given Duff's concession about prediction, and the point just made about the connection between crime and other forms of anti-social behaviour, this argument might seem odd. It makes more sense in context, for it is framed as an argument for a conduct requirement in criminal law: an argument against simply punishing for character, even for a character which we can predict with some confidence will develop into criminality. Returning to the example of Dave, one way to apply Duff's argument would be to frame it in terms of proof. Before he committed the racially aggravated assault, we might have had our suspicions, but we could not be sure beyond reasonable doubt that Dave would commit an offence. He might have had criminal tendencies, but he did not have a criminal character. That analysis seems reasonable. A truly radical character theorist might possibly be prepared to give up the idea of punishing for criminal conduct, and welcome a move to focus on the underlying anti-social traits, but given that most

---

[83] D. Farrington, 'Human Development and Criminal Careers' in M. Maguire, R. Morgan, and R. Reiner (eds), *Oxford Handbook of Criminology* (Oxford: Oxford University Press, 1997), 380.
[84] Roberts, *Punishing Persistent Offenders*, 86–7.   [85] Duff, 'Choice, Character', 373.
[86] Duff, 'Choice, Character', 373.   [87] Duff, 'Choice, Character', 373–4.

people would offend in sufficiently extreme circumstances, that would threaten to criminalize us all—a radical stance indeed.

Duff's argument, however, is not easily transposed to our concern: using non-criminal behaviour to prove whether Dave's assault is in character. Dave's non-criminal behaviour tells us something about his evaluative commitments—his lack of concern for other people—and the racially aggravated assault is a more extreme manifestation of this. If the anti-social behaviour has been proved, then casting Duff's argument in terms of proof seems to render it inapplicable here. The situation seems to be very similar to the one discussed in Chapter 4, where non-criminal behaviour is part of the evidence that a person has committed a crime. In *Norris*,[88] the case that Norris was involved in the racist murder of Stephen Lawrence included reliance on a video-recording in which Norris expressed extreme racist views—views which, however abhorrent, are not criminal. Even if we accept, in Duff's terms, that when Norris killed Lawrence this was a development of his character into criminality, and that at the time of the recording Norris did not have a criminal character, the tape-recording is still probative. The evidence shows that Norris has a comparative propensity to commit racist violence. Put in the language of the current discussion, the evidence helps to show that Norris's crime was in character, or, to be more precise, less out of character than it would have been had he never expressed racist views (although it would be more in character still if he had previously committed racist assaults).

If Duff's argument fails, then we cannot rule out the argument that, by taking character to mitigate and perhaps aggravate sentence, we are committing ourselves to a sentencing process which involves a wide-ranging moral audit of the defendant's life. However, there do seem to be a number of other responses to the moral audit problem, and these provide some reassurance.[89] The strongest argument builds on the fact that we are not taking the offender's character to be relevant to culpability. The claim, instead, is that it informs a judgment about his likely response to censure. Surely here what are most relevant are convictions. That Dave has committed anti-social behaviour in the past does not tell us much about how he will respond when censured: when the wrongdoing is marked by the formal process of conviction and sentence. If he has been censured before but continued to offend, that is far more telling. While I think this is a weighty argument for confining character-based aggravation and mitigation to previous convictions, it may not be definitive. Especially for first offenders, non-criminal

---

[88] [2013] EWCA Crim 712. For more context on the video, see <http://www.telegraph.co.uk/news/uknews/crime/8989641/Stephen-Lawrence-murder-damning-video-that-led-to-the-conviction-of-Gary-Dobson-and-David-Norris.html>.

[89] In his earliest development of progressive loss of mitigation ('Desert', 610–13), von Hirsch acknowledged the problem of inviting scrutiny of D's non-criminal wrongdoing. His response was that '[i]f the criminal laws ought not regulate such behavior directly—for reasons of privacy, autonomy, or for other reasons—then it should not involve itself with such conduct indirectly through the sentencing process' (611). It seems to me, though, that these factors are rarely weighty ones in the decision to criminalize: the identification of 'public wrongs' is more important.

behaviour, whether good or bad, might tell us something about whether a person
has the moral resources to respond appropriately to censure.

Before moving on to consider other arguments, we should note that the sentencing process does already range quite widely over the defendant's life. As we
have seen, at the sentencing stage offenders may call character evidence, and
'offence out of character'—which refers to something more than absence of criminal record—is a common mitigating factor noted by judges. While it is largely
the defendant who makes the running here, bringing in favourable factors, the
pre-sentence report may mention more negative factors, such as attitude to the
offence and anti-social attitudes connected to the offence.[90] However, on the evidence of the Crown Court Survey, these issues are rarely mentioned as aggravating factors by sentencers, so there seems to be a pronounced asymmetry in the
use of personal information in sentencing: it tends to mitigate, but not aggravate.
This asymmetry is also found in the use of character evidence to prove guilt.
Defendants can call witnesses to attest to their good character, but the prosecution does not usually produce witnesses to impugn the character of a defendant
like Dave. When the prosecution does use 'non-criminal bad character evidence'
(see discussion in Chapters 4 and 7), it tends to have a reasonably specific link
to the facts of the crime, as in *Norris*. For those who worry about the sentencing
process becoming a general moral audit of the defendant, then, the experience in
the law of evidence offers some reassurance. Although in theory the provisions in
the Criminal Justice Act 2003 allow the prosecution to dig into the defendant's
past and attack his character through non-criminal evidence, this does not really
happen. Evidence law has not leapt far into the bog.

To note the asymmetry in the treatment of good and bad character in evidence
law and sentencing is not to say that it is justified. Perhaps prosecutors should
be more proactive in presenting evidence of the defendant's non-criminal bad
character. There is, however, something to be said for asymmetry. In sentencing,
we saw that aggravation and mitigation have to be thought about in relation to
a starting point—the normal sentence for the offence. Evidence to suggest that
an offence is out of character can mitigate by pulling the offence down from the
starting point, but even supposing, in line with the earlier discussion, that previous convictions can aggravate, such aggravation should be modest and will be
dominated by convictions (non-criminal evidence would not seem to add much
if convictions are present). Non-criminal bad character would have its most significant role in a case where D has no criminal record and that is taken as a
mitigating factor—a case like Dave's.[91] The bad character evidence might reduce

[90] See Probation Circular 12/2007: Pre-Sentence Reports.
[91] It would also be relevant to rebut any non-criminal good character evidence adduced by D,
a practice which seems reasonable. While prosecutors in England and Wales do not argue for a
particular sentence, part of their role is to 'challenge any assertion made by the defence in mitigation that is inaccurate, misleading or derogatory'. See: <http://www.cps.gov.uk/legal/s_to_u/
sentencing_-_general_principles/#a01>.

the mitigation afforded by the absence of convictions. We can therefore focus our arguments on this example.

Even in Dave's case, there may be reason not to pursue the bad character arguments. The anti-social behaviour would have to be investigated and proved in court (to the criminal standard),[92] and it might also be disputed. Exploring it might simply not be worthwhile.[93] This is especially true because non-criminal character evidence may have limited probative value. In Chapter 2, we reviewed some of the empirical findings on the stability of character, and found evidence that many character traits are frail and fragmentary. While convictions for the more serious criminal offences can tell us that a person has a significant propensity to commit crime, it is rather less clear that a person's non-criminal anti-social actions say much about their overall character and therefore whether offending would be out of character for that person. The case law is replete with examples of people whose offending appears to be completely out of character.[94] In *Attorney General's Reference (No 64, 65 and 66 of 2013)*,[95] the offenders had been involved in a pre-planned attack on an acquaintance, resulting in convictions for GBH with intent. At sentencing, all presented good character evidence: none had shown any hint of anti-social behaviour before the assault. One of them was described as 'sweet, kind, polite and well-mannered. She goes out of her way to help others less fortunate than herself and has never been any trouble to her teachers or her parents. She was described as a model child and she is now a model prisoner.'[96] Her involvement in the attack 'might have come as something of a shock to those who know her or thought they knew her well'.[97] In *O'Bryan*, a case mentioned earlier, two of the defendants involved in an armed robbery 'had dedicated considerable time and energy to their communities which, prior to this offence, held them in considerable regard'.[98] One of them 'had been a member of a cancer fundraising team, and had been active in several charities—one dedicated to raising awareness of the devastating effects of knife crime, and another relating to sick children. He had been a committed amateur boxer. He had trained as a plasterer and, prior to this offence, had been industrious in working as such.'[99] While the good character evidence presented by the defence may not give the full picture, the disconnection is still striking. And although these examples involve good character, the same concerns surely apply to bad character too. Dave could be a pretty obnoxious person in many aspects of his life, but that may not tell us very much about the extent to which his crime reflects his evaluative commitments. People are complex, and behave differently in different aspects of their lives.[100]

---

[92] See Ashworth, *Sentencing*, 376.

[93] Although sometimes, as in the *Norris* example, it will have been proved during the trial itself.

[94] The frequency with which 'offence out of character' is recorded in the Crown Court Sentencing Survey is further evidence that this is a common situation.

[95] [2013] EWCA Crim 2477.   [96] *AG's Reference (No 64, 65 and 66 of 2013)*, [25].

[97] *AG's Reference (No 64, 65 and 66 of 2013)*, [33].

[98] [2013] 2 Cr App R (S) 16, [2012] EWCA Crim 2661, [26].   [99] *O'Bryan*, [23].

[100] Jimmy Savile being an obvious recent example of someone who seems to have combined doing vast amounts of charitable work with frequent sexual offending. For the more ambitious

This is not to deny that offending tends to be 'one element of a larger syn-drome of anti-social behaviour'. The point is that disjointed behaviour is not uncommon. Were Dave's case to be one of using bad character to prove guilt, it might be enough to say that his anti-social conduct made it slightly more likely that he was guilty—although even here we might doubt whether the snapshot of his behaviour told the whole story. This probability-based argument, how-ever, is less convincing in the sentencing context where we want to know if the defendant is likely to respond to censure, not whether he is somewhat less likely to than other people.

Apart from the fact that in sentencing the basis for mitigation only needs to be proved on the balance of probabilities,[101] these arguments about the fragil-ity of character obviously apply to mitigation through good character evidence as much as they do to aggravation by bad character. If there is nothing very unusual about the situation in *Attorney General's Reference*, where an appar-ently polite and caring teenage girl becomes involved in a vicious attack, then should we put so much reliance on good character evidence in sentencing? I am in fact fairly sceptical about the value of this sort of good character evidence in telling us much about what offenders are really like. But there are reasons not to be too dismissive of good character evidence in sentencing contexts. We know that offenders are sensitive to the way in which they are treated in the sentencing process, and allowing good character evidence can help them to think that the courts engage with them rather than simply concentrating on the offence.[102] This may encourage respect for the law.[103] Maruna found that the move to desistance depends in part on offenders developing positive narratives about their lives.[104] If the sentencing process can underline the message that an offence is out of character, and that the offender has the moral resources to respond appropriately to censure, this may encourage desistence.[105] Character in sentencing may, in Alfano's terms, be a useful moral fiction,[106] and modest mitigation based on it should not be ruled out.

argument that the frailty of character undermines the character theory of excuses, see J. M. Doris, 'Out of Character: On the Psychology of Excuses in Criminal Law' in H. LaFollette (ed), *Ethics in Practice* (3rd edn, Oxford: Blackwell, 2006).

[101] See Ashworth, *Sentencing*, 376.

[102] See the discussion in Chapter 3.

[103] T. R. Tyler, *Why People Obey the Law* (Princeton: Princeton University Press, 2006).

[104] S. Maruna, *Making Good: How Ex-Convicts Reform and Rebuild Their Lives* (Washington, DC: American Psychological Association, 2000).

[105] See also T. P. LeBel, R. Burnett, S. Maruna, and S. Bushway, 'The "Chicken and Egg" of Subjective and Social Factors in Desistance from Crime' (2008) 5 *European J Criminol* 131; S. Maruna, 'Why Our Beliefs Matter in Offender Management' 192 *Prison Service Journal* (November 2010), 22; and A. Bottoms and J. Shapland, 'Steps Towards Desistance among Male Young Adult Recidivists' in S. Farrall, M. Hough, S. Maruna, and R. Sparks (eds), *Escape Routes: Contemporary Perspectives on Life after Punishment* (Abingdon: Routledge, 2011), 71. See also the emphasis on hope and self-belief in R. Burnett and S. Maruna, 'So "Prison Works", Does It? The Criminal Careers of 130 Men Released from Prison under Home Secretary, Michael Howard' (2004) 43 *Howard J* 390.

[106] M. Alfano, *Character as Moral Fiction* (Cambridge: Cambridge University Press, 2013). See discussion in section 4.8, Chapter 4.

11.6 Alternative Accounts

In the discussion so far, I have developed a theory of the relevance of previous convictions to sentence which uses the concept of actions which are more or less out of character. The theory relies on von Hirsch's lapse theory of progressive loss of mitigation, although it is more receptive to the idea that criminal record can have a modest aggravating effect. What of other accounts?

Roberts approves of the 'out of character' idea, but does not flesh it out in detail.[107] More developed is his argument that previous convictions affect culpability in a manner akin to premeditation: they show that the offender was aware of the wrongness of what he did (an argument once used, but later rejected, by von Hirsch).[108] An offender who has carefully planned his offence is usually judged to be more culpable than one who offends on the spur of the moment. Previous convictions speak to the offender's 'state of mind with respect to the commission of the current offence'.[109] 'Awareness of...previous legal censure should recall the individual to respect the law; the offender who reoffends is therefore similar to the offender who plans the offence.'[110] The consequence of this is that while a first offence should mitigate, subsequent convictions should aggravate. A problem with Roberts's account is that much offending is impulsive, so it is hard to see how the defendant's awareness of wrongdoing can play a role. Nor is it clear that there is much gap between first and subsequent offenders in terms of awareness of wrongness.[111]

Lee defends the recidivist premium via an argument that when a defendant is convicted, his relationship with the state changes.[112] Conviction marks the wrongness of what the offender did, and conveys the message that he should not offend again. This changes the offender's normative position, placing him under an obligation to take steps to avoid offending in future—for example, avoiding certain acquaintances or tempting situations. If he reoffends, his sentence should be enhanced to reflect the breach of this obligation, although if the sentencer was convinced that the recidivist offender had made the requisite efforts to avoid reoffending, but had been subject to temptation through no fault of his own, the recidivist premium might be reduced or even waived.

Lee's account shares some ground with the theory put forward here. I have endorsed von Hirsch's argument that the discount for initial offences respects the offender's capacity to respond to censure by making an effort of will to desist: an

---

[107] Roberts, *Punishing Persistent Offenders*, 82.   [108] See above n 89.
[109] Roberts, *Punishing Persistent Offenders*, 82.
[110] J. V. Roberts, 'Revisiting the Recidivist Sentencing Premium' in von Hirsch et al, *Principled Sentencing*, 154.
[111] For further critical discussion, see Lee, 'Repeat Offenders', 54–7; and von Hirsch, 'Discount', 161.
[112] 'Repeat Offenders'.

effort that might, but need not, involve the sort of avoidance strategies mentioned by Lee. Von Hirsch goes so far as to say that offenders should make an effort to change.[113] Lee's argument is phrased carefully. He denies that conviction carries with it a command that offenders 'get their acts together',[114] preferring the language of 'normative expectation'.[115] But while the theories may look to be more or less equivalent, there are significant differences. Under Lee's account, it is not easy to see how an aggravated sentence could be justified unless the offender is under an obligation to take precautionary steps, in which case conviction does express a command—if a very unspecific one—to change one's ways. The specifics will vary from case to case, but might involve, for example, cutting off from one's friends, avoiding visiting shops, or seeking employment (and perhaps all of them at once). These are significant burdens. And while, as we saw, Lee questions whether a character theory of recidivist sentencing can avoid the descent to moral audit, the same concern might be levelled at his theory. We know that marriage and employment are connected to desistance.[116] If a defendant argues that he should avoid the recidivist premium because he has tried to repair a fraying marriage, or secure his job by being a moral employee, these issues will be ripe for exploration at the sentencing hearing.

No doubt there is a moral sense in which offenders should make efforts to desist. But once we attach penal consequences to a failure to do so, we are on dangerous ground. This prompts the question of whether von Hirsch's account might be vulnerable to the criticisms just described. For von Hirsch, the discount for initial offences is given in recognition of the offender's 'assumed capacity to make an effort of will to desist from further offending'.[117] This rewards the defendant before we know whether or not he will make an attempt to desist. It is true that if he does reoffend the next sentence will be higher, but there is no need to enquire whether the offender did make efforts to change because the discount has already been given. On this account, the moral duty to make efforts to desist really is a normative expectation. This seems to be a preferable way to structure things, for it avoids creating potentially onerous obligations which invite extensive scrutiny of an offender's life.

11.7 Sentencing Practice Revisited

Having considered the justifications for taking previous convictions and other forms of character evidence into account when determining sentence, we are now

[113] 'Proportionality', 9.   [114] 'Repeat Offenders', 64.   [115] 'Repeat Offenders', 64.
[116] See J. H. Laub and R. J. Sampson, *Shared Beginnings, Divergent Lives: Delinquent Boys to Age 70* (Harvard: Harvard University Press, 2006). For evidence that employment is not causative—desistence precedes it—see T. Skardhamar and J. Savolainen, 'Changes in Criminal Offending Around the Time of Job Entry: A Study of Employment and Desistance' (2014) 52 *Criminology* 263.
[117] 'Proportionality', 10.

in a position to return to an evaluation of sentencing practice. We saw that the key legislative provision is section 143 of the CJA 2003, which suggests that previous convictions aggravate, directing sentencers to 'the nature of the offence to which the conviction relates and its relevance to the current offence' and 'the time that has elapsed since the conviction'. While there are examples from the post-CJA case law where non-cognate offences are treated as aggravating, more emphasis does seem to be put on similar offences, and the research, as well as pre-CJA practice,[118] bears this out. If an offender commits a violent offence, but has a number of previous convictions for non-violent offences, should the violence be treated as out of character and lead to some mitigation (or at least convert the potentially aggravating record into a neutral factor)? It is hard to see why the similarity of offences should make a difference in sentencing. The criminological research reviewed in Chapter 2 suggests that most offenders are versatile rather than specialist. With regard to violence, the strongest predictor is the number of criminal offences rather than their type: any persistent offender has a good chance of collecting a conviction for violence at some point. In terms of the underlying theory, the idea is that offenders with good character or few convictions may have the moral resources to respond appropriately to censure from the courts, and offence similarity does not appear to be significant from this perspective.

Would this even apply to sexual offences? There is a tendency to see sex offenders as somehow different from other criminals, and we saw in the previous chapter that in the law of evidence this has even led to some courts giving a modified good character direction to juries in cases where D, charged with a sexual offence, has a criminal record for non-sexual offences.[119] The jury will be instructed that the absence of sexual convictions is some evidence in D's favour. In sentencing, the courts have sometimes taken the fact that an offender is being sentenced for his first sexual offence to be mitigation.[120] On the other hand, sexual offences are often serious offences, and this brings another factor into play. Should the absence of convictions and other good character evidence mitigate in the usual way? In its consultation on sentencing for sexual offences, the Sentencing Council suggested that the absence of previous convictions and other good character evidence would have limited impact in serious cases.[121] This approach was confirmed in the consultation response, which suggests a general principle that the more serious the offence, the less weight good character should receive.[122]

Starting with the question of offence similarity in relation to sexual offences, there is little criminological evidence to support the view that sex offenders are

---

[118] Baker and Ashworth, 'The Role of Previous Convictions', 191–3.

[119] See Chapter 10.

[120] See, eg, *Davies* [2006] 1 Cr App R (S) 37, [2005] EWCA Crim 1363; *Graham* [2006] EWCA Crim 2411; and *Gary C* [2005] EWCA Crim 147.

[121] Sentencing Council, *Sexual Offences Guideline Consultation* (London: Sentencing Council, 2012), 25. There was already authority for this: *Millberry* [2003] 1 Cr App R (S) 25, [2002] EWCA Crim 2891.

[122] Sentencing Council, *Sexual Offences: Response to Consultation* (London: Sentencing Council, 2013), 19.

different, so this should not be factored into the sentencing decision.[123] As for seriousness, one view is that a first serious offence should receive mitigation even if the offender has a considerable record of less serious offences.[124] Another, taken by the Sentencing Council in relation to sexual offences, is that seriousness blunts the impact of good character. My own view lies somewhere in between. A record of less serious offences is significant: if the offender has not responded to censure in minor matters, he should not be accorded the benefit of the doubt in more serious ones. But if the offender's first offence is a serious one, there might still be grounds for thinking he has the moral resources to respond to censure—although perhaps not if the offence was carefully planned or involved serious cruelty.

While it is hard to justify CJA, section 143's thinking about the similarity of previous convictions, the reference to time-lapse is far more sensible. An offence should be seen as out of character, and there should be potential for mitigation (or neutralization of aggravation) even if the offender has several previous convictions, as long as there has been a significant gap in time between the last offence and the current one. This may be a sign that the offender is starting to desist from crime. The research portrays desistance as a slow and sometimes stop-start process.[125] Signs of desistance will suggest that the offender has the moral resources to take the latest censure seriously, and to respond appropriately.

Time-lapse and offence similarity are minor footnotes to section 143's primary message: previous convictions aggravate. I have suggested that criminal record might play a minor aggravating role. Once mitigation has been lost, further convictions could aggravate, although only to a minor and diminishing extent. Sentencing practice appears to be partly in line with this—each conviction has a diminishing impact—but convictions almost certainly play a greater aggravating role than is justified. It is not just concerns about whether offending is out of or in character which are relevant here. If, as I am assuming, sentencing should largely be governed by retributive considerations, then sentences should generally be proportional to offence seriousness. If criminal record comes to play too large a role, then proportionality, and the sentence's ability to express the gravity of the offence relative to other offences, is threatened.

Moving beyond section 143, character may play other roles in the sentencing process. In some cases, an offender's good deeds unrelated to the offence are taken to mitigate. For instance, in *Wenman*, D was convicted of causing death by careless driving.[126] He had been drunk at the time of the accident and until the day of the trial had claimed that it was his wife who had been driving. Shortly before sentencing, he had come across a car which had skidded on the road and run into

---

[123] See discussion in Chapter 7, and F. E. Zimring, W. G. Jennings, A. R. Piquero, and S. Hayes, 'Investigating the Continuity of Sex Offending: Evidence from the Second Philadelphia Birth Cohort' (2009) 26 *Justice Quarterly* 58.

[124] Von Hirsch and Ashworth, *Proportionate Sentencing*, 154.

[125] Maruna, *Making Good*. See also S. Farrall and A. Calverely, *Understanding Desistance from Crime* (Milton Keynes: Open University Press, 2006); and Bottoms and Shapland, 'Steps Towards Desistance'.

[126] [2005] 2 Cr App R (S) 3, [2004] EWCA Crim 2995.

a ditch. Wenman stood in the ditch holding the driver's head above water until help arrived. The Court thought he was entitled to 'substantial credit for his selfless and courageous conduct',[127] and reduced the custodial sentence from four to three years. As Ashworth notes, what may be going on here is a form of 'social accounting', with the court feeling it should give credit for good deeds unconnected to the offence.[128] In his critique of retributivism, Tadros has suggested that this sort of thinking flows from a commitment to desert.[129] If wrongdoers deserve to suffer, then those who do good deeds deserve to have their lives go better, and there is no obvious desert-based reason why the state should seek to bring about the former but not the latter. The appeal of the notion of overarching desert might help to explain why the courts do sometimes engage in social accounting, but it is surely something they are ill-equipped to do. The courtroom is not an appropriate place to try to account for all the pluses and minuses in a person's life, and for every Wenman whose good deed is rewarded there must be dozens of offenders whose positive social contributions—caring for an elderly relative, say—go unnoticed. The other explanation for what occurs in cases like *Wenman* is that the courts see the good deed as evidence that the offence was out of character and that the offender has the moral resources to respond appropriately to censure. This justification should not be dismissed entirely, but what has been said above should surely make us doubt whether a response to an incident such as the one in *Wenmam* really tells us much about a person's overall character.

The assessment of character in sentencing is not just a matter of looking at the defendant's past behaviour. The sentencing process gives the court a chance to assess the defendant's response to the offence. 'Genuine remorse' is the most commonly mentioned mitigating factor in the Crown Court Sentencing Survey.[130] Remorse is probably best seen as an indication that the offender will respond to censure by making efforts to desist, and so is closely linked to the character factors we have been considering.[131] Another factor often mentioned by sentencing judges is whether the offender is addressing underlying problems, such as drug and alcohol abuse. It seems that judges often try to engage with offenders to see whether they are genuinely committed to changing their lives. Hough, Jacobson, and Millie found that sentencers making decisions at the custody threshold 'were casting around for some reason to avoid a custodial sentence. This could be an indication—of any kind—that a prolific offender was willing or able to change his behaviour, or that a first-time offender would not offend again.'[132] These

---

[127] *Wenman*, [11].

[128] A. Ashworth, 'Re-Evaluating the Justifications for Aggravation and Mitigation at Sentencing' in J. V. Roberts (ed), *Mitigation and Aggravation at Sentencing* (Cambridge: Cambridge University Press, 2011), 28–9.

[129] Tadros, *Criminal Responsibility*, 70–1.   [130] *Crown Court Sentencing Survey 2012*, 23.

[131] See H. Maslen and J. V. Roberts, 'Remorse and Sentencing: An Analysis of Sentencing Guidelines and Sentencing Practice' in Ashworth and Roberts, *Sentencing Guidelines*.

[132] Hough et al, *The Decision to Imprison*, 41. As Baker and Ashworth note, this is pre-CJA 2003 research and it might be questioned whether such practices still prevail ('The Role of Previous Convictions', 201). The *Crown Court Sentencing Survey* is some indication that they do. There are examples in the past case law where such glimmers of hope make a profound difference to sentence.

practices do seem appropriate. As noted above, we punish offenders, not offences. Where there is reason to think that an offender will respond appropriately to censure, there is reason to mitigate the sentence. Desistance is not a straightforward process, but a defendant's commitment to change is an important part of it and indicator of its possible success.[133] Courts should engage with these attitudes, not ignore them.

11.8 Conclusion

Character plays an important role in decision-making on sentence. In this chapter, I have argued that character's influence on sentence is partly justified. Drawing on von Hirsch's theory of progressive loss of mitigation, I have suggested that, while character does not seem to be relevant to culpability, it helps to inform judgments about whether an offender will take censure seriously. This allows character to mitigate, and to play a limited aggravating role. While arguing that character is relevant to sentence raises fears about the sentencing process becoming a detailed enquiry into an offender's life, I have explored various factors which help to allay these fears, especially where bad character is concerned.

By rejecting a link between culpability and character in the sentencing domain, the weight of the argument for the relevance of character hangs on the claim that sentencers should take account of D's likely response to censure. While this argument was made from a retributive perspective, the thinking here is not necessarily distinct from a more crime-reductionist approach to sentencing. While I argued earlier that the empirical evidence does not support basing sentencing policy on deterrence, the focus there was on increasing sentence severity to reflect criminal record. It presumably follows from the same research that shortening a sentence to reflect good character is unlikely to undermine deterrence, whether individual or general. Given the criminogenic effects of imprisonment,[134] and the possibility, noted above, that a reduced sentence may help to mould an offender's self-perception and encourage desistence, the argument for the mitigating effect of good character could be made on reductionist grounds. Whichever justification is emphasized, an appealing aspect of the practice of mitigation is the way in which it respects the offender's moral agency. A crime committed in the past may be the necessary basis for punishment, but it is an offender, with an ongoing life, who is punished. Just as character provides the link between the offender and the crime, so character may influence the amount of punishment which is fitting.

See, eg, *Bowles* [1996] Cr App R (S) 248; and *Attorney General's Reference no 45 of 2009* [2009] EWCA Crim 1759.

[133] See Bottoms and Shapland, 'Steps Towards Desistance', 64. See also Burnett and Maruna, 'So "Prison Works", Does It?'.

[134] See Kazemian, 'Assessing the Impact'; Nagin et al, 'Imprisonment and Reoffending'; and Nagin and Snodgrass, 'The Effect of Incarceration on Re-Offending'.

12

Dangerous Characters

The recent history of criminal justice has seen an increasing emphasis on identifying 'dangerous' offenders—typically those thought likely to commit violent and sexual offences—and incapacitating them by giving them extended sentences. In England and Wales, this led to the notorious scheme of 'imprisonment for public protection' (IPP) under which offenders classified as dangerous were sentenced to indeterminate periods of imprisonment, with release conditional on an assessment by the Parole Board that they no longer were dangerous. IPP was abandoned in 2012, but English law still contains several provisions designed to give longer than normal sentences to certain offenders. It is in this context that character—past behaviour, as well as a description of a person as dangerous—plays what is probably its most significant role in the criminal trial. Here, character not only helps to prove guilt or results in a somewhat harsher or more lenient sentence, but can lead to a very significant extra period of imprisonment or even to a life sentence—with no guarantee of release after the minimum term—which would not otherwise be imposed. The aim of this chapter is to examine some of the dangerousness provisions in English sentencing law and to ask whether the role played by character in their application can be justified. The focus is on offenders who are not classified as mentally disordered.

12.1 Dangerousness Provisions in England and Wales

The key provisions are found in the Criminal Justice Act 2003, Chapter 5 of Part 12 of which is entitled 'Dangerous Offenders'.[1] The current provisions reflect significant changes made by the Legal Aid, Sentencing and Punishment of Offenders Act 2012 (LASPO),[2] not least the abolition of IPP. In the first incarnation of IPP, offenders were presumed to be dangerous if they had committed a specified offence (one of 96 serious offences listed in a schedule to the Act), and an indeterminate sentence had to be passed if the presumption was not

---

[1] For other examples, see Powers of Criminal Courts (Sentencing) Act 2000, s 100 (minimum of seven years for a third Class A drug trafficking offence) and s 111 (minimum of three years for third domestic burglary).

[2] See D. A. Thomas, 'The Legal Aid, Sentencing and Punishment of Offenders Act 2012: The Sentencing Provisions' [2012] *Crim LR* 572.

Dangerous Characters

rebutted.[3] A minimum term was set by the judge; on expiry of the minimum term the offender could be released if the Parole Board was convinced that he no longer posed a significant risk to the public. The sentence was widely used, with the minimum term often being low,[4] suggesting that the offence for which the offender was sentenced was not all that serious. Offenders found it hard to convince a risk-averse Parole Board that they were no longer dangerous, and IPP led to a rapid rise in the number of prisoners serving indeterminate sentences,[5] putting strain on the prison service. There were insufficient resources for offenders to attend programmes which might have helped them to address their offending behaviour, a situation which led to censure in the English courts[6] and the European Court of Human Rights.[7] Amendments in the Criminal Justice and Immigration Act 2008 shifted the threshold for IPP upwards. The sentence could only be imposed if the offence merited a four-year determinate sentence, and in most cases the minimum term had to be more than two years. Even after amendment, and with the Court of Appeal emphasizing that IPP should be used as a last resort,[8] the sentence proved popular with judges and its use did not decline as rapidly as had been hoped.[9] The decision was therefore made to abolish IPP, but the incapacitative strategy was not abandoned completely.

Turning to the current provisions, section 225 of the CJA imposes a mandatory life sentence on offenders convicted of a serious offence where the offender is judged to be dangerous, ie where 'there is a significant risk to members of the public of serious harm' (which can include psychological injury)[10] resulting from further specified offences committed by the offender. The offence for which the offender is being sentenced must be one for which a life sentence is otherwise available, and must be serious enough to merit a life sentence. The specified offences are found in a long list of violent and sexual offences.[11] Under section 224A, there is a life sentence for offenders who commit a second 'listed offence'. Here, there is no requirement for a finding of dangerousness. The current offence must be one for which a sentence of ten years or more would otherwise be given, and the previous offence must be one of those listed in Schedule 15B—a list of reasonably serious violent and sexual offences—and have been met with a ten-year sentence or a life sentence with a minimum term of five years. The court has a discretion not to impose a life sentence if to do so would be unjust. An 'extended sentence' for violent or sexual offences is provided for in section 226A of the Act. Where

[3] For an overview of IPP, see J. Peay, *Mental Health and Crime* (London: Routledge, 2011), ch 12.
[4] J. Jacobson and M. Hough, *Unjust Deserts: Imprisonment for Public Protection* (London: Prison Reform Trust, 2010), 12.
[5] *The Story of the Prison Population: 1993–2012, England and Wales* (London: Ministry of Justice, 2013), 15. IPP certainly had an impact on the overall prison population, but calculating the size of the impact is not straightforward: see Jacobson and Hough, *Unjust Deserts*, 17–19.
[6] *R (on the application of Wells)* v *Parole Board* [2009] 2 WLR 1149, [2009] UKHL 22.
[7] *James, Wells and Lee* v *United Kingdom* (2013) 56 EHRR 399.
[8] *Attorney General's Reference (No 55 of 2008)* [2009] 2 Cr App R (S) 22, [2008] EWCA Crim 2790.
[9] Jacobson and Hough, *Unjust Deserts*, 11.   [10] CJA 2003, s 224 (3).
[11] Schedule 15, pts 1 and 2.

the offender has been convicted of a specified offence, has previously committed a Schedule 15B offence or would otherwise be sentenced to four years' custody, and poses a significant risk of serious harm, then an extension period may be added to the appropriate custodial sentence. The extension period is judged on the basis of public protection, but is capped at five years for violent offences and eight years for sexual offences. The effect of an extended sentence is that an offender will not be considered for release until he has served two-thirds of the custodial sentence (in normal cases release can be considered at the half-way point). In less serious cases (basically those where the custodial part of the sentence was less than ten years), the offender will then be released on licence (thus being subject to recall to serve the remainder of the extension period in custody); in more serious cases offenders will only be released on licence if the Parole Board considers that confinement is no longer necessary for the protection of the public, but all offenders must be released at the end of the custodial period.

These dangerousness provisions were considered by the Court of Appeal in *Burinskas*.[12] While IPP is no more, offenders who would have been sentenced to IPP will not necessarily be treated less harshly under the new regime. While some will be given an extended sentence, the Court made clear that some will now be given a discretionary life sentence under section 225. What this means is that, while the sentencing judge will set a minimum term, release is conditional on a decision by the Parole Board that imprisonment is no longer necessary for protection of the public. In practice, then, the abolition of IPP may not make that much difference, because an indeterminate sentence is still available. In *Burinskas*, the Court was aware that this makes the test for imposing a life sentence under section 225 critical. The section requires that a life sentence be justified by the seriousness of the current offence, and the Court interpreted seriousness as incorporating not only the seriousness of the offence itself, but also the defendant's previous convictions (referring here to CJA, section 143(2)), 'the level of danger to the public posed by the defendant and whether there is a reliable estimate of the length of time he will remain a danger', and the available alternative sentences.[13] This is a rather capacious test of seriousness. And the reference to a reliable estimate of the length of time for which D remains dangerous is alarming—it is extremely doubtful that risk assessments can deliver such estimates.

In several of the cases in the combined appeals heard in *Burinskas*, the trial judges seem to have seen section 225 as a new form of IPP, emphasizing the need for indeterminate sentences to reflect uncertainty about the offender's length of time at risk (uncertainty that, as noted, is probably inevitable). 'The judge concluded that he could not say when the appellant could safely be released; the only appropriate sentence therefore was life imprisonment';[14] 'there was no material upon which [the judge] could decide when it would be safe to release [D]. A life sentence was, therefore, the only safe sentence that he could pass';[15] '[the

---

12 [2014] EWCA Crim 334.   13 *Burinskas*, [22].   14 *Burinskas*, [93].
15 *Burinskas*, [133].

judge] was satisfied that an extended sentence was not appropriate because he could not, in the light of the reports, have any confidence as to whether the risk presented by the appellant would ever reduce'.[16] The Court of Appeal suggested that this approach should not be taken too far: the seriousness criterion in section 225 means that not just any risky offender can be given a life sentence. Thus, in the case of *Smith*, where the defendant had been convicted of kidnapping in an incident which, while disturbing, was less serious than his previous offending, it commented:

We do not consider that the seriousness of the offence justified a life sentence under s.225(2)(b) of the CJA 2003. Although we have no doubt that under the sentencing regime between 2005 and 2012 a sentence of IPP would have been passed, this case illustrates the position that amendments made by LASPO to the CJA 2003 do not permit the court to impose a life sentence for reasons solely of public protection.[17]

But there is some ambivalence on this point. While a life sentence was not said to be justified on the facts of *Smith* because the offence was not sufficiently serious, we saw that seriousness as defined by the Court of Appeal includes an assessment of dangerousness including whether 'there is a reliable estimate of the length of time [D] will remain a danger'. In another of the appeals, which admittedly involved a more serious crime than *Smith*, the Court held that the trial judge had been wrong to give an extended sentence:

it is not possible to say with any degree of confidence when [D] will no longer be dangerous. That is a matter for assessment at a much later stage. An extended sentence which requires his release at the end of the custodial term does not adequately protect the public. We are satisfied that the seriousness of this offence is such as to justify the imposition of a sentence of life imprisonment.[18]

Whatever the exact threshold for a life sentence under section 225, it is clear that dangerousness plays a significant role in sentencing. Sometimes it triggers what is effectively an indeterminate sentence under section 225, at others a significant extension to the sentence under section 226A. While the life sentence for a second serious offence (section 224A) does not require a finding of dangerousness, there can be little doubt that a desire to incapacitate the dangerous is part of the thinking behind this provision. The obvious question is whether a sentencing regime which puts so much emphasis on past and likely future behaviour can be justified.

12.2 Justifying Preventive Sentencing

The sentencing provisions just surveyed are in part preventive. They aim to incapacitate offenders judged to be dangerous. In the previous chapter, I argued that because retributivism struggles to justify institutions of punishment by itself,

---

[16] *Burinskas*, [150].   [17] *Burinskas*, [138].   [18] *Burinskas*, [62].

crime reduction concerns—deterrence and incapacitation—play a role in justi-fying state punishment. I also allowed that deterrence and incapacitation might play a role in justifying particular sentences, but went on to argue that the empiri-cal evidence ruled out crime-reduction concerns as a justification for applying a recidivist premium across the board. The question now is whether incapacitation might justify extended sentences for a subset of offenders—those classified as dan-gerous, where the cost-benefit issues noted in the previous chapter might not rule out incapacitation. I start by discussing theoretical concerns, before moving on to issues about our ability to predict serious violence, and to do so justly.

Incapacitation is a controversial sentencing rationale. Kramer's assessment (made in the context of the death penalty, but the arguments do not seem spe-cific to that context) is typical: incapacitation 'discounts the significance of moral responsibility...It deals with dangerously violent people as if they were wild ani-mals or rabid dogs, instead of dealing with them as moral agents who are respon-sible for their misdeeds'.[19] Similarly, Meyerson: 'preventive measures assume that people who are capable of choosing not to cause harm will cause harm, thereby denying them the opportunity to choose differently. They are treated as "predict-able objects" or "dangerous animals", rather than as individuals with capacity for free choice.'[20] And Ferzan: 'The State must respect that a responsible agent may choose not to commit an offence. It cannot detain an actor for who he is. It must wait to see what he will do.'[21]

These arguments need some unpacking. The rather emotive language—'rabid dogs', 'dangerous animals'—may in part be due to the focus of debates about preventive sentencing so often being on the risk of serious violence. Perhaps, then, we should consider a less extreme example. Vollaard's study of selective incapaci-tation in the Netherlands found that a sentence enhancement for habitual offend-ers whereby a prison term which might normally be a few weeks or months was increased to two years had a significant effect on crime rates, cutting the rate of burglary and theft from a car by 40 per cent in some areas.[22] Suppose the enhanced sentence could not be justified on grounds of desert: was the Dutch strategy wrong? Did it treat offenders like animals? It is not clear to me that it was or that it did. The crime-reduction benefits of the policy were substantial. Offenders were not treated like animals in the sense of having no rights at all.[23] What may lie behind the animals metaphor, however, is a concern that people are

---

[19] M. H. Kramer, *The Ethics of Capital Punishment: A Philosophical Investigation of Evil and Its Consequences* (Oxford: Oxford University Press, 2011), 147.

[20] D. Meyerson, 'Risks, Rights, Statistics and Compulsory Measures' (2009) 31 *Sydney L Rev* 507, 527–8 (citations omitted). See also A. Ashworth and L. Zedner, *Preventive Justice* (Oxford: Oxford University Press, 2014), 151–2.

[21] K. Kessler Ferzan, 'Beyond Crime and Commitment: Justifying Liberty Deprivations of the Dangerous and Responsible' (2011) 96 *Minnesota L Rev* 141, 142.

[22] B. Vollaard, 'Preventing Crime through Selective Incapacitation' (2013) 123 *Economic J* 262. I explain in Chapter 11 why this does not lend much support to a general recidivist premium.

[23] See A. Walen, 'A Punitive Precondition for Preventive Detention: Lost Status as a Foundation for a Lost Immunity' (2011) 48 *San Diego L Rev* 1229, 1262–3.

treated as responding only to threats and barriers rather than to moral communi-cation: they are not treated as moral agents.[24] I do not find that claim convincing.

One aspect of the moral agency argument is that incapacitation treats people as though they do not have free choice. I argued in Chapter 4 that a prediction that a person is likely to act in a certain way does not imply that she lacks free choice. Incapacitation is justified on the basis of risk, not inevitability. However, in the current context things are slightly different from the situation considered in Chapter 4, where the issue was using bad character as evidence of guilt. With incapacitation we are not just predicting, but intervening to prevent the pre-dicted choice being made. In some contexts, such intervention may be regarded as unproblematic. Self-defence is an example, and is a useful analogy for strategies of incapacitation.[25] Ferzan in fact allows that incapacitation may be justified on the basis of self-defence, but only where the actor has formed an intention to commit a crime. She explains:

It may be that we can predict with equal confidence that both A and B will commit a crime. If A has formed the intention, but B hasn't, why let the intention matter? The answer is that we take B's autonomy seriously by waiting. Although it may be an act of caring or kindness to order for a friend or a spouse before he arrives at a restaurant, predicting—even predictable choices—takes responsibility out of our hands.[26]

Why is removing choice such a bad thing? We remove certain choices from people when we lock and fit immobilisers to our cars, but Ferzan does not regard this as problematic.[27] Choice can certainly be pleasurable: in the restaurant example the friend would be denied the pleasure of choosing from the menu, but surely the pleasure of choice is not something we should give any weight to in the context of crime prevention. It is correct that we take responsibility out of the friend's hands by choosing for him, but if we do that to prevent him choosing the *foie gras*, and eating *foie gras* is, as we believe, seriously wrong, it is hard to see that, on balance, we have done anything which can be criticized.[28] Finally, if we choose for the friend on the basis of what we know about his preferences (he is not mad on spicy food, but really likes fish), it does seem that we are respecting his autonomy to some extent—more so than if we tossed a coin to make the decision. Likewise, where we sentence an offender on the basis of what his past behaviour reveals about what he is likely to do in the future: the sentence reflects his agency.

---

[24] See von Hirsch's discussion of 'tiger control' in A. von Hirsch, *Censure and Sanctions* (Oxford: Oxford University Press, 1993), 11–14.
[25] See S. J. Morse, 'Neither Desert Nor Disease' (1999) 5 *Legal Theory* 265, 294–303; and A. Ellis, *The Philosophy of Punishment* (Charlottesville, VA: Imprint Academic, 2012), 150–3.
[26] Ferzan, 'Beyond Crime and Commitment', 189.
[27] Ferzan, 'Beyond Crime and Commitment', 178.
[28] This is not to deny that people have the right to do wrong (see J. Waldron, 'A Right to Do Wrong' in *Liberal Rights: Collected Papers 1981–1991* (Cambridge: Cambridge University Press, 1993)). Hence in the hypothetical eating *foie gras* is seriously wrong, to keep the analogy with crimes the prevention of which is the rationale of the CJA provisions. Nor is it to deny that there is value in trusting people to make their own decisions; the claim is that this value is sometimes outweighed by other concerns.

Part of Ferzan's argument is that we should not punish people for who they are. One well-known concern about embracing incapacitation as an aim of punishment is that it would justify punishing people who have never committed a crime if they can nevertheless be shown to be dangerous. That is a genuine worry, which I consider later because it is helpful to address it after reviewing the reliability of risk assessment. If we concentrate, for now, on the situation in English sentencing law where an offender may be given a longer than normal sentence on grounds of dangerousness, then it is hard to deny that he is being punished at least in part for who he is: he is dangerous. But if incapacitation is a valid sentencing aim, then it is legitimate to punish people for who they are. That is the whole point of incapacitation.

There is more to say about the legitimacy of incapacitative sentencing, and I return to these issues below, discussing whether it is proper to regard incapacitation as punishment and the spectre of locking up non-offenders. So far, I hope to have shown that there is a case to be made for the sort of preventive sentencing found in the CJA. But to argue that preventive sentencing meets a legitimate sentencing rationale and respects moral agency is not to meet all of the criticisms levelled at it. Some of the worries are empirical: can we predict future wrongdoing well enough to justify incapacitation? But there are also other concerns, several of which echo issues discussed in previous chapters.

12.3 Actuarial Risk Assessment: Initial Concerns

We have seen that some of the preventive provisions in the CJA depend on a judgment that an offender is dangerous: that he poses 'a significant risk to members of the public of serious harm'. Some commentators seem especially worried that assessments of dangerousness often rely on actuarial risk assessment instruments (ARAIs). ARAIs score offenders on the basis of whether they have attributes which have been found to be associated—positively or negatively—with reoffending. For example, the Offender Assessment System (OASys), which is commonly used in England and Wales, includes the OASys Violence Predictor (OVP), which examines the following factors: offending history; age; sex; recognizes impact of offending; accommodation; employability; alcohol misuse; psychiatric treatment; temper control; and attitudes.[29] A score on a 100-point scale is generated from this. The OVP can then inform a broader 'Risk of Serious Harm' analysis, under which an offender is assessed as being a low, medium, high, or very high risk of serious harm, to the public in general and/or to other groups. For example, in *Fearon* it was said that: 'From the information collected in OASys [the appellant] is currently assessed as posing a high risk of serious harm to the public and a high risk of serious harm to staff, specifically police officers.'[30]

---

[29] See P. D. Howard and L. Dixon, 'The Construction and Validation of the OASys Violence Predictor' (2012) 39 *Criminal Justice & Behavior* 287, 297.
[30] [2012] EWCA Crim 2463, [11].

Another ARAI used in England and Wales is Risk Matrix 2000, commonly used for sex offenders. While the OVP includes several dynamic variables (variables which might be altered through deliberate intervention) such as alcohol misuse and employability, RM2000 focuses on static variables—variables which are unlikely to change while the offender is in custody. For sex offenders, the variables include age at onset of offending, number of sex offence convictions, number of convictions, whether the subject has targeted a male victim, whether he has targeted a stranger victim, and whether he has been in a two-year relationship.[31] The risk assessment uses the same scale as the OASys risk of serious harm analysis: low, medium, high, very high. In *Jubb*,[32] the pre-sentence report described the defendant as having a high risk of reconviction for a sexual offence and this was held to justify imposing an extended sentence: a five-year extension period to the eight-year sentence. Other ARAIs, such as VRAG—the Violence Risk Appraisal guide—are also sometimes used.[33]

The OVP differs in various ways from RM2000. While RM2000 could be applied by anyone with the protocol and sufficient detail about the offender's history, the OVP requires a degree of judgment and interpretation. The offender needs to be interviewed and such things as his attitudes assessed in order to be scored and fed into the assessment. But while this may suggest that RM2000 is more automatic and inflexible than the OVP, in practice this will not always be the case. In England and Wales, ARAIs often seem to be used to inform rather than direct a conclusion as to risk. Assessors frequently modify the ARAI conclusion by taking other factors into account.[34]

This brief review helps to put some of the criticisms of ARAIs into context. An over-arching concern is that making decisions about risk on the basis of ARAIs ignores the individual. This worry appears in various slightly different forms. '[I]t seems wrong,' Justice Coyne complained, 'to confine any person...on the basis of statistical evidence regarding the behaviour of other people.'[35] Ferzan protests that the sort of 'naked statistical evidence' used to assess dangerousness 'does not point to anything the detainee can disprove',[36] involves 'impersonal prediction',[37] and that 'reference class selection alters how dangerous the individual appears to be'.[38]

These criticisms are unconvincing. The behaviour of other people informs the assessment of much evidence used in criminal trials, such as evidence that D was seen running away from the scene of crime: such behaviour is only suspicious because of generalizations drawn from our experience of how people

[31] See D. Grubin, 'A Large-Scale Evaluation of Risk Matrix 2000 in Scotland' (2011) 23 *Sexual Abuse* 419, 421.
[32] [2014] EWCA Crim 755, [9].
[33] *Beesley* [2012] 1 Cr App R (S) 15, [2011] EWCA Crim 1021.
[34] M. Ansbro, 'The Nuts and Bolts of Risk Assessment: When the Clinical and Actuarial Conflict' (2010) 49 *Howard J* 252. The case law provides several examples: eg *Ashford* [2013] EWCA Crim 270; and *Neal* [2006] EWCA Crim 3416.
[35] *In re Linehan* (1994) 518 NW 2d 609, 616.
[36] 'Beyond Crime and Commitment', 157.   [37] 'Beyond Crime and Commitment', 157.
[38] 'Beyond Crime and Commitment', 156.

generally behave when having committed (or not committed) a crime. In any case, both the OVP and RM2000 rely heavily on facts about the offender's own behaviour: his offending, his temper control.[39] It is not easy to understand the complaint about the offender not being able to disprove the ARAI-based assessment. If the assessor miscalculated the offender's offending history or did not assess his thinking and behaviour competently, then the offender can object.[40] But perhaps the real concern here is that once someone has certain characteristics, the existence of which is hard to dispute, then under, say, RM2000 they will be categorized as high risk and that is that, even if factors not included in RM2000 suggest otherwise. No doubt there are instances of unreflective use of ARAIs: Cooke gives the example of an offender classified as high risk under RM2000 partly because his victim was a stranger (although they had been in telephone contact), and because he had never had a two-year relationship (although as a 19-year-old student it might have been surprising if he had).[41] However, surely any expert evidence can fall victim to the unreflective application of decision tools, and where it is it should be challenged, as it was in the case described by Cooke. In any case, in England and Wales it seems common for assessors to override actuarial conclusions, and common for defendants to dispute risk assessments.[42]

As for the reference class problem, we saw in Chapter 3 that this is an issue which can be raised in respect of any evidence. With ARAIs, the factors used for risk classification are not arbitrary: they have been found to be associated with recidivism in certain groups of offenders, and certain other factors will have been rejected, or given less weight than others, in building the model. Of course, it is possible that different ARAIs could be applied to the same individual and produce different results. Once more, though, this is unlikely to be a problem unique to assessments of dangerousness. Different models for analysing DNA evidence will produce different results, and this is a useful reminder that in forensic science, as in forensic risk assessment, we should not regard the probabilities produced by models as completely objective.[43] With ARAIs, there may sometimes be reason to prefer one model over another: the VRAG, for example, includes questions relating to psychopathy and schizophrenia which might make it a more appropriate instrument to use in some cases. But different ARAIs are unlikely to produce radically different results in an individual case. There is evidence that ARAIs are largely interchangeable, and have similar levels

[39] See C. Slobogin, 'Dangerousness and Expertise Redux' (2006) 56 *Emory LJ* 276, 297–8.
[40] Indeed, because ARAIs operate transparently, the evidence may be easier to dispute than forms of risk assessment which rely more heavily on judgment.
[41] D. Cooke, 'More Prejudicial than Probative?' [2010] *Journal of the Law Soc of Scotland: Online*, 8 January 2010.
[42] See Ansbro, 'The Nuts and Bolts of Risk Assessment'; *Ashford*; and *Neal*.
[43] For philosophical background, see A. Hajék, 'The Reference Class Problem is Your Problem Too' (2007) 156 *Synthese* 563.

of accuracy, presumably because they all tend to measure the same underlying features associated with offending.[44]

The initial objections to ARAIs, introduced above, are unconvincing. There are, however, various more serious criticisms of ARAIs, and some of these still pick up on the general point about their lack of individualization.[45] Generally speaking, these criticisms challenge the reliability of assessments based on ARAIs. A starting point is Meyerson's claim that when an ARAI shows that 75 per cent of individuals in a group reoffend, 'strictly speaking it does not make sense to say of any particular individual that he or she has a 75 per cent risk of re-offending or that she is likely to re-offend'.[46] Meyerson's explanation of the reason for this does not convince,[47] but it is important to think about the problem here: what secures the inference from group to individual?[48] One issue is whether the characteristics of the group on which the ARAI was based are a good fit for the individual who is being assessed.[49] VRAG, for example, was developed from research on a group of patients released from a maximum security psychiatric hospital in Canada.[50] We might question the application of such a tool to an offender in England and Wales who has no psychiatric problems.[51] The OVP, however, is based on a general sample of offenders in England and Wales.[52] RM2000 was also based on research in England and Wales.[53] Although that research is now dated—and rates of sex offence recidivism have changed in the meantime—more recent research on

[44] M. Yang, S. C. P. Wong, and J. Coid, 'The Efficacy of Violence Prediction: A Meta-Analytic Comparison of Nine Risk Assessment Tools' (2010) 136 *Psychol Bull* 740. See also D. G. Kroner, J. F. Mills, and J. R. Reddon, 'A Coffee Can, Factor Analysis, and Prediction of Antisocial Behavior: The Structure of Criminal Risk' (2005) 28 *Int J Law & Psychiatry* 360.

[45] A useful overview of the issues is M. Hamilton, 'Adventures in Risk: Predicting Violent and Sexual Recidivism in Sentencing Law' *Arizona State LJ* (forthcoming), available at <http://papers. ssrn.com/sol3/papers.cfm?abstract_id = 2416918>.

[46] 'Risks, Rights, Statistics', 521.

[47] 'The fact is that 75 per cent of the individuals in the group will certainly re-offend (the probability of their re-offending is 1) and 25 of them will certainly not re-offend (the probability of their re-offending is 0), and it is only because we are not in possession of all the relevant information that we are unable to make these finer distinctions within the group' (Meyerson, 'Risks, Rights, Statistics', 521). It is not the case that 75 per cent will definitely reoffend: this is the expectation, the most likely number to reoffend, but it is perfectly possible that more or less people will. It is true that there may be information we lack, but this is always the case in matters of evidence, and is precisely why we need to rely on probabilities (would Meyerson say that it makes no sense to say that a tossed coin has a 0.5 chance of landing heads?)

[48] For general discussion, see D. L. Faigman, J. Monahan, and C. Slobogin, 'Group to Individual Inference in Scientific Testimony' (2014) 81 *U Chicago L Rev* 417.

[49] See D. Mossman, 'Another Look at Interpreting Risk Categories' (2006) 18 *Sexual Abuse* 41.

[50] See Hamilton, 'Adventures in Risk', 34.

[51] The VRAG has been found to perform poorly (in terms of calibration) on a general criminal justice population in Switzerland: see A. Rossegger, J. Endrass, J. Gerth, and J. P. Singh, 'Replicating the Violence Risk Appraisal Guide: A Total Forensic Cohort Study' (2014) 9 *PLoS ONE* doi: 10.1371/journal.pone.0091845.

[52] See Howard and Dixon, 'Construction and Validation'.

[53] See Cooke, 'More Prejudicial than Probative?', for some examples of inappropriate use of RM2000: experts have applied it in cases of internet-based offending and to first offenders, types of case not included in the original research.

offenders in Scotland found RM2000 to predict sexual reoffending with a similar degree of reliability to the original research.[54]

Even if we think that the ARAI was developed using a group which is sufficiently similar to the offender being assessed, there might still be doubts about drawing the inference from group to individual. If members of the research group sharing the offender's characteristics had a five-year violence reconviction rate of 47 per cent, does that mean that the offender has a 47 per cent chance of violent reoffending within five years? In some cases, there may be obvious reasons to think that he does not: the offender may recently have lost an arm in a car accident, for example. Less dramatic characteristics are more likely to have been present in the research sample and thus taken into account if they made a significant difference to reoffending. Still, there is a good case for presenting results in a way which emphasizes the possible gap between group and individual. Thus, in *Neal*, the pre-sentence report suggested that: 'The RM2000 static risk test assessed [Neal's] risk as 2 in 10 over 20 years—that is to say a group of 10 other men with his static risk factors followed over 20 years would result in two members of that group committing a sexual offence.'[55] Further, where an ARAI includes dynamic risk factors, any indication that the offender is willing to work to address those factors—giving up drugs, for example—would be a significant point to take into account.[56]

12.4 How Reliable Is Risk Assessment?

The points made towards the end of the previous section are essentially about variability between individuals. While on average two in ten offend, we do not know if there are factors which make the offender more or less likely to be one of those two. This issue has given rise to a complex technical debate about the reliability of ARAIs. While we may be able to say that, on average, 50 per cent of people in the relevant group offend, applying the group average to the individual creates considerable uncertainty. Hart and Cooke suggest that for a generic ARAI, the 95 per cent confidence intervals around the mean risk scores for different offenders are wide and overlapping.[57] That is, while X might be said to have a 50 per cent chance of reoffending within three years, that means that the average person like X has a 50 per cent chance, but it is quite possible that the figure is higher or lower. All we can say is that in 95 per cent of cases, the chance of reoffending would be between 80 and 25 per cent, so X's chance of reoffending might in fact be the same as Y's, Y having been assessed as having a 15 per cent chance of reoffending.[58] This degree of imprecision is due in part to 'the inherent variability across

[54] See Grubin, 'A Large-Scale Evaluation'.
[55] [2006] EWCA Crim 3416, [6].
[56] See, eg, *Beesley* [2012] 1 Cr App R (S) 15, [2011] EWCA Crim 1021, [26]–[27].
[57] S. D. Hart and D. J. Cooke, 'Another Look at the (Im-)Precision of Individual Risk Estimates Made Using Actuarial Risk Assessment Instruments' (2013) 31 *Behav Sci & Law* 81.
[58] These figures reflect those calculated in Hart and Cooke, 'Another Look'.

individuals—and within individuals and their circumstances across time—and the multitudinous causes that result in violent crime'.[59] While there is a technical dispute about whether it is appropriate to apply confidence intervals in this context,[60] an analysis of the issue using a different (Bayesian) methodology comes to a reasonably similar conclusion: there is considerable uncertainty associated with predictions of reoffending.[61]

It is not easy to say what the significance of this is. The average is still the average, and there is an argument for taking this as the basis for fact-finding decisions.[62] If we were to think about the uncertainty associated with other evidence in a criminal trial, no doubt this would be considerable too. Perhaps we think that most eyewitnesses like W are accurate, but we cannot be too sure that in fact very many or only a few are. There may, however, be reason to treat assessments of dangerousness more rigorously than other types of evidence. When using evidence to decide on guilt or innocence, there are usually multiple sources of evidence providing mutual support. But when assessments of violence are undertaken at sentencing, the result could depend on the application of a single ARAI. Further, the assessment is often doing something more ambitious than much expert evidence does. Where guilt determination is concerned, there are good reasons to restrict experts to testifying about the degree of support their evidence lends to the prosecution case, for instance, by saying that 'my analysis provides strong support for the hypothesis that the defendant's shoe left the mark found at the scene of crime'. A principal reason for this is logical: if the expert says 'the defendant's shoe left the mark', she is making assumptions about the prior odds on guilt—in less technical terms, about the other evidence in the case. For example, there might be strong evidence that D was seen wearing the shoes at a different location at the time the crime was committed. For similar reasons, in the discussion of the probative value of bad character evidence in earlier chapters, the evidence was analysed as a multiplier: making the defendant's guilt more likely. But ARAIs classify—the offender is high risk, or has a 50 per cent probability of offending—rather than just saying that he is so many times more likely to offend than the average offender.[63] This is a grander claim, and may give the impression that other evidence cannot affect the risk. The claim also makes assumptions about base rates—an issue to which I

[59] D. J. Cooke and C. Michie, 'Limitations of Diagnostic Precision and Predictive Utility in the Individual Case: A Challenge for Forensic Practice' (2010) 34 *Law & Human Behav* 259, 270.

[60] '[I]t is simply unintelligible to employ frequentist confidence intervals to describe the precision of actuarial risk estimates': N. Scurich and R. S. John, 'A Bayesian Approach to the Group Versus Individual Prediction Controversy in Actuarial Risk Assessment' (2012) 36 *Law & Human Behav* 237, 243. See also D. Mossman and T. M. Selke, 'Avoiding Errors about "Margins of Error"' (2007) 191 *Brit J Psychiatry* 561; G. T. Harris, M. E. Rice, and V. L. Quinsey, 'Shall Evidence-Based Risk Assessment Be Abandoned?' (2008) 192 *Brit J Psychiatry* 154; and R. K. Hanson and P. D. Howard, 'Individual Confidence Intervals Do Not Inform Decision-Makers about the Accuracy of Risk Assessment Evaluations' (2010) 34 *Law & Human Behav* 275.

[61] Scurich and John, 'A Bayesian Approach'.

[62] See Harris et al, 'Shall Evidence-Based Risk Assessment Be Abandoned?'.

[63] Hart and Cooke, 'Another Look', at 96–7, suggest that this sort of comparative assessment would be less objectionable, as long as it avoids spurious precision.

return below. For now, the point is that assessments of dangerousness potentially make strong claims.

Experts disagree on the implications of wide confidence intervals for forensic practice. While Hart and Cooke seem to be in favour of abandoning predictions of violence,[64] others are less concerned.[65] One point in favour of current practice in England and Wales is that OASys and RM2000 tend to use broad risk categories—low, medium, high, very high—thus avoiding giving the impression that they can be especially precise—as they would if they talked about, say, a 47 per cent chance of reoffending. There are, however, other problems with ARAIs. Even ignoring the issue of confidence levels for individual offenders, they have limited accuracy in predicting offending. The most common way of assessing the reliability of ARAIs has been to use a statistic called 'area under the curve' (AUC). ARAIs typically have an AUC of around 0.72.[66] What this means is that if for a particular ARAI the AUC is 0.75, then if a person is chosen at random from the pool of recidivists and another is chosen at random from the pool of non-recidivists, there is a 75 per cent chance that the recidivist would have a higher score for risk of reoffending than the non-recidivist. An AUC of 0.75 is considerably better than chance (0.5), although some way off perfection. The AUC statistic measures discrimination, how well the instrument distinguishes between recidivists and non-recidivists. Discrimination, however, gives limited insight regarding the performance of an ARAI. If an ARAI classified all recidivists as having a 0.95 risk of reoffending, and all non-recidivists as having a 0.90 risk, the AUC would be 1. But this would not be much comfort to the non-recidivists, who might well be detained on the basis of their supposed high risk of offending. The AUC tells us little about the ability of an ARAI to predict recidivism.[67]

Assessing the predictive ability, or calibration, of an ARAI, is not straightforward (this is one reason why analysis in terms of AUC became popular). Tables 12.1 and 12.2 give some figures from research using the OVP (OASys Violence Predictor), with a two-year follow-up period.[68] The OVP has an AUC of around 0.74, which suggests that it discriminates slightly better than most ARAIs.[69]

For homicide and wounding (Table 12.1), recidivism is very rare. This is unsurprising, as serious violence is rare. There are a large number of false positives (1,459) even when a high risk threshold is used as the prediction criterion. But

[64] 'Another Look', 98–9.

[65] See Scurich and John, 'A Bayesian Approach'; and J. L. Skeem and J. Monahan, 'Current Directions in Violence Risk Assessment' (2011) 21 *Current Directions in Psychol Sci* 38.

[66] See S. Fazel, J. P. Singh, H. Doll, and M. Grann, 'Use of Risk Assessment Instruments to Predict Violence and Antisocial Behaviour in 73 Samples Involving 24 827 People: Systematic Review and Meta-Analysis' (2012) *BMJ* 345:e4692; doi: 10.1136/bmj.e4692, 4.

[67] J. P. Singh, 'Predictive Validity Performance Indicators in Violence Risk Assessment: A Methodological Primer' (2013) 31 *Behav Sci & Law* 8, 19.

[68] From Howard and Dixon, 'Construction and Validation', 301. It should be stressed that the risk categories (medium/very high) are not the actual ones used when the OVP is applied—they were constructed in order to compare OVP with another risk assessment instrument for research purposes. The data, however, are useful to illustrate the complexities of prediction, which is the reason I make use of them here.

[69] Howard and Dixon, 'Construction and Validation', 299.

Table 12.1 Homicide and Wounding (10,000 Offender Sample)

	Offend	Predicted	TP	FP	FN	TN	PPV
Medium risk or above	90	8,841	89	8,752	1	1,158	1%
Very high risk	90	1,495	36	1,459	54	8,451	2%

TP = true positives; FP = false positives; FN = false negatives; TN = true negatives; PPV = positive predictive value

Table 12.2 All Violent Offences (10,000 Offender Sample)

	Offend	Predicted	TP	FP	FN	TN	PPV
Medium risk or above	2,750	8,840	2,705	6,135	45	1,115	31%
Very high risk	2,750	1,495	856	639	1,893	6,612	57%

TP = true positives; FP = false positives; FN = false negatives; TN = true negatives; PPV = positive predictive value

when a low risk threshold is used, there are few false negatives (one): very few seriously violent offenders escape the net. That, however, comes at a high cost: if we detain all those predicted to be violent, then nearly 9,000 offenders are detained in order to prevent 90 very serious offences. With a higher risk threshold, fewer would be detained, but the majority of those would still be false positives and there would be a considerable number of false negatives. The final column in the table gives figures for positive predictive value (PPV), which is the proportion of offenders predicted to reoffend who do reoffend.[70] If we are interested in how many false positives there will be if we adopt a certain risk level for decisions about incapacitation, this is a useful measure. The PPVs for homicide and wounding are very low, reflecting the high proportion of false positives at both risk levels.

Once the focus shifts to violence in general (Table 12.2), the higher risk threshold gives a much lower number of false positives (639). By detaining 1,495 offenders we would expect to prevent 856 violent offences. There will be a large number of false negatives which we could reduce (from 1,893 to 45) by opting for the lower threshold, but this would come at the cost of detaining many more people and a near tenfold increase in the number of false positives. Perhaps, then, it would be tempting to use the higher risk threshold for policy purposes, and detain those judged to be at very high risk in order to prevent many violent offences. But 'violent offences' is a broad category, including homicide, assault, threats and harassment, violent acquisitive offences, public order, criminal damage, and weapon possession.[71] Many offences in this category would be relatively trivial

[70] PPV can be calculated by the following formula: PPV = TP/(TP + FP). See Singh, 'Predictive Validity Performance Indicators', 10.

[71] Howard and Dixon, 'Construction and Validation', 291.

(and would not meet the CJA's 'serious harm' criterion for dangerousness), so it is by no means obvious that a strategy of incapacitation would be worthwhile. This reflects the point made in the previous chapter, that while there is some evidence that incapacitation works, incapacitative strategies come at a high cost in terms of an increased prison population, so that unless serious crime is prevented, the policy may fail on cost-benefit grounds.

The foregoing is not intended as a criticism of OVP, but rather to illustrate some of the complications involved in assessing the predictive ability of an ARAI. There are obvious trade-offs: if we lower the threshold, this will decrease false negatives, but increase false positives. The base-rate of offending also has an impact: the rarer the type of offending, the more difficult it is to predict recidivism, leading to significant numbers of false positives and false negatives. And more serious types of offending—those where we might think an incapacitative strategy worthwhile—tend, of course, to be rarer.

The figures derived from the study of the OVP are probably reasonably representative. Recent meta-analyses of several ARAIs find that the mean rate of violence for individuals classified as high risk (ie PPV) was 55 per cent,[72] while the rate of violence for those classified as moderate or high risk was 41 per cent.[73] Prediction of sexual offending seems to be less successful: 23 per cent of those judged to be moderate or high risk go on to commit a sexual offence.[74] But, as the example using the OVP helps to show, these figures are sensitive to the base rate of violence, and base rates vary between studies: 'although the median annual rate of violence in high-risk groups is 12.9 per cent, half of samples reported rates which were either below 6.5 per cent or above 19.0 per cent'.[75] As many ARAIs were developed using research on populations with relatively high base rates of violence, the predictive ability of the instruments might be much less when used on a general criminal justice population.[76] The OVP research, however, was based on a general sample of offenders in England and Wales,[77] so the quoted PPV is probably a good indication of the OVP's predictive ability in this jurisdiction at the current time.

---

[72] J. P. Singh, S. Fazel, R. Gueorguiva, and A. Buchanan, 'Rates of Violence in Patients Classified as High Risk by Structured Risk Assessment Instruments' (2014) 204 *BJ Psych* 180, 182.

[73] Fazel et al, 'Use of Risk Assessment Instruments', 4.

[74] Fazel et al, 'Use of Risk Assessment Instruments', 4.

[75] Singh et al, 'Rates of Violence', 183.

[76] See A. Buchanan, 'Re: "Use of Risk Assessment Instruments to Predict Violence and Antisocial Behaviour in 73 Samples Involving 24 827 People: Systematic Review and Meta-Analysis"' Letter, (2012) *BMJ*, at <http://www.bmj.com/content/345/bmj.e4692/rr/598010>. For research illustrating this, see Rossegger et al, 'Replicating the Violence Risk Appraisal Guide', showing that when VRAG was replicated on a general criminal justice population in Switzerland, 43 per cent of those in the highest risk bin offended, compared to 100 per cent in the original study; 50 per cent in the second highest bin offended, compared to 76 per cent. The base rate in the original sample was 31 per cent, compared to 17 per cent in the Swiss study.

[77] See Howard and Dixon, 'Construction and Validation', 292. The sample included 'all OASys assessments of offenders subject to pre-sentence reports, commencing community sentences, or supervision upon release from custody'. Thus, the least serious offenders will have been excluded, but this is still a broad sample.

What are the implications of these figures? Some writers are critical of the predictive ability of ARAIs. After an analysis of discriminatory ability, Yang, Wong, and Coid conclude that 'because of their moderate level of predictive accuracy, [risk assessment instruments] should not be used as the sole or primary means for clinical or criminal justice decision making that is contingent on a high level of predictive accuracy, such as preventive detention'.[78] Focussing on predictive ability, Fazel et al suggest that 'risk assessment tools in their current form can only be used to roughly classify individuals at the group level, and not to safely determine criminal prognosis in an individual case'.[79] Perhaps this lends some justification to what seems to be the dominant practice in England and Wales: to use broad risk categories and to combine the use of ARAIs with judgment. But what is more debatable is whether the level of certainty of reoffending associated with even vague categorizations such as 'high' or 'very high' risk justifies the preventive detention practices found in the Criminal Justice Act.

Before trying to address that question, it is worth making a couple of clarifications. First, while the discussion has concentrated on ARAIs, the focus on a particular type of risk assessment is not significant when it comes to questions of predictive ability. Actuarial assessment is often contrasted with clinical judgment, but we have no reason to think that the latter would predict with more accuracy (indeed, the opposite is probably the case).[80] 'Structured professional judgment' lies somewhere between the two—clinical analysis is guided by prescribed risk factors, but scoring is not automatic—and seems to be as accurate as actuarial assessment.[81] Second, by some measures ARAIs perform remarkably well. The criticism is sometimes made that a PPV of 50 per cent 'is the level of chance prediction, or, in other words, only as accurate as tossing a coin'.[82] But looking at the figures for the OPV, in the condition where the PPV is 57 per cent, only 1,495 of 10,000 offenders were predicted to recidivate; this prediction was right in just over half of cases. Given a base rate of 28 per cent, that is quite impressive. Had we tossed a coin, we might expect to predict recidivism in 5,000 of the 10,000 cases. If we were right in half of the cases where the offender did reoffend (chance level), then we would get it right in 1,375 cases, but wrong in the remaining 3,625, achieving a PPV of 28 per cent. Even in the homicide and wounding example, where OVP's PPV is an unimpressive 2 per cent, coin tossing would do

[78] 'The Efficacy of Violence Prediction', 761.

[79] 'Use of Risk Assessment Instruments', 5. Cf M. E. Rice, G. T. Harris, and C. Lang, 'Validation of and Revision to the VRAG and SORAG: The Violence Risk Appraisal Guide—Revised (VRAG-R)' (2013) 25 *Psychol Assessment* 951, 961. The authors note Fazel et al's sceptical conclusion, and comment: 'this leaves practitioners and criminal justice professionals, when decisions must be made, with no better method to use instead'. This is true, and it may be that for some decisions, such as treatment or supervision decisions, ARAIs should be used. But the critical question is whether current risk assessment technologies are good enough to justify policies of incapacitation, or whether such policies should be abandoned.

[80] See Skeem and Monahan, 'Current Directions in Violence Risk Assessment'.

[81] Singh et al, 'Rates of Violence', 184.

[82] A. Roychowdhury and G. Adshead, 'Violence Risk Assessment as Medical Intervention: Ethical Tensions' (2014) 38 *Psychiatric Bull* 75, 79.

far worse (0.1 per cent). There can be no question that ARAIs identify factors associated with recidivism. The question is whether they do so well enough to justify preventive detention.

12.5 How Dangerous Is Dangerous?

The account above depicts ARAIs as having limited predictive ability. The statistics given for the OVP, however, do not show that instrument in its best light. When OVP scores are broken down into a more refined 10-point scale, then the two highest risk categories do a good job of predicting a middling category of violence: homicide and assault. 63 per cent of those with a score of 80 to 90 reoffended, as did 75.5 per cent with a score of 90 to 100.[83] Small numbers of offenders in a general criminal justice population, then, can be predicted to be violent—where violence excludes such things as criminal damage and public order offences, but is not limited to the most serious offences—with a reasonable degree of reliability.[84]

At this point, it may be useful to introduce another technical measure. The number needed to detain (NND) is the number of individuals we need to detain in order to prevent a single offence, given the predictive ability of a risk assessment tool. NND is simply the inverse of PPV.[85] Returning to the OVP figures in the tables above, the 2 per cent PPV for very high risk classifications of homicide and wounding gives an NND of 50; the 57 per cent PPV for very high risk classifications of violence in general gives an NND of 2. The trade-off is again obvious: serious violence is well worth preventing but difficult to spot, while once a very wide definition of violence is adopted, prediction is much easier. But with the score of 90 and above for homicide and assault, noted in the previous paragraph, the NND would be close to 1. An incapacitative sentencing strategy which concentrated on such an extremely high risk category might be justifiable: there would be relatively few false positives. It would, however, apply to very few offenders.

The approach to dangerousness in the Criminal Justice Act is much wider than this. The Act defines dangerousness as 'significant risk to members of the public of serious harm', including psychological harm.[86] 'Significant' has been interpreted as 'a higher threshold than mere possibility of occurrence and...can be taken to mean (as in the Oxford Dictionary) "noteworthy, of considerable amount or

---

[83] Howard and Dixon, 'Construction and Validation', 299. That this is a small group is obvious from a comparison with the figures in table 7, at 301.

[84] A new version of the VRAG (VRAG-R) also performs very well in the top risk category, with an 80 per cent five-year violence recidivism rate using a fairly robust definition of violence (see Rice et al, 'Validation of and Revision to the VRAG and SORAG'). About 10 per cent of the sample fell into this category. However, the high base rate (50 per cent) and the fact that many subjects in the study had been found not guilty by reason of insanity make this of questionable relevance to the typical defendant at risk of incapacitation under the CJA provisions.

[85] See Singh, 'Predictive Validity Performance Indicators', 10.   [86] CJA 2003, s 224.

importance".'[87] This does not even seem to require that violence is more likely than not. Can we predict that well? The OVP figures for homicide and wounding (a category which may be a reasonable fit for 'serious harm') suggest not: a 2 per cent risk of violence is not really 'significant'. But suppose we can predict serious harm to the sort of level envisaged by the CJA provisions. If we can identify a group with a 33 per cent risk of causing serious harm,[88] that might meet the 'significant' criterion. The NND would be 3.

Should we submit three offenders to preventive detention in order to prevent one crime which causes serious harm? Even under a purely desert-based sentencing model we would be imprisoning such people for some period of time; the question is whether the sentence should be enhanced on preventive grounds. It is not a question which can be answered easily. Supposing that the enhanced sentence prevented crime in the ratio suggested by the NND, the question—should we detain the three—seems to be one which is purely about trade-offs. I shall not attempt to answer it, except to suggest that an NND of 3 (and this can only be a subjective opinion) looks to be at the borderline of what is acceptable. In reality, any attempt to predict who among a group of violent offenders will cause serious harm in the future probably has to accept a much higher NND, one which will be extremely hard to defend.

12.6 Prediction, Incapacitation, and Time

There is one very significant complication to the discussion of predictive ability which has not been mentioned so far. As Ashworth points out,[89] an offender who has committed an offence serious enough to be considered under the provisions of the CJA described at the beginning of this chapter will often face a substantial term of imprisonment even if preventive concerns are not considered. So what we really need to be able to do is to predict whether an offender may reoffend after, say, five or ten years' imprisonment. We know that risk of offending declines over time, and this may mean that the longer the normal sentence, the less risk the offender will pose when released.[90] On the other hand, as noted in the previous

[87] *Lang* [2006] 2 Cr App R (S) 3, [2005] EWCA Crim 2864, [17].

[88] For the OVP, this is exactly the level of prediction for a very high risk category in relation to homicide and assault. See Howard and Dixon, 'Construction and Validation', 301.

[89] A. Ashworth, *Sentencing and Criminal Justice* (5th edn, Cambridge: Cambridge University Press, 2010), 237. See also A. von Hirsch and L. Kazemian, 'Predictive Sentencing and Selective Incapacitation' in A. von Hirsch, A. Ashworth, and J. Roberts (eds), *Principled Sentencing: Readings on Theory and Policy* (3rd edn, Oxford: Hart Publishing, 2009), 98.

[90] This problem helps to make the case for indeterminate sentences such as IPP. Because it is hard to predict risk in five years' time—especially as imprisonment should offer offenders the chance to address the causes of their offending—there is in theory a case to be made for reassessing risk after the offender has served a certain number of years, and conditioning release on this. See, generally, C. Slobogin, 'Prevention as the Primary Goal of Sentencing: The Modern Case for Indeterminate Dispositions in Criminal Cases' (2011) 48 *San Diego L Rev* 1127. However, IPP was such a disaster that the case for indeterminate sentencing has not been made out in practice.

chapter, there is some support for the view that time spent in prison does not decrease risk. Building on the finding that recidivism rates tend to be similar between those released from custody and those serving non-custodial sentences, Macleod, Grove, and Farrington argue that:

There is... no evidence... that criminal careers terminate during incarceration rather than at the point of conviction, in fact to the contrary. We therefore conclude that there is no overall crime reduction brought about by incapacitation except where offenders are incarcerated for a large proportion of their adult lives.[91]

This is a serious problem for preventive sentencing strategies. Either incapacitation works, in which case there is yet another source of doubt about the predictions on which incapacitation is based, or incapacitation is ineffective, and extended sentences—unless they are extremely long—merely delay reoffending.

12.7 Pure Preventive Detention

I have argued that incapacitative sentencing can be justified in theory, on the basis that crime prevention is a legitimate aim of punishment, and that incapacitation does not treat offenders as lacking moral agency. As noted earlier, this sort of argument faces an obvious criticism. It could potentially justify what might be called pure preventive detention:[92] the incapacitation of someone who fits certain risk factors, but who has not committed a crime.

This issue is one which has arisen in different guises at various points in this book. If we accept that previous convictions can be used to prove guilt, then it may be hard to argue against using evidence of the defendant's non-criminal behaviour—such as his bad temper—as evidence of guilt. Some might find this unsettling. A similar problem was noted in the previous chapter. If the absence of previous convictions is relevant to sentence on the basis of progressive loss of mitigation, it would seem that the prosecution should be allowed to dig into the offender's past to see if he really does have a good character. But in the present context, the stakes look to be even higher. Locking up law-abiding citizens because they have traits which can be used to classify them as dangerous is rather more disturbing than using a defendant's anti-social behaviour as evidence of guilt or as a reason for rejecting the mitigating force of a clean criminal record. Indeed, that arguments for incapacitative sentencing threaten to slide into arguments for pure preventive detention might be seen as a *reductio ad absurdum* of the incapacitative argument.[93]

---

[91] J. F. Macleod, P. G. Grove, and D. P. Farrington, *Explaining Criminal Careers: Implications for Justice Policy* (Oxford: Oxford University Press, 2012), 220.

[92] The phrase is used in S. J. Morse, 'Neither Desert Nor Disease' (1999) 5 *Legal Theory* 265.

[93] See P. Ramsay, 'Imprisonment under the Precautionary Principle' in G. R. Sullivan and I. Dennis (eds), *Seeking Security: Pre-Empting the Commission of Criminal Harms* (Oxford: Hart Publishing, 2012), 199; and Kramer, *The Ethics of Capital Punishment*, 147–8. Wood takes the argument further, arguing that embracing incapacitation as a punishment aim entails *punishing* dangerous

One way to resist the *reductio* argument is to contend that there is something special about criminal conviction which permits the state to take coercive action. The Floud report talked of a presumption of harmlessness which is lost on conviction,[94] and Walen takes a similar approach, endorsing a presumption of law-abidingness.[95] As I suggested in Chapter 4, it is not obvious what would justify a presumption of harmlessness which would operate in this way, in particular being lost on conviction rather than eroded by evidence of dangerousness. Further, if the presumption of harmlessness is a sound normative principle, then it also appears to apply in the context of criminal evidence. If so, then, as we saw, it would rule out using evidence of non-criminal behaviour as bad character evidence in the proof of guilt. While the use of non-criminal bad character evidence to prove guilt might sound disturbing, once certain examples become the point of focus—such as *Lewis*,[96] where possession of legal paedophile literature is used to prove child abuse, and *Norris*,[97] where expressions of extreme racism are used to prove racially motivated homicide—it seems to me to be problematic to insist on a sharp crime/non-crime distinction in the evidence context. This, then, provides a further reason to be suspicious of a strong presumption of harmlessness.

It might be argued that the threshold of criminal conviction is significant for another reason, connected to rule of law values. It is generally good if people are able to avoid punishment by making appropriate choices about their conduct, and no doubt the same applies to other liberty-depriving measures such as pure preventive detention.[98] Using conviction for a serious criminal offence as the trigger for preventive detention respects an 'opportunity to avoid' principle,[99] even if some of the factors which inform the assessment of dangerousness are unchosen (age and not having lived with both parents to age 16 would be examples of unchosen factors).[100] The obvious response to this, however, is that using chosen factors, such as anti-social behaviour, as the primary requirement for pure preventive detention

---

non-offenders: D. Wood, 'Dangerous Offenders and the Morality of Protective Sentencing' [1988] *Crim LR* 424.

[94] J. E. Floud and W. Young, *Dangerousness and Criminal Justice* (London: Heinemann, 1981), 44.

[95] A. Walen, 'A Punitive Precondition for Preventive Detention: Lost Status as a Foundation for a Lost Immunity' (2011) 48 *San Diego L Rev* 1229.

[96] (1983) 76 Cr App R 33.   [97] [2013] EWCA Crim 712.

[98] Cf Morse, 'Neither Desert Nor Disease', 298, who argues that because desert is not involved, legality is not an issue in pure preventive detention.

[99] On the importance of fair opportunity to avoid in criminal law, see, eg, D. O. Brink and D. K. Nelkin, 'Fairness and the Architecture of Responsibility' in D. Shoemaker (ed), *Oxford Studies in Agency and Responsibility: Volume 1* (Oxford: Oxford University Press, 2013). More practically, note the judgment of the ECtHR in *M* v *Germany* (2010) 51 EHRR 41, [90]: 'where a national law authorises deprivation of liberty it must be sufficiently accessible, precise and foreseeable in its application, in order to avoid all risk of arbitrariness. The standard of "lawfulness" set by the Convention thus requires that all law be sufficiently precise to allow the person—if need be, with appropriate advice—to foresee, to a degree that is reasonable in the circumstances, the consequences which a given action may entail.'

[100] The latter is a factor scored in VRAG (death of a parent is an exception).

would respect the opportunity to avoid principle, especially if the factors were publicized in advance.[101] But in any case, while an opportunity to avoid liberty-depriving measures may be desirable, the principle does not appear to be absolute. We permit pure preventive detention of the mentally disordered and those with contagious diseases.[102]

Several commentators think that the detention of the mentally disordered can be distinguished from the detention of other dangerous people: the former, unlike the latter, lack autonomy.[103] But this does not seem to me to be a useful distinction. I have argued that preventive detention does not show a lack of respect for autonomy. Nor is there a bright line between the mentally disordered and others. While we treat mentally disordered people as lacking responsibility for the purposes of criminal liability, it is too sweeping to say that the mentally disordered who might be subject to preventive civil commitment lack autonomy, while on the other side of the line many of those subject to incapacitation under the CJA provisions will have personality disorders or other mental health problems, so might be thought to lack full autonomy.[104] Indeed, Szmukler suggests that allowing the mentally disordered, but not others, to be subject to civil preventive detention is discriminatory, especially as there is little reason to think that one group is more treatable than the other.[105]

I am not convinced, therefore, that there is a way for those who endorse incapacitation as a sentencing aim to resist the push of the *reductio* argument: the possibility of pure preventive detention does seem to follow from incapacitative sentencing. But I do doubt that the *reductio* leads to absurdity given that we allow preventive detention in other contexts. Further, it is hard to see how a person could be classified as dangerous with anything like the degree of rigour which would be needed to justify liberty deprivation unless he had committed a serious criminal offence. Previous criminal behaviour is the best predictor of future criminal behaviour. Even in the sentencing context, I have questioned whether our predictive ability is good enough to justify the use of incapacitation in the vast majority of cases. The evidential base for pure preventive detention is even less likely to be satisfied, especially given the low base rate for serious violence among the general population.

[101] Another way to respond to concerns about legality would be to criminalize dangerousness. See D. Husak, 'Lifting the Cloak: Preventive Detention as Punishment' (2011) 48 *San Diego L Rev* 1173; and D. Husak, 'Preventive Detention as Punishment? Some Possible Obstacles' in A. Ashworth, L. Zedner, and P. Tomlin (eds), *Prevention and the Limits of the Criminal Law* (Oxford: Oxford University Press, 2013).

[102] See Ashworth and Zedner, *Preventive Justice*, ch 9.

[103] See S. J. Schulhofer, 'Two Systems of Social Protection: Comments on the Civil-Criminal Distinction, with Particular Reference to Sexually Violent Predator Laws' (1996) 7 *J Contemp Legal Issues* 69. For similar arguments, see Morse, 'Neither Desert Nor Disease', and Ferzan, 'Beyond Crime and Commitment', although both allow that some dangerous non-offenders might be detained under an analogy with self-defence.

[104] This was the case for IPP, and no doubt will continue to be the situation under the CJA dangerousness provisions: see Peay, *Mental Health and Crime*.

[105] G. Szmukler, 'Risk Assessment: "Numbers" and "Values"' (2003) 27 *Psychiatric Bull* 205.

The above considerations suggest that there is a good pragmatic case for requiring conviction for a serious crime before allowing preventive detention on grounds of criminal dangerousness, at least for those who do not fall under the provisions of the Mental Health Act.[106] This would act as a 'failsafe', in von Hirsch and Ashworth's terms,[107] giving some assurance that the evidential threshold was met, and would also speak to the principle of fair opportunity to avoid.

So far, I have suggested that the spectre of pure preventive detention does not undermine the case for adopting incapacitation as a sentencing aim. A further question is whether it is right to classify prevention as punishment: perhaps incapacitation under a sentencing regime is really pure preventive detention. Suppose D commits GBH, and would normally be given a sentence of ten years for the crime on the basis of retributive considerations. Because he is classified as dangerous, however, he is given a life sentence under CJA, section 224A, and may be imprisoned for much longer than the five years which would be the normal release date for a ten-year sentence. What is the connection between the extra time for which D is detained and the offence of GBH which he committed? When detained for the extra time, is D really being punished? 'One can "restrain," "detain," or "incapacitate" a dangerous person,' claims Robinson, 'but one cannot logically "punish" dangerousness.'[108] This matters because if incapacitation is not punishment, it might be better taken out of the criminal courts. Indeed, Robinson's argument is that incapacitation should be separated from the criminal law because it has come to distort punishment: among other problems, the incapacitative part of the sentence is not deserved, and the offender should be held in non-punitive conditions. Others, however, think there are reasons to keep incapacitation of the non-mentally disordered within the criminal law, with its high level of procedural protections.[109]

One way to bring incapacitation within the ambit of punishment is to argue that being dangerous is blameworthy. There is reason to think we can rightly be blamed for our characters. As Sher notes, much behaviour flows fairly directly from character.[110] When S shows indifference to the suffering of other people, we might criticize her. If she responds 'that's just the way I am, I find it hard to care about other people', it is unlikely that we would change our attitude to her. In this

---

[106] Although note Szmukler's argument (in 'Risk Assessment') that this should be the threshold for all preventive detention.

[107] A. von Hirsch and A. Ashworth, *Proportionate Sentencing: Exploring the Principles* (Oxford: Oxford University Press, 2005), 56.

[108] P. H. Robinson, *Distributive Principles of Criminal Law: Who Should be Punished How Much* (Oxford: Oxford University Press, 2008), 113.

[109] See Husak, 'Lifting the Cloak'; and Slobogin, 'Prevention as the Primary Goal of Sentencing'. The ECtHR is also suspicious of attempts to avoid procedural protections by classifying measures as non-penal: see *M* v *Germany*, (2010) 51 EHRR 41, [126]–[127].

[110] G. Sher, *In Praise of Blame* (Oxford: Oxford University Press, 2006), ch 4. For similar arguments, see A. M. Smith, 'Control, Responsibility, and Moral Assessment' (2008) 138 *Phil Studies* 367; R. M. Adams, 'Involuntary Sins' (1985) 94 *Phil Rev* 3; and T. M. Scanlon, *What We Owe to Each Other* (Harvard: Harvard University Press, 1998), 267–94.

example, we seem to be blaming S for who she is. It would be artificial to distinguish between S's failure to care about others and S herself.[111] This implies that punishment for character traits might be appropriate, a conclusion Sher memorably describes as 'a bit too interesting'.[112] The move to punishing for character might be questioned by noting that there are plenty of things which are morally wrong and blameworthy which we do not punish—lying and having racist views, for example. Criminal law stops far short of attempting to mirror morality, and the role of principles such as the harm principle in restraining criminal law's reach is well known.[113] But where dangerousness is concerned, harm does play a role in justifying state intervention. Might the combination of risk of future harm and blameworthiness suggest that there is a desert basis for preventive detention? Under this approach, D's extra time in custody would be justified as being deserved punishment for the 'wrong' of dangerousness.[114] That is a possible way of thinking about dangerousness and punishment. Indeed, Husak has argued that in some instances of incapacitation, long sentences will be justified as being proportional to the underlying wrong.[115] His paradigm example, however, is terrorists who pose risks of mass destruction, and in the sort of case which concerns us—an offender who poses a risk of causing death or serious harm—the proportionality question is not so easy to resolve.

While the desert argument might play some role in justifying the fairness of punishing for dangerousness, I am cautious about putting too much weight on it. An alternative argument is that incapacitation can be classified as punishment on non-desert grounds. Note that the argument against classifying the incapacitative part of a sentence as punishment could equally be applied to a sentence justified on the basis of deterrence. If the reason for sentencing D to custody is not desert, but to deter him from reoffending, or to deter others from offending, then in what sense is he being punished for the crime of GBH which he committed? But to conclude that the sentence imposed to deter is not punishment would be to allow desert to answer all questions about punishment.[116] If it is reasonable to say that the deterrent sentence is punishment, then surely the same can be said for an incapacitative sentence. If commission of a serious crime such as GBH is required before an incapacitative sentence is imposed, then it seems appropriate to call that sentence punishment. Classifying the sentence as punishment, however, does not

---

[111] Sher also argues that blame for character does not depend on whether S is responsible for her character, although in the criminal context this would raise issues about opportunity to avoid, discussed above.

[112] *In Praise of Blame*, 67.

[113] See D. Husak, *Overcriminalization: The Limits of the Criminal Law* (Oxford: Oxford University Press, 2007). See also R. A. Duff, *Answering for Crime: Responsibility and Liability in the Criminal Law* (Oxford: Hart Publishing, 2007), ch 4; and A. P. Simester and A. von Hirsch, *Crimes, Harms, and Wrongs* (Oxford: Hart Publishing, 2011).

[114] See Ramsay, 'Imprisonment'.

[115] Husak, 'Preventive Detention as Punishment?', 192. Husak is here discussing proportionality in a context where possessing certain attributes predictive of terrorism has been made a specific criminal offence.

[116] See T. McPherson, 'Punishment: Definition and Justification' (1967) 28 *Analysis* 21.

entail that the conditions of detention should be punitive. If desert requires hard treatment, then it might be the case that the desert part of a sentence should be served in punitive conditions, whereas the extended incapacitative part should be served in non-punitive conditions.[117]

12.8 Conclusion

In this chapter, I have noted the significance of dangerousness in modern sentencing law and explored the justifications for incapacitation as a sentencing aim. While I suggested that incapacitation can be justified theoretically, in practice things are much bleaker. In some ways, risk assessment instruments perform remarkably well, picking out factors connected with recidivism and predicting violence well above chance level. But in populations with a relatively low base rate for violence, such as a general criminal justice population, there are very significant doubts as to whether risk assessment instruments predict serious violence well enough to justify preventive detention in more than a few cases. The NND statistic was used as a way of exploring this. Of course, it is possible that risk assessment instruments will improve on current predictive ability: that is one reason why it is worth exploring arguments around incapacitation rather than writing it off as a lost cause. Some, however, suspect that we have more or less reached the limits of prediction.[118] In any case, there is an even more worrying possibility: that incapacitation simply does not work, because it delays reoffending rather than shortens an offender's career.

While IPP has been abolished, the Criminal Justice Act still contains provisions which allow dangerous offenders to be subjected to longer than normal sentences and indeterminate (life) sentences. Even if I am wrong to criticize the policy of incapacitation, there is little reason to think that the new scheme will operate well. Whatever their limitations, carefully applied risk assessment tools are our best means of assessing dangerousness. Yet under IPP trial judges often relied on their own hunches about dangerousness.[119] This is unlikely to change; indeed, one can discern a similarly complacent attitude in the Court of Appeal's treatment of the post-LASPO provisions.[120] Judges are not bound by the risk

---

[117] This is not a straightforward issue. It is certainly questionable just how punitive the conditions of a desert-based custodial sentence should be, given that liberty deprivation is in itself hard treatment (see K. Drenkhahn, C. Morgenstern, and D. van Zyl Smit, 'What Is in a Name? Preventive Detention in Germany in the Shadow of European Human Rights Law' [2012] *Crim LR* 167, 186). Further, if, as suggested above, there is some desert basis for punishing dangerousness, the gap between the desert and incapacitative regimes may not be that large—and no doubt, in practice, that is one reason why incapacitative sentences are regarded as penal.

[118] See Yang et al, 'The Efficacy of Violence Prediction', 761. Cf Rice et al, 'Validation of and Revision to the VRAG and SORAG', 961.

[119] See Jacobson and Hough, *Unjust Deserts*, 29.

[120] See *Burinskas*, [2014] EWCA Crim 334, [80] ('by any measure he is highly dangerous'); [180] ('[w]e have not the slightest doubt that the judge was entitled to find the appellant dangerous and was correct to do so. No one who has listened to the facts could come to a different conclusion').

assessment in the pre-sentence report,[121] and in any case the risk levels in OASys and the OVP are expressed in terms of low, medium, high, and very high, so there is room for manoeuvre in linking these to the CJA requirement of significant risk. Only 6 per cent of offenders given IPP sentences were classified as being very high risk ('imminent risk of harm'); 68 per cent were high risk ('identifiable indicators of risk . . . [violence] could happen any time'); and the remaining 26 per cent were classified as low ('no significant, current indicators of risk of harm') or medium risk ('unlikely to [cause harm] unless there is a change of circumstances').[122] Even taking these designations at face value, there can surely be little justification for that last quarter being given preventive sentences.

Throughout this book, I have argued that character has a legitimate role to play in fact-finding and sentencing decisions in the criminal trial. But asking character to predict reoffending with sufficient certainty to justify incapacitation of large numbers of offenders is to ask too much of it. In this chapter, I have shown how certain technical measures, such as positive predictive value and number needed to detain, can be used to give a rough assessment of what we do when we use risk assessment in preventive sentencing. If we are to continue to go down the incapacitative path, as no doubt we will, policy-makers and judges should at least use these measures to explain who they think should be incapacitated and what they expect to gain from it.

---

[121] See *Lang*, [2006] 2 Cr App R (S) 3, [2005] EWCA Crim 2864, [17].
[122] See M. Debidin (ed), *A Compendium of Research and Analysis on the Offender Management System (OASys) 2006–2009* (London: Ministry of Justice, 2009), 225. The risk descriptors can be found in L. Gianquitto, 'Highly Subjective Assessment' (2010) *Inside Time* at: <http://www.inside-time.co.uk/articleview.asp?a=722&c=highly_subjective_assessment>.

13

Conclusion

Across the course of this book, I have examined the use of the defendant's character in evidence law and sentencing, and also looked briefly at character theories of criminal liability. In all of these domains, character is controversial and its use raises complex theoretical and empirical issues. In this brief conclusion, I summarize some of the ground covered in earlier chapters, and then look more broadly at the significance of the trend of increasing reliance on character in the criminal trial.

13.1 Summary

During the course of the twentieth century, the law of evidence in common law jurisdictions was sceptical of admitting evidence of the defendant's bad character as propensity evidence—to show that because the defendant has committed crimes before he is more likely to have committed the current crime. In England and Wales, that situation has now changed, with the Criminal Justice Act 2003 ushering in a much more liberal admissibility regime. This has brought evidence law more into line with sentencing, where character has played a more prominent role. I argued that the CJA provisions on propensity evidence were by and large a sensible reform of evidence law. This argument proceeded in several steps: I reviewed the empirical evidence on recidivism and on the prejudicial nature of bad character evidence. I also examined the reasoning process underlying the use of propensity evidence and scrutinized the law prior to the CJA, showing that none of the formulations of the common law rule was satisfactory. There is plenty to criticize in the new law, but the courts seem to me to be drawing the admissibility line in a reasonable place. We have not moved to automatic admissibility: only convictions for cognate offences tend to come in, and the courts show a reasonable amount of awareness of the problems of stale convictions. No doubt many will not be persuaded by this argument. One issue is the uncertainty of admissibility under the new law. That uncertainty is put into perspective by the lack of predictability under the previous law and the difficulty of crafting any determinate rule which treats admissibility as a function of probative value. Some might prefer a higher admissibility threshold for bad character evidence. That is a respectable argument: one cannot be confident that bad character evidence poses no risk to trial fairness. But the story of the common law is, in part, a story of the failure of higher admissibility thresholds. It is true that the CJA requires 'substantial probative value' (rather than mere relevance) before bad character evidence is admitted against witnesses or by one defendant against another,[1] and this formulation might be thought to provide a model for a higher admissibility threshold where the prosecution seeks to use propensity evidence against a defendant. But in practice, the higher threshold seems to have had little impact in the co-defendant and witness contexts and a basic assessment of relevance governs admissibility. This may well be because once relevance has been established—especially as the thinking is that relevance requires some similarity between offences—it is not easy to conclude that probative value is not significant.

A recurrent theme in this book is the importance of analysing evidence carefully. Part of the case against the common law position on bad character evidence was that it was founded on a failure to understand how bad character evidence works—a failure often compounded by commentators. And if the basic admissibility scheme for propensity evidence under the CJA has worked well, with judges attuned to many of the significant factors affecting probative value, the confusions of the common law have not been entirely vanquished.[2] A reference to coincidence is too often a front for shoddy reasoning, and while this practice is often fairly innocuous, there are times when it leads to the strength of a case against a defendant being exaggerated, or not being analysed as carefully as it should be. Finally, when it comes to the use of bad character evidence to show a defendant's lack of credibility, the justifications simply do not stand up to close analysis.

If bad character evidence is often regarded with suspicion, good character evidence is usually seen in a much more favourable light. In the short review of the law in Chapter 10, I concluded that the practice of telling the jury when the defendant has no convictions is welcome. The consideration of good character provides a bridge to sentencing. The absence of previous convictions is regarded as a mitigating factor in sentencing, as is evidence of the offender's general good behaviour and positive social contributions. This may seem puzzling if things are seen from the perspective of culpability. That an offence is out of character does not, I suggested, make it less culpable. The best explanation of the relevance of character to sentence seems to be along the lines of von Hirsch's theory of progressive loss of mitigation: the defendant with good character is more likely to attend to the message of censure inherent in criminal conviction—a conclusion which could also be explained in terms of there being less need for deterrence and even by the possible utility of shaping offenders' self-conceptions as people who are

---

[1] Criminal Justice Act 2003, ss 100 and 101(1)(3). The Law Commission proposed that propensity evidence should only be admitted against a defendant where it had substantial probative value: Law Commission, *Evidence of Bad Character in Criminal Proceedings*, Law Com No 273 (London: TSO, 2001), 214.

[2] This was the argument in Chapter 8, on the basis of a reading of the case law. Here, as before the CJA came into force, commentators have helped to lead the courts astray. See, eg, the reference to common law cases and styles of argument in *Blackstone's Criminal Practice 2014* (Oxford: Oxford University Press, 2014), F12.48–12.61.

not doomed to recidivate. This line of thought might justify a modest recidivist premium, but after a few convictions flat-rate sentencing should prevail. While the courts may place too much weight on previous convictions in sentencing, the empirical evidence suggests that the aggravating effect of criminal record does not accumulate indefinitely, so practice is not too far removed from what seems to be justified in theory. If the use of character in the criminal trial often raises fears about stigmatizing offenders, this analysis of good character in sentencing suggests that character has a role to play in humanizing the trial, and making some defendants feel that the courts engage with them as individuals.

The negative, stigmatizing face of character is most apparent when it comes to the sentencing of offenders who are regarded as dangerous. Here, criminal record, and other aspects of an offender's character such as his attitudes, can have a substantial impact on sentence. Some of the questions in this area are theoretical, and I argued that incapacitation is a valid sentencing aim. But other issues are evidential, and the empirical case for using risk assessments—including judicial hunches—as the basis for incapacitative sentencing is, in the vast majority of cases, extremely weak. Here, character is asked to carry more weight than it can bear.

13.2 The Uses of Character

While character evidence was hardly absent from the criminal trial before the introduction of the Criminal Justice Act 2003,[3] the Act certainly gives it more prominence, allowing jurors to draw inferences to guilt on the basis of the defendant's propensity to offend. This presumably makes it easier for the prosecution to prove its case, but might the increased prominence of character have other implications for the criminal trial, and criminal law more generally?

One possible link between character and the criminal law is the law of attempts. It is sometimes noted that if the *actus reus* of attempt liability is drawn widely, there will be more pressure to introduce character evidence. This is because, where D has not yet engaged in any overtly threatening conduct but is simply preparing to, it will be hard to prove his criminal intentions. Character evidence is an obvious way to show what those intentions are.[4] And it is possible that things may work the other way: with character evidence more widely admissible, broad offences of preparatory liability may become more acceptable. We have certainly seen several such offences enacted in recent years: conduct in preparation of an

---

[3] One research study found that, where D had previous convictions, the jury became aware of them in about 20 per cent of cases. M. Zander and P. Henderson, *Crown Court Study* (London: HMSO, 1993), 118.

[4] A good example is *Geddes* [1996] Crim LR 894, CA 25 June 1996, where D was charged with attempted false imprisonment. The prosecution tried to introduce evidence of conversations he had had where 'he revealed that he harboured designs against young boys and wished to kidnap a child for sexual purposes'. This was ruled inadmissible, but would have more chance of being admitted today under the provisions of the CJA.

act of terrorism;[5] possessing an article for use in connection with fraud;[6] committing an offence with intent to commit a sexual offence;[7] and arranging or facilitating the commission of a child sexual offence.[8] But while the admissibility of character evidence meshes with the 'pre-emptive turn' in criminal justice,[9] it is likely that these offences would have been created even without changes to the law of evidence. A more plausible story, explored in the next section, is that the pre-emptive turn and the changes to the law on character evidence are both products of the same historical forces which have prompted other significant changes to the criminal justice system in recent years. Further, while it is possible that character evidence will fuel arguably repressive trends, such as the expansion of attempt liability into broader preparatory offences, at this level of speculation there are less worrying things which the wider use of character evidence might be thought to prompt. It might, for example, undermine arguments that reverse burdens on defences to possession offences are necessary.[10]

Another way in which character might impact on criminal law is by encouraging a character conception of criminal culpability. The wider admissibility of character evidence, Lacey suggests, 'will inevitably shape the practice of attributing criminal responsibility in the trial process', because it allows judge and jury to 'form evaluative, character-based assumptions which will supplement legal capacity-based tests wherever—as is usually the case—they are sufficiently open-ended to admit of character-based inferences'.[11] This is an intriguing possibility, but needs careful assessment. Character evidence might be useful in assessing whether a defendant meets various different culpability standards. To start with a straightforwardly cognitive standard such as intention: suppose D admits hitting V, but claims it was accidental—he raised his arm to balance himself when he stumbled. If D has previous convictions for assault, we might think it more likely that he would have hit V intentionally than if he had a clean record. The case of recklessness is a little more complex, but, assuming a simple cognitive view of recklessness—taking a foreseen unreasonable risk—we might think D more likely to have foreseen the risk because we consider that someone whose criminal

---

[5] Terrorism Act 2006, s 5.   [6] Fraud Act 2006, s 6.
[7] Sexual Offences Act 2003, s 62.   [8] Sexual Offences Act 2003, s 14.
[9] As well as new preparatory offences, other examples of the phenomenon are ASBOs, control orders, and the sex offenders' register. See generally A. Ashworth and L. Zedner, *Preventive Justice* (Oxford: Oxford University Press, 2014); A. Ashworth, L. Zedner, and P. Tomlin (eds), *Prevention and the Limits of the Criminal Law* (Oxford: Oxford University Press, 2013); and G. R. Sullivan and I. Dennis (eds), *Seeking Security: Pre-Empting the Commission of Criminal Harms* (Oxford: Hart Publishing, 2012).
[10] Eg, in *Lambert* [2002] 2 AC 545, there was considerable discussion as to whether 'reading down' the reverse burden of proof on the knowledge element in drug possession with intent to supply would make the offence too difficult to prove.
[11] N. Lacey, 'Space, Time and Function: Intersecting Principles of Responsibility across the Terrain of Criminal Justice' (2007) 1 *Crim Law & Philos* 233, 243. See also N. Lacey, 'The Resurgence of Character: Responsibility in the Context of Criminalization' in R. A. Duff and S. Green (eds), *Philosophical Foundations of Criminal Law* (Oxford: Oxford University Press, 2011). Cf V. Tadros, 'Distinguishing General Theory, Doctrine and Evidence in Criminal Responsibility: A Response to Lacey' (2007) 1 *Crim Law & Philos* 259.

record shows a lack of regard for the well-being of other people would go ahead with his actions in the face of a foreseen risk, while a person of good character would not. In these examples, the inference to the existence of *mens rea* involves an assumption that D's past behaviour is relevant to current behaviour, but it does not seem to change the nature of *mens rea*: the focus is still on what was going through D's mind at a particular point in time. The *mens rea* standard can still, in Lacey's terms, be purely capacity-based (ie interpreted in terms of choice and opportunity rather than in the more character-based language of whether D has a settled disposition to behave in a certain way).

The same seems to hold for more attitudinal conceptions of recklessness. Recklessness can be interpreted as involving 'standards of character'[12] such as indifference or the display of the vice of lack of regard for others.[13] The question of whether D displayed such bad character standards can still be confined to a narrow window of time around the alleged offence: 'was D indifferent at time *T*, given his reasons for acting?', not 'is D generally indifferent?' Evidence about D's past actions displaying bad character might still be relevant, just as it is with the cognitive *mens rea* standards. Knowing that D has shown a lack of regard for others in the past by committing assault could be used to assess the plausibility of different scenarios: was his inattention while driving due to his just having heard that his son was ill or because he was rushing to get home to watch the football?[14] As with the cognitive *mens rea* standards, character evidence can help us to determine the question of whether D displayed indifference without making the *mens rea* standard any more character-based than it already is.

It seems to me, then, that the wider admissibility of character evidence does not mean that the law's assessment of culpability must become more character-based. Using character to prove culpability does not necessarily change the culpability standard. Nor does the use of character evidence favour attitudinal *mens rea* terms over cognitive ones: character is as useful in proving intention as it is in proving indifference. This is not to deny that heavier reliance on character evidence could encourage jurors,[15] judges, and policy-makers to analyse culpability in more character-based terms, where D is blamed to the extent that his act is in character. Whether that occurs remains to be seen, and as with the broadening of attempt liability it will not be easy to trace causation.

Neither does the argument that evidence and culpability can be kept separate deny that the broader use of character evidence in evidence and sentencing affects what Lacey refers to as 'practices of criminalization'—the collection of criminal justice practices which determine D's likelihood of conviction and degree of

---

[12] See J. Gardner, 'The Gist of Excuses' (1997–98) 1 *Buffalo Crim L Rev* 575, 576–7.

[13] On the latter as underpinning an attitudinal version of recklessness, see V. Tadros, *Criminal Responsibility* (Oxford: Oxford University Press, 2005), ch 9.

[14] For these examples, see Tadros, *Criminal Responsibility*, ch 9.

[15] Nadler's empirical work, discussed in Chapter 3, is suggestive, but the points made above show just how hard it is to interpret the finding that character evidence affects judgments of responsibility.

punishment.[16] In the final section of this chapter—and of the book—I reflect on why character has come to take on a larger role in such practices, a development which, as Lacey observes, seems to take us back to the eighteenth century trial, where character played a central role.

13.3 Character's Renaissance

One notable thing about the legal provisions examined in this book is that the vast majority are found in the Criminal Justice Act 2003. Sections 98 to 113 of the Act brought in the new admissibility scheme for bad character evidence; sections 224 to 236 deal with dangerous offenders, and section 143, under the heading 'determining the seriousness of an offence', provides that when sentencing a court 'must treat each previous conviction as an aggravating factor if...the court considers that it can reasonably be so treated'. After the Act, then, defendants with previous convictions are doubly disadvantaged: their criminal record will be used not only to prove their guilt, but also to aggravate their sentence, or it might even trigger an extended sentence on grounds of dangerousness. This prompts the question: why, in 2003, did bad character come to play an enhanced role in the criminal trial?

The first thing to say in response to this question is that one needs to be cautious in attaching too much significance to 2003. It is true that the Criminal Justice Act 2003 was New Labour's flagship piece of criminal justice legislation. The White Paper which preceded the Act is notable for its emphasis on characteristic New Labour themes: satisfying victims, the problem of persistent offenders, and the need to modernize and rationalize—with archaic rules of evidence a prime target.[17] But it is not surprising to find that the character provisions in the Act have a history which preceded Labour's 1997 election victory. The changes to sentencing law in the 2003 Act were incremental. The Criminal Justice Act 1991 provided that, while a sentence should generally be commensurate with the seriousness of the offence, in the case of violent or sexual offences, the sentence should be for 'such longer term...as in the opinion of the court is necessary to protect the public from serious harm from the offender'. The Crime (Sentences) Act 1997 (passed under the outgoing Conservative administration, but with the key provisions implemented by Labour)[18] moved things on by providing for a life sentence for a second serious offence,[19] a minimum of seven years for a third Class A drug offence,[20] and a three-year minimum for a third domestic burglary.[21] So while the

---

[16] See Lacey, 'Intersecting' and 'Resurgence'.

[17] *Criminal Justice: The Way Ahead*, Cm 5074 (London: HMSO, 2001).

[18] See Lord Windlesham, *Dispensing Justice: Responses to Crime Volume 4* (Oxford: Oxford University Press, 2001), 43–57.

[19] Section 2. There was a relatively short list of serious offences, including murder, manslaughter, s 18 assault, rape, and armed robbery.

[20] Section 3.   [21] Section 4.

2003 Act went much further, especially with Imprisonment for Public Protection (IPP), which vastly expanded the pool of offences for which an incapacitative sentence was available, the policy of targeting the more dangerous offenders had been a feature of legislation since the early 1990s, and had been a focus of debate since the 1970s.[22] As for the general recidivist premium in section 143 of the Act, its precursor was introduced in the 1993 Criminal Justice Act: 'in considering the seriousness of any offence, the court may take into account any previous convictions of the offender or any failure of his to respond to previous sentences'.[23] While the 2003 Act replaces 'may' with 'must', the 1993 provision was doubtless intended to reflect the judicial practice of imposing a recidivist premium after an attempt to prevent judges from sentencing on criminal record had met with controversy.[24]

The 2003 Act's innovations in relation to bad character evidence were much more radical. However, these too have a history. The Law Commission's Report recommending the reforms that were the basis for the legislation was published in 2001,[25] but its work on character evidence was prompted by a reference made in 1994, which in turn was due to a recommendation made by the Royal Commission on Criminal Justice in 1993. The Royal Commission had been set up in response to the miscarriages of justice of the late 1980s and early 1990s, but took itself to have a broad rationalizing and modernizing agenda.[26] It remarked that the law on character evidence 'is...difficult to comprehend, embodied as it is in a series of judgments that are not always readily reconcilable'.[27]

If the reforms in the 2003 Act did not spring from nowhere, it remains significant that the Labour Government moulded them and put them into legislation. But, as the precursors to the 2003 provisions suggest, New Labour's concerns about victims and recidivists were the product of a larger historical process. A further sign of this is the judicial reaction to the reforms. As we saw in Chapter 12, the judges liked sentencing 'dangerous' offenders to IPP to such an extent that the prisons began to fill with offenders serving indeterminate sentences. The IPP provisions had to be amended to restrict their use and were then abandoned in 2012. The enthusiasm for IPP was not inevitable—and was not predicted by policy-makers. Nor was it inevitable that the provisions widening the admissibility of bad character evidence would be interpreted so liberally by the courts. In 2003, my own prediction would have been that the judges would use the common law's ways of thinking about character evidence—which often involved denying that it

[22] See A. E. Bottoms, 'Reflections on the Renaissance of Dangerousness' (1977) 16 *Howard J* 70.
[23] Section 66(6), replacing s 29 of the Criminal Justice Act 1991.
[24] The story is told in Lord Windlesham, *Responses to Crime Volume 3: Legislating with the Tide* (Oxford: Oxford University Press, 1996), ch 1; and N. Lacey, 'Government as Manager, Citizen as Consumer: The Case of the Criminal Justice Act 1991' (1994) 57 *MLR* 534.
[25] *Evidence of Bad Character*, Law Com No 273.
[26] See L. Bridges and M. McConville, 'Keeping Faith with Their Own Convictions' (1994) 57 *MLR* 75; and R. V. Ericson, 'The Royal Commission on Criminal Justice System Surveillance' in M. McConville and L. Bridges (eds), *Criminal Justice in Crisis* (Aldershot: Edward Elgar, 1994).
[27] Royal Commission on Criminal Justice, *Report*, Cm 2263 (London: HMSO, 1993), ch 8, para 30.

was relevant—to restrict admissibility. Even the fairness-based exclusionary provision in section 101(3) of the CJA has been little used. There is, however, one potential complexity in this story. Section 143 of the CJA (the court 'must treat each previous conviction as an aggravating factor...') may have had some impact on sentencing, but it does not appear to have had as dramatic an effect as the other provisions. After a certain number of convictions, flat-rate sentencing prevails, whereas the wording of the section would allow each new offence to increase the sentence indefinitely.

Much has been written about the social, political, and economic forces which have shaped criminal justice policy in the last 40 years, pushing it in a more punitive direction.[28] The basic story is that with the decline of welfare-based approaches to penal policy in the 1970s, criminal justice became politicized. Once the Labour party realized that its stance on law and order was an electoral liability, it began, in the 1990s, to mimic Conservative political rhetoric on being tough on crime. With the two major political parties locked in a law and order arms race, the prison population began to grow at an alarming rate, more than doubling between 1993 and 2011.[29] This growth in the prison population implicates the judiciary, for it occurred at a time of falling crime rates and is best explained by an increase in sentencing levels.[30] Judges were probably responsive to the wider penal climate: the political rhetoric, which in turn seems to have stoked media portrayals of crime and justice. Behind this surface story of why we have the criminal justice system we have today are narratives about the deeper, underlying forces. Here, there is a little less consensus, but significant explanations include majoritarian politics, neo-liberalism, the rise of an economic mentality with its toolkit of actuarialism and risk assessment, and governments, frustrated by their lack of ability to control crime, simply venting their rage on offenders.[31]

Against this background, it is no surprise to find an increasing emphasis on character in the criminal trial. Targeting recidivists is an obvious way to get tough on crime, and recidivists pose an increased risk which it is tempting to try to

---

[28] For the account which follows, see T. Newburn, '"Tough on Crime": Penal Policy in England and Wales' (2007) 36 *Crime & Justice* 425; R. Reiner, *Law and Order: An Honest Citizen's Guide to Crime and Control* (Cambridge: Polity, 2007), ch 5; and D. Downes and R. Morgan, 'The Skeletons in the Cupboard: The Politics of Law and Order at the Turn of the Millennium' in M. Maguire, R. Morgan, and R. Reiner (eds), *The Oxford Handbook of Criminology* (3rd edn, Oxford: Oxford University Press, 2002).

[29] See *Story of the Prison Population: 1993–2012 England and Wales* (London: Ministry of Justice, 2013). Since peaking in 2011, there has been a slight decline: see the figures archived at <http://www.howardleague.org/weekly-prison-watch/>, in particular the week-by-week breakdown since 2004.

[30] See M. Hough, J. Jacobson, and A. Millie, *The Decision to Imprison: Sentencing and the Prison Population* (London: Prison Reform Trust, 2003); and *A Presumption against Imprisonment: Social Order and Social Values* (London: British Academy, 2014), 32–41.

[31] See Reiner, *Law and Order*; N. Lacey, *The Prisoner's Dilemma: Political Economy and Punishment in Contemporary Democracies* (Cambridge, Cambridge University Press, 2008); L. Zedner, *Security* (Abingdon: Routledge, 2009), ch 4; L. Zedner, *Criminal Justice* (Oxford: Oxford University Press, 2004), ch 8; D. Garland, *The Culture of Control: Crime and Social Order in Contemporary Society* (Oxford: Oxford University Press, 2001); and B. E. Harcourt, *Against Prediction: Profiling, Policing, and Punishing in an Actuarial Age* (Chicago, IL: University of Chicago Press, 2007), ch 6.

control. The exclusionary aspect of such policies—which 'reinforce[] social divisions and exclusion'[32]—are easy to discount in an 'exclusive society'.[33]

These narratives have considerable force in explaining the increased emphasis on criminal record in guilt adjudication and sentencing.[34] The Law Commission's proposals on character evidence were obviously appealing to the Labour Government partly because of their tough-on-crime credentials. But in both evidence and sentencing, it is important not to over-simplify. As we have seen, as regards sentencing, the 2003 Act's invitation to impose an ever-increasing recidivist premium appears to have been rejected by the same judiciary which found IPP deeply attractive. Perhaps considerations of desert in sentencing sill hold some power, even where recidivists are concerned.[35] Moreover, in evidence law there are other narratives to explain why the law moved to admit more bad character evidence. Evidence law has its own trajectory, which involves eroding strict admissibility rules and placing increasing trust in the jury and judicial instructions.[36] While the character evidence provisions of the 2003 Act have some affinity with the sentencing provisions, they have as much, if not more, with the provisions in the same Act relaxing the law on hearsay,[37] provisions which are not quite so easy to fit into a 'tough on crime' narrative.[38] Even focussing just on character evidence, the Royal Commission's proposal that the law should be reviewed built on what was already happening. In 1991, the House of Lords in *DPP* v *P*[39] had taken a significant step towards rethinking the old similar facts rule, reading it in terms of a basic probative value/prejudicial effect test. A few years later, in *R* v *H*,[40] an invitation to tighten up the law was rejected, with Lord Griffiths commenting:

In the past when jurors were often uneducated and illiterate and the penal laws were of harsh severity...the judges began to fashion rules of evidence to protect the accused from a conviction that they feared might be based on emotion or prejudice rather than a fair evaluation of the facts of the case against him. The judges did not trust the jury to evaluate all the relevant material and evolved many restrictive rules which they deemed necessary to ensure that the accused had a fair trial in the climate of those times. Today with better educated and more literate juries the value of those old restrictive rules of evidence is being re-evaluated and many are being discarded or modified.[41]

Of course, it would be naïve to suppose that there were not also deeper social forces at work here. It is surely significant that both of these cases involved allegations

---

[32] Reiner, *Law and Order*, 167. See further Harcourt, *Against Prediction*, 168–9, 192.

[33] J. Young, *The Exclusive Society* (London: Sage, 1999).

[34] See further Lacey, 'Resurgence'.

[35] One reason why IPP may have been more attractive than the recidivist premium is that it allowed judges to pass the buck to the Parole Board, which made the ultimate decision about release.

[36] See discussion in chapter 7 and P. Roberts and A. Zuckerman, *Criminal Evidence* (2nd edn, Oxford: Oxford University Press, 2010), 700–2.

[37] Sections 114–36.

[38] The provisions apply equally to both prosecution and defence. That said, in practice it is the prosecution which is more likely to benefit from wider admissibility of hearsay, as it tends to generate more evidence in the form of witness statements.

[39] [1991] 2 AC 447.   [40] [1995] 2 AC 596.

[41] *R* v *H*, 613. Griffiths identified the decision in *DPP* v *P* as an example of this trend.

of child abuse, a crime which was of increasing public concern in the 1990s, and which might be hard to prove without character evidence.

Just as we should not over-simplify the forces shaping legal change, so too we should be wary of viewing negatively all law reforms which have been influenced by the often toxic criminal justice politics of the last 20 years. In this book, I have tried to judge the CJA's character provisions on their own terms. Very simply, while I have been critical of policies which augment sentences for recidivists, I have argued that the increased use of bad character evidence in the guilt-determination stage of the trial is defensible.

Index